Opening Day, April 9, 1985
Cubs 2, Pirates 1

The New Era Cubs 1941-1985

by Eddie Gold
and Art Ahrens

BONUS BOOKS *Chicago, 1985*

89 88 87 86 85 5 4 3 2 1

Text photos: Supplied by Art Ahrens from his personal collection

Book Design: Productotemp, Inc./Newton Jacobson

Endpaper photo: Kesh Sorensen

Library of Congress Catalog Card Number:
85-60183

International Standard Book Number:
0-933893-04-3

Bonus Books, Inc.
160 East Illinois Street
Chicago, Illinois 60611

Printed in the United States of America

Table of Contents

Acknowledgments

The authors wish to express their heartfelt gratitude to the following: Dr. Steve Boren, L. Robert Davids, Bill Loughman, Emil Rothe, Jim Rowe, John C. Tattersall, Richard Topp, all the members of SABR, and the Chicago Public Library, where we loitered for eons looking at roll after roll of microfilm.

Foreword

During our many years as cellmates in the sports department of the *Chicago Sun-Times,* Eddie Gold often appeared at my desk with sheets of yellow copy paper in his ink-stained hands.

"This is my Dallessandro," he would say, or "Do you want to read my Speake?"

Itinerant newsmen who had drifted in from other cities would stare in our direction as though we had lost our minds. We knew what they were thinking. What is a Dallessandro? How does a guy read a Speake?

We knew, though. Gold and Gleason knew.

Those outsiders didn't understand us. Gold is a Cubs fan. I am a Sox fan. We were talking a language they did not comprehend.

For a long time I did not comprehend Gold. Because my lifetime has been spent ever so joyously on Chicago's Great Sout' Side, I'd never met a person quite like Gold. I'd never really known a Cubs fan.

It had not occurred to me that a man could care as deeply about the Cubs as I care about my cherished White Sox. Until Gold I had thought that Sox fans were the only Chicagoans who worried, suffered, and bled, pitch-by-pitch, play-by-play, inning-by-inning, game-by-game, season-by-season, into eternity.

Those sheets of yellow paper were Eddie's proof, Eddie's personal tributes to the heroes, the hotdogs, the hell-raisers of his childhood, his boyhood, his manhood, his middle age. His stories about "Dim Dom Dal" Dallessandro and Bob Speake were not written for the newspaper or for me, but for himself. He had a need to put his memories and his impressions on the record, and because he has sufficient energy to propel Wrigley Field to the moon, he wrote those stories in his *spare* time.

In my files I have scores of those Golden mini-manuscripts, some of them dating back to the time when the Cubs were the Chicago White Stockings. His Dallessandro and his Speake mesmerized me because they were, so obviously, labors of adoration.

Magically those yellow sheets became part of this book because Gold finally took seriously the caustic advice of those who demanded that he share his singular insights with those who love the Cubs and with those who hate the Cubs.

There is no other person in the world who knows more about the Cubs than Gold does, who understands, as he does, the eccentrics who have owned the Cubs, managed the Cubs, played for the Cubs. There is, however, a man much younger than Gold who one day may succeed Eddie as the world's most knowledgeable Cubs fan. He is that tall, slender southpaw, Art Ahrens, Gold's friend and collaborator.

This is the third book Gold and Ahrens have written in partnership. They are to the history of the Cubs what Ernie Banks and Billy Williams are to the home runs of the Cubs. Eddie and Art were brought together by their consuming interest in baseball research. Then each discovered the other to be the rarest of beings, one who truly understands the Cubs.

The famous players, the superstars, the stars, and the very good are here in these pages, but because my fondest memories are of White Sox players named Jack "The Mop" Wallasea and Smead Jolley, I am enchanted by the histories of those Cubs who are memorable rather than immortal.

Gold and Ahrens devote much of their space to jarring the memory, to reminding us of truths we have forgotten or never knew.

I had forgotten that catcher Clyde McCullough, my very own all-time favorite Cub nut, was so tough he sometimes caught without a chest protector.

I had never known that outfielder Bill Nicholson, one of two players in history who *almost* hit a baseball into the Wrigley Field scoreboard, was a failure as a minor league batter until his career was salvaged by an ex-Cubs outfielder who is in the Hall of Fame. (You don't actually expect me to identify that Hall of Famer, do you? Read the book.)

I had never known that outfielder Dominic Dallessandro, "Dim Dom Dal" to you out-of-towners, was drafted into the army because he made the mistake of hitting .304 one season.

I had forgotten that outfielder Jim Hickman, one of the most pleasant men to wear a baseball uniform, was almost 31 years old when the Cubs acquired him.

I had never known that shortstop Roy Smalley, Sr., fondly remembered for throwing baseballs into the stands above and beyond first base, once threw a ball into the center field bleachers.

I had forgotten that pitcher Bob Anderson's arm touched off the "two-balls-in-play" episode that has a well-deserved niche in Chicago lore.

And although I had known that infielder Emil Verban was a proficient player and not the clown that he's made out to be by dilettantes of the so-called Emil Verban Society, I had not appreciated how good Verban was. He went to bat 2,911 times in the major leagues, but struck out only 74 times. (When you get into the book, you'll find more of Verban's sterling accomplishments.)

Gold and Ahrens are collectors of the bizarre, but they also understand the nuances of inside baseball.

Every Cubs fan knows that Keith Moreland was the catalytic player in the drive to a division championship in 1984. Eddie and Art tell us the reason *why* the right fielder became the "gun of August."

The authors remind us that Ryne Sandberg's batting average, no more than .261 in 1983, soared to .314 in '84. Then they reveal the source of the batting tip that propelled Sandberg from mediocrity to excellence.

Do I have any complaints? Only two.

First, Gold and Ahrens left out Al Heist, who seemed destined to be the Cubs *last* outstanding defensive centerfielder until Bob Dernier arrived in Wrigley Field.

Second, and this is more complicated, there is a rousing song that is fast becoming the anthem of Chicago's Great Sout' Side. Written by three gentlemen who perform at the

Reilly's Daughter Pub, its title is (appropriately) *South Side Irish,* and the last lines go like this:

And when it comes to baseball,
We have two favorite clubs,
The Go! Go! White Sox . . . .
And whoever plays the Cubs.

But for accidents of location and birth, Gold and Ahrens would have been Sox fans. They should have been.

Bill Gleason

Bill Gleason
April, 1985

SECTION ONE 1941-1945 Wrigley Wartime Heroes

In the summer of 1941, the winds of war were blowing ever closer to American shores. For Cub fans, however, the World War II period was more memorable for laughs than victories. During the early '40s, Cub players wore their own version of the zoot suit, a uniform featuring cutoff, sleeveless jerseys, the first in major league history. It lasted three years.

Springtime at training camp at Catalina Island, near Los Angeles, found the Cubs with a new general manager, James Gallagher, and a new field boss, Jimmy Wilson. Together, they embarked on a series of deals that made the Cubs look like a farm club for the Dodgers.

Billy Herman was traded for a couple of glorified Triple A players and cash. Lou Stringer, Herman's replacement at second, could not hold a candle to Billy, either as a hitter or a gloveman.

Later in the year, Larry French and Augie Galan were handed to Brooklyn on a silver platter. The result? The Dodgers won the pennant while the Cubs skidded to sixth.

When Pearl Harbor came, the big leagues heard the call from Uncle Sam. While the 1942 season was almost up to prewar standards, things went downhill thereafter. With most of the real talent being gobbled up by the military, rosters brimmed with fuzzy-faced teenagers, minor league journeymen, and has-beens who were too old to be drafted.

For the Cubs, it was a time when such legendary characters as Lennie Merullo, Lou Novikoff, Dom Dallessandro, Hiram Bithorn, and Heinz Becker flourished.

Weak up the middle and with few quality pitchers, the Cubs repeated their sixth-place finish in 1942. Fans could look with pride only to the steady work of Stan Hack and husky catcher Clyde McCullough, the slugging of Bill Nicholson, the pitching of Claude Passeau, and the hustling of Phil Cavarretta, who had been recycled at first base after several years as a utility outfielder. Outfielder

The Chicago Cubs, 1945 National League Champions

Peanuts Lowrey and pitcher Hank Wyse were also given brief trials.

The following year the Cubs inched up to fifth, as Cavarretta and Nicholson approached their peaks. Lowrey looked good in the outfield, Wyse worked his way into the regular rotation, and Eddie Stanky showed promise at second base. However, when Don Johnson was brought up late in the season, the Cubs soured on Stanky prematurely. The following June he was traded to—you guessed it—Brooklyn.

In 1944 the Cubs got off to their worst start in history, losing 13 in a row after winning the opener. Jimmy Wilson's head rolled, and in his place returned Charlie Grimm, after coach Roy Johnson served one day as interim manager.

The Cubs recuperated steadily, eventually finishing in fourth place. Don Johnson proved to be a pleasant surprise at second base, as was center fielder Andy Pafko. Both had been brought up late in the previous year.

During the spring of '45, most writers predicted the Cubs would finish no higher than second or third behind the Cardinals, who had already won three straight pennants and two World Series. When the team started off slowly, it looked as if the scribes would be right.

But Chicago soon built up steam, capturing the lead July 8—with St. Louis snapping at the Cubs' heels every minute.

On July 27, Gallagher pulled a steal by obtaining pitcher Hank Borowy from the Yankees. Borowy turned out to be just the right tonic for the stretch drive. He was the only one on the staff who was effective against the Cardinals.

The Cubs finally clinched the pennant on Sept. 29, with the Cardinals only three games back. The Cubs had a good lineup by wartime standards, but these were not as high as in peacetime.

The Cardinals, for example, had lost Stan Musial to the navy, and he would likely have made the difference. Even so, a pennant was still a pennant and a welcome treat to war-weary Cub fans.

The Cubs met the Tigers for the fourth time in the World Series. When asked his pick, Chicago sports columnist Warren Brown replied, "I don't think either team can win it." He was almost right. In a series filled with mishaps and oddball plays, Detroit finally squeezed by in seven games. It was the closest the Cubs had come to a world championship since 1908. With scores of players returning home from overseas, the future was anybody's guess.

JIMMY WILSON

WILSON, JAMES
B. July 23, 1900, Philadelphia, Pa.
D. May 31, 1947, Bradenton, Fla.
BR TR 6′1½″ 200 lb.

Hack Wilson was one of the most popular players in a Cub uniform. Jimmy Wilson was perhaps the most unpopular. He fought criticism and dissent throughout his three years and two weeks as Cub manager.

When Wilson stuck his neck out of the Cub dugout he usually was greeted with a barrage of razzberries. Most of it was undeserved, but he was *there,* the only one in full view of the fans.

Wilson enjoyed a long career as a catcher from 1923 to '40 with the Philadelphia Phillies, St. Louis Cardinals, and Cincinnati Reds. His career average was .284, and he was a fine handler of pitchers.

He was named playing-manager of the Phillies in 1934 and lasted through the 1938 season. The Phils were dreadful during the Depression. They finished last twice and seventh three times under Wilson.

The black-haired backstop signed on as a coach with the Reds in 1939. The following season he was on a pennant winner. Then tragedy struck. Catcher Willard Hershberger committed suicide, and first-string catcher Ernie Lombardi was injured.

The desperate Reds took the 40-year-old Wilson out of the coaching box and put him behind the plate for the World Series against the Detroit Tigers.

The old man had no business playing in that series, but he emerged as a hero with a .353 average as Cincinnati won in seven games. In addition, he stole the lone base and took it home to Philadelphia as a momento.

Wilson's heroics impressed Cub owner P. K. Wrigley and General Manager James T. Gallagher. The Cubs had finished fifth in 1940, dropping out of the first division for the first time since 1925.

Gabby Hartnett, who only two years earlier hit his famed "Homer in the Gloamin' " to help win the 1938 pennant, was fired and replaced by Wilson. It wasn't a popular move with Cub fans.

The team had a tradition of playing managers from the days of Cap Anson and Frank Chance to Rogers Hornsby, Charlie Grimm, and Hartnett. If Hartnett had to go, why not turn over the reins to second baseman Billy Herman?

Guess who was the first Cub to go? Herman was dealt to the hated Brooklyn Dodgers for two nonentities and $40,000. The fans were livid, but the press was vicious. One columnist started calling Gallagher and Wilson the "James Boys."

Later that season, the Cubs waived the popular Larry French and Augie Galan to the Dodgers, who were pennant-bound under manager Leo Durocher. Herman, French, and Galan joined such former Cubs as Hugh Casey, Dolph Camilli, Curt Davis, Kirby Higbe, and Babe Phelps in the Dodger livery.

One newspaper, the *Daily Times,* ran a daily box score entitled "What The Ex-Cubs Did Today." Gallagher could hide in the front office, but Wilson carried the brunt of the abuse.

After one gut-wrenching loss to the Braves, Wilson was tossing and turning in bed. For comfort, he turned on the radio and was just in time to hear a broadcast from a Boston night club.

The announcer said: "And now ladies and gentlemen, here's Lou Novikoff of the Chicago Cubs, singing 'Trees.' " Wilson looked at the clock. It was past curfew. He stormed from the hotel, hailed a cab, and sped to the night club.

Novikoff spotted his manager and summoned him to the stage for a duet. It was "timber" for the "Trees" warbler. He didn't carry much lumber to the plate for the rest of the season.

In Wilson's three seasons, the Cubs finished sixth twice and made a jump to fifth the other year. The Cubs won their 1944 opener, but then dropped nine games in a row. Wilson resigned. "I cannot explain the slump, but it is here," said Wilson. "And in baseball, when you don't win you have to get out."

A few days later Wilson rejoined the Reds as a coach. But worse luck followed. His son Robert was killed in the Pacific while on a B-29 bombing mission.

At the end of the 1946 season, Wilson retired from baseball and entered the citrus fruit business in Bradenton, Fla. He died of a heart attack at the age of 47 on May 31, 1947.

STAN HACK

HACK, STANLEY CAMFIELD
B. Dec. 6, 1909, Sacramento, Calif.
D. Dec. 15, 1979, Dixon, Ill.
BL TR 6' 175 lb.

One of only six players in Cub history to collect more than 2,000 hits, Smiling Stan Hack was a fixture at third base throughout most of the 1930s and '40s. He gathered 2,193 base hits and had a 16-year lifetime batting average of .301. But statistics alone cannot begin to tell of his many accomplishments.

Hack made his professional debut with Sacramento of the Pacific Coast League in 1931, batting a whopping .352. The Cubs brought him up the following year, but he was not yet ready for the big time, batting only .236 in 72 games.

Stan did, however, replace the departed Hack Wilson as Pat Malone's drinking partner, and the two polished off many a bottle. In the beginning, the youthful Hack could not hold as much "hooch" as the seasoned drinker Malone, so Pat frequently had to carry Stan back to the hotel on his shoulders.

In 1933 Stan was sent down to Albany of the International League, then recalled near the end of the season. This time he was ready for the majors, responding with a .350 average in 20 games. From that point on, the third base job was his.

Stan had his first complete .300 season in 1935, hitting .311 as the Cubs won the pennant. From 1936 through '41 he tied a National League record by scoring 100 or more runs for six consecutive years. Primarily a singles and doubles hitter, Stan seldom went for the fences, never hitting more than eight home runs in one year.

The 1938 season is best remembered for the pennant sparked by Gabby Hartnett's famous twilight homer against Pittsburgh. What is often forgotten is that the team's leading hitter was the dependable Stan Hack, batting .320 with 195 hits. Although the Yanks creamed the Cubs in four straight in the World Series, it was no fault of Stan's. He batted .471, making eight hits in 17 trips.

With his genial, outgoing personality, Hack earned the nickname "Smiling Stan" to teammates, fans, and writers alike. He became one of the most popular Cubs of all time. Because Charlie Grimm called him "Stanislaus," many thought that Stan was Polish, when actually he was of English descent. But nobody cared, so long as he could play ball.

As a glove man, Stan had a smooth, easy style that made the toughest plays look routine. He led the league at his position twice in fielding average, five times in putouts, and twice in assists.

From April 30 to July 4, 1942 (second game), Hack set a National League record (since broken) by playing 54 consecutive games without an error, handling 154 chances at third base. When Stan finally made a boot, it was on a grounder off the bat of another Stan—Musial of the Cardinals—who would soon become famous himself. Hack was also a competent baserunner, twice winning the league lead in thefts.

After batting .289 in 1943, Stan retired, in part, because he did not get along with Cub manager Jimmy Wilson. But Wilson was dismissed the following May and Charlie Grimm returned to the job. "Jolly Cholly" talked "Stanislaus" out of retirement, and Hack returned to the Cubs in mid-June.

After four appearances as a pinch hitter, Hack returned to the starting lineup on June 28, 1944. Grinning like a Cheshire cat, Grimm hauled Stan out of the dugout in a wheelbarrow and dumped him on third base. Hack went two-for-four in the opener and one-for-four in the nightcap as the Cubs took a pair from the Dodgers 12-6 and 6-2.

Coming out of retirement was the smartest decision of his career. In 1945 Stan had his best season at the plate, batting .323, second only to Phil Cavarretta. For good measure, he was the league's top fielding third baseman as the Cubs won their first pennant in seven years.

On Aug. 30 he garnished his 2,000th major league hit, a single to open the first inning off the Pirates' Preacher Roe, but the Cubs came back to win 6-4.

It took the Tigers seven games to edge the Cubs in the '45 series, with Stan batting .367. It was in the sixth game, Oct. 8, that Stan had his most shining hour. The score was tied at seven in the bottom of the 12th. Darkness was enveloping Wrigley Field.

With two out and Bill Schuster on first, Hack slashed a liner to left field. The ball hit a sprinkler faucet and took a bounce over Hank Greenberg's shoulder. By the time he chased down the ball, Schuster had crossed the plate with the winning run.

After hours of deliberation, the hit was ruled a double, thereby absolving Greenberg of any guilt. Either way, it had kept Cub hopes alive, which was all that mattered.

Hack was back at third base in 1946, but not as frequently. Advancing age and a broken hand began to catch up with him. After playing only part time the following year, Stan retired.

Following his retirement from active play, Hack managed in the Cub farm system for several years before returning to the parent club in 1954. In three seasons as Cub skipper, Stan brought a largely talentless team home seventh, sixth, and eighth before his head rolled.

He then coached for the Cardinals for two years, serving briefly as interim manager in 1958. After a couple of more managerial assignments in the minors, Stan left the game for keeps in 1966.

In his later years, Stan operated a restaurant in Grand Detour, Ill., talking about his favorite subject—baseball—while tending bar for his customers. To his last breath, he was still "Smiling Stan" to one and all.

PHIL CAVARRETTA

CAVARRETTA, PHILIP JOSEPH
B. July 19, 1916, Chicago, Ill.
BL TL 5′11½″ 175 lb.

A star pitcher on a softball team developed a reputation as a neighborhood menace by breaking several windows some distance from the playing field. Word of his prowess drifted to Percy Moore, Lane Tech High School's famed baseball coach.

Moore envisioned a muscular athlete. Instead, he saw a slight boy with knickers, shirt, face, and hands grimy after furious slides into the bases. The youngster was Phil Cavarretta, the third child of Italian immigrant parents who settled on Chicago's North Side in 1911.

The black-haired, gray-eyed Cavarretta became Lane Tech's star pitcher. He led them to three straight city championships and Moore's American Legion team to the junior world championship.

But the year 1934 was a tough one for a working man trying to support a wife and three children. Construction work was at a standstill. Michael, the oldest boy, was working at odd jobs, and daughter Sarah was turning over her small earnings to the family fund.

Young Phil had been allowed to escape toil because he was Michael and Sarah's favorite. Each year they persuaded their parents that "he's happy and having so much fun—let him enjoy himself playing baseball."

But in this Depression month of May 1934, a decision had come. Phil should say farewell to baseball. Young Cavarretta approached Coach Moore and broke the news in a choked voice.

"Coach, my folks are having a hard time. I've got to quit school and find a job right away."

Moore visited the Cavarretta home. He wanted to know what the family would think about Phil trying to find a job in baseball. Papa

Cavarretta gave Moore the fishy eye. Who would be fool enough to pay a boy to throw a little ball at another boy?

The coach made an appointment with Cubs' manager Charlie Grimm and Cavarretta appeared early on a Saturday morning at Wrigley Field. Grimm observed that the youngster was carrying two gloves: a finger mitt, used by pitchers and outfielders, and a first baseman's glove.

"Can't you make up your mind where you want to play?" Grimm joked.

Earnestly young Phil replied, "I want to try out for pitcher, outfielder, and first baseman."

In batting practice, Cavy got hold of a fastball thrown by Cub star pitcher Pat Malone and knocked it into the right field bleachers. Grimm said, "OK, we'll give him $125 a month and send him to Peoria."

Before departing for Peoria, Moore told Cavarretta, "Hustle. Hustle from the first inning until the last man is out. The fans will forgive an error, but they never forgive a man who doesn't give his best."

Cavy played well in Peoria, batting .316 in 34 games before the Central League folded. He was then shipped to Reading of the New York-Penn League where he played first base and batted .308. Finally, the big day came. He was recalled by the Cubs at the tender age of 18.

In his major league debut on Sept. 25, 1934, Cavarretta homered off Whitey Wistert of the Cincinnati Reds and the Cubs won 1-0. In seven games, Phillibuck, as he was fondly called by Grimm, hit a rousing .381.

The following season Grimm gave his first base job to Cavarretta. The young rookie responded with a .275 average that included 28 doubles, 12 triples, 8 homers, and 62 RBI.

Cavy was part of a galaxy of stars that included infielders Billy Herman, Billy Jurges, and Stan Hack; outfielders Frank Demaree, Augie Galan, and Chuck Klein; a pitching staff of Lon Warneke, Bill Lee, Larry French, and Charlie Root; and the capable Gabby Hartnett behind the plate.

A 21-game winning streak in the September stretch carried the Cubs to the 1935 pennant. During that streak Cavy celebrated his first anniversary in the majors (Sept. 25) by hitting a homer to beat the St. Louis Cardinals 1-0.

When the Cubs again won the pennant in 1938, all attention was focused on Hartnett's homer, which turned back the Pittsburgh Pirates.

Forgotten was a single play by Cavy late that season. The Pirates had the tying run on first base and Paul Waner slashed a hit to right field. Cavy scooped up the ball on the first hop and fired to third to nail the runner and save the game.

Cavarretta grew up in a Cub uniform. Soon, he and Hack were the lone survivors from the Cubs' halcyon days. When Hack retired after the 1943 season, Cavy was made team captain. He had earned his stripes by hustling.

The Cubs spun their wheels at the outset of the 1944 season and Grimm was summoned again to take control. He enticed Hack out of retirement, but retained Cavarretta as captain. That season, Cavy set an All-Star Game record by reaching base safely five straight times on a triple, single, and three walks.

But the best was to come. In 1945 he led the Cubs to the pennant, hitting .355 to win the batting championship and was voted the National League's Most Valuable Player. In the World Series, Phil hit .423, but the Cubs lost to the Detroit Tigers in seven games.

The next year he lost his job. Slick-fielding Eddie Waitkus was handed the first base spot, and without a whimper, Cavy grabbed another glove and played the outfield.

The seasons raced by. Waitkus was traded to Philadelphia. Cavy quietly went back to first. He was still the Cub mainstay.

On July 21, 1951, Cavarretta realized a dream he had always nurtured. He became manager of the Cubs, inheriting a last-place ballclub from Frankie Frisch. Then followed his greatest playing day.

The Cubs had lost five in a row when they encountered the Phillies in a doubleheader on July 29 at Wrigley Field. The Cubs had been held scoreless in 31 innings going into the last of the sixth inning of the first game.

There were two on base with the Cubs trailing 1-0. Before stepping into the batter's box, Cavarretta spit in the air and hit the glob with his bat. It was a ritual. This time he spit out a triple, giving the Cubs a 2-1 lead. He later drove in another run with a single and the Cubs won 5-4.

The second game was something else. It was 4-4 in the last of the seventh. The bases were loaded and Robin Roberts, the Phillies' first Robin of fling, was on the mound.

A big roar went up from the crowd of 35,000 as pinch hitter Cavarretta emerged from the dugout. The manager had put himself on the spot. Cavy leaned into Roberts' first pitch and drove the ball over the right field screen for a grand-slam homer.

The Cubs went on to win a doubleheader with their manager driving in seven runs. Cavy had made the right move. In a clutch situation, he sent in his best hitter—himself.

In Cavy's first full season as manager, the Cubs were a .500 ballclub, thanks mainly to the slugging of Hank Sauer, who won the MVP Award. But in 1953 Sauer broke his thumb and the team fell back to seventh.

Then came spring training 1954. The club played poorly during the exhibitions. Cavy reported to owner P. K. Wrigley and with rare candor told the boss that the Cubs were candidates for the second division and owned few players of promise.

Cavarretta's report was diagnosed as "defeatism" and he was bounced, the first major league manager to be fired during spring training. "I thought it my duty to give Mr. Wrigley frank views on the ballclub's ability," sighed the deposed pilot.

So much for honesty.

After that shock came another. Cavy signed with the hated crosstown White Sox. He was handed his familiar No. 44 jersey and batted .316 in a utility role. On Aug. 3 he smashed a grand-slam homer to help beat the Boston Red Sox. But Cavy drew his release early in the 1955 season after going hitless in four at bats.

The only player-managers to hit pinch grand-slam homers were Rogers Hornsby in 1931 and Phil Cavarretta in 1951. Both were Cubs.

Abandoned and homeless, Cavarretta wandered in the baseball wilderness. He managed for a while in the minor leagues, coached with the Detroit Tigers, and served as coach and minor league batting instructor with the New York Mets.

"Cub catcher Jody Davis was one of my pupils in the Mets' system," said Cavarretta. "You could see he had raw power then. He kept swinging from the heels and wasn't making contact. But he was willing to listen. I'm glad to see him do well."

Cavarretta, now 68, enjoys the good life in Palm Harbor, Fla., fishing, playing golf, and romping with his six grandchildren.

"Now that I'm retired as Mets' hitting instructor, I'm free to root for the Cubbies," said No. 44.

CLAUDE PASSEAU

PASSEAU, CLAUDE WILLIAM
B. April 9, 1909, Waynesboro, Miss.
BR TR 6'3" 198 lb.

Claude Passeau had so many floating bone chips in his elbow that his pitching arm rattled like a dice box. Yet, he once pitched a one-hitter in the World Series.

The lantern-jawed, leathery-faced pitcher won 19 games the year he had his appendix frozen and was held to 14 wins the season he had several broken ribs and a torn muscle in his back. He once pitched and won while wearing a black patch over his right eye. Passeau was a 20-game winner that year.

In another World Series game, a line drive tore the nail off his forefinger. He went on throwing a blood-splattered ball. "My pitching hand was badly swollen and caked with blood," said Passeau, who was lifted under protest.

Passeau had as much guts as any pitcher and spilled a lot of it during a 13-year career that saw him win 162 games and lose 150. The rangy right-hander had his most productive seasons in a Cub uniform, posting a 124-94 record from 1939 through '47.

Besides pitching, Passeau was a remarkable fielder. He went from Sept. 21, 1941, to May 20, 1946, without committing an error, accepting 273 chances cleanly. The remarkable achievement was done while wearing the smallest glove used by any major league pitcher.

"I was permitted to use the glove because I have a crippled left hand," revealed Passeau, now 76. "The third and little finger are bent down so they almost touch my palm and are powerless.

"As a youngster, I was ridin' in a truck, headin' for the ol' fishin' hole. My friend asked me to pick up his gun off the floor of the back seat. I reached back and caught the gun by the end of the barrel. The truck hit a bump and the gun went off. A bullet plowed through my hand and came outside my wrist."

Passeau's father was a 6′4″, 240-pound lumberjack, who worked in a sawmill outside Lucedale. Young Passeau helped with the farm chores and played a bit of baseball during the summer. But his father insisted that an education came first.

Passeau graduated from Millsaps College in 1932 with a bachelor of science degree. That didn't mean much then. It was hard getting a job. He worked as a pipe fitter and then became a fireman on a merchant marine ship. After shipping around the world in freighters, Passeau decided on a baseball career.

From China, Japan, Australia, and the South Seas, Passeau flitted about Decatur, Moline, Shreveport, Beaumont, Williamsport, Grand Rapids, and Charleston with little success.

It wasn't until he won 20 games with Des Moines of the Western League in 1935 that his contract was purchased by the Pittsburgh Pirates. In his first game, Passeau was mauled for seven hits and four runs in three innings. That marked his lone Pirate appearance.

The Pirates swapped catchers, sending Earl Grace to the Philadelphia Phillies for Al Todd and threw in Passeau for good measure. The Phillies were perennial losers and Passeau got a chance to pitch.

From 1936 through '38 Passeau won 36 and lost 51, but was among the leaders in innings pitched, games started, and strikeouts. He was traded to the Cubs on May 29, 1939, for outfielder Joe Marty and pitchers Kirby Higbe and Ray Harrell.

Passeau became the ace of the Cubs' staff, winning 20 in 1940. He also became a Dodger nemesis during their beanball wars of that era. His particular target was Dodger player-manager Leo Durocher.

In one game, Durocher stepped to the plate. Passeau hitched his belt, tugged at his cap, wiped his lips with his pitching hand, rubbed his hand on his shirt front, hitched his shoulder, and delivered in a quick herky-jerky motion. Durocher watched his act and struck out.

Leo remembered. In retaliation on July 19, 1940, he had pitcher Hugh Casey plunk Passeau with a pitch between the shoulder blades. Passeau then threw his bat at Casey and a free-for-all began. When the umpires and police restored order, Passeau's uniform was half torn and he was banished. But he departed with an 11-4 victory.

On May 19, 1941, Passeau hit a grand-slam homer at Wrigley Field to cap a 14-1 triumph over Leo's Dodgers. His victim? Hugh Casey. For years, Durocher tried unsuccessfully to pry Passeau from the Cubs.

Bone chips were discovered in his elbow during the 1945 season, and Cub manager Charlie Grimm asked Passeau whether he wanted to have them cut out. "Hell no," replied the veteran pitcher. "We've got a chance to win the pennant." Later Passeau said, "Every time I threw a ball it was like a dozen needles shooting through my arm."

"Mr. Chips" hung up a 17-9 record in the Cubs' pennant triumph and Grimm selected him to pitch the third game of the World Series against the Detroit Tigers at Briggs Stadium.

Passeau's arm hurt so severely that tears ran down his cheeks as he warmed up before a throng of 55,500 on this gray, misty Oct. 5 afternoon. But he pitched through the soreness and etched one of the greatest World Series performances, a one-hit 3-0 victory.

With one out in the second inning, Rudy York hit a "little looping liner to left" for a clean single. But York was erased in a double play. In the sixth inning, Passeau walked Bob Swift. "Nobody mentions that I drove in a run with a long fly in that game," recalled Passeau, whose bat produced 15 lifetime homers. In all, Passeau faced 28 batters and threw 109 pitches—72 strikes and 37 balls.

"The sore arm made me a good pitcher. When I couldn't throw hard, I began to pitch here and there, giving the hitters a little of this and a little of that."

Three days later, Grimm called on Passeau to pitch the sixth game at Wrigley Field. The Tigers went into the match, leading three games to two.

Passeau's shoulder ached and his elbow rattled, but he drum-majored a 5-1 lead through six innings. Then in the seventh, a line smash through the box tore off a fingernail. After he departed, the Tigers went on to tie, but the Cubs bounced back to win 8-7 in the 12th inning when Stan Hack's hit bounced over Hank Greenberg's shoulder.

The Tigers won in seven games, but that never convinced Passeau. "If it hadn't been for this finger, I'm sure I'd have beaten them.

"Heck, I liked to finish what I started. Used to pitch about 20 complete games a year. And there's nothin' wrong with Wrigley Field. I loved that park. All you had to do was throw the lefty batters low and outside and the righty batters high and inside. I always led the league in fewest homers allowed. You can look it up.

"And I never threw a curve. I had what was called a "slurve." Some batters claimed I threw a spitter. Heck, I wouldn't know what to do with a wet baseball."

The injuries and the years held Passeau to a 9-8 record in 1946 (his eighth straight winning season). Following spinal surgery he fell to 2-6 in 1947.

On Sept. 26, 1947, the Cubs made a wholesale severance of ties with a quartet of favorites. Drawing their releases were Hack, Billy Jurges, Bill Lee, and Claude Passeau. It was good-bye Mr. Chips.

Passeau went back to his Lucedale farm, but didn't lack for action. He was selected sheriff and wore a .38 on his hip. "My job was to keep peace in the county," drawled Passeau.

"There never is much trouble. Oh, every now and then, there's a bit of excitement. I shot a couple guys one time. They just wouldn't stop fightin'. I didn't shoot to hit 'em though. Just shot at their feet. They stopped."

Throughout his career Passeau wore No. 13. "That's my lucky number. My auto tag number is 13. The serial on my rifle is 13. The last two digits on my insurance policy are 13, and my address is 113 London Street."

BILL NICHOLSON

NICHOLSON, WILLIAM BECK
B. Dec. 11, 1914, Chestertown, Md.
BL TR 6'0" 205 lb.

It all started in Brooklyn's Ebbets Field. The fans would be oohing and aahing at Bill Nicholson's every move. It became a ritual. Big Nick would select his favorite warclub, tap his spikes with the bat, and step into the batter's box.

His left cheek bulged with tobacco. He squeezed the bat so hard that sawdust was oozing out. And that swing. The Dodger fans would yell "Swish" every time Nicholson took a tremendous swipe with the bat.

It soon carried across the borough to the Polo Grounds, Nicholson's favorite playpen. It was there that "Swish" became "Swat." It reached a climax on July 23, 1944, with one of the most unusual bits of baseball strategy.

The Giants were leading the Cubs 12-9 in the second game of a doubleheader. It was the seventh inning, and the Cubs had the bases loaded. The next batter? Swish Nicholson.

Giants' manager Mel Ott wore a path to the mound. He ordered rookie Andy Hansen, the seventh Giant pitcher of the game, to walk Nicholson *intentionally,* forcing in a run. "I couldn't believe it," said Nicholson. "I was the most surprised guy in the ballpark."

The strategy worked. The Giants went on to win 12-10 and gain a split. Why an intentional pass with the bases loaded? Well, Nicholson had already tied major league records with four homers in a row and four in a doubleheader.

His weekend destruction included nine runs scored, nine base hits, nine runs batted in, and six homers. The six homers came within 40 hours—a major league record.

It wasn't always that way. In the summer of 1936, William Beck Nicholson came out of Washington College in Chestertown, Md., to join the Philadelphia Athletics.

The dairy farmer with the broad back and muscular shoulders was a plunging fullback and prodigious slugger in college. He got into a dozen games as a pinch hitter with the A's and did nothing.

Manager Connie Mack watched him in the batting cage and muttered, "I can't understand that fellow. He broke down the fences in college." Nicholson just couldn't hit low outside curveballs and high hard ones under his chin.

After hitting .167 at Oklahoma City in 1936 and .217 at

Williamsport, Mack soon tired of the husky prospect who either "broke his bat or hit a homer or did both." He was sold to Chattanooga for $25,000 and an outfielder name Dee Miles.

Nicholson's manager at Chattanooga was Kiki Cuyler, the former Cub star. Cuyler made Nicholson open his stance, stop lunging at the ball, and get set for each pitch. The results were phenomenal. His batting average soared to .364 and he started splintering the fences.

Cuyler informed the Cubs of the outstanding prospect, just the power hitter they needed. Finally, on June 26, 1939, the Cubs heeded Cuyler's pleas and purchased Nicholson for $35,000 with shipment to the majors by August.

Nicholson departed Chattanooga with a .334 average and a league-leading 23 home runs. In his Wrigley Field debut on Aug. 1, Nicholson homered off Wayman Kerksieck of the Philadelphia Phillies.

He immediately became Chicago's favorite ballplayer of the 1940s, not only for his towering home runs but also for his ability to play the sunbathed right field position at Wrigley Field. In addition, he had a good, strong throwing arm.

Some of Nicholson's feats became legend. He once launched a rocket that just went to the right of the Wrigley Field scoreboard. "It had to be my longest homer," recalled Nicholson.

"I remember getting the fat part of the bat and driving the ball high and deep to right-center off Al Brazle of the Cardinals. The ball landed to the right of the scoreboard onto Sheffield Avenue." The Pirates Roberto Clemente once hit one to the left of the scoreboard, but nobody ever reached it with a batted ball.

On June 10, 1942, Nicholson hit the longest single in Wrigley Field history. Jimmie Foxx was on second and Rip Russell on first when Nicholson hit a towering fly over Pirate center fielder Lloyd Waner's head. Both Foxx and Russell thought the ball would be caught and advanced only one base after the ball struck the 400-foot marker.

Some players considered the annual All-Star Game a bore, seeking excuses to avoid that extra day of work. Nicholson said it was an honor to be treasured. He wasn't fit to play in 1944 when he was chosen for the National League squad for the fourth time.

One hand was swollen and so painful he couldn't hold a bat. He spent all day soaking his hand in a hot salt solution. By evening he was ready. The American League was leading 1-0 in the fifth inning at Pittsburgh's Forbes Field when Nicholson batted for Ken Raffensberger and doubled home a run. Then he scored on a hit to put the National League ahead 2-1 en route to a 7-1 triumph.

At the conclusion of the 1944 season, Nicholson was nosed out by one vote to the Cardinals' Marty Marion for Most Valuable Player, 190-189. That season, Nicholson's 33 homers were more than the 23 hit by the entire White Sox team. He also tied a record, joining Babe Ruth and Foxx, by leading the league in homers and RBI for two consecutive seasons.

Slugger Bill Nicholson is the only Cub to be walked intentionally with the bases loaded. The Giants gave up the easy run at the Polo Grounds.

Then he fell in the clutches of one of the most amazing slumps. Besides being diabetic, Nicholson is color blind. He couldn't follow the pitches because of the poor background at Wrigley. "It was hard to see. I kept losing the ball among the white-shirted fans in the bleachers." That kicked off many remedies, which were finally resolved by blocking off the seats.

The Cubs went on to win the 1945 pennant, but Nicholson's average dipped to .243 and his homer production to 13. However, in the World Series against the Detroit Tigers, Nicholson tied a record with eight RBI.

Nicholson continued to lead the Cubs in homers, topping the team eight years in a row. But he never regained his stride of the early 1940s. His strikeouts increased, but he received cheers every time he came to the plate. The fans loved him despite his shortcomings.

Once in a while there was still the old spark. One occasion was Aug. 8, 1947, against Ewell Blackwell of the Cincinnati Reds. Blackwell, known as the Whip, was baseball's premier pitcher that season. He had already won 16 in a row, pitched a no-hitter, and was en route to a 22-win season.

The gangling 6′6″ right-hander resembled a fly rod with ears. When he delivered his buggy whip sidearm, he looked like a man falling from a tree. Nicholson and the rest of the Cubs couldn't solve Blackwell, but battled him to a 1-1 tie into the 11th inning.

Nicholson came to the plate that inning, tapped his shoetops, hitched his belt, and got set. All he hit was a foul ball. But catcher Ray Lamanno dropped the ball. Nicholson got a reprieve.

Blackwell then pumped and delivered and Nicholson connected. The ball was hit high and deep. It landed on the right field catwalk for a game-winning homer. Big Nick grinned from ear to ear as he rounded the bases.

The Nicholson Cub era came to an end on Oct. 29, 1948, when he was traded to the Phillies for outfielder Harry "The Hat" Walker. It was a former home run champ for an ex-batting champ.

In his decade with the Cubs, Nicholson hit 205 homers, second only to Gabby Hartnett. Eight of them were with the bases loaded. The trade wasn't popular, but Walker was soon dealt to the Reds for Hank Sauer, and the Cubs had a new homer hero.

Nicholson lasted four seasons with the Phillies, mostly as a pinch hitter. In 1950, it was disclosed that Nicholson had diabetes. He was rushed to the hospital after complaining of feeling weak and losing 20 pounds. Big Nick thus missed playing in the World Series against the New York Yankees that season.

The 39-year-old Nicholson drew his Phillies release after the 1953 season, finishing his career with 235 homers. How does Nicholson like the many changes since he left baseball?

"Well, the designated hitter is OK. It probably would have kept me in the game longer. And we could've used batting helmets. I can still feel a knot in my forehead. I was leaning in and a pitch by Ace Adams of the Giants came in high and tight and bopped me.

"But I hate those magic carpets. The ball bounces around like a yo-yo. I was standing in the outfield at Philadelphia's Veterans Stadium and could feel the heat rising. Just give me grass, daylight ball, and another pennant flying over Wrigley Field."

When he's not doing chores around his 120-acre Maryland farm, Nicholson spends most of his leisure time fishing and hunting Canadian geese—and talking baseball. "I still get cards and letters from fans seeking autographs," said Nicholson, whose lifetime batting average was .268.

DOM DALLESSANDRO

DALLESSANDRO, NICHOLAS DOMINIC
B. Oct. 3, 1913, Reading, Pa.
BL TL 5′6″
165 to 180 lb.

Rumor has it that Dom Dallessandro once leaped against the center field wall at Wrigley Field and was left dangling in the ivy vines. If true, it's a good bet that "Dim Dom Dal" was clutching the ball.

One time, Dim Dom was playing left field, which is almost out of sight from the Cubs' dugout on the third base side. The Phillies, meanwhile, were in the middle of a rally. Cub manager Charlie Grimm called time to relax his team and have fun with the umpires.

Ump Beans Reardon raced toward Grimm and yelled, "What's goin' on?" Grimm looked out toward the high grass in left field real hard and replied, "I can't find Dim Dom."

Dim Dom Dal was short for Diminutive Dominic Dallessandro. And at 5′6″ he was short, but stocky and heavily muscled. Dallessandro was built along the lines of a former Cub great—an Italian version of Hack Wilson.

At times he was called a "Fire Hydrant," a "Larruping Liliputian," or a "Tree Stump That Walked Like a Man." Dallessandro, whose round face usually sported a grin, said, "I don't care what you call me, just so you call me at meal times."

Trivia buffs would be delighted to know that little Dim Dom was once traded for tall Ted Williams. After starting his baseball career in his native Reading in 1933, Dallessandro made it to the Boston Red Sox in 1937.

The left-handed hitting outfielder got into 68 games and batted only .231. He was then sent to San Diego, where in turn, the Red Sox obtained the rights to Williams.

At San Diego, Dallessandro hit like Williams, leading the Pacific Coast League in batting with a .368 average in 1939. His 199 hits included 50 doubles, 9 triples, 18 homers, and 98 RBI.

The Cubs then purchased his contract for $17,500 and two players. He became an instant favorite with Cub fans who tuned in when his piano legs pursued a fly ball.

Dallessandro replaced the highly touted Lou Novikoff in 1941. He responded with a .272 average, socking 36 doubles, scoring 73 runs, and batting home 85.

But Dallessandro was mostly an irregular regular, filling in at all three outfield positions and pinch-hitting. In 1944 it was discovered that Dim Dom needed eyeglasses.

After donning the specs he hit a satisfying .304. Twice classified as 4-F, the U.S. Army took another look at the .300 hitter and inducted him prior to the 1945 season. Dallessandro thus missed being a member of the Cubs last pennant winner.

During his career, Dallessandro hit three grand-slam homers, including a pinch job with two out in the ninth inning that beat the Giants in the Polo Grounds. He also stole home once after misreading a sign from the bench.

Perhaps his most memorable game was the one in which Dodger manager Leo Durocher tore what little hair he had from his scalp. It happened at Wrigley Field on April 30, 1946.

The Cubs and Brooklyn were tied 1-1 in the 11th inning and the Cubs had the bases loaded with none out. Manager Charlie Grimm called on his midget to pinch-hit.

Dallessandro, recently discharged from the army and back in a utility role, strode to the plate against reliever Hugh Casey, who stood about six inches taller. It was Dominic vs. Goliath.

Dallessandro dug into the plate as Casey fired the first pitch high for a ball. Dim Dom spread his legs in the batter's box and now appeared 5′3″. The next pitch was high for ball two.

The cagey Dallessandro then added a crouch to his stance and now stood about 4′11″. The flustered Casey wiped his brow and threw high again for ball three. Durocher called time and rushed to the mound. The towering Casey nodded his head to Durocher's animated gestures and was set again.

Dim Dom was now Tom Thumb. He stood in a crouch, feet spread and knees bent. If he were any lower he'd have been under the plate. Dodger catcher Ferrell Anderson, another strapping chap, was almost in a prone position, trying to find a suitable strike zone for Casey.

Casey rocked back and fired. The ball was medium high, but sailed past Dim Dom's cap for ball four. The little guy was a big factor as the Cubs walked away with the victory.

But Dallessandro got his walking papers following the 1947 season. It happens to all ballplayers—even those who were traded for Ted Williams.

Dim Dom was a career .267 hitter with 22 home runs.

PAUL ERICKSON

ERICKSON, PAUL WALFORD
B. Dec. 14, 1916, Zion, Ill.
BR TR 6′2″ 200 lb.

Paul Erickson will always be remembered as the pitcher whose clutch strikeout clinched the 1945 pennant for the Cubs.

The Cubs were leading the Pittsburgh Pirates 4-3 with two out and runners on second and third in the ninth inning at Forbes Field on Sept. 29.

Manager Charlie Grimm summoned Erickson from the bullpen to face pinch hitter Tommy O'Brien. O'Brien fouled off the first pitch. The runners were edging off the bases. Erickson was set for his second delivery.

The strapping right-hander, who could throw the ball through a brick wall—if he could find the wall, let loose with a fastball that was headed for the screen.

O'Brien ducked. Luckily the ball struck his bat for strike two. Grimm gasped. Catcher Dewey Williams called time and raced to the mound.

Everyone was expecting another fastball. But Williams called for a curve. Erickson followed orders and threw a sweeping curve. O'Brien was fooled. He took a third strike and the Cubs won the pennant.

Tall Paul, who was a Chicago milkman during the off-season, was dubbed Li'l Abner despite his blond hair. A product of the Zion, Ill., sandlots, Erickson joined the Cubs in 1941 and had a modest 5-7 record. Among his victories was a 1-0 one-hit victory over the Pirates on Aug. 8. In addition, he showed promise by allowing only one home run in 141 innings pitched.

The following season, Erickson was a big disappointment, winning only one and dropping six. Despite his blazer, Erickson remained a fringe pitcher. His top season was a 9-7 mark in 1946.

Erickson remained in the majors until 1948, dividing his last season with the Cubs, Phillies, and Giants. His career record was 37-48. As a Cub he was 35-48.

CLYDE MCCULLOUGH

MCCULLOUGH, CLYDE EDWARD
B. March 4, 1917, Nashville, Tenn.
D. Sept. 18, 1982, San Francisco, Calif.
BR TR 5'11½"
180 lb.

Clyde McCullough looked like a cross between your local army recruiter and the village hangman. He had a battered nose, a bull neck, barrel chest, gray-squinting eyes, blond-grayish-balding hair, and a slingshot arm.

McClint, as he was called by his Cub mates, always was in baseball somewhere. He was the type whose uniform had to be torn off, but no one ever tried it.

McCullough, the youngest of 13 children and the admitted "runt of the litter," ended his formal education in the second year of high school in Nashville, Tenn., in 1934. His reason for departure: "I quit school so I could eat." He joined Lafayette, La., in the Evangeline League for $60 a month.

The peppery catcher was New York Yankee property for five years before the Cubs purchased him from Kansas City in 1939. He approached Cub manager Gabby Hartnett and said, "You're the tops as a catcher; I want you to watch me when I throw."

Mac then displayed his gifted right arm, and Hartnett replied, "All I can tell you is to keep on throwing." Hartnett then tossed McCullough to Buffalo where he batted .324, hit 27 homers, and drove in 89 runs. He also set an International League record by throwing out 40 baserunners.

In 1941 Jimmie Wilson, another ex-catcher, became the Cubs' manager. He made the talkative pepperpot his No. 1 catcher. Mac yelled at pitchers who were his seniors and displayed his colorful flair by throwing away his protective chest protector during a wilting hot spell. "Why didn't I wear it? Because it was too darn hot," replied McCullough, who hit nine homers in his rookie season, one in every park.

Perhaps Mac's greatest thrill came on July 26, 1942, against the Philadelphia Phillies at Shibe Park. As McCullough put it, "I hit three consecutive homers in a row." But nobody picked up the Big Mac attack and the Cubs lost 4-3.

McCullough broke his left ankle in the 1943 opener and missed the first seven weeks. He returned in time to receive his draft notice. He entered the navy and was stationed at Norfolk, Va.

One afternoon his navy team played the Washington Senators and George Case, who was baseball's biggest burglar. Five times Case tried to steal and five times McCullough threw him out.

McCullough left the navy just in time to take a third strike against the Tigers' Hal Newhouser in the final game of the 1945 World Series. He then declared himself the No. 1 catcher for 1946. The tough, gruff backstop, however, shared the job with Bob Scheffing, Mickey Livingston, and others.

Relegated to the bench, McCullough announced within earshot of manager Charlie Grimm that "you can't catch on this club unless you can play the banjo," a crack about Grimm's hobby. The Cubs traded McCullough and pitcher Cliff Chambers to the Pittsburgh Pirates for infielder Frankie Gustine and pitcher Cal McLish after the 1948 season.

McCullough was reacquired by the Cubs after four years at Pittsburgh. He was older, but just as brash. Mac walked up to Willie Mays when the Giants were in town and cracked, "You know Willie, somebody should take a picture of us together. We're the best two players in the league. You with your bat and your speed and me with my great arm and brains."

McCullough caught his lone no-hitter, a masterpiece by Sad Sam Jones, against the Pirates at Wrigley Field on May 12, 1955. By then, the sun had painted the great outdoors on his face. McClint was in his 21st season of pro ball.

In the ninth inning, Jones walked the first three batters. Cub manager Stan Hack called time and rushed to the mound with McCullough, who broke the silence by saying, "Sam, one more walk and yer outta there."

Jones then struck out Dick Groat, Roberto Clemente, and Frank Thomas. The last strike was a McCullough special. With the count 2-and-2 on Thomas, Jones fired away. Mac sprang from behind the plate as the ball hit his glove. Umpire Art Gore had no alternative but to call "Strike three!"

Midway through the 1956 season, McCullough received a shock.

He was dropped from the roster to make room for an $80,000 bonus pitcher, Myron "Moe" Drabowsky.

Ironically, it was McCullough who caught Drabowsky's flickering fastball in practice. When some players became inquisitive, Mac simply told them that the "fellow out there is Moe McCullough, my kid brother."

McCullough left with a lifetime batting average of .252, which he attributed to his position. "We're constantly getting hit on the arms, hands, thighs, and feet. And the sponge in the glove doesn't absorb all the shock of a sizzling fastball," said Mac.

"The worst part are the foul tips that bounce off your bare hand and arms. Sometimes your hands get so sore you can't grip a bat. That's the real answer why catchers don't bat for higher averages."

McCullough died of a heart attack at age 65 in San Francisco, while scouting for the San Diego Padres.

LENNIE MERULLO

MERULLO, LEONARD RICHARD
B. May 5, 1917, Boston, Mass.
BR TR 5′11½″
166 lb.

Lennie Merullo was nervously pacing between second and third base. There was one out in the second inning of the second game of a doubleheader at Braves Field on Sept. 13, 1942.

Clyde Kluttz of the Braves hit an easy grounder to Cub shortstop Merullo, who booted the ball for an error. Ducky Detweiler singled to right and Merullo fumbled Bill Nicholson's throw-in. That put Braves' runners on second and third and gave Merullo two consecutive errors.

Tommy Holmes was next up and he bounced an easy grounder to Merullo, who, oops, bobbled the ball. One run in, men on first and third and three successive errors for Merullo.

Merullo picked up some pebbles, juggled them, and tossed them aside as Al Roberge stepped to the plate. Roberge swung mightily and topped the ball. It was headed in Merullo's direction. Lennie scooped it up, juggled it, and watched it trickle away from him. Another run scored.

Merullo had set a major league record by committing four errors in an inning, and they came on four successive plays. But all turned out well on this memorable occasion. The Cubs went on to outlast the Braves, tagging the defeat on a scrawny, hooked-nosed rookie named Warren Spahn. The score was 12-8.

At a nearby hospital in Boston, another rookie arrived on the scene. He checked in at 7 pounds, 12 ounces. Mrs. Lennie Merullo had given birth to a bouncing baby boy, who was aptly named "Boots."

Now Boots has a son named Matt. He's an 18-year-old catcher, a sophomore at North Carolina," said Merullo, who resides in Reading, Mass., a Boston suburb. "He's a big (6′2″ and 200 pounds) redhead with freckles. Has the size, strength, and the tools to be a big leaguer," boasted Grandpop Merullo.

Lennie played baseball and hockey in high school around East Boston. As a youngster his hero was Cub catcher Gabby Hartnett. Every time the Cubs played the Braves, Merullo would bring his old, battered glove to Braves Field and work out with the Cubs.

It was natural that when Lennie decided to make baseball his career, he'd sign with the Cubs. But an education came first. Merullo enrolled at Villanova. At the same time, Fordham boasted a pitching phenom named Hank Borowy, who was unbeaten in college play.

Villanova defeated Fordham 5-4, ending Borowy's winning streak. It was Merullo who made the key plays at short and came up with the timely hits. The two were later teammates on the Cubs' 1945 pennant winner.

Merullo dropped out of Villanova with a semester to go. He joined the Cubs minor league club at Moline, Ill., in 1939, but later resumed his studies and earned a Bachelor of Science degree at Boston College.

The wiry Italian lad made his Cub debut at the tail end of the 1941 season and showed promise with a .353 average, collecting six hits in 17 trips in the final seven games.

Merullo replaced Bobby Sturgeon in 1942 and was the regular shortstop the next two seasons. He yielded the position to Roy Hughes in 1944, when his average dipped to .212. Merullo had superior range and a stronger arm, but Hughes was less prone to errors and wielded a stronger bat. The two shared the job in the pennant-winning season. Hughes, however, took over in the World Series, batting .294 to Merullo's .000.

Merullo, never a favorite with Cub fans, gained their respect in the spring of 1946 during a heated battle with Dem Bums of Brooklyn at Ebbets Field.

Dixie Walker, the "People's Cherce" of the Dodgers, slid hard into second base "and hit me behind the ear," recalled Merullo. "We sprang to our feet, the players made a big circle and let us square off."

Dixie (6′1″ and 175 pounds) chopped a right to Merullo's brow . . . Lennie countered with a combination left and right and dumped Dixie to the dirt . . . Merullo then flailed away and Dixie was groggy. . . .

The result? Merullo had a black eye and Walker lost one tooth and chipped another. Walker could no longer whistle "Dixie." When the Cubs returned to Wrigley Field, Merullo was accorded a royal welcome.

"Years later, there was a baseball banquet in New York. I met Walker in the men's room. He saw me and kiddingly took two steps back. Then we shook hands," laughed Merullo.

A sciatic condition in his back shortened Merullo's career, which concluded after the 1947 season. He was one of the Cubs' stopgap shortstops between the Billy Jurges and Ernie Banks eras. Merullo's talent was evident, but he never fulfilled his promise. He fought with himself and the result was that it made him so tight that his fielding was erratic.

Merullo had one grand slam and was involved in three triple plays. However, he is best remembered for his four errors in an inning and his fight with Walker. He hit only six homers and batted .240 in his seven-year Cub stay.

Lennie remained active in the game and brought pitcher Moe Drabowsky to the Cubs. He recommended Red Sox farmhand Glenn Beckert to the Cubs as an $8,000 waiver draftee.

Merullo is now a member of the Major League Scouting Bureau, and is based in the East. "I remember Ryne Sandberg and Rick Sutcliffe when they played in the Eastern League," said Merullo.

"Ryne wasn't that impressive. Some questioned whether he was a big league prospect, perhaps because he did everything too effortlessly. He was a tall, skinny shortstop and was sure-handed. And he always hit between the gaps in left and right center. It appears today that he has more power.

"Sutcliffe was more of a side-armer then, like Ewell Blackwell. He always seemed to have a smile on his face. Now, he has that red beard and appears meaner. He really stares them down. That sinker and slider were always tough to hit, even then."

LOU NOVIKOFF

NOVIKOFF, LOUIS ALEXANDER
B. Oct. 12, 1915, Glendale, Ariz.
D. Sept. 30, 1970, South Gate, Calif.
BR TR 5'10" 185 lb.

A fly ball is hit to deep left field. There is a long pause. Finally, the left fielder appears with a hot dog in one hand and a Coke in the other. But no ball. Well, that's Lou Novikoff.

The moon-faced, barrel-chested Novikoff ran like an animated duck, played the harmonica, sang a mean baritone, liked to draw pictures—and could he ever hit!

Novikoff, one of 12 children, spoke nothing but Russian until he was ten. Playing softball under the name of Lou Nova, "The Mad Russian" once struck out 22 batters in an eight-inning game.

He then turned to hardball and became the scourge of the minor leagues, hitting .351 at Ponca City, .367 at Moline, .361 at Tulsa, and .363 at Los Angeles.

They loved him in LA. His 1940 statistics were outstanding. In 174 games, Novikoff scored 147 runs, had 259 hits, 44 doubles, 6 triples, 41 homers, and 171 RBI to go with his .363 average.

On June 2, 1940, Novikoff graciously accepted *The Sporting News* trophy as the top minor league player. He responded by hitting two home runs, two singles, and throwing out a runner at the plate.

Novikoff then grabbed the microphone and sang "My Wild Irish Rose," with an encore of "Down By The Old Mill Stream." Somehow, he forgot his harmonica.

Was the much-ballyhooed "Commissar" fact or fiction? By now, Cub fans were clamoring for Novikoff. After all, Red Sox fans had their Ted Williams, and Yankee fans had their Joe DiMaggio.

He reported to the Cubs in 1941 and worked with Cub coach

Kiki Cuyler to get rid of his duck waddle. He hit well enough, but his fielding was atrocious. He treated the ivy vines at Wrigley Field as if they were poison ivy.

Cub traveling secretary Bob Lewis, thinking Novikoff had hay fever, took him to the wall. Lewis grabbed the vines off the wall and rubbed it all over his hands and face. Lewis even chewed a few leaves. Novikoff then smiled and asked if they were okay for smoking.

Then Novikoff developed another phobia. He said he couldn't play left field at Wrigley Field because the "foul lines were crooked." When his batting average took a crooked turn to .241, Novikoff was dispatched to Milwaukee to regain his confidence.

Novikoff reported to manager Charlie Grimm and immediately complained about the bumps in left field at Borchert Field. Grimm told Novikoff to fall down in front of the ball or wait until the ball stopped rolling. That way they could cut 'em down to triples.

Grimm then took Novikoff for a stroll around the field. "Look at all those people," said Grimm. "Do you think they're out here to see our lousy ballclub? No. They're out here to see you hit. You wouldn't let 'em down, would you?"

Novikoff puffed his chest and went out and won his fourth minor league batting title, hitting .370 to Lou Klein's .367. The Mad Russian was now ready for major league pitching.

It was agreed by the Cub brass to play Novikoff regularly in 1942, no matter how he fielded. By June 10, the team was floundering in the second division and Novikoff was batting .206. Always noted as a bad ball hitter, Novikoff was swinging at anything.

Even his wife, the former Esther Volkoff, would come out to the park and yell "strike out the bum." She then decided what Lou needed was some "hoopsa," the Russian equivalent of hamburger. It is rolled in cabbage leaves and served on a bun. Suddenly, the Mad Russian became the "Socking Soviet." For a stretch of more than four weeks, in late July and August, Novikoff was hitting better than .375.

He joined right fielder Bill Nicholson as a "game-breaker," finishing second to Big Nick in RBI. He got his average up to the magic .300 in the final week of the season to tie Stan Hack for team leadership.

The following season, Novikoff staged his famous holdout, seeking a $10,000 contract. The Cubs won only seven of their first 26 games without their balding slugger. He finally reported in late May for a compromise salary reported to be $8,500.

Cub fans were elated. In one of his first games, he went to the wall for a fly ball and suddenly froze. His shoulders scraped the bricks, but he jumped too late. The ball got away for an extra-base hit. The next ball came to him on the first hop and hit him on the chest. Novikoff was back in form. So was Esther. "If you aren't the lousiest ballplayer I ever saw," she hollered.

Novikoff was soon benched, despite his .279 average. The Cubs had Peanuts Lowrey in from LA and Andy Pafko waiting in the wings. And neither wore gloves to keep their hands warm.

The Mad Russian again played sparingly in 1944, hitting .281, and was sent to Los Angeles the following winter. He was welcomed by Angel fans and hit a cool .455 in his first five games, collecting 10 hits in 22 trips. He even stole a base. After finishing with a .310 average, Novikoff was purchased for $7,500 by the Phillies and hit .304 but was released after only 17 games in 1946.

Novikoff then returned to his first love—softball. He worked as a stevedore and starred for the world champion Long Beach (Calif.) Nitehawks. He was still playing at age 53, when he duck waddled into the Hall of Fame. No, not the one in Cooperstown, N.Y.—the Softball Hall of Fame in Rock Island, Ill.

The Mad Russian died of emphysema at age 54 in South Gate, Calif.

CY BLOCK

BLOCK, SEYMOUR
B. May 4, 1919, Brooklyn, N.Y.
BR TR 6'0" 180 lb.

Who was the only major leaguer to appear on a gigantic billboard in New York's Times Square? The Babe? DiMag? Yogi? Nope, not even Reggie Jackson. It was Cy Block.

Amidst the hustle and bustle of the Great White Way was an advertisement reading: "Cy Block says 'Life Insurance Is The Home Run Investment... With It You Can't Strike Out. Your Life Is My Business.' "

Also depicted was a player completing his swing. Under the photo it read: "Cy Block Chicago Cubs 1942-1947."

Yes, there was a Cy Block, and he did play for the Cubs. Block had a lifetime batting average of .302, including a rousing .364 in 1942. But Block only played in 17 major league games.

Cy was a third baseman, but the Cubs had a fixture at that position named Stan Hack. Block grew old waiting for Hack to age. By the time Hack retired, Block was ready for the insurance business.

The Block story began on the sandlots in Brooklyn. There were the usual stickball games on hot, summer afternoons just outside the shadow of Ebbets Field.

Block's mother wanted little Seymour to study to become a doctor or a lawyer. Ballplayers, in her eyes, were beer drinkers and loafers. All Block ever wanted was to play baseball.

He and his companions used to scale the wooden bleacher fence at Ebbets Field to see Dazzy Vance dazzle the hitters with his fastball and Babe Herman drop countless flyballs in the outfield. Inevitably, there was the usual fat police officer, ready to boot Block and his buddies out of the ballpark.

But baseball was in his blood. He started as a second baseman in 1938 with Paragould, Ark., in the Class D North East Arkansas League. Among his early instructors was Cub immortal Joe Tinker, who told Block he had the determination and spirit to overcome what he lacked in natural ability. Tinker assured him he would make it to the big leagues.

After hitting .325 and earning $65 per month at Paragould, our hero was invited to spring training with the Memphis Chicks. There he ran afoul of the fun-loving Hugh Casey, who used to snip off Cy's neckties and throw his baggage off moving trains.

But Block was excess baggage with the Chicks. He was shipped to Greenville, Miss., of the Class C Cotton States League, where he batted .315. Then it was on to Macon where his double-play partner and roommate was Eddie Stanky.

If Stanky was a tough hombre in the majors, he was a holy terror in the minors. In an exhibition game against Kansas City, Phil Rizzuto stole second by sliding head first under Stanky's tag. The next time Rizzuto tried it, Stanky gave him the knee and knocked him out cold.

Stanky toughened Block for the major leagues. In his final season at Macon, Block led the Sally League with a .357 average and was voted the Most Valuable Player.

Block was invited to the Cubs spring training camp at Catalina Island, but lost out to second baseman Lou Stringer. He was advised to try third base because Hack couldn't last forever.

Block batted .276 at Tulsa and was recalled late in the 1942 season. He replaced Hack for a Labor Day doubleheader against the Cincinnati Reds and fastballing Johnny VanderMeer, who once pitched back-to-back no-hitters.

Vandy struck out Block on three fastballs in his first big league at bat. Old slugger Jimmy Foxx told Block not to worry. Foxx said he should wait patiently for the curve. Sure enough, Vandy threw a curve and Block singled home a run. Block then rapped a double off the left field wall in his third try against VanderMeer.

There was a hot pennant race that season between Brooklyn and St. Louis. Commissioner K. M. Landis said no rookies could be used in games against the Cardinals or Dodgers. Thus, Block was barred from playing against Dem Bums at Ebbets Field before the home folks.

That winter, Block enlisted in the coast guard and missed three full seasons. He returned in time to appear as a pinch runner for the Cubs in the 1945 World Series against the Detroit Tigers.

But Hack was still at third base and Block drifted from Los Angeles to Nashville to Buffalo. Then he recalled his mother's words: "Don't be a baseball bum." After 15 years in baseball, Block joined the Mutual Benefit Life Insurance Co., where he became a life member of the Million Dollar Round Table.

Roberto Clemente was Puerto Rico's all-time sports hero. The Pirates' outfielder died tragically on New Year's Eve, 1972, in a plane crash a few miles from his birthplace on a mission to aid earthquake victims in Nicaragua.

Hi Bithorn was Puerto Rico's first baseball hero. He, too, died tragically—of a gunshot wound on New Year's Day, 20 years earlier.

HI BITHORN

BITHORN, HIRAM GABRIEL
B. March 18, 1916, Santurce, Puerto Rico
D. Jan. 1, 1952, El Mante, Mexico
BR TR 6'1" 200 lb.

Hiram Gabriel Bithorn, a burly pitcher of Danish-Spanish extraction, left Puerto Rico's tropical shores and entered the New York Yankees chain at Norfolk in 1936, where he had a 16-9 record.

The next year he was 10-1 at midseason, a .909 percentage, and boasted a 1.90 ERA. The Yankees moved him up to Binghamton, where he finished with 7-8.

In 1938 the Yankees sent Bithorn to their top farm club at Newark. It was then that he developed a growth on his elbow and wound up at Johns Hopkins Hospital for consultation. An operation was advised.

"I was in the X-ray room," said Bithorn, "when suddenly the doctor wanted to know who was going to pay for surgery. I told them the Newark club was. They called the Newark Bears' secretary and he said 'No.' " The operation was called off.

The Yanks shipped Bithorn to Oakland. He wound up at Hollywood in 1940 and that fall was operated on. "At their expense," added Bithorn, who repaid the Stars with a 17-15 record that included a league-leading 12 shutouts and 228 innings pitched.

Bithorn was picked up for $7,500 by the Cubs in the 1942 winter draft and combined with Cuban catcher Sal Hernandez as baseball's first Latin battery. They were called the Castilian Caballeros and enjoyed heckling in Spanish to upset the enemy batters.

Bithorn, who had a 9-14 rookie season with the Cubs, displayed a keen sense of humor that was flavored with his delightful accent. Harry Hazlewood, a Wrigley Field groundskeeper, once asked Bithorn, "You're pitching today; what do you want me to do with the mound today, Hi?"

"Well," retorted Bithorn, "you might move it 10 feet closer to home plate."

Hi Bithorn and Sal Hernandez of the 1942 Cubs formed the first Latin battery in big league history.

Bithorn also possessed a volatile temper. He was pitching against the Dodgers in Brooklyn, and instead of throwing toward the plate, he whizzed a fastball into the Dodger dugout, just missing manager Leo Durocher, who was needling him. Hi drew a $50 fine from NL president Ford Frick.

The next time the Cubs were in Brooklyn, Cub manager Jimmy Wilson noticed Bithorn hanging around first base, near the Dodger dugout. "What are you doing here?" asked Wilson. "I wait for that Durocher," said Bithorn. "If he comes out of the dugout I'll kill him."

The following season, Bithorn killed the opposition. The speed baller added a little cunning to his repertoire and compiled an 18-12 record with a nifty 2.60 ERA. He pitched 250 innings, had 19 complete games and led the league with seven shutouts that included two two-hitters and a three-hitter.

Bithorn was also a big thorn to the world champion Cardinals, beating St. Louis four of five times. Soon, everyone took notice, including the U.S. Navy, who welcomed Hi aboard on Nov. 26, 1943.

Navy chow apparently agreed with Bithorn, who ballooned to 225 pounds before his discharge two years later. In addition to his expanded waist line, Bithorn came up with a sore arm and had a disappointing 6-5 record in 1946.

The Cubs sold Bithorn to Pittsburgh on waivers at the end of the season. When the Pirates dropped him from their spring roster, he was picked up by the White Sox, where he pitched only two innings and had a 1-0 mark before returning to Caribbean baseball.

Bithorn operated a tavern in Santurce, umpired in the Class C Pioneer League, and was another forgotten ballplayer—until New Year's Eve, 1951.

Perhaps the true story of his death will never be known. Bithorn was on a trip to visit his mother in Mexico City when he was arrested for trying to sell a 1947 car for $350 without proper documents.

Police officer Ambrosio Castillo Cano said Bithorn had no papers for the car and there were no license plates on it. The two got into the car and started for the El Mante, Mexico, police station.

Officer Cano testified that Bithorn suddenly struck him and tried to get out of the car. Claiming self defense, Officer Cano fired a .45 into Bithorn's stomach. He was taken to the nearest hospital, where he died.

Adding mystery to his testimony, Officer Cano claimed that Bithorn gasped, "I am a member of a communist cell on an important mission," as he lay dying.

An investigation followed. Officer Cano was found guilty of simple homicide and was sentenced to eight years in state prison. Bithorn's body was shipped to Puerto Rico where an estimated 6,000 mourners filed past the bier in Sixto Escobar Park.

As a memorial to Puerto Rico's first baseball hero, a ballpark bears the name: Hiram Bithorn Stadium.

PEANUTS LOWREY

LOWREY, HARRY LEE
B. Aug. 27, 1918, Culver City, Calif.
BR TR 5'8½"
170 lb.

When Harry Lee Lowrey was born, an uncle took one look and said, "He's no bigger than a peanut." Lowrey grew to be a ballplayer, but at 5'8½", he remained Peanuts.

Before he entered the baseball scene, Lowrey was a scene-stealer in the movies. His grandfather had a ranch in Culver City, the home of Metro-Goldwyn-Mayer Studios. And the ranch was used as a backdrop for *Our Gang* comedies.

Lowrey was a toddler when he made his film debut, sitting in a street car, next to Thelma Todd. He was supposed to look out the window, but instead, kept mugging at the camera. She promised to take him to the circus and buy him peanuts if he stopped mugging. That did it. Little Peanuts looked at her soulfully and played it straight.

Lowrey soon went from mugging to stealing bases as a shortstop with St. Augustine's of Culver City in the CYO League. He started his pro career with Moline in 1937, and the following season joined Ponca City, which was loaded with future Cubbies.

The Ponca City alumni of 1938 included Paul Erickson, Emil Kush, Lou Novikoff, Vern Olsen, Rip Russell, and Lou Stringer. Peanuts was the least heralded of the lot as they worked their way to Los Angeles, the Cubs' top farm club.

Lowrey became the Cubs' regular center fielder in 1943, leading the club in stolen bases and hitting .292. In 1944 he turned in his bat for a rifle. Upon his return from the army, Lowrey found Andy Pafko in center field.

Peanuts switched to left field and hit a solid .283 with 89 RBI as the Cubs won the 1945 National League pennant. He batted .310 as the Cubs lost the World Series in seven games to the Detroit Tigers.

Perhaps his most productive day as a Cub was July 12, 1946, when he drove in seven runs with two singles and a three-run homer to beat the Brooklyn Dodgers 13-2.

But his most memorable was the day he quelled a near-riot with one stroke of the bat. The Cubs were playing the Boston Braves in the second game of a doubleheader at Wrigley Field on Aug. 26, 1948.

The Braves were leading 1-0 in the third inning. The Cubs had runners on first and second with Phil Cavarretta at bat. Cavy knocked the first pitch against the left field wall. Braves' left fielder Jeff Heath pretended to lose the ball in the ivy vines as Cavy circled the bases with a three-run inside-the-park homer.

The ball was in full view of the bleacher fans and Heath, who kicked it aside. But the umpires fell for Heath's act and called it a ground-rule double, allowing only one run to score.

Angry fans showered the field with beer bottles, hot dog wrappers, and raw fruit. Some stormed onto the field. Play was held up and the umps threatened to forfeit the game in Boston's favor.

When order was restored, the popular Pafko was intentionally walked. That set off more booing and another barrage of debris. A few minutes later, Lowrey cleared the bases with a game-winning triple. It was Heath who had to chase the ball into the left field corner.

Lowrey, a real handyman who played every position except first base, pitcher, and catcher, remained a Cub favorite until he was traded with Harry "The Hat" Walker to the Cincinnati Reds for Hank Sauer and Frankie Baumholtz in the spring of 1949.

He remained with Cincy one season before beginning a new career with the Cardinals. It was at St. Louis that Peanuts Lowrey became Pinch Lowrey. One season he batted almost .500 in the pinch with 13 hits in 27 at bats. The next year he collected a league high 22 pinch hits.

Lowrey closed out his career with the Philadelphia Phillies in 1955. He then joined ex-Cub teammate Cavarretta as a player-coach at Buffalo in 1956. One day, Buffalo had the bases loaded in the 14th inning. Cavy looked down his bench for a pinch hitter. He called for Lowrey, and little Peanuts reached into his back pocket and came up with another triple.

Meanwhile, during the off-season Lowrey remained a handyman in the films. And he didn't have to change uniforms. Peanuts had bit roles in *Pride of the Yankees, The Stratton Story,* and *The Winning Team.*

Lowrey's biggest role was in *The Winning Team* with Ronald Reagan as pitcher Grover Alexander. Lowrey was the shortstop that plunked Reagan with the ball between the eyes as he was heading for second.

"We used a cotton ball, and when I hit him, I shouted, 'Look out.' But the director said, 'Cut!' He figured I would get an extra $350 for having a speaking role," said Lowrey.

"So we reshot the scene, and after I hit Reagan, I had to look sad and keep my face down as Reagan was sprawled on the ground. I looked plenty sad, thinking of the lost $350," added Lowrey.

Peanuts, who is acknowledged as one of the foremost golfers among the ballplayers, was also in demand as a major league coach during the past two decades.

He served with the Phillies, Giants, Expos, Angels, and Cubs from 1960 through '79. Peanuts was the Cubs' third base coach during the stormy Leo Durocher and Herman Franks eras.

"Let me tell you about Durocher," said Lowrey. "When I was a player, I hated him. When I was one of his coaches, I loved the guy. He got all over a player and got the most out of him. The Cubs didn't blow it in 1969. The darn Mets kept winning. They played like hell and deserved it.

"And don't listen to that stuff about playing all day games wearing you out. I loved it. That's just a poor excuse. The players just couldn't cut it and they had to blame it on something."

Lowrey spends much of his time taking on his golf buddies in playing gin rummy at the Riveria Club near his Inglewood, Calif., home. "Just had a gall bladder operation. Can't play too much golf," added Peanuts, who shelled the pitchers for 1,177 hits and batted .273 in 13 seasons.

Hank Wyse was the Cubs' workhorse during World War II. The moon-faced moundsman pitched 536 innings in the 1944-45 seasons. He won 38 games, lost 25, and lasted through 37 complete games.

Called Hankus Pankus by manager Charlie Grimm, the pudgy

pitcher perfected his control by throwing hour after hour at a target erected on the back of a barn on the family's farm in Lunsford, Ark.

With the country mired in the Depression, Wyse went up to Kansas City to look for work in 1937. The employment manager of a steel tank company asked Wyse if he could play ball.

"I can pitch," replied the 19-year-old Wyse, who is of Cherokee, English, and Irish stock.

"We have an important game tomorrow. You're the pitcher," said the personnel employer, who also managed the company team. "If you lose, you're through before you even start. If you win, I'll have a job for you."

Wyse went out and pitched a no-hitter, in which nary a fly ball was hit to the outfield. He landed the job.

Wyse entered organized ball with Tulsa in 1940. There he had a 2-2 record before being shipped to Moline of the storied Three-I League. It was at Moline that the first of his back injuries struck.

While fielding a bunt, Henry made a quick, twisting motion to get off a throw. He doesn't remember whether he got the runner, but he does recall the jabbing pain.

Wyse began wearing a corset to sooth his injured back. He became a pain to rival batsmen as he reeled off 20-4 and 20-11 records with Tulsa in 1941 and '42. That earned him a late-season trial with the Cubs.

Hank broke into the National League by beating Johnny VanderMeer and the Cincinnati Reds 6-3. He won another and dropped one before the season ended.

Prior to reporting to the Cubs camp in 1943, Wyse suffered a setback. His wife died shortly after giving birth to their son, David. Wyse continued on and showed promise with a 9-7 rookie season, walking only 34 batters in 156 innings and compiling a 2.98 ERA.

During the off-season, Wyse fell off a ladder while working as a welder. The fall resulted in a spine injury—a misplaced vertebra. It was painful for Hank to sit down, but apparently, standing and pitching didn't bother him.

The rubber-armed Wyse won 16 and dropped 15 with his deadly sinker and change-up. He refused to submit to back surgery and it proved a Wyse decision as he won 22 and lost 10, leading the Cubs to the 1945 pennant.

Possibly Wyse's best performance was his one-hitter on April 27 at Wrigley Field. It was a cold and windy day as Hank flirted with and lost his bid for a no-hitter.

He held the Pirates hitless until one out in the eighth inning. Wyse got two strikes on rookie catcher Bill Salkeld, but grooved the next pitch. Salkeld drove a line single to right-center. It was the lone hit as the Cubs won 6-0 for their sixth straight win.

Wyse was involved in another streak midway in the season. The Cubs had won 10 in a row when they took the field against the visiting Boston Braves on July 12. For Boston, outfielder Tommy

HANK WYSE

WYSE, HENRY WASHINGTON
B. March 1, 1918, Lunsford, Ark.
BR TR 5'11½"
185 lb.

Holmes had hit safely in 37 consecutive games.

"Tommy was a fine gentleman," recalled Wyse. "I held him hitless in three trips before he came to bat with two out in the ninth. I threw him two wide ones for balls and he fouled off another. Then I threw a half speed pitch.

"Holmes hit a two hopper to me and I tossed him out. I remember Holmes saying, 'Damn you, Hank,' as he ran down the line."

The Cubs had beaten the Braves on Wyse's three-hitter for their 11th victory in a row. After the game, Cub manager Charlie Grimm compared Wyse with Grover Cleveland Alexander.

"Give Ol' Alex a quick lead and he'll just breeze through," said Grimm. "Wyse is just like that. No strain. No pressure."

Wyse breezed through the season until the second game of the World Series against the Tigers. He met another Hank (Greenberg) who tagged him for a three-run homer in the sixth inning, turning a 1-0 Cub lead into a 4-1 defeat. Wyse was a series disappointment. His earned-run average was 7.04, after a 2.68 mark during the season.

Wyse finally submitted to back surgery during the winter of 1945 and came back to win 14 and lose 12. But he slipped to 6-9 in 1947 and drew his Cub release.

After an 18-8 season at Shreveport in 1949, Wyse was drafted by the Philadelphia A's, where he was 9-14 in 1950. He split his final big league season with the A's and Washington Senators in 1951, with a 1-2 record.

After baseball, Wyse started from scratch by going to the dogs. He settled in Pryor, Okla., near Tulsa, and raised bird dogs for field trials. "I still train them," said Wyse. "One of 'em, Rex, is probably one of the best hunting dogs in the state."

When not hunting or fishing, Wyse follows baseball via cable TV. "What I don't understand is why pitchers can't go the distance," said the 64-year-old ex-hurler. "We went to spring training and got into shape to go nine innings. Nobody ever wanted to come out. I completed 23 games when we won the pennant."

If you need any pointers on baseball or bow wows, one word from Wyse is sufficient.

MICKEY LIVINGSTON

LIVINGSTON, THOMPSON ORVILLE
B. Nov. 15, 1914, Newberry, S.C.
D. April 3, 1983, Newberry, S.C.
BR TR 6'1½"
185 lb.

Thompson Orville Livingston sounds like someone belonging in the social register. Mickey Livingston sounds more like a catcher.

Livingston received his nickname when he was playing American Legion ball. At that time, Mickey Cochrane was one of the oustanding catchers, so his teammates slipped Thompson Orville a "Mickey."

The lanky Livingston started as a first baseman in Newberry High. When the team needed a catcher, he was nominated. Mickey signed originally with the St. Louis Cardinals in 1934 and was given the runaround in their vast farm chain.

"The Cardinals sent me to one of their tryout camps at Greensboro, N.C., after I graduated from high school," said Livingston. "They then sent me to spring camp the following year.

"I was there six weeks and then my traveling began. First I was shipped to Rochester for two weeks. Next stop was Columbus for a week and then they sent me to Asheville, N.C.

"I was there only for a few days when they wanted to ship me on to Huntington, W. Va. That was too much. I told 'em I was through and went back home."

Mickey next signed with Chattanooga in 1937 and jumped to the big leagues the following season. His stay with the Washington Senators was brief, but eventful.

Livingston played two games and pounded out three hits in four trips for a .750 average. Two of his hits were doubles, so his slugging average was a delightful 1.250.

But his .750 batting average was higher than his .667 fielding average. The poor rookie had a terrible time catching Dutch Leonard's knuckleball. "The ball did all tricks. It acted like a butterfly," lamented Livingston, who didn't surface back to the majors until 1941 with the Phillies.

By this time he was an accomplished catcher, but batted like a butterfly. Livingston larruped a lusty .203 and improved his stickwork to .205 in 1942. He was now ripe for the Cubs.

Livingston was acquired from the Phillies for pitcher Bill Lee on Aug. 2, 1943. He hit a homer in his first trip to the plate against the Reds.

He cracked out seven hits, including two homers and a double in 15 times at bat for a .467 average as a Cub. The sudden spurt was due to a change in his batting style suggested by coach Kiki Cuyler.

"Kiki Cuyler told me I'd probably do better if I held my bat out a little farther, away from my body. I tried it and it seems to have made a difference," said Livingston.

Livingston finished the season at .254 (.261 as a Cub) and was inducted into the army on Feb. 20, 1944. His service stint was short, having received his honorable discharge on Nov. 8, 1944, at Camp Atterbury, Ind.

Mickey shared the catching with Paul Gillespie in 1945 as the Cubs swept to the pennant. Gillespie was famed as the first Cub to sport a crew-cut. Livingston was famed for hitting the lone homer in a 24-2 rout over Boston at Braves Field on July 3.

Livingston's robust hitting put Gillespie on the bench during the World Series against Detroit. Mickey batted .364, banging out eight hits, including three doubles, and drove in four runs. But it was Livingston, who popped to catcher Paul Richards for the final out as the Tigers won in seven games.

Livingston shared the catching with Clyde McCullough and Bob

Scheffing, two service returnees in 1946. He got into 66 games and batted .256.

The handsome backstop was waived to the Giants midway through the 1947 season, but saw little action with Walker Cooper enjoying a 35-homer year behind the plate. From there he went to the Braves and wound up his career with the 1951 Dodgers.

He then bounced around the bushes as a manager at Shreveport, Beaumont, Boise, and Colorado Springs, before returning to Newberry. It wasn't learned that Livingston was ill until the Cubs held an old-timers game on June 14, 1980, at Wrigley Field for their 1945 pennant heroes.

Livingston died April 3, 1983, at age 58 in Newberry.

Mickey's lifetime average was .238 with 19 homers and 354 hits, most of them as a Cub.

DON JOHNSON

JOHNSON, DONALD SPORE
B. Dec. 7, 1911, Chicago, Ill.
BR TR 6'0" 170 lb.

"Don Johnson was *our* Ryne Sandberg," said teammate Lennie Merullo. "If anyone was an unsung hero on the pennant-winning Cubs of 1945, it was Johnson. He ignited many a rally with a timely hit, and was an expert at advancing a man with a bunt."

Johnson inherited his baseball ability from his father, Ernie Johnson, a journeyman infielder, who played for several teams during the 1910s and '20s, including two stints with the White Sox, where he batted .295 in 1921.

"Dad was a backup to Yankee shortstop Everett Scott when they opened Yankee Stadium," recalled the younger Johnson, now 73 and a resident of Laguna Beach, Calif.

Don languished in the minors for 10 seasons before World War II breathed new life into his career, just as it seemed doomed to stagnation.

"I remember those rattling buses and overheated trains," said Johnson, who began his career in 1933 in Seattle. He made stops in Sacramento, San Francisco, Hollywood, Tulsa, and Milwaukee.

"I never hit much," admitted Johnson, who was brought up to the Cubs in September 1943 at the ripened age of 32. The Cubs were so impressed with his play the following spring that he took the regular second baseman's job away from Eddie Stanky.

Stanky was traded to Brooklyn for southpaw pitcher Bob Chipman and ultimately became the better player of the two. Still Johnson proved to be a wise investment.

In 1944 Don played in all 154 games, batted .278, led the Cubs in doubles with 37, and was selected to the National League All-Star team, although he did not play. It was an impressive rookie year, and the following campaign would be frosting on the cake.

On April 17, 1945—opening day of the season—Don drove in the winning run as the Cubs beat the Cardinals 3-2 to begin their long drive for the pennant.

This game was historic because the Cardinals never led the league for a *full* day in their pennant chase. It also marked the major league debut of Red Schoendienst, who played left field for St. Louis.

It was Schoendienst's throw that Bill Nicholson slid under to score the winning run on Johnson's single in the bottom of the ninth.

Perhaps Don's biggest day came July 3 at Boston, where he collected three singles and two doubles in seven trips, scored five runs, and knocked home another four.

After grounding out in the first inning, Don doubled to lead off the third, then scored on Nicholson's double. In the fourth inning, Johnson slapped a single over second to send Merullo across the plate. The sixth inning was almost a repeat of the third, as Don doubled and scored on Nicholson's single.

In the next inning, Don drove in Claude Passeau with a sacrifice fly, followed by a single in the eighth. Finally, in the ninth he sent two more runners home with another single. The Cubs scalped the Braves 24-2 in their version of the Boston Massacre.

But the most vivid game in Johnson's memory was the pennant clincher at Pittsburgh's Forbes Field on Sept. 29. "We were ahead 4-3, but the Pirates had runners on first and third with two out," recalled Johnson.

"Just one more out and we win the pennant. Erickson's first pitch was a fastball for a strike. I'll never forget that next pitch," shuddered Johnson.

"It was another blazer and Paul lost control of it. I almost lost my uppers and lowers. Al Gionfriddo was racing home with the tying run as the ball was headed for the backstop.

"But pinch hitter Tommy O'Brien ducked and the wild heave somehow struck his bat for strike two. Erickson continued to be off target as O'Brien ran the count to two balls and two strikes.

"Standing at second base, I expected another fast one. But catcher Dewey Williams wisely called for a curve. I can still picture O'Brien taking the next pitch—a beautiful curve—for strike three. What a pleasureful moment. The pennant was ours."

For the season, Johnson batted .302 and scored 94 runs. Don was a disappointment in the World Series, batting only .172 as the Tigers outlasted the Cubs in seven games.

Thereafter, he left his best days behind him as advancing age, aggravating injuries, and postwar competition took their toll. In 1946 he missed nearly half the season with a broken hand as his average fell to .242.

He was back in the daily lineup the following year, but had slowed down considerably at second base. Johnson played his final game on May 16, 1948, then retired, a lifetime .273 hitter with 528 base hits.

ANDY PAFKO

PAFKO, ANDREW
B. Feb. 21, 1921,
Boyceville, Wis.
BR TR 6'0" 190 lb.

Andy Pafko, the eternal farmboy from Boyceville, Wis., will be remembered for his odd batting stance. He crouched with his bat cocked high at one end and his protruding rump at the other.

"People made fun of Stan Musial's stance, too," laughed Pafko. "As long as I was comfortable—and got results, I stayed with it."

The thick-chested Pafko patrolled center field with easy loping strides, diving for low liners and climbing the vines for high arching smashes. His arm was the archenemy of all baserunners.

He was loose-jointed with wavy hair and a bobbing Adam's apple and was a favorite of Cub fans for almost a decade. Handy Andy was traded before his time. More than 30 years have passed and the Cubs are still without an equal in center field. Except for possibly Bob Dernier.

"Dernier can really go get 'em," said Pafko, who resides in Mount Prospect, Ill. "He gets a jump on the ball and goes into the gaps. All winning teams need a fleet center fielder, whether it's a cozy ballpark or a huge carpeted stadium."

Although Dernier is faster afield and on the basepaths, he lacks Pafko's powerful arm and home run bat.

Pafko, one of six sons of Slovak immigrants, grew up hayin' and feedin' on the family farm. When those chores were done, there were always cows to milk. "Nothin' like milkin' to strengthen the wrists," said the boyish-looking Pafko.

And then there was baseball. Andy, Frank, and Eddie, the three youngest Pafkos, had their chores before they could give any thought to playing. The trio struck up an idea. They pushed the clock an hour ahead. It was pitch dark when the alarm went off. But it worked.

His mom and dad never knew about it. "We had an extra hour of daylight for baseball. And we did it regularly," chuckled Pafko. He also had time for football. As captain and halfback of Boyceville High, Pafko scored all four touchdowns and placekicked all the points to win the homecoming game from Woodville by a single point.

Pafko then suffered a setback. On his 17th birthday he and his chum, Paul Yurik, were attending Sunday school. It was a bitterly cold day and the gas stove was turned on full blast. Suddenly there was an explosion. Fire swept the premises.

Yurik pulled Pafko from the flames. Paul died shortly thereafter and Andy was badly burned about the face. Dr. Francis Butler of Menominee preserved Pafko's eyesight and the youngster recovered slowly.

In the spring of 1940, without his parents' consent, Pafko paid his own way to Eau Claire, Wis., for a tryout with the Northern League Bears. After hitting only .209 in 67 games, he was released.

The next season, the Green Bay club held a throwing contest and Pafko won it. "I threw the ball over the grandstand," recalled Pafko. And he batted .349 with 13 homers. Macon was the next stop in 1942. There Pafko batted .300 and set a Sally League record with 18 triples.

"I was supposed to play in Milwaukee in 1943," said Pafko. "That made me feel good. I was lonesome at Macon and wanted to be around home so my family and friends could come to the games. All of a sudden I was told to report to Los Angeles. It made me mad.

"I decided to give up baseball. But my kid brother, Eddie, talked me out of it." At LA, Pafko was the toast of the coast, winning the batting title with a .356 average, scoring 109 runs, collecting 215 hits, with 31 doubles, 13 triples, 18 homers, and 118 RBI.

Pafko, who had never seen a major league game, was told to report to the Cubs at the tailend of the season. He rode the train three days from Los Angeles, then took a taxi straight to Wrigley Field, where that day's game was played in cold temperatures and a freezing drizzle.

Facing ex-Cub Bill Lee, Pafko smacked the first pitch, lining a single over third. He added a double and wound up with four RBI as the Cubs beat the Phillies in a rain-shortened game. There were only 314 fans in attendance for Pafko's debut, the smallest crowd in modern-day Wrigley Field history. In 13 games, the young outfielder showed his potential by hitting a rousing .379.

After Peanuts Lowrey was drafted into the army, Pafko opened his rookie season in center field in 1944. The new idol of the bleacher fans batted only .269, but led the league with 24 assists with his overpowering arm.

"The next season I was last in assists. They learned to stop running on me," said Pafko, who was affectionately called "Prushka" by manager Charlie Grimm.

The Cubs won the pennant in 1945. Prushka batted .298, hit 12 homers, 12 triples, 24 doubles, and drove in 110 runs. In addition, the slugging Slovak finally received his mother's blessing to play ball instead of trying to work for a living.

The Cubs were playing the Pirates on Sept. 23, 1945, at Wrigley Field. It was rainy and cold, but Andy's mom and dad were among the 45,000 fans in the stands. Some friends made it "Andy Pafko Day." "I didn't get a car or anything like that," said Pafko. "Just some luggage and a watch.

"Preacher Roe struck me out the first time up. I went back to the bench thinking, 'They give you a 'day' and you stink out the joint. Good thing mom doesn't know anything about the game.'

"But then I came up in the third inning with the bases loaded and the Bucs ahead 3-2. Roe threw the ball high and inside. I swung. The ball hooked down the left field line. It looked like it was going foul. Then a blast of cold wind swept in from the west and helped keep it inside the line. It went out of the park almost at the foul pole for a grand-slam homer. We went on to win.

"People were hollering and jumping. They were shaking her hands and yelling, 'That's your boy.' She didn't know what happened and my father was too excited to explain it. After the game she was clinging to my arm and crying and saying, 'Yes, good

. . . that's good.' Mom never saw another game. She died the following summer."

The following summer wasn't much for Pafko. He stepped on a ball during warmups on June 1 and suffered a bone separation in his right ankle that sidelined him for almost two months. Then he broke his right elbow when he crashed into the fence while making a circus catch of a drive by Walker Cooper to preserve a 2-1 victory over the Giants on Aug. 27. That put him out of action for the season.

Pafko bounced back in 1947, batting .302 and making the All-Star team. He switched to third base in 1948, although he never played that position before, hitting a career-high .312 and adding 26 homers. In 1949 Pafko returned to center field and was involved in a bizarre episode.

The Cubs were leading St. Louis 3-2 with two out in the ninth inning at Wrigley Field. A Cardinal runner stood on first. Pinch hitter Rocky Nelson swung and Pafko made a shoestring catch in short left-center to supposedly win the game.

But umpire Al Barlick, stationed near second base, ruled that Pafko had trapped the ball. As Pafko was holding the ball aloft and racing to the dugout in glee, two Cardinals were streaking around the bases.

By the time he figured out what was happening, his throw to the plate plunked Nelson squarely on the back. The Cards won 4-3. "I caught it in the pocket, not the webbing. I even kept my glove off the ground so it would be easy to see," said Pafko.

Andy combined with slugger Hank Sauer to give the Cubs baseball's most potent one-two punch in 1950. Pafko hit 36 homers and the Honker added 32 for 68. The next season Pafko was traded.

It happened on June 15, 1951, a date Cub followers have long lamented. One day before the eight-player swap, Pafko was taking batting practice. One of the visiting pitchers, Don Newcombe, approached him and said, "You're going to be a Dodger tomorrow."

The following day, Pafko was a Bum. He went to Brooklyn with pitcher Johnny Schmitz, infielder Wayne Terwilliger, and catcher Rube Walker. In return, the Cubs received a sore-armed pitcher, a sore-armed catcher, a utility infielder, and a utility outfielder—Joe Hatten, Bruce Edwards, Eddie Miksis, and Gene Hermanski.

The trade made little sense. It created a gaping hole in center field that has been patrolled the past 30 years by stop-gap journeymen and young phenoms who never developed. It also hurt the box office. Pafko was one of the few Cub attractions.

Andy, meanwhile, joined an all-star cast of Dodgers that included perhaps baseball's best armed outfield. Pafko shifted to left field because center was Duke Snider territory and right belonged to the Reading Rifle, Carl Furillo.

The Dodgers were on their way to the pennant that season until Bobby Thomson of the Giants smacked one over Pafko's head into the left field bleachers with two out and two on in the bottom of the ninth inning at the Polo Grounds.

Two years later, Pafko came home to Wisconsin. The Braves shifted their franchise from Boston to Milwaukee, and Pafko was dealt to dairyland, rejoining old Cub manager Grimm. Andy won the team's cow-milking contest and was voted the most popular Brave.

But in 1954 he yielded his outfield position to a youngster named Hank Aaron. "He can run and hit with the best of 'em," predicted Pafko. "It feels funny, warming the bench," added Andy, who continued in a utility role until 1959.

In his 17-year career, Pafko batted .285 with 1,796 hits and 213 homers—126 as a Cub. Now 63, semiretired, and living in Mount Prospect, a Chicago suburb, Pafko looks fit and trim. He appears as if he could still back-peddle to the vines in Wrigley to snatch a sure base hit off the top of the fence.

Grantland Rice once wrote about famed jockey Earle Sande: "Gimme a handy guy like Sande, booting the winners home." He could have added: "Gimme a handy guy like Andy, driving those runners home."

ROY HUGHES

HUGHES, ROY JOHN
B. Jan. 11, 1911, Cincinnati, Ohio
BR TR 5'10½" 167 lb.

Roy Hughes was more than a wartime retread with the Cubs. In fact, the team got a lot of mileage out of the well-traveled infielder.

The Cincinnati native started with Zanesville in the Mid-Atlantic League in 1932 and played with nine clubs in six circuits before landing with the Cubs in 1944.

Hughes was a wiry second baseman with speed to burn when he reported to the Cleveland Indians in 1935. He was inserted into the leadoff spot by manager Steve O'Neill and responded with a .293 average.

Nicknamed "Jeep" because of his speed, Hughes hit on all cylinders in 1936, scoring 112 runs, collecting 188 hits, with 35 doubles, 9 triples, and 20 stolen bases. But his .295 average was only sixth best on a club that batted .304 overall.

Perhaps it was his lack of homer production (only one in three seasons) that reduced Hughes to a utility role the following season. In 1938 he was traded to the St. Louis Browns for catcher Rollie Hemsley, and in 1939 he bounced from the Brownies to the Yankees to Newark to the Phillies.

Then it was back to the bushes. Hughes was with Montreal of the International League when he suffered a setback on May 28, 1940.

He slid into Creepy Crespi at second base. "He came down on my right shoulder and something popped," recalled Hughes. "I couldn't even raise my arm the rest of the season and the doctors told me I was through."

His career was salvaged that winter by an explosion of a tar can that blew him helter skelter and severely burned him on the arms and shoulders. "That explosion blew me back into shape," said Hughes. "The doctors said it was a miracle.

"I was trying to thaw out some tar in the basement of my home. The heat of the explosion sort of sealed those damaged muscles. It welded them together again. I walked out of the hospital with new life in a dead arm."

After two big seasons with the Los Angeles Angels, then the Cubs' top farm club, Hughes was summoned to the Cubs after veteran third baseman Stan Hack decided to retire to his Oregon apple ranch at the outset of the 1944 season.

The handy Hughes was hitting a hefty .322 at third base, when Cub manager Charlie Grimm sweet-talked Hack out of retirement. The fun-loving Jolly Cholly carted Hack onto the field in a wheelbarrow and dumped him at third in special ceremonies at Wrigley Field.

Meanwhile, shortstop Len Merullo went into a tailspin, his batting average dipping to .212. The Jeep rode to the rescue and plugged the gap at short. Hughes finished with a .287 average and led the club with 16 stolen bases.

Roy played 36 games at short, 21 at second, 9 at third, and 2 at first as the Cubs waved a wartime flag, winning the pennant by three games over the Cardinals. Although the Cubs lost the World Series to the Tigers in seven games, Hughes was quite productive, hitting .294 and driving in three runs on five hits in 17 trips.

The Cubs sold Hughes to the Phillies for the $7,500 waiver price on Jan. 21, 1946. Roy concluded his 16-year up-and-down career with a .273 big league average.

Before he departed, Hughes helped lay the ground work for the players' pension fund. Today, he enjoys his role as a grandfather in Cincinnati and is one of a handful of retired players active in the Society for American Baseball Research. He attends all their summer conventions and revels in trivia talk about all aspects of the game.

FRANK SECORY

SECORY, FRANK EDWARD
B. Aug. 24, 1912, Mason City, Iowa.
BR TR 6'1" 200 lb.

Mason City, Iowa, was the hometown of *The Music Man's* Meredith Willson. Outfielder-umpire Frank Secory wasn't one of the 76 trombones in the big parade, but he did help drum-major the Cubs to the '45 flag.

Secory, nicknamed the "Deacon" because of his impeccable dress, had one sip of coffee with the Detroit Tigers in 1940, going to bat once and whiffing away.

He emerged again in 1942 with the Cincinnati Reds. There he had five gulps of java before he was gone. After batting .290 with the Milwaukee Brewers of the American Association, Secory started to percolate with the Cubs at the tail end of the 1944 season.

The Deacon collected 18 hits, including four homers, in 56 trips for a .321 average and a .554 slugging percentage. But with Bill Nicholson, Andy Pafko, and Peanuts Lowrey as the regular outfield trio, Secory provided right-handed bench strength.

In fact, Secory delivered perhaps the biggest clutch hit of the season. Thanks to an 11-game winning streak, the Cubs shook off everybody but the St. Louis Cardinals going into September. Their lead over the Cards was a half game, when they clashed in a crucial doubleheader in St. Louis.

The Cardinals won the opener, a 4-0 shutout by Red Barrett, and overtook the Cubs by a half-game. "We were tied 1-1 in the 10th inning," recalled Secory, who is now retired and resides in Port Huron, Mich.

"We had the bases loaded and two out and I was fidgeting in the dugout. Manager Charlie Grimm was about to send in Paul Gillespie to pinch-hit, when I mentioned that I hit pitcher George Dockins pretty good when we were in the Texas League.

"Grimm overheard me and sent me up to bat. I cleared the bases with a double against the wall in right-center, driving home Pafko, Reggie Otero, and Lowrey. We won 4-1 and left St. Louis with a half-game lead."

Secory also served as a pinch hitter in the World Series against the Tigers, batting .400 with two hits in five trips. He saw limited action the following season and drew his Cub release.

Before he departed, Secory bid adieu by stroking a pinch grand slammer off the Giants' Dave Koslo to turn a 12th inning 6-6 tie into a 10-6 Cub victory at Wrigley Field.

"I wanted to stay in baseball, but didn't care for coaching or managing. I figured an umpire was responsible only for himself, so I started in the West Texas-New Mexico League and soon graduated to the Texas League.

"Then I was fortunate," said Secory. "The National League expanded its umpiring crew to 16 in 1952, and I was welcomed aboard. Veteran umps Larry Goetz and Lou Jorda warned me about manager Leo Durocher. They said, 'Don't let Leo get one step ahead or he'll run you right out of the league.' Durocher and I got along, somehow.

"My most difficult decision? Oh, that was easy. It happened at Wrigley Field. The Cubs were playing the Reds, and Hal Jeffcoat broke for home and missed the plate. And Cincy catcher Hobie Landrith missed the tag.

"I delayed making a decision and just stood there and watched as both crawled toward the plate. Meanwhile, Cubs' manager Phil Cavarretta and Reds' manager Rogers Hornsby both stormed from their dugouts.

"Jeffcoat struggled and put a few pinkies on the plate and I signaled 'safe.' "

Secory retired as an umpire in 1970 with fond memories. "If I had to pick out the nicest gentlemen to come to bat, I'd select Stan

Musial, Billy Williams, Gil Hodges, and, of course, Ernie Banks."

HANK BOROWY

BOROWY, HENRY LUDWIG
B. May 12, 1916, Bloomfield, N.J.
BR TR 6'0" 175 lb.

If only Hank Borowy hadn't had blisters to go with his blistering fastball, he would have had a more blissful career. But the slim right-hander was a blessing for the Chicago Cubs in 1945.

The Cubs completed their famous deal with the New York Yankees, buying Borowy's contract for a reported $97,500 on July 27, 1945. Borowy went on to win 11 and lose only 2 as the Cubs charged to the National League pennant.

Success had ridden tandem with Borowy ever since he first pitched as a stripling for the Bloomfield, N.J., Grey Caps. The sandlot team drew its name from its one item of regulation equipment, grey caps.

The lanky Polish lad then pitched Bloomfield High to the state championship in 1935, winning 13 and losing 1. Among his victories were a no-hitter and a 26-strikeout performance.

At Fordham University the frail-looking Borowy won 24 of 25 games. His lone loss was 5-4 to Villanova. A shortstop named Lennie Merullo made several great stops and a couple of timely hits to decide the game. Merullo and Borowy later became mates aboard the Cub pennant winner.

During his six years of high school and college ball, Borowy compiled a 52-3 won-lost record. Before he had finished his sophomore year at Fordham, more scouts were camped at the Borowy doorstep than there were bobby soxers after Frank Sinatra.

Scout Paul Krichell, who discovered Lou Gehrig among others, signed Borowy to a Yankee contract in the spring of 1938, when Hank was in his junior year at Fordham. The blond youngster with the knife-bridged nose and narrow chin agreed to sign for an $8,000 bonus.

As he started to inscribe his formal Henry Ludwig Borowy on the dotted line, nothing happened. Krichell went in search of ink. When he returned, Borowy said softly, but firmly, "I've had more time to think it over and I think I'm worth another $500."

Krichell gulped, then paid off and replied, "That was the most expensive ink I've ever put in my pen." They also agreed that Borowy was to be shipped to Newark, the Yankees' top farm club.

Borowy spent three seasons at Newark, compiling 9-7, 12-10, and 17-10 records. He was ready to don the famed Yankee pinstripes in 1942. Manager Joe McCarthy worked Borowy into the regular rotation, and Hank responded with a 15-4 rookie record.

One of Borowy's victories was a near no-hitter on Sept. 3. Harlond Clift of the St. Louis Browns skittered a grounder off second baseman Joe Gordon's glove in the first inning. Gordon knocked it down, but his throw to first was late. After much deliberation, it was ruled a hit.

Borowy soon emerged as the mainstay of the Yanks' war-riddled pitching staff. He had a 14-9 mark in 1943 and a 17-10 record in 1944. Then followed one of baseball's most puzzling deals.

Despite his 10-5 record, Yankee owner Larry MacPhail placed Borowy's name on the waiver list. That meant the other seven American League teams could pick him up for $7,500. The catch was that waivers could then be withdrawn. The other teams, figuring it was a wasted effort, didn't bother putting in a bid for Borowy.

That cleared the way. MacPhail phoned Cubs' general manager Jim Gallagher and said Borowy was available. The Cubs, locked in a pennant battle with the St. Louis Cardinals, closed the deal for a reported $100,000. It was later substantiated as $97,500.

Hank immediately proved his worth by winning 11 and losing 2 down the stretch drive. His lone losses were by 2-1 and 1-0 scores. In the latter he tossed a three-hitter, but bowed to Cub nemesis Harry "The Cat" Brecheen of the Cardinals.

Borowy gained revenge on the Cardinals on Sept. 19 in St. Louis. The Cards had a 1-0 lead going into the ninth inning. Card third baseman Whitey Kurowski opened the inning by booting Don Johnson's grounder. Peanuts Lowrey bunted Johnson to second, but Phil Cavarretta fouled out.

That brought up Andy Pafko, who took two quick strikes. One more and there would be a tie for first. But Handy Andy singled to short center, scoring Eddie Sauer, running for Johnson, with the tying marker.

In the 10th inning, Bill "Swish" Nicholson's pinch single with the bases loaded sealed a 4-1 Cub triumph, putting them two games up. Cub manager Charlie Grimm raced out of the dugout and hugged the wan, sweaty Borowy.

One week later, the Cubs clinched the pennant as Borowy, with ninth-inning relief help from Paul Erickson, edged the Pittsburgh Pirates 4-3. Having won 10 games for the Yankees before the deal, Borowy thus equaled Joe McGinnity's record for reaching the 20-game victory class in one season, pitching in both leagues. His overall record was 21-7.

Borowy won the World Series opener, blanking Hal Newhouser and the Detroit Tigers 9-0. Newhouser gained revenge over Borowy in the fifth game, but Hank came back to pitch four scoreless innings of relief to win the sixth. He then started the seventh and deciding game, but discovered he had pitched himself out. The Tigers, with Newhouser on the mound, took the series.

Although Borowy spent only a half season with the Cubs, he was voted a full share of the series loot. After all, he got them there. Perhaps the Cubs remembered when another ex-Yankee, Mark Koenig, hit .353 after being acquired in midseason 1932 and was voted only a half-share. The Yankees, especially Babe Ruth, never let them forget during the fall classic.

Borowy never recaptured the effectiveness of that 1945 season. Instead of blistering his opponents, he kept blistering his fingers. By exercising pressure on his fingers when applying spin to his fastball Borowy had grown a bumper crop of calluses.

The calluses would dig into the flesh and blisters would develop. Sometimes blood would spurt all over the ball. The tender-fingered Borowy tried creams, wood-rubbing, bone-honing, staining, finger dipping into goop, umpice, and alom to toughen the tender digits.

But all the finger rubbing worked in reverse. The skin became raw instead of rough. During the next three seasons, Borowy's records fell to 12-10, 8-12, and 5-10. He was traded with first baseman Eddie Waitkus to the Philadelphia Phillies for pitchers Walt Dubiel and Dutch Leonard after the 1948 season.

He did have a last hurrah. On Aug. 1, 1948, he held the Brooklyn Dodgers to one hit in a 3-0 victory before 45,531 fans at Wrigley Field. Gene Hermanski's single over second base in the second inning was the spoiler. Hermanski was cut down trying to steal as Borowy went on to face the minimum 27 batters. He worked his raw fingers to the bone for that win.

After two seasons with the Phillies, Borowy was waived to the Pittsburgh Pirates. He wound up his career with the Tigers in 1951. Borowy then went back to his hometown of Bloomfield, N.J., and entered the real estate business. His first purchase was a firehouse.

Borowy's overall record was 108-82. In a Cub uniform Mister Blister was 36-34, but his outstanding pitching performance in 1945 fingered him as one of the most unforgettable Cubs.

SECTION TWO 1946-1953 Sauer Sweet, But Sour Seasons

The Cubs had not been hurt by the draft as badly as other clubs, but in 1946 this temporary advantage vanished. Furthermore, many of the Cub stars were aging players whose "last hurrah" had been the '45 pennant. They could not withstand the stiffer competition. Consequently, the defending champions slipped to a distant third.

Cub players back from military duty included Johnny Schmitz, Bob Scheffing, Emil Kush, Clyde McCullough, Eddie Waitkus, and some lesser names. Waitkus was an immediate hit at first base, pushing Phil Cavarretta back into the outfield. Schmitz was a hard-luck lefty whose statistics belied the quality of his pitching. Kush was a competent fireman, and Scheffing, a catcher, had a couple of good seasons ahead of him. But they were not enough to keep the Cubs in contention.

By 1947 the old men were a year older as the Cubs sank to sixth. During the off-season, many familiar names disappeared from the roster.

The following spring the Cubs went for youth, bringing up youngster after youngster from their farm system. Unfortunately, only a few of them had noteworthy careers, and even some of those could be better described as anti-heroes than heroes.

Roy Smalley, the new shortstop, had great range, but was as likely to fire the ball into the grandstand as not. He became the symbol of Cub frustration during the postwar era. Bob Rush, like Schmitz, was a tough-luck hurler whose record should have been far better. Outfielder Hal Jeffcoat had a bazooka throwing arm, but a squirt gun batting average. He was later converted to a pitcher. Meanwhile, the Cubs finished dead last for the first time in 23 years.

Marv Rickert and Eddie Waitkus hit the only back-to-back inside-the-park homers in National League history in the fourth inning at the Polo Grounds on June 23, 1946.

In June 1949 Frankie Frisch replaced the beleaguered Charlie Grimm as Cub manager. A few days later, the Cubs obtained outfielders Hank Sauer and Frankie Baumholtz from the Reds in a first-class steal. Sauer replaced the departed Bill Nicholson as the Cubs' new home run hero, while Baumholtz was a fine singles hitter. Nevertheless, they could not prevent the team from finishing in the cellar once again.

Over the winter Jim Gallagher was kicked upstairs. Wid Matthews, a blind optimist, became Director of Player Personnel. In a short time, he would make Gallagher look like a genius by comparison.

The Cubs went on a home run binge in 1950, belting 161 baseballs over the fence, their most since the Hack Wilson halcyon days of 1930. However, everything else continued dismally. The Cubs escaped the basement by only one rung. The sieve-like infield of Preston Ward, Wayne Terwilliger, Smalley, and Bill Serena committed 201 errors to lead both leagues.

By the following season, the Cubs had returned to the dungeon, during a year that witnessed Phil Cavarretta taking Frisch's place as manager. Wid Matthews dealt Andy Pafko and three others to Brooklyn for four players, all of whom put together were not worth

Pafko. Just *why* Andy was traded has never been made clear.

Even so, there were signs of hope in rookie first baseman Dee Fondy and sophomore third baseman Ransom Jackson, both of whom proved to be solid performers.

In 1952 the Cubs were the surprise of the league, climbing up to fifth place with a .500 record. Sauer was Most Valuable Player and Baumholtz challenged Stan Musial's monopoly on the batting title. Fine pitching came from Rush, Warren Hacker, Paul Minner, and bullpen ace Dutch Leonard. Compared to what Cub fans had been through, it was a satisfying year.

Just as the Cubs were beginning to look respectable, they reverted to previous form, dropping to seventh in 1953. That was the year they picked up Ralph Kiner from the Pirates to complete the hallowed outfield troika of Kiner in left, Baumholtz in center, and Sauer in right. Cynics claimed that Baumholtz had to play all three positions. Although obviously an exaggeration, it typified Cub anti-heroics in the late '40s and early '50s.

JOHNNY SCHMITZ

SCHMITZ, JOHN ALBERT
B. Nov. 27, 1920, Wausau, Wis.
BR TL 6'2" 170 lb.

Spring training had not officially opened. Many of the Cubs had assembled at Catalina Island in 1946 to take a scenic hiking tour. They hiked over the hilly trails and then reported to trainer Andy Lotshaw with blisters and aching bunions.

Not so with pitcher Johnny Schmitz, who spent the winter hacking holes in ice-bound lakes and hunting in the wintry woods of Wisconsin. Two hours after the hike he was off playing 18 holes of golf. Add that to his size-14 brogans and you get the nickname "Bear Tracks."

Bear Tracks was not for wise cracks. He was a silent, slim southpaw. While others perspired to melt away surplus blubber in steamy sweat boxes, Long John was always trying to butter up on his 6'2" torso.

The modest and reserved Schmitz, the second of six children, came from a poor family in Wausau, Wis. During the Depression, his dad, a fireman, was out of work. But there was always time for athletics.

Schmitz began as a left-handed third baseman on a softball team. He then switched to pitching and never lost a game for Wausau High School, despite weighing only 150 pounds.

He was signed by Rudy Schaefer of the Milwaukee Brewers and was sent to Hopkinsville, Ky., of the Kitty League in 1938. There he posted an .846 percentage on 11 victories and 2 defeats. The next season he made the jump to the Brewers, who were managed by Charlie Grimm.

Although the Brewers had trouble winning, Schmitz was a big hero, being of German descent. Whenever Grimm took Schmitz out of a game, a cry would come from the stands: "What's the matter, Sharley? . . . Sharley, he was just getting warmed up."

It was Grimm who recommended Schmitz to the Cubs. Johnny made his big league debut on Sept. 10, 1941, and chalked up his first victory on one pitch. He came in to face Cookie Lavagetto with two on and one out with the Dodgers leading 4-2 in the top of the ninth inning at Wrigley Field.

Johnny Schmitz threw only one pitch and was the winning pitcher in his big league debut in 1941.

Cookie hit the first pitch and grounded into a double play. The Cubs rallied with three runs in the bottom of the ninth to win 5-4. A win for Schmitz on one pitch. A Dodger killer was born.

Schmitz was 2-0 that season and had a 3-7 record before enlisting in the navy midway through the 1942 season. After 19 months in such steaming places as New Caledonia, Guadalcanal, and Tulagi, where he picked up those annoying tropical ailments, Schmitz reported to the Cubs in 1946.

Although he was an unknown quality at the outset of the season, he wound up as the ace of the pitching staff, leading the National League in strikeouts with 135. His record was a modest 11-11.

One of those games will always be remembered. It was the final game of the season at Wrigley Field. It was the Cubs against the St. Louis Cardinals. All St. Louis had to do was win the game to clinch the pennant. If the Cardinals lost, it would mean a playoff between Brooklyn and St. Louis for the flag.

Stan Musial homered off Schmitz for an early lead. But the Cubs scored five runs in the sixth inning and went on to win 8-3. Schmitz drove in the go-ahead runs.

The score was tied 3-3 when Grimm let Schmitz bat for himself with the bases loaded in the sixth. Schmitz hit a high bouncer that handcuffed first baseman Musial, whose throw to first was high, enabling two runs to score.

Grimm then announced for all to hear, that Schmitz was the best southpaw in the league, better than Warren Spahn, Johnny "Double-No-Hit" VanderMeer, and the Cards' pair of Howie Pollet and Harry "The Cat" Brecheen.

Schmitz encountered the emaciated-looking Brecheen early in the 1947 season and tossed a two-hitter, but the Cat prevailed 1-0. It was that kind of year for Schmitz, who won only 13 while losing 18.

But 1948 was something else. Schmitz *was* the best southpaw. He pitched 18 complete games and reversed his 1947 record, winning 18 and losing 13 with a last-place ballclub. In addition, Schmitz was credited with a one-hitter, three two-hitters, four four-hitters, two five-hitters and four six-hitters.

He almost lost that one-hitter. He trailed the New York Giants 2-0 at the Polo Grounds going into the top of the ninth inning, the Giants scoring both runs in the eighth without a hit. But Handy Andy Pafko homered with two on and the Cubs won 3-2 for Schmitz.

The Eastern writers took notice of the slat-like southpaw that season. He was called the "Dodger Killer," beating them five times.

Schmitz took a delight in beating Brooklyn. His career lists 18 victories against the Dodgers.

His nemesis was the Cardinals, especially with Brecheen on the mound. On April 30, 1950, the two hooked up on a damp, chilly afternoon at Sportsman's Park in St. Louis.

In one stretch, Brecheen retired 19 batters in a row. Schmitz did even better. He had knocked off 20 batters in succession. But in the 13th inning, Del Rice poled a 400-foot homer off Schmitz. The Cardinals won 1-0.

On May 15, 1951, the Cubs and Dodgers were involved in an eight-player swap. It was one-sided in Brooklyn's favor. They received Pafko, Schmitz, second baseman Wayne Terwilliger, and catcher Rube Walker. The Cubs got stuck with second baseman Eddie Miksis, pitcher Joe Hatten, catcher Bruce Edwards, and outfielder Gene Hermanski. At last, the Dodgers would no longer be tormented by Schmitz.

But Bear Tracks had trouble getting untracked in Dodger flannels. In the next five seasons he bounced from the Dodgers to the Reds, to the Yankees, to the Senators, to the Red Sox, and finally to the Orioles. He closed his career in 1956 with a 93-114 record. As a Cub Schmitz was 69-80.

He then resumed fishing through the ice, a pastime that engrossed him every winter. Sometimes he gets 100 perch a day. When he gets tired of this, he switches to hunting rabbits. In addition, Schmitz serves as the greenskeeper at the Wausau golf course.

EDDIE WAITKUS

WAITKUS, EDWARD STEPHEN
B. Sept. 4, 1919, Cambridge, Mass.
D. Sept. 15, 1972, Boston, Mass.
BL TL 6'0" 170 lb.

Eddie Waitkus was like a vacuum cleaner at first base. He scooped up everything hit his way without raising any dust. One time he almost bit the dust after being felled by a .22 calibre rifle shot fired by a crazed teenager.

Waitkus might never have become a major leaguer if he hadn't decided to forego a Saturday afternoon movie back in 1936, in his home town of Cambridge, Mass.

The first baseman of a local semipro team was injured, and Ralph Wheeler, who served as manager of the team and as a Chicago Cubs scout, called a half dozen youngsters.

Waitkus, who had decided to see a Hoot Gibson western, was persuaded to play. The lean and lanky Waitkus starred for the team and eventually signed a Cub contract. After three minor league seasons, Waitkus joined the Cubs in 1941.

But World War II intervened. Waitkus became a machine gunner in the Pacific theatre. There he earned four battle stars, seeing action in the New Guinea, Bougainville, and Luzon invasions.

Waitkus had another battle on his hands when he returned home after 32 months of combat. Stationed at first base for the Cubs was veteran Phil Cavarretta, who was coming off a 1945 campaign in which he led the National League in batting with a .355 average and was named Most Valuable Player.

Cub manager Charlie Grimm, quite a first baseman in his heyday, greeted his rookie at the outset of spring training and told him to trot over to the bag to see how he handled some grounders. Grimm tried to smash the ball past Waitkus for 15 futile minutes.

Grimm was flustered, but ecstatic. The conclusion? Cavy was shifted to the outfield and Waitkus won his first battle. He finished his rookie season with a .304 average, tops on the Cubs. But it was his fancy fielding that fractured the fans.

Waitkus was deadly on bunts. He would race in, grab the ball, and fire to second to thwart the opposition's sacrifice strategy. He stopped almost all liners hit his way and could leap skyward for errant throws.

He was also Steady Eddie at the plate, following his rookie year with .292 and .296 seasons. Waitkus, in addition, made his way into the record books on June 23, 1946, when he combined with Marv Rickert in hitting back-to-back inside-the-park homers at the old Polo Grounds, a National League feat never equaled.

In 1949 Waitkus was dispatched to the Philadelphia Phillies in another horrible Cub trade. Waitkus wore the Phillies' red pinstripes when they invaded Wrigley Field for a three-game series with the Cubs on June 15.

A love-sick 19-year-old girl named Ruth Steinhagen reserved a room at the Edgewater Beach Hotel, where the Phillies checked in. She gave a bellboy $5 and a note to deliver to Eddie's room on the third floor.

Waitkus helped the Phillies defeat the Cubs 9-2 that afternoon. Following the game Waitkus had dinner with his roommate, outfielder Bill Nicholson, another old Cub hero. It was 11:30 p.m. before Waitkus found the message in his room.

He knocked on her door. She admitted him and greeted him with the rifle. Waitkus asked what this was all about, but the young woman shouted, "Now, you're going to die."

She fired at close range. The bullet penetrated Eddie's chest, pierced a lung, passed near his heart, and lodged close to the spine. Steinhagen picked up the phone and told the switchboard operator, "I've just shot a man."

Waitkus was rushed to Illinois Masonic Hospital, where he underwent surgery. He was listed in critical condition for several days. Steinhagen, who collected photos of Waitkus and said she was infatuated with him, was committed to a mental hospital.

But Waitkus won another battle. He returned to action the following season as a member of the Phillies' famed "Whiz Kids." They won the pennant, with Waitkus hitting a solid .284 and again fielding like Eddie Waitkus.

That winter he won the Comeback of the Year Award. The old, flawless mitt master was acclaimed the Phillies' lifesaver after he escaped death.

Waitkus played less frequently from 1953 on, retiring two years later with a .285 lifetime average and 1,214 hits.

BOB SCHEFFING

SCHEFFING, ROBERT BODEN
B. Aug. 11, 1915, Overland, Mo.
BR TR 6'2" 180 lb.

Bob Scheffing was just another catcher buried in Branch Rickey's far-flung farm chain. He knocked about the minor leagues, sporting batting averages of .189, .199, .231, and .210.

The parent St. Louis Cardinals had two kid catchers of high promise named Mickey Owen and Walker Cooper. To make matters worse, while playing for Mobile in 1938, Scheffing broke his right shoulder when he blocked a runner sliding into home plate.

Rickey offered the 23-year-old Scheffing a job managing Washington, Pa., in the Class D Penn State Association at $75 a month.

"Do you want to manage Washington?" asked Rickey.

"Not particularly," replied Scheffing.

"Well, you get your release if you don't," said Rickey.

"In that case, I'll take it," said Scheffing.

Class D was the lowest rung in organized baseball, but Scheffing's club boasted a Warneke and a Sisler. Not Lon Warneke and George Sisler, but Warneke's nephew and Sisler's son.

Scheffing was told to play first base even though he couldn't throw across the infield. The result? Scheffing led the league in fielding and drove in 96 runs while batting .330. Washington won the 1939 postseason playoff championship.

Scheffing earned a promotion to Rochester in the International League and was drafted by the Cubs in the spring of 1941. Scheffing was the Cubs' second-string catcher behind hard-throwing Clyde McCullough. He hit one homer that season.

That homer came with the bases loaded as a pinch hit in the ninth inning and beat the Cardinals 7-3 when St. Louis was fighting for the National League pennant.

Scheffing's average dipped to .196 in 1942. But the military service also takes chaps with unhealthy batting averages. He thus missed the next three seasons while serving in the U.S. Navy.

Scheffing was a bit rusty when he returned to the Cubs for the opener of the 1946 season. The Cubs were facing the Cincinnati Reds at Crosley Field. Joe Beggs held the Cubs to a lone single and Cincy led 3-0 going into the ninth inning.

Then Stan Hack singled, Don Johnson doubled, Peanuts Lowrey and Phil Cavarretta singled, and the Cubs trailed 3-2. Cub manager Charlie Grimm had used every available player and went fishing for someone to pinch-hit for Bobby Sturgeon.

He looked down his bench and had only Scheffing left. The

ex-sailor was the last hope to keep the Cubs afloat. It was anchors aweigh as Scheffing lined a single to left-center, bringing home the tying and go-ahead runs. The Cubs went on to win the opener 4-3.

Scheffing led the league in pinch hits that season, while sharing the catching chores with McCullough. In 1948 he managed to bat .300. Scheffing remained a Cub until June 7, 1950, when he was traded to the Reds for Ron Northey.

He retired as a player in 1951 and joined the St. Louis Browns in 1952 as a coach under Rogers Hornsby. In midseason, however, the Browns rebelled against Hornsby. Club owner Bill Veeck fired Hornsby and received a loving cup from his players for the greatest play since the Emancipation Proclamation. Scheffing refused to indulge in the theatrics. He was the lone member of the Browns' cast not to have his named inscribed.

Scheffing rejoined the Cubs as a coach in 1954, then took over as manager of their top farm club, the Los Angeles Angels. He brought the Angels home third, just two games out of first, then won the 1956 pennant by 16 games, the widest margin in any professional league that season.

Scheffing replaced Hack as Cub manager in 1957 and started rebuilding the team. Fans flocked back to Wrigley Field to watch the power-hitting Cubs in action. His 1958 lineup included Ernie Banks,47 homers; Moose Moryn, 26; Lee Walls, 24; Bobby Thomson, 21; and Dale Long, 20. Scheffing brought back Hornsby as a batting coach, and it was Hornsby who picked out Ron Santo and Billy Williams from among the Cub minor league crop as future batting stars.

When the Cubs finished only 13 games out of first place with an inexperienced pitching staff, Scheffing was mentioned as a leading candidate for Manager of the Year in 1959. He was summoned by owner P. K. Wrigley and marched into his office with a grin, expecting a fat raise.

Wrigley said Bob had done "a helluva fine job," but he wanted to "make a change." Scheffing was fired.

The genial ex-catcher eventually won Manager of the Year honors, but it came two years later in a Detroit uniform, leading the Tigers to a 101-61 record and finishing two games behind the New York Yankees.

Scheffing was let out by the Tigers in June 1963, again listening to a familiar tune. This time it was echoed by Detroit GM Jim Campbell. "I'm sorry Scheff, but we've got to make a change," said Campbell.

It was his last managerial job. From there, Scheffing became farm director of the New York Mets, eventually being elevated to the post of vice-president and general manager in 1970. He was now in a position to hire and fire managers.

Scheffing is now retired and resides in Scottsdale, Ariz. His 35-year baseball career took him from a $75-a-month minor leaguer in Branch Rickey's chain to player, coach, manager, scout, and executive.

In the majors he was a .263 lifetime hitter with 357 hits.

HAL JEFFCOAT

JEFFCOAT, HAROLD BENTLEY
B. Sept. 6, 1924, West Columbia, S.C.
BR TR 5'10½" 185 lb.

Hal Jeffcoat was a strong-armed outfielder who threw like a pitcher. But, alas, he also hit like one. Jeffcoat came from a family of pitchers. His brother George won 7 and lost 11 with the Dodgers and Braves during the 1930s. Brother Bill pitched in the Giants' farm system, and Charlie was in the Yankees' vast minor league chain.

But Hal wanted to be an outfielder. He starred in football, basketball, and baseball at West Columbia (S.C.) High. When he was 17 he signed on as a semipro with a Jacksonville (Fla.) shipyards team. He played several games a week in his spare time from work on the battlewagons.

The stocky, sandy-haired Jeffcoat was drafted into the army in 1944. He was a combat paratrooper, making the jump into southern France. He later saw action at Anzio.

Following the war Jeffcoat signed with Larry Gilbert's Nashville Vols of the Southern Association and was sent to Shelby, N.C., of the Tri-State League.

Hal's best day in the minors came during the summer of 1946 at Shelby. In the first game his sixth-inning homer was the decisive blow in a 4-3 victory. In the second game his 16th-inning homer broke a 4-4 tie.

Jeffcoat was promoted to Nashville in 1947. There he batted a solid .346, but finished way behind Memphis slugger Ted Kluszewski, who led with a .377 average. Jeffcoat did lead with 218 hits and his 118 RBI were second to a chap named Albert Flair, who drove in 128. In addition, Hal scored 120 runs and collected 36 doubles and 13 triples.

The 23-year-old's contract was purchased by the Cubs later that year. Manager Charlie Grimm saw him uncork some potent throws from deep center field during spring training at Catalina Island. Grimm was convinced he had a young phenom. Grimm shifted Andy Pafko to third base and installed Jeffcoat in center field, although Hal was as green as the Wrigley Field ivy. Grimm's plan worked. Pafko, a natural athlete, proved better than adequate at third base, the spot vacated by the retired Stan Hack. Jeffcoat, combining speed and natural instincts, in addition to his strong arm, was one of the best center fielders in the league.

He even hit. On May 2, 1948, Jeffcoat had two doubles in one inning. He drove in three runs in a seven-run eighth inning as the Cubs ripped the Cardinals 13-4 in St. Louis. Grimm nicknamed the youngster "Hotfoot Hal," a moniker that somehow never took hold. The handsome Jeffcoat, however, became a darling of the bobby-soxers.

There was one day that season that Jeffcoat never forgot. It started out to be a grand day. Mrs. Jeffcoat presented Hal with their second son, John Philip Jeffcoat, on Aug. 28.

That afternoon, the Cubs went into the ninth inning, leading the Boston Braves 4-2 at Wrigley Field. There were two on, two out, and two strikes on Jeff Heath. Heath lined one to center field. Jeffcoat misjudged the ball, coming in too fast for it. Then he darted back, crashed into the wall, and was knocked unconscious.

By the time right fielder Bill Nicholson could retrieve the ball, Heath had rounded the bases for an inside-the-park homer. Three runs were in and the Braves won 5-4.

Nevertheless, Jeffcoat did rank among the standout rookies. He hit .279 with 132 hits, including 16 doubles and 53 runs scored. Hotfoot Hal cooled off in 1949, hitting only .245 and losing his center field job to Pafko. His lone consolation was leading the club in stolen bases with 12, including home plate twice.

There was more woe for Jeffcoat the following season. On May 14, 1950, Jeffcoat made a diving stab at Pirate Pete Castiglione's double to right-center and landed on his left shoulder. He was sidelined two months with a broken collarbone.

"I was in combat two and one-half years as a paratrooper," lamented Jeffcoat. "I made 13 jumps out of an airplane and never got a scratch. Now I get busted up for two months just chasing a little white ball."

From then on Jeffcoat was a utility outfielder. By the spring of 1954, Jeffcoat feared his career might be at an end. Stan Hack, who took over the managerial reigns during spring training, was told by his coaching staff that Jeffcoat might be able to help as a pitcher.

During an exhibition game against the Orioles, Jeffcoat was summoned in the fifth inning. He borrowed a glove and forgot about a toe plate. He held the Orioles scoreless, allowing only two hits. Jeffcoat earned his first victory on a five-hit eight-inning bullpen stint against the Dodgers on May 6 at Wrigley Field. He finished the season with a 5-6 record.

Perhaps his finest day as a Cub was on May 18, 1955. He came in with the tying and winning runs on base and none out in the ninth inning against the Phillies. He saved a 3-2 victory for Sad Sam Jones.

Jeffcoat was back in the second game. He entered in the fourth inning with the Cubs trailing 4-2. Jeffcoat permitted one run the rest of the way as the Cubs rallied for a 7-5 victory on homers by Bob Speake, Ted Tappe, and a chap named Ernie Banks. Jeffcoat was now the Cubs' leading reliever, winding up with an 8-6 record.

The Cubs thanked him by trading him on Thanksgiving Day for a turkey of a catcher named Hobie Landrith. The Reds got the gravy. Jeffcoat was among the top firemen in 1956 with an 8-2 record. He won a dozen games the following season and a half dozen in 1958.

Jeffcoat was sent to the Cardinals in midseason 1959 in a swap of ex-Cubbies. In exchange for Jeffcoat the Reds received Jim Brosnan.

Jeffcoat retired after the 1959 season, a .248 lifetime hitter and a 39-37 hurler.

ROY SMALLEY

SMALLEY, ROY FREDERICK
B. June 9, 1926, Springfield, Mo.
BR TR 6'3" 190 lb.

Roy Smalley, Cub shortstop of the late 1940s and early '50s, could be best described as an "anti-hero." He replaced Lennie Merullo at the position in 1948 and immediately drew the attention of fans and writers. Touted as the next Marty Marion by the Cubs' organization, Smalley covered ground as if it were going out of style, diving to his left and diving to his right. He would make a miraculous stop, only to ruin it by heaving the ball into the grandstand.

In his first season, Roy batted .216 and led the league's shortstops in errors with 34. The next year, he upped his batting average to .245 and his miscue count to 39, again leading the league.

When Wayne Terwilliger arrived at second base in August 1949, the post-war version of Tinker-to-Evers-to-Chance was born; namely, "Terwilliger to Smalley to the dugout." Chicago racetrack announcer Phil Georgeff, when he was not horsing around, penned this rhyme:

On edge was the crowd,
The Braves had the bases loaded.
From Elliott's bat the ball exploded.
It bounded into Terwilliger's glove,
Sailed to Smalley like a dove.
"Out at second," the umpire accursed.
Smalley uncoiled, threw to first.
'Twas an easy play, that tremendous clout,
"Terwilliger to Smalley—to the dugout."

When Eddie Miksis replaced Terwilliger in 1951, the main verse was changed to "Miksis to Smalley to Addison Street."

In fairness, Roy's wild throws were not entirely his own fault. He had a deformed middle finger on his throwing hand, the result of an injury suffered in 1945 when he was in the navy. As to the strength of Smalley's arm, there could be no doubt. In 1949 a throwing contest was held at Wrigley Field, and only three Cubs could fire the ball from home plate into the center field bleachers, a distance of more than 400 feet. They were Andy Pafko, Hal Jeffcoat, . . . and Smalley.

In 1950—the year the Cubs put Smalley on milk shakes to gain weight—Roy had his best season—and his worst. Afield, he played every game and topped the league at his position in putouts (332), assists (541), double plays (115), total chances per game (6.0)—and errors (51).

He displayed power at the plate, smashing 21 homers and

driving in 85 runs. However, he batted only .230 and led the league in strikeouts with 114. On June 28, he became one of only 10 Cubs to hit for the cycle, getting a single, double, triple, and homer in the same game. Phil Cavarretta and Andy Pafko added homers as the Cubs trounced the Cardinals 15-3. On Aug. 5, he married Jolene Mauch, sister of former Cub teammate Gene Mauch.

Early the following season, Roy broke his ankle sliding into third base and was never the same after he returned to the lineup, playing on and off regularly thereafter.

In 1953 he reached a career high with a .249 batting average, but came to the plate only 253 times. By then the Cubs had brought up the youthful Ernie Banks, and Roy was dealt to Milwaukee the following spring.

In 1955 the Braves traded him to the Phillies, where he finished his career three years later. His son, Roy Junior, is a shortstop with the Twins.

Lifetime, Roy was .227 with 61 homers.

BOB RUSH

RUSH, ROBERT RANSOM
B. Dec. 21, 1925, Battle Creek, Mich.
BR TR 6′5″ 205 lb.

Harry Rush was a minor league pitcher who came up to the St. Louis Browns for a cup of coffee in 1923. He never got to sip the nectar. After being measured for a uniform he was sent back to the bushes.

Harry Rush vowed that his only son, Robert Ransom, would be a major league pitcher some day. From the time young Bob was big enough to toss a baseball, the two worked hours on end.

Rush pitched three no-hitters for South Bend's Riley High, two in succession, and played semipro ball for Pop Frankel's team. Frankel, who was in his 70s when he spotted Rush, was a bird dog of sorts. He first detected big league possibilities in Freddie Fitzsimmons and later uncovered Eddie Hanyzewski for the Cubs. It was Pop who recommended the fast-growing Rush.

The Cubs went to South Bend for an exhibition game and invited young Rush to throw a few for observation. Cub coach Roy Johnson watched in awe and declared, "Don't let that kid get away."

After signing a Cub contract Rush went into the army and fought with the Fourth Armored Division of General George Patton's Third Army in Europe. He was a machine gunner in a jeep in a reconnaissance platoon.

Following the war Rush took up his pro career at Des Moines in 1947. The fire-balling right-hander won six-of-seven, recorded a 1.61 ERA, and was promoted to Nashville where he finished at 9-7.

With a scant season in the minors Rush was set for delivery to the Cubs. One look at the towering 6′5″ pitcher had everyone bugeyed. He would kick his left foot higher than a chorus girl before delivering the ball.

Writers blinked at his style and dashed for their typewriters for superlatives. He was called the "South Bend Buzzsaw," the "Skyscraping Speedballer," and the "Hoosier Hurricane."

Rush's high-kicking motion had to be modified because the baserunners took liberties. And he was tipping off his pitches, be it curve or fastball. It was obvious the Cubs brought him up too soon after he registered a 5-11 rookie season in 1948.

Three seasons later, Rush's career won-lost record was 39-61. He was a 20-game loser in 1950. Gone were the superlatives. He was just plain Bob Rush. It was tough to be a winning pitcher with second-division ballclubs.

In 1952 the Rush act was of star quality. He won 17 games, including a two-hitter, a three-hitter, four four-hitters and three five-hitters. With a little luck, Rush could have been a 20-game winner.

He lost two 1-0 games, two 2-0 games, a 3-0 game and dropped five others by one run in low scoring contests. From May 3 to June 8 Rush pitched three straight shutouts in winning seven in a row, and ran up a string of 32 straight scoreless innings.

Against the Reds on May 30, Rush had a perfect game until Grady Hatton doubled with two out in the seventh inning. In addition, Rush developed as a hitter, getting 28 hits in 96 trips for a .292 average.

He also gained a spot on the National League All-Star team, winding up as the winning pitcher when teammate Hank Sauer slammed a two-run homer for a 2-1 win in a rain-shortened contest at Philadelphia's Connie Mack Stadium.

Rush was the Cubs most dependable pitcher for a decade, winning 110 games with mediocre teams. Later in his career, Rush developed an astigmatism. He saw double. It was corrected with glasses that enabled him to see the catcher's signs. "At one time I wondered how the catcher could have 10 fingers on one hand," said Rush.

After absorbing 140 Cub losses, Rush became a winner in one day. He was traded from the last-place Cubs to the world champion Milwaukee Braves on Dec. 5, 1957. He left with mixed emotions. "I hate to leave Chicago," said Rush. "The fans are the best in the country."

But then there was new Cub manager Bob Scheffing, who declared, "Rush just isn't a winning pitcher. That's why we traded him."

Rush, ever the gentleman, didn't return any brickbats. "I don't pay much attention to his remarks," said Rush. "It takes a better baseball man than Scheffing to bother me."

Rush had the last word. He had a winning record (10-6) and Milwaukee won the pennant. At last a World Series. Braves manager Fred Haney elected Rush to start the third game against the New York Yankees. A throng of 71,599 shoehorned into Yankee Stadium on Oct. 4, 1958. It was Rush against Don Larsen, the gent who pitched a perfect game against the Dodgers in the 1956

World Series.

It was a scoreless contest and Rush had allowed only an infield single going into the fifth inning. Then he walked the bases full. There were two out with Hank Bauer at bat. Rush delivered. Bauer broke his bat and hit a pop fly to short right. It fell in for a hit and two runs scored. Rush was taken out for a pinch hitter in the seventh and the Yankees went on to win.

Rush had lost a lot of tough games. But this one hurt. It was a good pitch. He was beaten by a broken-bat blooper. He sat alone on a stool with only the stony silence of an empty clubhouse.

Rush remained with the Braves until midseason 1960, when he was waived to the White Sox. With the South Siders, Rush was relegated to a relief role. He closed out his career with a 127-152 record.

Today, Rush resides in Arizona. Among his neighbors is Scheffing.

WARREN HACKER

HACKER, WARREN LOUIS
B. Nov. 21, 1924, Marissa, Ill.
BR TR 6'1" 185 lb.

There has always seemed to be some sort of Hack on the Cubs. Hack Miller, Hack Wilson, and Stan Hack were all .300 hitters. Warren Hacker was a pitcher, and a hard-luck one at that. The Cub bats were usually silent with Hacker on the mound.

Although his Cub record was a dismal 52-70, the blond right-hander did manage to have one memorable season and one memorable game. He compiled a 15-9 record in 1952 and tossed a near no-hitter in 1955.

Hacker's father was a miner in Marissa, a dusky coal region in Southern Illinois. But he would have no part of his son pursuing that occupation. "Dad was determined that I would be a ballplayer," recalled Hacker.

Almost from the time he was big enough to carry a glove, Warren was taught the rudiments of baseball by his dad. Hacker never took the game seriously until he went overseas with the marines during World War II.

Warren was a bomber crew chief with missions over Midway and Majura. He was awarded the Presidential Citation and three battle stars for combat. In between he pitched for a marine ballclub.

One of his buddies recommended Hacker to Grover Seitz, manager of Pampa in the West Texas-New Mexico League. Young Hacker, whose lone pitch was a fastball, lost his first game and finished with a 20-4 record for Pampa in 1946.

A 17-14 record with Shreveport in 1948 earned Hacker a late season shot with the Cubs. In his lone start, Hacker was hit for seven runs in three innings, giving him a 0-1 record and a 21.00 earned-run average.

The next four seasons Hacker kept packing his satchel for up-and-down trials with the Cubs. Warren did have one good effort during those lean seasons. He relieved Johnny Schmitz with the bases full and none out in the first inning. He allowed one hit, a fifth-inning single by Elbie Fletcher, to beat the Boston Braves in 1949.

But the miner's son was marked for shipment to the minors. At Los Angeles in 1951, Hacker had a dubious 8-15 record. That mark was misleading. Five of his victories were shutouts and one was a no-hitter.

When Hacker reported to the Cubs' training camp in 1952, most experts doubted he would stick. After all, he failed in four previous trials.

Hacker was the forgotten man on the pitching staff at the outset of the season. It wasn't until June 7 that he got his first chance to start a ballgame. He won it, beating the Braves 9-3, mixing his fastball and curve with a knuckler and a screwball.

Hacker then completed 12-of-20 starts that included five shutouts. From June 12 on, he never walked more than two batters in any game. He pitched five games without issuing a pass.

Hacker concluded the season with a 15-9 record and only 31 walks in 185 innings. His 2.58 earned-run average was lower than such aces as Warren Spahn, Robin Roberts and Sal Maglie. He was beaten out for the ERA title by a little-known rookie reliever named Hoyt Wilhelm, who knuckled down with a 2.43 average.

Trailing 8-2 with two out and nobody on base in the ninth inning, the Cubs rallied for seven runs and a 9-8 victory over the Reds in 1952 at Crosley Field.

Then it was back to tough luck. He was the same Hacker in 1953. But the Cub bats betrayed him and he wound up at 12-19. The square-shouldered Hacker dropped two 1-0 games, two 2-0 games, and during one stretch worked 30 innings without the Cubs scoring a run.

To his credit, Hacker didn't rant or rave or tear apart any furniture when the Cubs booted away another game. "I guess those things go with this game," said Hacker. "You can't let it get you down."

Warren was on the verge of oblivion until May 21, 1955. It was a brisk Saturday afternoon in Milwaukee's County Stadium as the Cubs took the field against the Braves.

Hacker held the Braves hitless for five innings, issuing only a fourth-inning walk to Chuck Tanner. And in the sixth inning, an error by young Hank Aaron and a homer by Dee Fondy gave the Cubs a 2-0 lead.

Hacker had retired 13 batters in a row going into the ninth inning. He disposed of the first batter, bringing up George Crowe, a bespectacled pinch hitter.

Hacker threw a knuckler that broke belt high and Crowe belted it about 10 rows into the wooden seats in right-center for a homer that broke up the no-hitter.

Hacker got the next two batters for a 2-1 Cub victory. "I was glad it was a good hard shot, rather than a dinky hit," lamented Hacker, who didn't strike out a single batter.

The hard-luck hurler later pitched for the Reds and Phillies before winding up his career as a reliever with the White Sox in

1961. He finished with a 62-89 record, which easily could have been reversed.

EMIL VERBAN

VERBAN, EMIL MATTHEW
B. Aug. 27, 1915, Lincoln, Ill.
BR TR 5′11″
165 lb.

Emil Verban, whose name rhymes with bourbon, must be getting his kicks today. The supposedly long-forgotten journeyman second baseman of the 1940s is the current darling of the Washington elite.

Prominent politicians and pundits, including columnists George Will and David Broder and a chap named Ronald Reagan, are members of the so-called "Emil Verban Society." The group has adopted Verban as a symbol of Cub mediocrity. But the last laugh is on them.

In reality, Verban was a smooth fielder, a fleet runner, and although he lacked power, boasted a .272 career batting average, just two points below Ernie Banks. In addition, the Lincoln (Ill.) product was one of the toughest batsmen to strike out.

Verban rattled around the Cardinals' farm chain for eight seasons, hitting such whistle stops as Paducah, Fremont, Tiffin, Alexander, Decatur, and Asheville before advancing to Columbus and Houston, and finally, St. Louis, in 1944.

Playing alongside "the Octopus," shortstop Marty Marion, Verban became known as "the Antelope." The slender, silent rookie batted only .257, but struck out only 14 times as the Cardinals won the 1944 pennant.

Verban wasn't tight-lipped in the World Series against the St. Louis Browns that autumn. He became enraged at Browns' owner Donald Barnes, who allegedly put Mrs. Verban behind a post while alloting seats.

"I'd punch him in the nose if he wasn't so darn fat," threatened Verban, who saved his best hits for the Brownie pitchers. Verban led all Cardinal batters with a .412 average. In the sixth and deciding game, he collected three hits and drove in the winning run.

The wiry Croatian upped his average to .278 in 1945, but was supplanted in the lineup the following spring by a young redhead named Albert Schoendienst. Verban was soon dispatched to the Philadelphia Phillies for catcher Clyde Kluttz.

The Antelope was no klutz afield or at bat as he enjoyed his most brilliant season in 1947. He batted .285 and led all second basemen with a .982 fielding average, committing only 17 errors.

In addition, Verban was the toughest batter to fan in either league. Choking up on his heavy 38-ounce Johnny Mize model, Verban struck out only eight times in 540 at bats—once every 67.5 trips to the plate.

He was sidelined with an injury at the outset of the 1948 season and was soon replaced by another phenom named Granny

Hamner. On Aug. 2, 1948, Verban was purchased on waivers by the Cubs.

He had now gone 2,128 trips to the plate without hitting a home run. It took only a month in Cub flannels before Verban broke that spell. It came on a damp, drizzly day in Cincinnati's Crosley Field and there were no heroics involved.

The date was Sept. 6, 1948. There were two out and none on in the seventh inning when Verban strode to the plate to face fastballing Johnny VanderMeer. With one swipe of the bat, Verban sent the ball high over the left field wall.

It was the Cubs' lone run of the game. Vandy threw a four-hitter as the Reds won 3-1, dropping the Cubs into the National League cellar. In his short two-month Cub stint Verban batted .294.

The Cubs remained in the cellar in 1949 and the Antelope found heavy traffic around second base, sharing the position with such storied athletes as Twig Terwilliger, Bob Ramazotti, and Gene Mauch.

Why Verban had to share second base is a mystery. His .289 average was best of the quartet. Mauch had a .247 batting mark, the Twig was .223, and Ramazotti was .179.

Get a whiff of Verban's strikeout ratio. He fanned twice in 343 at bats—once every 171.5 trips.

Verban lost his job entirely in 1950. He injured his right hand at the outset of the season and couldn't hold a bat or throw for over a month. When he returned he rode the bench with his .108 average before being waived to the Boston Braves in the closing weeks of the season.

After two years with Springfield (Mass.) of the International League, Verban announced his retirement at age 37. He then entered the shale business with his brother to go with his 300-acre farm near Elkhart, Ill.

Undoubtedly the most remarkable aspect of Verban's career is his strikeout ratio. He fanned only 74 times in 2,911 trips. Heck, Dave Kingman can strike out 74 times in one month.

FRANKIE FRISCH

FRISCH, FRANK FRANCIS
B. Sept. 9, 1898, Queens, N.Y.
D. March 12, 1973, Wilmington, Del.
BB TR 5'11"
165 lb.

Frankie Frisch went from the Giants' Fordham Flash to pilot light of the Cardinals' Gashouse Gang to plain Onkel Franz with the lowly Cubs. Frisch's brief fling as Cub manager was the low point in a brilliant baseball career.

Frisch grew up in the Bronx, about five miles north of the Polo Grounds, home of the Giants. The son of a well-heeled lace-linen manufacturer was captain of the baseball, football, and basketball squads at Fordham University.

Known as the "Fordham Flash," Frisch became a Giants' regular in 1920. He helped the team win four straight pennants, starting in 1921. He hit .300, .471, .400, and .333, being the only batter to hit better than .300 in four successive World Series.

The young switch-hitting second baseman, who was to bat above .300 a dozen years in a row, soon became captain of the Giants. Many said he was groomed as McGraw's managerial successor.

However, there were drawbacks in being captain. He immediately became the tyrannical McGraw's whipping boy. McGraw always berated his captains for mistakes of others. Thus a breach developed between the fiery pair.

Meanwhile, in St. Louis, the Cardinals won their first pennant in 1926 under playing-manager Rogers Hornsby. When Hornsby demanded a three-year contract, Cardinals' owner Sam Breadon vehemently objected.

That set the stage for one of baseball's biggest trades. The Cards sent second baseman Hornsby to the Giants for second baseman Frisch, plus pitcher Jimmy Ring.

Frisch took over as playing-manager midway through the 1933 season. He led baseball's most colorful ballclub, the 1934 Gashouse Gang.

Never had one team assembled so many zany characters. There were Ducky Medwick, Wild Bill Hallahan, Lippy Durocher, Pepper Martin, Ripper Collins, and of course, Dizzy Dean, and his brother Paul, who was sometimes known as Daffy Dean.

The Gashouse Gang roared to the pennant and won the World Series, beating the Detroit Tigers in seven games. The Dean brothers won two series games each. However, it was Frisch's lone pennant winner.

The Gang ran out of gas by 1937 and so did Frisch. He got into only 17 games and batted .219, closing with a career average of .316 and 2,880 hits.

Frisch was replaced by Mike Gonzalez as Cardinal manager at the tailend of the 1938 season. He soon caught on as a Boston Braves' broadcaster. "It was wonderful," recalled the Flash. "I could witness a grand slam and get a good night's sleep."

He resumed the headache of managing, taking over the Pittsburgh Pirates in 1940 and lasting through the '46 season. The many faceted Frisch was elected to baseball's Hall of Fame in 1947. When Durocher took command of the Giants, he pulled Frisch out of the Giants' radio booth and invited his old pilot and double-play sidekick as a coach.

Frisch got that managerial itch again and this time he had to start from scratch. The Cubs were floundering under Charlie Grimm. The Grimm reaper came during a nine-game losing streak and the not so Jolly Cholly was replaced on June 10, 1949.

Frankie was Grimm's personal choice as his successor. Grimm was kicked upstairs as vice president of baseball operations. The day Frisch took over, the Cubs dropped into the cellar.

The Old Flash was now 50. The years had put a lot of gray in his short-cropped hair. The flying feet were replaced by a slow waddle. The new Cub pilot said he was going to stress speed. All the time, Frisch knew he had inherited a ballclub that could barely crawl.

The Grimm-Frisch combo, however, made a great move in their

first time out of the gate. They sent veteran outfielders Peanuts Lowrey and Harry Walker to the Reds for outfielders Frankie Baumholtz and Hank Sauer.

Sauer, combining with Andy Pafko, gave the team a one-two power punch, but they were lacking elsewhere and finished a lackluster last. They were 19-31 under Grimm and 42-62 under Frisch.

Although Cub fans tried to admire Frisch's tirades with the umpires, they too, tired of his early exits. Sometimes Frantic Frankie was tossed out of games before his pitchers were shelled from the mound. But there was one episode that endeared him to none. It happened on July 26, 1950.

Cub pitcher Monk Dubiel had a 4-0 lead going into the sixth inning against the Phillies in Philadelphia. Eddie Waitkus singled to open the inning. Dick Sisler walked and Del Ennis poked a double to right, scoring one run. Dubiel walked the next five in succession, forcing in five runs. In one stretch he threw 14 consecutive balls.

Frisch offered no relief. "I don't care if the Phils had scored 99 runs," bellowed Frisch. "I'm sick and tired of seeing a pitcher look to the bullpen everytime he gets into a little jam. It's time some of 'em learned to pitch their way out of trouble."

It was a troubled season for the Cubs. Pafko hit 36 homers and Sauer added 32, but the best they could do was 64-89 to beat out the Pirates for seventh place.

The following month Onkel Franz resigned. He caught wind the Cubs were grooming Stan Hack as manager for 1952. "As long as that was the case, I figured I might as well end things now," said Frisch, who was replaced by Phil Cavarretta as manager "for the rest of the season."

The Cubs were 35-45 when Frisch departed and 141-196 during his turbulent tenure.

FRANKIE BAUMHOLTZ

BAUMHOLTZ, FRANK CONRAD
B. Oct. 7, 1918, Midvale, Ohio
BL TL 5'10½"
175 lb.

A flyball is hit to the outfield. Left fielder Ralph Kiner and right fielder Hank Sauer cup their hands to their mouths and shout in unison, "Take it, Frankie." And center fielder Frankie Baumholtz wearily pursues the ball.

Any ball hit to the Cubs' outfield in the mid-50s was fair game for the busy Baumholtz, who was flanked by two lumbering "gazelles"—Kiner and Sauer—both in the lineup because of their booming bats.

But Baumholtz made other outfielders give chase as he hit the ball to all fields en route to a lifetime batting average of .290. Baumholtz's most productive years were in a Cub uniform.

As a youngster, Baumholtz was an all-around athlete. He concentrated on basketball and gained All-American honors at Ohio University. He was voted Most Valuable Player in the 1941

NIT. If Sauer and Kiner would have been in the audience, they could have shouted, "Dribble it, Frankie."

Baumholtz turned pro in 1941 and starred for the Cleveland Rebels of the American Basketball League, one of those loose leagues that sprang up one night and disappeared the next. Meanwhile, he also played baseball, spending two years in the Cincinnati Reds' farm system.

But before he reached the majors, the war came. Baumholtz's four and one-half years of service in the navy included combat duty in air and submarine battles in the Atlantic and Mediterranean. He was awarded the Bronze Star for heroic duty in commanding a mortar group in the Iwo Jima campaign. He was also in the battle for Okinawa. Baumholtz emerged from the navy a lieutenant.

Frankie gave up basketball for baseball and hit .343 for Columbia in the Sally League, good for second honors behind Ted Kluszewski, his teammate, who batted .352.

Promoted to the Reds in 1947, Baumholtz hit .283 in his rookie season. He led the Reds with a .296 performance in 1948 and then was shipped along with Sauer on June 15, 1949, in what many regard as the Cubs' finest trade. In return the Reds received outfielders Peanuts Lowrey and Harry "The Hat" Walker.

While Sauer went on a homer binge and emerged as the "Mayor of Wrigley Field," Baumholtz's average dipped to .229. He was sent to the Los Angeles Angels of the Pacific Coast League in 1950.

Baumholtz immediately proved he was no minor leaguer by leading the Coast League with a .379 average. His lofty record included 126 runs, 254 hits, 53 doubles, 10 triples, 15 homers, 89 RBI, and 372 total bases.

He returned to the Cubs in 1951 and was back in stride with a .284 average. But the best was yet to come. The following season Baumholtz battled Stan Musial for the batting title. Going into the final weeks, Baumholtz trailed Musial .333 to .332.

On the final day of the season, Musial volunteered to pitch against Baumholtz. The Cardinal slugger was a pitcher in the minors until he encountered arm trouble. Stan kicked and pumped in fine southpaw style, and Baumholtz, who always cocked his bat high in the air, turned around and batted right-handed. He hit a grounder that was bobbled by third baseman Solly Hemus. It was a standoff, but good publicity. Musial, however, finished with a .336 mark to Baumholtz's .325. Stan, incidentally, thought Baumholtz should have been given a hit.

With the arrival of Kiner the following season, Sauer shifted to Baumholtz's right field spot, with Frankie moving to center field. Baumholtz was the only one of the three with any semblance of speed. When he wasn't chasing flyballs, Baumholtz found time to hit .306 and .297 the next two seasons. By 1955, Kiner was gone, Sauer was fading, and Baumholtz was worn out. Frankie maintained a .289 average, but yielded playing time to youngsters Bob Speake, Jim Bolger, and Jim King.

Baumholtz accepted his utility role. On June 5, 1955, the New

York Giants were leading the Cubs 1-0 with two out at the Polo Grounds. Then Ernie Banks singled and Dee Fondy walked.

The ruddy-cheeked Baumholtz was summoned by manager Stan Hack as a pinch hitter. Pitcher Jim Hearn threw two wide ones to Baumholtz. Giant manager Leo Durocher pulled Hearn for reliever Marv Grissom.

Grissom threw one pitch and Baumholtz connected for a three-run homer and a 3-1 Cub victory. This time it was, "Hit it, Frankie."

HANK SAUER

SAUER, HENRY JOHN
B. March 17, 1919, Pittsburgh, Pa.
BR TR 6'2" 198 lb.

Left field resembled Tobacco Road following a bumper crop of Hank Sauer home runs. It was a Wrigley Field ritual for bleacher fans to toss packets of tobacco onto the field as Sauer returned to his position after hitting another homer.

But it was a long road for the pipe-smoking Sauer. Hammering Hank began his career as a first baseman in the New York Yankees' chain, but wasn't destined to reach the big leagues for good until 11 seasons had passed.

Called "the Honker" because of his prominent proboscis, Sauer was drafted by the Cincinnati Reds in 1940, but couldn't get to first base with the veteran Frank McCormick on the bag.

Then followed three seasons in the minors as a converted outfielder and two years in the U.S. Coast Guard. The turning point came in 1947 at Syracuse when manager Jewell Ens asked Sauer to swing a heavier bat.

Sauer discarded his 35-ounce bat for a 40-ounce Chick Hafey model. Overnight, the boy from Syracuse became a slugger, hitting 50 homers with 141 RBI and a .336 average.

After being named Minor League Player of the Year, Sauer returned to the majors for good, clouting 35 homers, the most in a season in Reds' history up to that time. In addition, Sauer drove in 97 runs.

Came 1949 and Sauer got off to a slow start. That precipitated one of the few trades that tipped the scales in the Cubs' favor. Sauer and Frankie Baumholtz went to Chicago for outfielders Peanuts Lowrey and Harry "The Hat" Walker.

Sauer had found a home for his homers. He loved jawing with the bleacher fans and soon was bestowed with the title "Mayor of Wrigley Field."

However, there was no love affair between Cub fans, Sauer, and Manager Burt Shotton of the Brooklyn Dodgers. Sauer was voted along with Ralph Kiner and Enos Slaughter as the three National League outfielders for the 1950 All-Star team. It happened that all three were left fielders.

Shotton suggested replacing Sauer with Duke Snider, his own center fielder. After storms of protest from Chicagoans (the game was to be held at Comiskey Park) NL president Ford Frick ruled

Sauer, Kiner, and Slaughter must play at least the first three innings before Shotton could make any lineup changes.

Shotton obeyed and opened with Kiner in left, Slaughter in center, and Sauer in right field. Shotton did pull Sauer after the third inning, but diplomatically replaced him with Andy Pafko, a Cub teammate, who *was* a center fielder.

Sauer saved his All-Star heroics for the 1952 classic at Philadelphia's Shibe Park. Thunderclouds were forming as the raw-boned Sauer strode to the plate to face Bob Lemon. The National League was trailing 2-1 in the fourth inning.

Sauer supplied some thunder of his own by unloading a two-run homer into the left field seats. Sauer's clout must have shook a few clouds as the game was called after five innings with the National League winning 3-2. Shotton, however, wasn't on the scene, having retired from baseball.

Sauer hit 37 homers that season, tying him with Kiner for the league lead. Sauer's 121 RBI topped the majors. He carried a mediocre Cub team to fifth place with a .500 record.

As a reward, Sauer was named Most Valuable Player for the year. That set off more controversy. Robin Roberts won 28 games for the Philadelphia Phillies and the Eastern writers demanded a recount of the MVP ballots.

In 1953 the Cubs acquired Kiner from the Pittsburgh Pirates in an eight-player trade. Kiner could play only left field. So, the Mayor and his constituents moved to right field and Baumholtz shifted to center. With Kiner and Sauer on the flanks, Baumholtz had to cover most of the ground.

There was some bitterness by Cub fans toward Kiner, who drew twice Sauer's salary and only hit half as many homers (41 to 22) in 1954.

Kiner was dealt to Cleveland in 1955 and left field again was strewn with tobacco for Sauer's return. Then followed the jolting news. Cub general manager Wid Matthews proudly announced the next spring that the Cubs had traded Sauer to the St. Louis Cardinals for outfielder Pete Whisenant.

Hank Sauer twice hit three homers in one game off the same pitcher — Curt Simmons of the Phillies.

"What is a Whisenant?" was the question asked by all.

In seven Cub seasons Sauer had hit 198 homers and had driven in 587 runs. He set records for most homers in a season by a Cub left fielder (37) and a Cub right fielder (41), (both since broken by Dave Kingman and Billy Williams).

And Sauer became the first Cub to hit three homers in a game twice. Ironically, pitcher Curt Simmons of the Phillies was the same victim. And one of the games was a 3-0 affair. One newspaper headline read, "Sauer 3, Phillies 0."

The Cubs had traded all that for a fellow who hit .192 with the Boston Braves before slumping to .191 with the Cardinals. To this day, Cub fans still ponder, "What is a Whisenant?"

Sauer spent one season with St. Louis and parts of three with the New York and San Francisco Giants before becoming a scout and batting instructor in the Giants' farm system.

The Cubs staged an old-timers game in 1977 and old No. 9 sauntered out to left field and waved to the crowd. He was greeted with a shower of packaged tobacco.

The fans forgot about Whisenant, but they remembered Sauer.

Lifetime, Hank was a .266 hitter with 1,278 hits, 288 homers, and 876 RBI.

PAUL MINNER

MINNER, PAUL EDISON
B. July 30, 1923, New Wilmington, Pa.
BL TL 6′5″ 200 lb.

Tall Paul Minner's baseball career began and ended with neck injuries. In between, the lanky lefty was a pain in the neck to the St. Louis Cardinals. Although his career record was only 69-84, Minner compiled a 21-8 mark against the Redbirds.

The buck-toothed blond got his start in the New York Giants' farm system. He was signed by Hall of Famer and former Cub Fred Lindstrom in 1941. The following season Minner won 18, dropped only 2, and had a 1.41 ERA for Lindstrom's Elizabethton club in the Appalachian League.

But the war came along and it wasn't until 1946 that he returned to baseball, posting an impressive 16-11 mark for Mobile, a Brooklyn Dodger farm club. The Dodgers brought up Minner at the conclusion of the season and he lost his lone decision—to the Chicago Cubs.

Minner spent the next three seasons bouncing up and down the Dodger organization. The 6′5″ speedballer was up to stay in 1949, but spent most of the season in mop-up roles, with a 4-3 record.

He did get his first—and only—taste of World Series play, pitching the final inning of the final game against the New York Yankees. He held the Yankees scoreless, but it was too late. Brooklyn was already trailing 10-6.

Darkness had set in at Ebbets Field and the lights were turned on. Minner thus became the first hurler to pitch under the lights in World Series history.

Minner was noted for his fastball until one afternoon in Brooklyn. "I was fooling around with Pete Reiser, shagging balls in the outfield," said Minner. "I went after a low liner and when I stooped for it, something popped in my neck. The rest of the season, my head was pulled over toward my left shoulder. I never saw a runner on second base all year. Couldn't turn that far."

Minner was no longer a fastballer. Soon, he was no longer a Dodger. Minner and first baseman Preston Ward were sold to the Cubs on Oct. 13, 1949.

When Minner reported to the Cubs, he lost his two buck teeth. They were infected. Paul had a dental plate installed—just in time for Christmas.

Minner was far from a winner in his first two Cub seasons, winning 14 and losing 30. He then junked his tardy fastball for junk pitches that included a curve at two speeds, a palm ball, a screwball, and an occasional blooper.

The result was a 14-9 record in 1952, when he started gaining recognition as a Cardinal killer. "I can't explain it," said Minner. "Stan Musial, Enos Slaughter, and Red Schoendienst sure aren't easy guys to pitch to and they always get their hits off me. I don't think I've got 'em jinxed. I just get a lot of breaks when I'm pitching against them."

Here is a year-by-year breakdown of Minner breaking down the Cards: 1950 (2-3), 1951 (0-1), 1952 (2-0), 1953 (3-1), 1954 (5-1), 1955 (5-0), 1956 (0-1). With Brooklyn, Minner won 4 and lost 1 to St. Louis.

In addition, Minner was a robust hitter for a pitcher. His lifetime average was a modest .219, but he collected 19 doubles, 4 triples, 6 homers, and drove in 43 runs.

His pitching career ended abruptly in 1956, when he sustained a back injury.

RANDY JACKSON

JACKSON, RANSOM JOSEPH
B. Feb. 10, 1926, Little Rock, Ark.
BR TR 6'1½"
180 lb.

Handsome Ransom Jackson was quite a sobriquet. Actually, he resembled a Gregory Peck with meat on his bones. But, as Yogi Berra always said, "Ya don't hit the ball with your face."

Ransom Joseph Jackson, Sr., was a star third baseman at Princeton, Class of '22, and was eager to have his son in athletics. "All he wanted to do was come right home after school," said the senior Jackson. "He was just timid, I guess."

Randy played a little softball and touch football around the neighborhood in Little Rock, Ark., but never joined his high school team. When he went to Texas Christian University under the navy V-12 program, the elder Jackson had to badger him into entering athletics.

"I was in the navy and was in charge of cadets and knew the V-12 boys were excused from calisthenics only if they went out for sports," said the senior Jackson. "I painted a horrible picture of how strenuous and boring calisthenics were. That convinced him. He went out for baseball and football."

When young Randy reported for football practice, TCU coach Dutch Meyer asked him what position he played. "I told him I didn't have any position," said Randy. "So he ordered me to line up with the guards. While we were beating our heads together, I looked over and saw the backs just trotting around, kicking and tossing the football. I decided that's where I belonged.

"I went to coach Meyer and insisted I was really a backfield man. I always was pretty good at punting and running in touch football. I wound up punting for TCU and playing halfback. We won the Southwest Conference, too."

Randy also tried out for the baseball team in 1945. This time, he knew his position. He picked third base because that was his dad's position. Randy went on to hit .500 and win the Southwest Conference batting title.

After the war, Jackson transferred to the University of Texas, where he was a backfield teammate of the famed Bobby Layne. In addition, he hit .438 and .400 under coach Bib Falk, the former White Sox star, thus becoming the first player to win three straight Southwest Conference batting crowns.

That was enough to bring the scouts running. Scout Jimmy Payton convinced Jackson to sign with the Cubs, telling him veteran third baseman Stan Hack was about to retire, and his advancement to the majors would be rapid.

Jackson was placed in Hack's hands at Des Moines in 1948. He hit .322. After a .298 season with 19 homers and 109 RBI at Oklahoma City, Randy was ready for the Cubs.

He was matched against another rookie third sacker named Bill Serena, who was fresh from a 57 homer, 190 RBI, and .374 average at Lubbock, Tex. The two split the job during the spring. Jackson then received his first thrill and first jolt in the same week.

After hitting a game-winning homer in the last of the 10th inning off Clarence Podbelian to beat the Dodgers 7-6 on May 5, 1950, Jackson was sent to Springfield, Mass., for more seasoning. He was reunited with Hack and hit .315 with 20 homers to win International League Rookie of the Year honors.

Serena broke his wrist at the outset of the 1951 season and the Cubs were moaning. But Jackson stepped in, and in three games against the Dodgers and one against the Phillies, hit four homers, scored nine runs, and drove in 11 in just 14 times at bat.

But he still didn't satisfy manager Frankie Frisch, who wanted his quiet rookie to holler and hustle. It wasn't so with the opposite sex. Called "Handsome Ransom" by the lipstick set, he became the glamour boy of the Cubs.

The fem fans claimed he had soft, brown eyes, a chiseled face, and the kind of "little boy" smile that added up to swoon stuff. They either wanted to "mother" him or to "date" him, according to their ages.

The sheik of third base finished the season with 16 homers and 76 RBI, second to Hank Sauer. For the next five seasons, third base was his bag.

There were many broken hearts when Handsome Ransom announced he was marrying an airline stewardess, who knew little about baseball. Her first game was the Cubs' 1953 opener against the Reds at Wrigley Field.

Mrs. Jackson, the former Ruth Fowler, was among the 21, 229 fans who saw the Reds take a 2-1 lead into the eighth inning. Then with two out, Jackson doubled off the left field wall, driving home two runs for a 3-2 Cub win. "My heart did a handspring," she confessed.

In 1955 Jackson was named to the National League All-Star lineup as backup third baseman to the Braves' Eddie Mathews. The National League was losing 5-2 in the eighth inning, but tied the score on four straight singles by Willie Mays, Ted Kluszewski, Randy Jackson, and Hank Aaron. They eventually won on a

12th-inning homer by Stan Musial. Imagine, Say Hey, Big Klu, Hammerin' Henry, Stan the Man, and Handsome Ransom in the same breath.

Randy reached his peak that year with 21 homers, but the following spring was swapped to Brooklyn for third baseman Don Hoak and outfielder Moose Moryn. It was one of the few Cub-Dodger trades that swung in Chicago's favor.

Hoak was a pepper pot, as he later proved with the Reds and Pirates, but was a .215 bust in his lone Cub season. Moryn, however, gave the Cubs some outfield punch for the next five seasons.

Jackson, meanwhile, was joining the famed Boys of Summer, who were entering the autumn of their careers. But Randy couldn't dislodge Jackie Robinson from third base and was a semiregular in Brooklyn and LA the next two and one-half seasons.

He was then waived to the Indians in 1958 and was reacquired by the Cubs late in the 1959 season from Cleveland for the legendary Riverboat Smith.

Jackson retired at the end of the season, a .261 lifetime hitter. He entered the laundry business in Lawton, Okla. Of his 103 homers, 88 were in a Cubs' uniform. It was the most by a Cub third sacker until the Ron Santo era.

CHUCK CONNORS

CONNORS, KEVIN JOSEPH
B. April 10, 1921, Brooklyn, N.Y.
BL TL 6′5″ 215 lb.

Chuck Connors couldn't get to first base as a ballplayer, but he was right on target as TV's "Rifleman." Most biographies refer to Connors as a former Brooklyn Dodger, although he only made one plate appearance with Dem Bums as a pinch hitter in 1949.

However, he did play 66 games with the 1951 Cubs, hitting two homers and batting .239. So it is the Cubbies, not the Dodgers, who can lay claim to the colorful Connors.

Connors was brought up in a cold-water flat in Brookyn, and at 6′5″, should have been more prominent in basketball than baseball. He played center in the winter and first base in the spring at Adelphi Academy High in Brooklyn.

At 18 Connors signed a Dodger contract, receiving a $200 bonus. "When they gave me the $200, it was a check," recalled Connors. "I had never seen a check before in my life. I told them 'I don't want this. I want money.'

"So they went down to the bank and brought me ten $20 bills. I counted the money and said, 'Could you go back and get 200 $1 bills?' They laughed, but they did it. I took the money, ran home to my mother, and when I got into the kitchen, I threw it all up in the air and said, 'Ma, look. I'm a professional ballplayer and I'm going to make a lot of money.' "

During the off-season, Connors attended Seton Hall University, where he starred in basketball. He went to the Boston Celtics in 1946, breaking into the pros with a crash.

"We were taking our warmups before a game with the Chicago Stags and I went in for a shot, hung on to the hoop and shattered the glass backboard. The game was delayed a half hour while another backboard was borrowed," said Connors.

Chuck went on to play 49 games without any shattering statistics, averaging 4.9 points a game. The next season his average dipped to 3.0 and he went back to baseball full-time.

Drafted by the New York Yankees after the Dodgers failed to protect him, his first stop was Norfolk in the Piedmont League. He was reclaimed by Brooklyn and shifted from Newport News to Mobile and finally Montreal.

The blue-eyed, gangling first baseman with the blond crew-cut and lantern jaw wowed 'em in Montreal. Whenever he would make an error, he would throw down his glove, trot to the dugout, bow to the crowd, and then slowly, bang his head against the post in the dugout.

Somehow, he reported to the Dodgers. It was contract time. He reported to the bossman, the Mahatma, Branch Rickey. Connors sat in the outer office while teammate Gene Hermanski haggled over his contract. When Hermanski came out, Connors wanted to know the details.

"He asked me if I smoked," said Hermanski. "I said not too much. He asked me if I went out with women. I said not too much. Then he asked me if I drank. I said a little now and then. That's when Rickey hit the ceiling. So I didn't sign."

Connors hitched up his pants and went into Rickey's sanctum. Branch fired the same questions. Did he smoke? "No, Mr. Rickey." Go out with women? "No, Mr. Rickey."

Drink? Connors pounded the desk and shouted, "If I have to drink to stay in your organization, I'm leaving." Rickey dropped his cigar and gave Connors a fat raise.

But there was one roadblock. Gil Hodges was the Dodgers' first baseman. Connors sat on the bench. Rickey promised the rookie, "If Hodges runs into a slump, you're playing."

"I could've waited another 10 years for Hodges to slump," said Connors.

Meanwhile, the brash Brooklynite performed card tricks and recited "Casey At The Bat" and "The Face On The Barroom Floor" to the delight of his teammates.

When Connors did his imitations of Rickey and manager Burt Shotton, he was sold to the Cubs. Chuck joined the Cubs in the spring of 1951. He was pitted against Dee Fondy, another ex-Dodger, for the spot behind veteran first baseman Phil Cavarretta.

Fondy won the promotion and Connors was demoted to Los Angeles, where he got his chance to try out his act before the Hollywood crowd. He was a smash hit, batting .321 with 22 homers and 77 RBI, before trading jobs with Fondy in midseason.

In LA Connors would ham it up for the fans. After hitting a homer, he would turn cartwheels into second and slide into third.

But he was now with the staid Cubs. There were no acrobatics, but he remained a lively interview with the media and a holler guy on the field.

However, his bat remained silent. He did get a clutch double, driving home the tying run that set the stage for player-manager Cavarretta's famed pinch grand slam in a doubleheader sweep against the Phillies.

The next season Connors was clowning back on the coast. An MGM casting director offered Chuck a bit role as a policeman in the film, *Pat and Mike,* starring Spencer Tracy and Katherine Hepburn. He took the offer and quit baseball for a movie career.

Connors' thin smile was equally adaptable to roles as a hero or villain. Among his other films were such classics as *Geronimo, Move Over Darling, Broken Sabre, The Deserter, Pancho Villa, Mad Bomber,* and *Tourist Trap.*

His big break came in 1957, when he landed the role of Lucas McCain in the TV series "The Rifleman." Did anyone notice he fired his rifle from his hip, southpaw style?

Connors also starred in another TV western "Branded" and more recently as a mid-19th century slave owner in "Roots." In all the press releases Connors was called a former Dodger.

A Dodger? C'mon. In his lone Brooklyn at bat he hit into a double play. Connors was a Cub.

DEE FONDY

FONDY, DEE VIRGIL
B. Oct. 31, 1924, Slaton, Tex.
BL TL 6'3" 195 lb.

Had he been able to crack the majors at an earlier age, first baseman Dee Fondy might have enjoyed a spectacular career. As it was, he was around for eight years, most of them productive.

In 1941 Dee's high school coach took him to the Brooklyn tryout camp in Santa Barbara, Calif. The Dodgers wanted to sign him on the spot, but Dee's father insisted that he continue his schooling instead.

Then the war broke out and Dee served two years in the artillery on the European front, winning a Purple Heart for a shrapnel wound in the right foot. Consequently, Fondy did not play professional ball until 1946, when he finally made his debut with Santa Barbara.

In the ensuing years, Fondy moved up the ladder in the Dodger farm system, but by the late 1940s, Gil Hodges had a secure hold on the first baseman's job and Dee was an unneeded commodity.

On Oct. 10, 1950, Fondy and another first sacker, Kevin "Chuck" Connors, were traded to the Cubs for outfielder Hank Edwards and cash.

Came April 17, 1951, opening day at Wrigley Field and Fondy's major league debut as he was nearing 27. In the pregame ceremonies, Sam Snead became the only person to hit a ball over the Wrigley Field scoreboard in center field. However, it was a golf ball, not a baseball, so it did not count in the history books except as trivia.

But there was nothing trivial about Fondy's heroics as his bases-loaded triple in his first big league at bat led the Cubs to an 8-3 victory over the Reds.

Although he was batting .271, Fondy was optioned to the Cubs farm club in Los Angeles (Pacific Coast League) for more seasoning. After hitting .376 for Los Angeles, Dee was called back for keeps in 1952. Batting .300 in 145 games, he won the regular first baseman's job away from manager Phil Cavarretta, who aided Dee's hitting by teaching him the drag bunt.

In 1953 Dee was even better, batting .309 with 184 hits, both club highs that year. He also displayed power, socking 18 homers and driving in 78 runs. As a fielder, he was adequate, but nothing spectacular.

At this point, Dee appeared on the verge of superstardom, but he could never put it all together, showing only streaks of batting prowess. In 1954, his batting average was only .266 with 25 games left to play. Suddenly, Fondy began burning through the league like prairie fire, hitting a torrid .383 his last 25 games to bring his final average to .285.

Unchained on the basepaths, Dee stole 20 bases, the most by a Cub since Stan Hack's 21 back in 1940. But the following year, he got off to a worse start. By July 27, 1955, his batting average was an anemic .232. Then the bat caught fire again. From then to the end of the year, he batted .313 to jack his final mark up to .265.

Fondy's last full year as a Cub was 1956. On May 2, 1957, he and Gene Baker were dealt to the Pirates for Dale Long and Lee Walls. Dee hit .313 that year for his highest mark, but came to the plate only 374 times. After dropping to .218 with the Reds the following year, Dee retired. He left behind an even 1,000 hits and a .286 batting average.

EDDIE MIKSIS

MIKSIS, EDWARD THOMAS
B. Sept. 11, 1926, Burlington, N.J.
BR TR 5'6½" 185 lb.

The motto "Miksis will fix us" was a painful reminder of the notorious swindle that sent Cub favorite Andy Pafko to the Brooklyn Dodgers. Eddie Miksis was a Cub regular by default. They were short of talent during the dreary 1950s.

Miksis was a fuzzy-faced teenager of 17 when he joined the Dodgers during the wartime player shortage. The New Jersey native was an infielder with Trenton of the Inter-State League in 1944. Trenton was financially drained and the Dodgers were to contribute $10,000 for the privilege of selecting any player they wanted. Owner Branch Rickey sent scouts to look at the team. They took Miksis.

The highlight of his Dodger career came in the fourth game of the 1947 World Series. Needing one out for a no-hitter, Yankee pitcher Bill Bevens served a pinch double to Cookie Lavagetto, bringing across two runs for a 3-2 Dodger victory. It was Miksis, pinch-running for Pete Reiser, who slid home with the winning run.

But with Brooklyn, Miksis never had been able to break into the lineup because Eddie Stanky, Billy Cox, Pee Wee Reese, and Jackie Robinson rated ahead of him. The splendid bench-splinter once got to play for three straight weeks when Stanky was injured. He batted .350 during that stretch, but was yanked by manager Leo Durocher when Stanky had recovered.

"Leo explained that the team needed Stanky's fire," said Miksis with ire. "I spit fire when I got the news. Nearly every week I was in the front office demanding to be traded."

Miksis got his wish on June 15, 1951. The Dodgers sent sore-headed Miksis, plus sore-armed pitcher Joe Hatten, sore-shouldered catcher Bruce Edwards, and the not sorely needed outfielder, Gene Hermanski, to the Cubs for the popular Pafko, plus three others. General Manager Wid Matthews uttered the "Miksis-fix us" slogan at that time and it was nixed by Cub followers with not mixed emotions.

Miksis was handed the second base job and became part of the Cub double-play duo alongside the eratic Roy Smalley. Eddie's contribution was a .266 average, his personal high. He was a regular fella at last.

But in the 1952 opener he injured his right knee and hobbled about all season, finishing with a .232 average. There was one game, however, in which Eddie applied a dash of psychology, turning a 4-3 Phillies' "victory" into a 3-2 defeat. It happened on June 11 at Wrigley Field.

The Phillies had the bases loaded with two out and the score tied 1-1 in the fourth inning. Richie Ashburn lined a single to center, scoring Jack Mayo and Connie Ryan and sending Tommy Brown to third.

Miksis called for the ball and stepped on second. Umpire Al Barlick ruled Brown out for not touching second to retire the side, nullifying the two runs.

"I didn't see Brown miss second," said Miksis with a sly smile. "But when he rounded the bag he glanced back with a guilty look on his face. So I called for the ball. It was just a stab in the dark. I was playing a hunch. Psychology, you know."

While Miksis supplied the brains, teammate Hank Sauer supplied the brawn. Sauer hit three solo homers off pitcher Curt Simmons for the 3-2 Cub win. And Tommy Brown? He was dropped by the Phils and picked up by the Cubs the following week.

Miksis regained the second base job in 1953, getting into 142 games, a career high. Then it was back to the bench as the Cubs brought up the classy keystone combo of Ernie Banks and Gene Baker the following season. Eddie's stickwork fell to .202.

If Miksis couldn't break into the infield, he tried the outfield. Guess what? He made only three errors in right and center field to lead the National League with a .983 fielding average. Although he hit only .235, he contributed a personal high 9 homers and 41 RBI.

By this time Hatten, Edwards, and Hermanski were gone from the Cub scene. Miksis was the lone reminder of the Pafko misdeal. It was ironic that Miksis wound up in Pafko's old center field spot, minus the cannon arm and booming bat.

Perhaps Eddie's most memorable batting contribution came during an exhibition game. The Cubs were playing the White Sox in a charity game on Aug. 15, 1955, at Comiskey Park.

His two-run 10th-inning homer off Jack Harshman powered the Cubs to a 7-6 victory. That was one evening Cub fans could chant "Miksis will fix us" without a sneer.

Miksis spent much of the 1956 season pounding the pines again, then drifted from the Cardinals to the Orioles to the Reds.

He retired in 1958, a .236 hitter with 722 hits.

RALPH KINER

KINER, RALPH MCPHERRON
B. Oct. 27, 1922, Santa Rita, N.M.
BR TR 6'2" 195 lb.

Ralph Kiner, the slugger who turned "Greenberg Gardens" into "Kiner's Corner," was one of a handful of players who found the "Friendly Confines" of Wrigley Field a rather unwelcome spot.

Kiner played only a season and a half in a Cub uniform and ranked along with Dick Bartell, Jimmy Wilson, and Roy Smalley as a favorite target of the boobirds.

The record books are filled with Kiner's accomplishments. He hit 369 career homers. In his first seven years in the major leagues, he either tied or led in homers. Twice he hit more than 50 homers. Twelve of his homers were grand slams. And he was elected to baseball's Hall of Fame in 1975.

Why then was he so unpopular with Cub fans? The answer perhaps can be summed up in two words: Hank Sauer.

It all began on June 4, 1953, when Kiner was acquired from Pittsburgh in a 10-player trade. The Cubs sent pitcher Bob Schultz, catcher Toby Atwell, infielders Preston Ward and George Freese, outfielders Gene Hermanski and Bob Addis, and an estimated $100,000 to the Pirates for pitcher Howie Pollet, catcher Joe Garagiola, infielder Catfish Metkovich, and the big catch—Kiner.

The gigantic deal was well received in Chicago. Imagine, Kiner and Sauer, two sluggers, batting back to back. Both, however, played left field and were slow afoot. Sauer was the darling of the left field bleacherites. He was called the "Mayor of Wrigley Field" and after every homer would be peppered with packets of chewing tobacco.

Sauer agreed to shift to right field to accommodate Kiner. Kiner actually outhomered Sauer 15 to 13 at Wrigley Field that season. Overall, Kiner hit 35 homers, 28 as a Cub. Sauer, who missed part of the season with a broken thumb, finished with 19.

But the following season, Kiner was bothered by a bad back and his homer production fell to 22. Sauer bounced back with 41 homers, hitting 21 to Kiner's 9 before the home crowd.

Moreover, Kiner's salary was in the $90,000 bracket, then an astronomical figure. Sauer's paycheck was less than half that. Cub fans felt Kiner wasn't giving them their money's worth in comparison to Sauer. The Cubs solved that problem by dealing Kiner to the Cleveland Indians on Nov. 16, 1954, for pitcher Sam Jones, outfielder Gale Wade, and $60,000.

Kiner spent two seasons in Albany, N.Y., and one in Toronto. He was unimpressive, never getting more than 14 homers. He then spent three years as a navy pilot in the Pacific. He didn't see any action, but gained 30 pounds on navy chow.

Kiner reported to the Pirates in 1946 and was the talk of spring training, hitting 14 home runs. That earned him a spot in the opening day lineup. He batted only .247, but connected for 23 homers, nosing out Johnny Mize of the New York Giants by one and becoming the first rookie to lead the National League since Harry Lumley of the Brooklyn Dodgers in 1904.

The following season Hank Greenberg joined the Pirates and he took Kiner under his wing. The Pirates shortened the left field distance from 365 feet to 335 feet and named the inner fence "Greenberg Gardens."

Greenberg pumped only 25 homers, but Kiner pounded out 51 and the fenced-in area was renamed "Kiner's Korner." The 51 homers enabled Kiner to tie Mize for the home run title. In 1948 Kiner and Mize again shared the homer crown with 40 each.

On Sept. 11, 1948, Kiner enjoyed his favorite game. The Pirates were playing the Cubs at Wrigley Field. Kiner had the sniffles and a stomach ache and was scratched from the lineup. It was the first game Kiner didn't start all season.

He took some pills and was on the rubbing table. The game was a slugfest with the Cubs ahead 10-7 after seven innings. Kiner's temperature was 101° and his eyes were watery, but he grabbed his shoes, buttoned his shirt, and ran down the runway to the Pirates' dugout.

By the time he reached the bench, the Pirates had the bases loaded. Manager Billy Meyer asked Kiner if he could make it. "I can give it one good swing," sniffed Kiner.

His legs were weak, his stomach was doing flip flops, and his eyes were tearing as he ran the count full against Cub pitcher Hank Borowy. Hank threw a curve and Kiner hit it out of the ballpark for a grand-slam homer. He jogged around the bases and kept going right into the clubhouse. The Pirates went on to win 13-12.

The next year Kiner made his best run at Babe Ruth's record 60 homers, but fell short with 54. He again was the undisputed champ the following two seasons with 47 and 42. He tied Sauer with 37 in 1952. Kiner thus tied or led in homers his first seven seasons in the National League, an all-time record.

Following his short stint with the Cubs, Kiner closed out his career by hitting 18 homers with the Indians in 1955. An ailing back hastened his decision to quit. A lifetime .279 hitter, he concluded with 369 homers, averaging one per 14.1 at bats, second only to Ruth's 11.8 in consistency.

Kiner then turned to radio and TV sportscasting as one of the voices of the New York Mets. He was voted into the Hall of Fame in 1975 off his slugging exploits.

PAUL SCHRAMKA

SCHRAMKA, PAUL EDWARD
B. March 22, 1928, Milwaukee, Wis.
BL TL 6'0" 185 lb.

On Aug. 8, 1982, the Chicago Cubs officially retired Paul Schramka's number. Ernie Banks happened to be wearing jersey No. 14 during the ceremonies at Wrigley Field.

"I sent Ernie a telegram, saying 'I left all the base hits in the jersey for you,'" said Schramka, now a funeral director in his native Milwaukee.

The 6-foot, 185-pound outfielder played two games as a Cub and never got to bat in 1953. In the April 14th season opener at Cincinnati, Schramka ran for catcher Clyde McCullough in the seventh inning of a 3-2 Cub victory over the Reds.

Two days later Schramka replaced Gene Hermanski in left field in the eighth inning of a 3-0 loss to the Cardinals in St. Louis. A ball was never hit in his direction.

On April 24th, the injured Hank Sauer returned to the lineup. Schramka received the bad news. He was sent to Springfield, Mass., of the International League on 24-hour recall. He was never recalled.

"It was fun anyway," added Schramka. "I was lucky. How many people can say they played major league baseball?"

After leaving the Cubs, Schramka knocked about the next two seasons with stops at Springfield, Des Moines, Los Angeles, Beaumont, and Macon. But there was some fun along the way.

"Omaha had a second baseman, whom we dubbed the 'Banty Rooster,' a fellow named Earl Weaver," said Schramka. "In those days we used to leave our gloves on the field between innings.

"I pulled a plastic snake out of my pocket and put it in Weaver's glove. We watched intently from the dugout as Weaver went out to his position. Earl bent down, took one look, let out a screech, and started kicking his glove all the way to the outfield. I wonder whatever became of Weaver?"

Schramka was only 26 when he quit baseball. "I decided to fold it up, join my dad in the funeral business, and raise a family." Milwaukee is Brewer country, but Schramka still bleeds true Cub blue. "I have a soft touch in my heart for the Cubbies," said Schramka.

Now for another trivia question. Who wore Cub jersey No. 14 before Schramka? Researchers had to go back all the way to 1944 to uncover outfielder Lou Novikoff, the "Mad Russian."

SECTION THREE 1954-1960 Banks for the Memories

The mid-to-late 1950s are fondly recalled as the era of ducktail haircuts and black leather jackets, ponytails and pleated skirts. It was the time of 3-D movies, Davy Crockett caps, Mickey Mouse ears, hula hoops, and the birth of rock 'n roll. For the Cubs, the fabulous fifties were characterized by massive home run production but little else. The Cubs were the Edsels of the National League.

The spring of '54 opened on a sour note when manager Phil Cavarretta was fired for giving Phil Wrigley an honest evaluation of the team's chances. His accuracy was borne out by another seventh place finish under his successor, Stan Hack. The lone optimistic note was the arrival of black rookies Gene Baker at second and Ernie Banks at short. They gave the Cubs their best infield combination since Billy Herman and Billy Jurges.

The following season the Cubs got off to a fast start, but faded in July, finishing sixth. The year of Bill Haley and the Comets also witnessed the emergence of Ernie Banks as a full-fledged superstar, and Bob Speake as a would-be Babe Ruth. Speake hit 10 homers in May—and two for the rest of the year.

Over the winter the Cubs pulled what looked like yet another Brooklyn-inspired boner when they traded Ransom Jackson to the Dodgers for a part-time outfielder, Walt "Moose" Moryn. However, Jackson was never the same after leaving Chicago, while Moryn became a dependable clutch hitter and the hero of the blue collar fans.

Moryn and Banks gave the Cubs a good one-two punch, but the team still had a soft underbelly. In 1956 they "celebrated" their 10th straight year in the second division by tumbling to the basement. Clyde McCullough, the lone veteran of '45, played his last game in midseason.

Following that forgettable year, the heads of Matthews, Gallagher, and Hack rolled. The somber-looking John Holland, who looked better-fitted for running a funeral parlor, became the new general manager, while Bob Scheffing replaced Hack as field boss.

The only Cub to hit three homers in a game and hit for the cycle (single, double, triple, and homer) was Lee Walls.

Things did not fare much better during Scheffing's first year at the helm. The Cubs finished in a tie for seventh. Lee Walls joined Moryn in the outfield and Dale Long, another home run threat, became the new first baseman. Pitchers Dick Drott and Moe Drabowsky enjoyed splendid rookie seasons, but their accomplishments were sparse thereafter.

In 1958 the Cubs went on the biggest home run binge in their history, smashing a league-leading 182, still the club record. A record five Cubs slugged 20 or more homers—Banks, Moryn, Walls, Long, and Bobby Thomson. The Big Boppers of the league, they batted .265 as a team and scored 709 runs.

Even so, they could only move up to a tie for fifth place. Considering the near-total lack of dependable starters (rookie Glen Hobbie was the "ace" of the staff with 10 wins), Scheffing did a creditable job with what he had, and fans were appreciative.

The Cubs pulled an encore in 1959, again finishing in a tie for fifth as Banks won his second consecutive MVP Award. Hobbie won 16 games but pitching continued to be a problem as firemen Don Elston and Bill Henry were worn out by season's end.

Then came the bombshell. After giving the Cubs their best record (74-80) in seven years, Scheffing was given the axe. When asked why he fired Scheffing, P. K. Wrigley replied, "He lacked ginger"—whatever that meant.

An aging Charlie Grimm was recycled to manage the Cubs in 1960, but this time he found it to be too many headaches. After just 17 games, he switched places with radio color man Lou Boudreau for the remainder of the year.

The Cubs began poorly and played consistently so for the whole year, escaping the cellar by only one game. Moreover, they were again in the throes of an agonizing change. Most of their well-liked regulars of the late '50s—Moryn, Walls, Thomson, Long, Henry, Al Dark, and Tony Taylor—were gone by midseason, some by advancing age, others by bad trades. P. K. Wrigley was getting ready to drop the biggest bomb yet.

ERNIE BANKS

BANKS, ERNEST
B. Jan. 31, 1931,
Dallas, Tex.
BR TR 6'1" 186 lb.

When it comes to the Yankees, you think of Babe Ruth. When it comes to the Cardinals, you think of Stan Musial. When it comes to the Mets, you think of . . . well, Ed Kranepool? Maybe Marv Throneberry?

When it comes to the Cubs, there can be no doubt—Ernie Banks. Banks went through thin and thinner for 19 seasons with mostly woeful Cub teams. Yet, he remained "Effervescent Ernie."

Some detractors say his sunny disposition, enthusiasm, and optimism were a put-on. But none can doubt his 512 homers, his back-to-back MVP Awards, his five grand-slam homers in one season, or his historic 500th homer.

What memories. The cheerful slugger was a skinny, 22-year-old shortstop when he reported to the Cubs in the closing days of the 1953 season. He saw Wrigley Field for the first time on Sept. 14, 1953. Banks stepped into the batting cage, nervously wiggled his fingers while gripping his bat, and with his supple wrists, hit the first batting practice pitch into the left field bleachers. Welcome to the Friendly Confines.

The road to becoming the biggest celebrity in Chicago baseball history was not an easy one. The second of 12 children born to Eddie and Essie Banks, Ernie knew only poverty from birth. His father often worked from dawn to dusk seven days a week. As the oldest boy in the family, Ernie did most of the housework, keeping the kerosene lamps lit, carrying in wood for the stoves, and hauling in water from the back yard pump. He developed a strong body by picking cotton.

Banks first developed an interest in sports when he entered

Booker T. Washington High School in Dallas. There he played softball, football, and basketball. He caught the eye of Bill Blair, a former pitcher and outfielder for the Indianapolis Clowns.

In the summer of 1948 Blair arranged a meeting for Ernie with Johnny Carter, who owned and managed the Detroit Colts, a Negro touring team based in Amarillo, Tex. Banks spent the next two summers as shortstop for the Colts, playing before small town black audiences throughout Texas, New Mexico, Oklahoma, Kansas, and Nebraska.

Following graduation from high school in 1950, Ernie was recruited by the Kansas City Monarchs of the Negro American League for $300 a month. His manager was John "Buck" O'Neill, who later became a Cub coach (the first black coach in the majors). One of Ernie's teammates was Elston Howard, who would become the first black player on the Yankees.

Ernie's career was interrupted by two years in the army, but by 1953 he was back with the Monarchs. In the early 1950s the Cubs were grooming Gene Baker at their Triple A club in Los Angeles to be their first black player. They wanted a black roommate for Baker. When they learned Banks was available, they purchased him and pitcher Bill Dickey from the Monarchs on Sept. 8, 1953. Dickey was discarded shortly afterward, and the way was paved for Banks and Baker to come to Chicago.

Barely two weeks were left in the season when Ernie arrived on Chicago's North Side. "Green Hornet" streetcars clanged along Clark Street for 20 cents a ride and a row of coal bins stood like sentries along Seminary Avenue in front of Wrigley Field. Cub fans went to the park in double-breasted suits and wide-brimmed fedoras.

After taking batting practice only for three days, Ernie played his first game on Sept. 17. Understandably nervous, he went hitless in three trips and committed an error at shortstop in a 16-4 loss to the Phillies.

Banks hit his first homer in his third game as a Cub on Sept. 20, 1953. "It was against the Cardinals' Gerry Staley in Busch Stadium," recalled Banks. "Hank Sauer told me to watch out for his knuckleball and not to swing too hard. Just concentrate on meeting the ball.

"Staley threw me a knuckleball. A good knuckler. I was surprised when I hit it and I didn't think it would go far. It wasn't until I rounded first that I realized it was in the left field seats.

"As I was circling the bases, it seemed as if everything had stopped. The crowd was silent and all eyes were watching me. It was a strange feeling, but a great one."

Although the Cubs lost 11-6, Ernie's major league career was off to a good start. By the year's end he had batted .314 in his first 10 games.

Banks at short and Baker at second made the Cubs strong up the middle for the first time since the days of Billy Jurges and Billy Herman. Both hit .275 in 1954, and Ernie's 19 homers set a record for a Cub rookie, surpassing Bill Serena's 17 in 1950. Radio announcer Bert Wilson nicknamed Ernie "Bingo" and Gene "Bango"; hence the double-play combination of Bingo to Bango to Bilko (Steve Bilko, back-up first baseman to Dee Fondy). However, the nicknames never fully caught on and were soon forgotten.

By 1955 Banks had become a genuine superstar. With his .295 batting average, 44 homers, and 117 RBI, he replaced the fading Hank Sauer as the Cubs' new long ball threat. Moreover, five of his homers were grand slams, setting a major league record that has since been tied, but not exceeded.

Ernie Banks hit his first big league homer off Gerry Staley of the Cardinals in 1953 at Sportsman's Park.

Ernie's natural wrist action struck terror in the heart of every National League pitcher, his only weakness being a low, outside curve, which he often fanned on. On Aug. 4, 1955, he slammed three homers in one game for the first time in his career in an 11-10 slugfest win over the Pirates at Wrigley Field. Homer No. 40, on Sept. 2, set a record for a shortstop, eclipsing the old mark of 39 set by Vern Stephens of the Red Sox in 1949. In just two years, Ernie had gone from a nobody to the toast of Chicago.

Ernie had played 424 consecutive games when he was sidelined by a minor ailment on Aug. 11, 1956. That established a record for most consecutive games played from the start of a major league career. He suffered an off year by his standards. His home run total dipped to 28 and his RBI to 85.

The following year witnessed a welcome rebound as Ernie, frequently appearing at third base, socked 43 homers and drove home 102 runs. Career homer No. 100 came at Philadelphia on June 9, when he knocked a Robin Roberts offering out of Connie Mack Stadium during a 7-3 Cub win. On Sept. 14, 1957, Ernie did an encore of the three-homer act against the Pirates. All three were solo shots as the Cubs beat Pittsburgh 7-3 at Wrigley Field.

Banks was now reaching the pinnacle of his prowess. In 1958 the Cubs went on their biggest home run binge in history, clouting a club record 182. Ernie was at the top of the heap with a league-leading 47. This, combined with a career-high .313 average, 129 RBI, and 119 runs scored, earned him a well-deserved Most Valuable Player Award, not to mention *The Sporting News* Player of the Year honors.

Ernie's 200th home run came on June 14, 1959, off Carlton Willey of the Braves in the seventh inning at the Friendly Confines as the Cubs beat Milwaukee 6-0. But the Braves' Eddie Mathews beat Banks out of the home run crown, 46 to 45. Banks still batted .304, and his 143 RBI were tops in the league. In addition, his .985 fielding average set a record for a shortstop while his 12 errors set a new low. (Both, however, have since been broken). For good measure he led in assists with 519.

On Nov. 14, 1959, Ernie was voted Most Valuable Player for the second straight year, the first player in the National League so honored. *The Sporting News* quickly followed with another Player of the Year Award.

Cub manager Bob Scheffing recalled a few years later that

"during my first 26 years in baseball, Joe DiMaggio is the only player I'd ever consider rating ahead of Ernie Banks after the year Ernie had for me in 1959. He batted fourth behind three hitters, who didn't come even close to averaging .260, and still he batted in 143 runs. He also hit 45 homers, and I figured out that his bat was directly responsible for 27 of our 74 victories that season. Afield he was the equal of any shortstop I've seen."

In 1960 Ernie won his second and last home run title, giving the ball the kiss-off 41 times. On July 11 he hit his only All-Star Game homer and also contributed a double, driving in two runs as the National League prevailed 5-3 at Kansas City. Defensively, one could not ask for more. Banks led the league in putouts (283), assists (488), and fielding average (.977), to win *The Sporting News* Gold Glove Award.

After leading the league in games played for six of the last seven seasons, Ernie began to show signs of slowing down when he turned 30 in 1961. Hampered with eye and knee problems, he could no longer move around his position as quickly as before. His hitting also was affected; his power production fell to 29 homers and 80 RBI.

The first experiment was to place him in left field, and the less said about that the better. Then it was back to shortstop. Finally, as the season drew to a close, Ernie was relocated at first base.

That proved to be the rebirth of Ernie's career. He became the Cubs' best defensive first baseman since Eddie Waitkus. Between 1962 and '69 he led the league in assists five times, putouts three times, and fielding average once.

Now that he was more relaxed in his new position, Ernie's bat started booming again. In 1962 he poled 37 homers and drove in 104 runs for a horrendous Cub team that finished in ninth place behind the expansion Houston Colt .45s. On May 29 he again smashed three homers in one game, but the Braves outlasted the Cubs 11-9 in 10 innings.

Following his comeback, Banks suffered the worst season of his career in 1963. Sidelined for the entire month of September with the subclinical mumps, he saw his batting average plummet to .227 and he drove in only 64 runs. Even so, Ernie carved two more historic notches into his six-shooter. On May 9 he tied a major league record by making 22 putouts at first base as the Cubs beat the Pirates 3-1 on Dick Ellsworth's three-hitter. A month later, to the day, he belted three homers in a game for the fourth and last time. Two of the blows were off Dodger ace Sandy Koufax, but Los Angeles won 11-8.

Having completed his 10th full season with the club, Banks was now affectionately called "Mr. Cub." Although he was with a chronically losing team, Banks never lost faith in the Cubs.

It was fitting, then, that he was honored with an "Ernie Banks Day" at Wrigley Field on Aug. 15, 1964. His father came up from Texas for the celebration and proudly put on the baseball cap that had brought fame and glory to his son. After being awarded numerous gifts and testimonials, Ernie said, "First, I want to thank God for making me an American . . . and giving me the ability to be a major league baseball player . . . and, of course, all the wonderful Cub fans for your warmth and acceptance in making this day possible. I will be forever grateful to the fine Cub organization, the teammates here and beyond, and especially to Mr. Wrigley, who has been more than just an employer. I will never forget this day. I thank you all from the bottom of my heart."

As is often the case on such events, the Cubs lost to the Pirates 5-4, and the man of the hour went hitless in four at bats. Even so, the spirit was not dampened.

Like good wine, Banks was mellowing with age. In 1965 he initiated his annual season prediction, proclaiming, "The Cubs will come alive in '65." Although the Cubs played dead and finished in eighth place again, it was no fault of Banks, who drove in 106 runs with 28 homers. At first base he collected a whopping 1,682 putouts. Home run No. 400 came on Sept. 2, when Ernie connected off the Cardinals' Curt Simmons with two on in the third inning, en route to a 5-3 Cub victory.

In 1966 Leo Durocher was appointed Cub manager and Ernie announced, "The Cubs will shoot from the hip with Leo the Lip." Instead they finished tenth, and relations between Durocher and Banks were often strained. Although Ernie's batting average of .272 was his highest in five years, his homer total dropped to 15, his lowest yet.

Even so, he attained two more personal milestones. On June 11, 1966, he became only the fourth Cub player in history to hit three triples in one game as the Cubs routed Houston 8-2 at the Astrodome. The others were Marty Sullivan (1887), Bill Dahlen (1896 and 1898), and Charlie Hollocher (1922). On July 20 he collected the 2,000th hit of his career, but the Reds nipped the Cubs 5-4 at Wrigley Field.

The following year Ernie's prophecy was, "The Cubs will be heavenly in 'sixty-sevenly." This time he was right. Casting off their second division yoke for the first time since 1946, the Cubs climbed to a solid third place finish. Ernie's contributions were a .276 average, 23 homers, and 95 RBI.

His achievements continued to add up. On Sept. 15, 1968, he played his 2,254th game, surpassing Cap Anson's Cub record as the Cubs blanked the Phillies 4-0 at Philadelphia. The following day, telegrams of congratulations arrived from Anson's three surviving daughters. Ironically, Anson had been the prime force in the exclusion of blacks from the majors back in the 1880s.

By 1969 there was actually serious talk about the Cubs winning a pennant. Bumper stickers reading "C'mon Cubs—win it for Ernie" began popping up on cars. And the 38-year-old Banks played as if he had visited the fountain of youth. On May 13 he enjoyed one of his finest days, driving in seven runs and posting RBI number 1,500 as the Cubs shellacked the Padres 19-0 at Wrigley Field. Eleven days later, Ernie garnered his 12th and final grand-slam homer as the Cubs beat the Padres 7-5 at San Diego.

Banks led the league in RBI through the first half of the season as the Cubs appeared to be on the road to glory. But Ernie tailed off. By September the Cubs were in a tailspin, finishing second to the Mets. Ernie's batting average slipped to .253, but he still drove in 106 runs while leading the league in putouts and fielding average.

Age finally began to catch up with the seemingly ageless Banks in 1970. Arthritis in the knees limited his action to 72 games. On May 12, however, came the most historic moment of his career. The Braves were in town and Pat Jarvis was on the hill when Ernie came to bat with two out in the second inning. On the one-one count Jarvis served again, only to see it sail into the left field bleachers for Ernie's 500th homer! He was given a standing ovation as he crossed the plate, and the Cubs went on to win 4-3 in the 11th. Banks was given the historic ball and clicked his heels for the reporters.

But the magic was no longer in the once booming bat. Although Ernie still said, "Let's play two today," he was now lucky to make token appearances, coming to bat only 83 times in 1971. On July 21 he hit homer No. 511 to tie Mel Ott on the all-time list. His 512th and final home run came on Aug. 24 at Wrigley Field. The Cubs won both games 11-7 over the Mets and 4-3 over the Reds. Mr. Cub's final hit came in his final game on Sept. 26, a first inning single in a 5-1 loss to the Phillies at Wrigley Field.

Banks retired from the majors a .274 hitter with 2,583 hits in 2,528 games. On the all-time Cub list, he is first in games played, first in homers, first in extra base hits (1,009), first in total bases (4,706), second in hits, second in RBI (1,636), second in doubles (407), fourth in runs scored (1,305), fourth in slugging average (.500), and seventh in triples (90). When he appeared as a pinch hitter in the Boys Benefit game at Comiskey Park on Aug. 14, 1972, it was another standing ovation.

In the years that followed, Banks continued to serve in the Cubs' public relations department. For awhile, he was on the board of directors of the Chicago Transit Authority.

The honor of honors came on Feb. 14, 1977, when Ernie was voted into baseball's Hall of Fame, saying, "I consider my election to the Hall of Fame the highlight of my career and a tremendous personal honor. I owe a debt of gratitude to all the people connected with our fine game of baseball. It's always a beautiful day for baseball . . . LET'S PLAY TWO!"

The formal induction at Cooperstown came on Aug. 9. In his acceptance speech Banks said, "This is the happiest day of my life. I have read that a man's success depends on the people who believe in him. I owe so much to my parents for all they put up with me; and to my wife and children—you don't know what a baseball wife has to put up with.

"And there's one man who's not here. I've owed a great debt to him since I first met him in 1953, and I only wish that the late Mr. Phillip K. Wrigley could be here." Among those who congratulated

Ernie was Minnesota Twins' shortstop Roy Smalley, Jr., whose father Banks had replaced at short for the Cubs 24 years earlier.

After Banks had been part of the Cub organization for nearly 30 years, Cub fans were shocked to learn in June of 1983 that he was no longer with the club. He has since relocated to California, leaving his Cub days behind as a memory. To his admirers, however, he will always remain "Mr. Cub."

GENE BAKER

BAKER, EUGENE WALTER
B. June 15, 1925, Davenport, Iowa
BR TR 6'1"
170 lb.

The Cubs brought up Gene Baker too late and let him go too soon. But in between he teamed with Ernie Banks to form one of the Cubs' finest double-play combinations.

With the success of Jackie Robinson in 1947, the major leagues found a long-delayed mother lode of talent—the black ballplayer. Some teams followed the Brooklyn Dodgers lead by rapidly signing blacks, while others dawdled.

The Cubs waited until 1950 before signing Baker, a skinny shortstop from Davenport, Iowa. Baker was already 25 when the Cubs purchased his contract from the Kansas City Monarchs of the Negro League.

They assigned him to Springfield, Mass., and before the season was over, he was the regular shortstop for the Los Angeles Angels of the Pacific Coast League, the Cubs' top farm club.

Baker got into the LA lineup on July 8, 1950, and never left until Aug. 31, 1952, when he was taken out for a rest. Gene had played 420 consecutive games, an all-time Angels' record.

Meanwhile, the Cubs were floundering afield. They had enough power with a lineup that included Hank Sauer, Ralph Kiner, Randy Jackson, and Dee Fondy. But their fielding was atrocious.

At shortstop was Roy Smalley, perhaps the most maligned player in Cub history. Every Smalley error was magnified and he was the main target of the boobirds.

Why were the Cubs delaying a move to bring up Baker to replace Smalley? Gene was the outstanding shortstop on the West Coast. Rival scouts and managers called him "a definite big league prospect" and said he "was ready for an immediate opportunity to play in the majors." The Cub brass remained silent.

Four seasons had elapsed and Baker was still an Angel. He glided over the ground, had a bullwhip arm, was durable, and proved a clutch hitter. There were no outbursts from Baker, who did admit later, "I was just as good five years before I made the big leagues. Everybody who saw me play will tell you that. It's just that my time hadn't come."

After being held back, Baker and another slender shortstop named Ernie Banks came up at the tag end of the 1953 season. They were the Cubs' first black players.

"I ran out to shortstop but Ernie was already there," recalled Baker. "Ernie," I said, "what are you doing here?"

Banks just grinned and said, "Heck, I'm playing short. They got you playing second."

"I raced to the dugout and looked at the lineup card tacked to the wall. Sure enough, I was playing second base. I'd never played there before in my life."

The Cubs also needed a second baseman badly. Since Baker had more experience than Banks, the Cubs figured he could make the adjustment easier. Baker did learn how to play second. In addition, he taught young Banks everything he knew about shortstop.

Banks and Baker became as much a team as scotch and soda. They were inseparable on and off the field. Both hit .275 in 1954, their first full season.

The following year, Banks grabbed the spotlight with 44 homers, five of them grand slammers, and hit .295. Baker batted .268 and played alongside Banks in all of the Cubs' 154 games.

But Baker wasn't always in Banks' shadow. For instance, there was a Ladies Day game against the Dodgers on Aug. 8, 1955. A crowd of 41,860 jammed the Wrigley Field girders. They came to see Robinson, Roy Campanella, and Don Newcombe and stayed to cheer the Cubs' Toothpick Sam Jones and Baker.

It was a superb mound duel between Newcombe and Jones, the top two black pitchers in baseball. Baker had a first-inning single and a leadoff double in the third, but both were wasted. The game was scoreless until Baker strode to the plate in the eighth inning.

Newcombe's first pitch made Baker hit the dirt. Gene rose, wiped away the dust, and worked the count full, before hammering Newcombe's next pitch into the left field bleachers for a 1-0 Cub victory.

The Cubs weren't leading the league, but at least they had baseball's best double-play combination. It seemed that they were set for years at the keystone. But the Cubs had other ideas.

They were grooming a youngster named Casey Wise for second base and asked Baker to switch to third base during spring training of 1957. Baker quietly obliged and moved to third.

Then came another jolt. Baker was no longer a Cub. He was traded along with Fondy to the Pittsburgh Pirates for sluggers Dale Long and Lee Walls. The inseparable Banks-Baker combo was separated.

Baker played second, short, and third with Pittsburgh until he suffered a serious knee injury in 1958 that forced him on the inactive list for a season and a half. When he returned, he was relegated to a utility role.

The Pirates then released him as an active player in June 1961. They appointed him manager of their farm club at Batavia, N.Y., in the Class D New York-Penn League.

It was announced that Baker was the first black manager in organized baseball, but it was later disclosed that Nate Moreland piloted the Calexcio team in the Class C Arizona-Mexico League two years earlier.

Baker later rejoined the Pirates as a coach and today serves as a scout in their organization. Down through the years, Banks and Baker have retained their close relationship. When Banks was elected to baseball's Hall of Fame in 1977, the first person he contacted was his old double-play sidekick, Gene Baker.

In his eight seasons as a major leaguer, Baker was a .265 hitter with 590 hits and 39 homers.

SAM JONES

JONES, SAMUEL
B. Dec. 14, 1925, Stewartsville, Ohio.
D. Nov. 5, 1971, Morgantown, W. Va.
BR TR 6'4"
192 lb.

Sam Jones was known as Emperor, Sad Sam, and Toothpick Sam. Rival batsmen used other names after facing the rangy right-hander's sweeping curveball. It was that devastating.

Surprisingly, with all his raw talent, Jones's 12-year log was only 102 victories and 101 losses. He shuffled from team to team, performing for seven major league clubs.

It was his inability to control his pitches that prevented Sad Sam from being one of the greatest pitchers in the game. He led the National League in bases on balls four times, including 185 with the 1955 Cubs, a club record.

It was a long, hard pull for Jones to reach the majors. He started with the Cleveland Buckeyes of the Negro League in 1946. It was there that he learned how to throw a curveball. His teacher was Satchel Paige. Sam's curve had the batters fall away into the dirt before darting into the strike zone.

Jones caught the eye of the Cleveland Indians' scouts, but was up and down in their organization after being beset with bursitis. He was acquired by the Cubs in 1955 along with outfielder Gale Wade in the deal that sent slugger Ralph Kiner to Cleveland. Jones was 29. He knew this was his last chance to stick.

Few pitchers had a more spectacular or exciting first season than Jones in 1955. None present in Wrigley Field on May 12, 1955, could dispute that.

There were only 2,918 fans assembled on that gray, overcast day, when Jones faced the Pittsburgh Pirates. At least 50,000 fans swear they were in attendance for what probably was the most improbable ninth inning of any no-hitter.

The Cubs were leading 4-0. Jones, chewing on his ever-present toothpick, had walked four and fanned three going into the ninth inning.

Jones proceeded to walk Gene Freese, Preston Ward, and Tom Saffell to load the bases with none out. The next three hitters were the heart of the Pirate batting order—Dick Groat, Roberto Clemente, and Frank Thomas.

Cub manager Stan Hack raced out of the dugout for a conference with Jones and catcher Clyde McCullough. Would Hack yank a pitcher on the verge of a no-hitter? Hack looked toward the bullpen where several pitchers were warming up. But he decided to stick with Jones.

While Jones was chewing on his toothpick, everyone else was

chewing on his fingernails. Jones and McCullough decided to go with his best pitch, the sweeping curveball. Groat took three strikes. One down. Clemente went down swinging, on five pitches. Two gone.

The count went to 2-2 on the slugging Thomas. Jones tucked the toothpick in the corner of his mouth, reared back and fired. Thomas took it. McCullough literally sprang from behind the plate as the ball hit his glove. It was then that umpire Art Gore called, "Strike three."

Jones had struck out the side with the bases loaded and became the first black to pitch a major league no-hitter. It was also the first no-hitter at Wrigley Field in 38 years. After the game, Jones was presented a gold toothpick by sportscaster Harry Creighton.

Don Hoak struck out six times in one game for the Cubs in 1956.

By season's end Jones had a no-hitter, a two-hitter, a three-hitter, a four-hitter, and three five-hitters. He led the Cubs with 14 victories. His 20 defeats, 185 walks, and 198 strikeouts topped the National League.

The following season, Jones had a 9-14 record and again led in walks (115) and strikeouts (176). Jones was the ace of a mediocre pitching staff on a mediocre ballclub.

In 1957 there was a complete shakeup of the Cub organization. The incoming general manager, John Holland, probably never saw Sad Sam's sweeping curve because he swept him aside in another one-sided Cub trade.

Sad Sam was shunted to the St. Louis Cardinals with three other players for pitchers Tom Poholsky, Jackie Collum, and catcher Ray Katt. Poholsky and Collum won one game each in a Cub uniform and Katt was dealt before he could even don a Cub uniform.

And Jones? He won 26 games for the Cards in two seasons before going to the San Francisco Giants in 1959, where he pitched another no-hitter. He also had a one-hitter against the Los Angeles Dodgers. The lone Dodger hit was a roller by Junior Gilliam to shortstop Andre Rodgers, who bobbled the ball before throwing late to first base.

Jones won 21 games that season, led with a 2.83 ERA, and was acclaimed Pitcher of the Year. But there was another side to Jones that never showed in the statistics.

Jones, who never said two words if one word would do, took notice of a 12-year-old named Johnny, who wore a brace and dragged his right leg. Johnny, a polio victim, always showed up at the players' entrance for every Giants' home game.

The two became attracted to each other. Without fanfare, Jones saw to it that the youngster got in for every game and that the usherettes found him a seat.

Their friendship continued until Jones was shipped to the American League in 1962. It was during spring training with the Detroit Tigers that Jones had malignant lymph nodes removed from his neck. Following surgery, Jones came back to post a 2-4 record.

After a 2-0 mark with the Cardinals in 1963, Jones closed out his career in Baltimore, where he was 0-0 in 1964. Soon Jones was in and out of hospitals. He died of cancer on Nov. 5, 1971, at the age of 45.

His stay with the Cubs was brief. His record was 23 victories, 34 losses. He is remembered for pitching one of the most dramatic games in Wrigley Field history.

BOB SPEAKE

SPEAKE, BERT CHARLES
B. Aug. 22, 1930, Springfield, Mo.
BL TL 6'1" 178 lb.

Bob Speake could hardly be confused with Tris Speaker. Speaker played 22 years of solid baseball. Speake had one solid month. But what a month!

It started when Cub slugger Hank Sauer hurt his back on May 1, 1955. Cub manager Stan Hack asked rookie first baseman Bob Speake if he ever played the outfield. Speake nodded, "Yes." Then came the fireworks.

On May 3 Speake tripled with the bases loaded in a 6-0 victory over the Giants. Five days later his two-run homer in the eighth inning ruffled the Reds 5-3. On May 18, Speake hit a two-run homer to give the Cubs a 7-5 triumph over the Phillies.

Bleacher fans at Wrigley Field started chanting, "Speake to me," when Bob came to bat. He usually responded. And it didn't matter who was pitching.

The Cubs were playing the Milwaukee Braves May 20 at County Stadium. The score was 2-2 in the 10th inning when Warren Spahn made one of his rare relief appearances.

Speake strode to the plate with one out and one on. It was an ideal situation for the Braves, with a crafty veteran southpaw facing a raw rookie left-handed batsman. But Speake slashed Spahn's first pitch into the right field stands for a 4-2 Cub victory.

On May 25 his homer made it 1-0 over St. Louis. The next day he hit a two-run homer as the Cubs beat the Giants 3-0. On May 27 he hit another homer, but the Cubs lost 7-5 to the Braves.

Speake saved his best for a memorable Memorial Day double-header sweep over the Cardinals. He had five hits and five RBI, and all came in the clutch. His two-run homer in the ninth inning of the opener put the Cubs ahead 5-3, but the Cards tied the score in their half of the ninth.

He then singled home the go-ahead run in a four-run 10th and the Cubs won 9-5. In the second game he broke a 3-3 deadlock with an 11th-inning homer for the 4-3 triumph.

In the month of May, the Cubs won 20 and lost 9. Speake hit 10 home runs that month. Going into June he was batting .304 and had driven in 31 runs in 91 at bats. His clutch hits, which also included four doubles and two triples, provided the margin in 10 of the Cubs' 20 victories.

Speake was mentioned along with Cleveland southpaw Herb Score as the top two rookies in baseball. Fans across the nation took notice. Speake received 774,128 All-Star votes. He even pushed

Cub favorites Sauer and Ernie Banks into the background.

But just as quickly as he spurted, so did he falter. He hit only two more homers and finished the season with a dismal .218 batting average. The next season found Speake back in the minor leagues.

The Cubs brought him back in 1957. He hit 16 homers, but batted only .232. The May magic was gone. Speake was traded to the San Francisco Giants the following spring for Bobby Thomson, another former clutch hitter of note.

After hitting .211 and .091 and playing sparingly, Speake was heard no more. But he had some merry month of May.

MOOSE MORYN

MORYN, WALTER JOHN
B. April 12, 1926, St. Paul, Minn.
BL TR 6'2" 200 lb.

It was May 15, 1960. Cub pitcher Don Cardwell was nursing a 4-0 no-hitter against the Cardinals with one batter to go in the top of the ninth. Suddenly the batter, Joe Cunningham, rifled a sinking liner to left field. The Wrigley Field crowd of 33,000 suffered collective cardiac arrest. From all eyes, it looked like a sure hit.

But Cub left fielder Walt "Moose" Moryn charged in like a horseman of the Apocalypse and snagged the drive off his shoetops to save Cardwell's no-hitter. It was Cardwell's first start being traded to the Cubs from the Phillies two days earlier.

"I didn't even think about catching it when I started running in," the Moose recalled years later. "It was just a case of do or die." Whatever the case, Moryn's dramatic catch etched his name into the hearts of Cub fans forever.

A product of the Brooklyn Dodger farm system, Moryn rambled along the minor league trail from Sheboygan to Danville to Mobile to Montreal to St. Paul before being called up to the parent club in 1954. Even then, he was shuffled back and forth to St. Paul, seeing little action in Brooklyn.

On Dec. 6, 1955, Moryn and Don Hoak were traded to the Cubs for Ransom Jackson in what looked like another bum deal. Jackson was an established star, while Moryn and Hoak were unknown quantities.

But in Chicago Walt had a chance to play regularly and he made the most of it. His .285 batting average and 23 home runs were among the few highlights of a 1956 Cub team that finished last. Although not a fast outfielder, the Moose had a powerful throwing arm. His 18 assists were tops among National League outfielders.

The following year was even better as Moryn batted .289, drove in 88 runs, and enjoyed a 19-game hitting streak. More importantly, he was one of the best clutch hitters on the team.

By now, Moose had become the idol of the blue-collar bleacherites at Wrigley Field. Whenever the blond-haired, barrel-chested Moryn stepped to the plate, they chanted, "Moose! Moose! Moose!," and he seldom let them down. Whenever the

Cubs had their backs to the wall, Walt could always be counted on to save the day.

Things looked grim on May 2, 1958, when the Braves led the Cubs 7-0 after six innings. But the Cubs rallied to beat Milwaukee 8-7 on two Moose Moryn homers. The clincher came off Dick Littlefield in the bottom of the ninth.

Moose's greatest performance, however, came that Memorial Day in a doubleheader against the Dodgers. After propelling the Cubs to an eventual 3-2 victory with his game-tying double in the opener, the Moose smashed three homers in the nightcap as the Cubs outslugged the Bums 10-8.

Danny Murphy was the youngest Cub to hit a homer. He was 18 years and 20 days when he hit a homer to help beat the Reds in 1960.

The first blast came off Don Newcombe to center field, the second off Ed Roebuck to right, and number three off Sandy Koufax to left-center. Reflecting upon the day with two decades retrospect, the Moose said, "I wasn't aware of it at the time, but my mother and my niece were in the Wrigley Field grandstand praying the rosary that I would have a good day. It must have worked."

Moryn belted 26 homers that year and was selected to the NL All-Star team. In 1959 Walt suffered an off season, dropping to .248. His homer count dipped to 14. But even that did not prevent him from coming through with his patented heroics.

On May 12, Lew Burdette and the Braves nursed a 3-2 lead going into the bottom of the ninth. Three more outs and the Braves would have a victory in their pockets. Not if Moose Moryn could help it, however, as he knocked a Burdette fastball into the bleachers to tie up the game. Minutes later, Earl Averill walloped a sudden-death grand slammer to win it.

In 1960 Moryn was hitting at a .294 clip when the Cubs dealt him to the Cardinals. After roughly a year with the Redbirds, Moryn finished with the Pirates in 1961. He retired with a .266 batting average and 101 homers, most of them when they counted.

After leaving baseball, the Moose moved to a Chicago suburb and became a successful salesman for Montgomery Ward. If his fans had it their way, he would still be wearing Cub pinstripes and winning ball games.

JIM BROSNAN

BROSNAN, JAMES PATRICK
B. Oct. 24, 1929, Cincinnati, Ohio.
BR TR 6'4" 215 lb.

Too bad Jim Brosnan couldn't throw the book at the batters. Although he was tops in the literature league, Brosnan was not among the pros when it came to pitching.

Brosnan, a tall, bespectacled, pipe-smoking right-hander, was a baseball enigma. He not only read books without moving his lips, but wrote 'em as well.

A product of the Cubs' farm system, "Broz" spent eight seasons in the big leagues and compiled a 55-47 log. He was better known for his two best-sellers, *The Long Season* and *Pennant Race.*

The pitcher-author was an imposing figure on the mound at 6'4" and 215 pounds. But he toiled seven long seasons in the bushes before putting together a 17-10 record in 1955 with the Los Angeles Angels, the Cubs' top farm club.

As a Cub, Broz's main claim to fame was a faulty zipper. On June 21, 1957, Brosnan took to the mound against the Giants with the score tied 10-10 in the top of the 10th.

While warming up, his jersey got caught in his zipper, causing him to fall off the mound. He injured the Achilles' tendon in his left foot and was relieved by Darius Hillman, who was tagged for two runs.

The thinking man's pitcher had a 14-18 record in parts of four seasons with the Cubs. In that span he pitched only two complete games and had one shutout. He was traded to the Cardinals for veteran infielder Alvin Dark midway through the 1958 season—and that's when the fun began.

After finishing with a respectable 8-4 record with the Cards, Broz decided to write a diary. It soon developed into *The Long Season.* It was a major breakthrough of sorts, suggesting that ballplayers are not young gods.

The book was met with mixed reactions. Some hailed it as witty, perceptive, outspoken, realistic, and full of rare insights and views. It also became the book that bothered the baseball establishment.

He took the reader into the locker rooms and revealed that baseball heroes are made of flesh, bone, blood, and nonsense.

Broz's description of Cardinal batting coach Paul Waner was a classic: "Waner looks like a gnarled gnome, the figment of a wild Irish imagination. At his best playing weight, 140 pounds, he could have passed for an ex-jockey sidling up to tout a favorite horse."

Brosnan wasn't too keen on coach Johnny Keane, whom he called the Verbal Instructor: "Johnny Keane raised his fungo bat. All coaches religiously carry fungo bats in the spring to ward off suggestions that they aren't working. Keane looks like he sleeps with that fungo bat."

Pitching coach Sal Maglie was described as: "Machiavellian Maglie—he might have been the model for a medieval Italian woodcut."

Sportswriters didn't escape unscathed: "San Francisco writers describe the baseball scene with all the precision of a 3-year-old child, finger-painting in the playroom."

But Brosnan saved his best potshots for manager Solly Hemus and general manager Bing Devine. The result? Brosnan was dispatched to the Cincinnati Reds on June 8, 1959, for another ex-Cub, Hal Jeffcoat.

It was a homecoming for the Cincinnati-born Brosnan, a graduate of Xavier University. And it was a boon to the Cincy bullpen, where Brosnan and another former Cub, Bill Henry, formed the best righty-lefty relief duo in the league.

In four seasons with the Reds, Brosnan was 29-20 with a bundle of saves. Moreover, he was part of a pennant-winning team in

1961. He recreated it in his second literary effort, *The Pennant Race.*

Brosnan's second book lacked the acid of his first book, but this time he was with a winner. Some purists didn't appreciate one passage: "An extra shakerful of martinis was shaken, savored, and swallowed." They contend that martinis are stirred, not shaken. That bruises the gin.

On May 5, 1963, the White Sox went highbrow and acquired Brosnan for pitcher Dom Zanni in a waiver deal. Sox GM Ed Short announced that Brosnan would not be permitted to publish any newspaper stories or magazine articles or conduct a radio or TV show during the season.

Brosnan ripped the censorship and was the first ballplayer to be released "for right of free expression." He then placed an ad in *The Sporting News* that read:

"Bullpen operator, experienced . . . often effective imitator of big-league pitcher . . . free agent . . . respectfully requests permission to pursue harmless avocation of professional writer." There were no takers.

Today, Broz is still writing out of his Morton Grove, Ill., home, pouring out a couple of million words as a full-time free-lance writer. He was an original, one of the first to debunk America's sports heroes.

MOE DRABOWSKY

DRABOWSKY, MYRON WALTER
B. July 21, 1935, Ozanna, Poland.
BR TR 6'3" 190 lb.

Through some weird twist of fate, pitcher Moe Drabowsky has made a habit of being an historic loser.

When Stan Musial of the St. Louis Cardinals delivered the 3,000th hit of his distinguished career, Drabowsky was pitching for the Cubs.

When Early Wynn of the Cleveland Indians struggled to his 300th victory, Drabowsky was the losing pitcher.

When Dave Nicholson of the White Sox poled the ball over Comiskey Park's left field roof, who surrendered the homer? Yep, it was Mighty Moe.

There is another negative record behind Drabowsky's name. He tied the record for most hit batsman, plunking four in one game on June 2, 1957.

Drabowsky has another distinction. He is the only ballplayer from Poland. He was born in Ozanna in 1935 and has some memories of his early years. "I can remember the barnyard and the animals running about—the horses, the cows, and the others," said Drabowsky. "I can also remember the stream running through the backyard. I'd sit there and try to catch fish with my bare hands."

With the Nazis creating political unrest, the family fled to the United States in 1938, when Myron was three.

They settled in Hartford, Conn. "I couldn't speak English and when I started school, I got bad grades," recalled Drabowsky. "But with the advent of television, I started picking up some English and did better in school." Chalk one up for TV.

Meanwhile, scout Lennie Merullo, a former Cub shortstop, had been following young Moe since his high school days at Loomis High in Windsor, Conn. After Drabowsky, who was captain of the 1956 Trinity College team, pitched a no-hitter and struck out 16 Wesleyan College batters, Merullo, Drabowsky, and his parents were flown to Chicago.

Moe pitched batting practice with veteran Clyde McCullough catching. When some members of the New York Giants watched Moe's flickering fastballs, they became inquisitive. "That's Moe McCullough, my kid brother," boasted Clyde, who was playing minor league ball before Drabowsky was born.

The Cubs were so impressed they signed Drabowsky to a $50,000 bonus contract. Ironically, to make room for Moe, the Cubs asked waivers on the 38-year-old McCullough.

Cub manager Stan Hack found the proper spot to unveil his young phenom. With the Braves and Warren Spahn ahead 6-1 in the eighth inning on Aug. 8, 1956, Drabowsky pitched the final inning and escaped with a single and a walk around two strikeouts and a force play.

He drew his first start a week later against the White Sox in the annual charity game at Comiskey Park and was obviously nervous, pitching before 23,438. He walked three and hit two others to force home two runs in the first inning.

Then he settled down, allowing two hits before being taken out for a pinch hitter in the eighth inning. The Cubs viewed the 4-0 loss as a triumph because they discovered they had a real find.

Hack then used psychology. He didn't tell Drabowsky about his initial starting assignment in a regular-season game. "I was afraid the kid might lose some sleep if he knew about our plans beforehand," revealed Hack. Drabowsky wasn't told he was pitching until he reached the ballpark. It worked. Moe mowed down the Cardinals 8-1 in St. Louis.

The following season Drabowsky teamed with another rookie, Dick Drott, forming a combination known as the Gold Dust Twins. Both struck out 170 batters, with Drott winning 15 and Drab 13. Moe showed his foes some woe with a one-hitter and a two-hitter.

The one-hitter was against the Pirates at Wrigley Field. It took a dinky infield hit by Ted Kluszewski in the sixth inning to prevent Moe from a pitch niche. "We were playing the shift against Big Klu," recalled Drabowsky. "He hit a short grounder and second baseman Bobby Adams was too deep to throw him out."

The two-hitter took only 1 hour and 37 minutes, with the Cubs winning 1-0 on Ernie Banks's homer. Johnny Temple and pesky pinch hitter Jerry Lynch were the only ones to dent his deliveries.

Then the Cubs' gold turned to dust. Drott and Drabowsky

developed arm trouble. Drott soon dropped out of baseball while Drabowsky struggled through the next three seasons.

He was off and on after suffering a torn muscle fiber in his elbow, had his thumb broken by a line drive, and pulled a muscle in his chest throwing fastballs.

The Cubs finally gave up on Drabowsky, sending him to the Braves in the spring of 1961 for erratic shortstop Andre Rodgers. His five-year Cub tenure concluded with a 32-41 mark.

After leaving the Cubs, Drabowsky went from thrower to pitcher. The ex-bonus baby now combined brains with brawn after being banished to the bullpen.

He also became a pitching nomad with stints in Milwaukee, Cincinnati, Kansas City, Baltimore, St. Louis, and finally, the White Sox in 1972, where he was 0-0 in seven games.

Undoubtedly, his most enjoyable season was 1966 with the pennant-winning Orioles. Moe was 6-0 as a reliever and perfect as a prankster. Teammate Frank Robinson owned rubber snakes to frighten outfielder Paul Blair. Drabowsky once substituted a live snake for one of Robby's rubber ones and scared Blair out of the clubhouse.

Drabowsky was probably enjoying a prank while sitting in the bullpen beyond the outfield fence for the first game of the World Series at Dodger Stadium on Oct. 5.

Starter Dave McNally was staked to a 4-1 lead against the Dodgers when he suddenly lost control with one out in the third inning, walking three Dodgers in a row. Baltimore manager Hank Bauer summoned Moe from the bullpen.

Drabowsky picked up his glove and windbreaker and trudged in from the bullpen to face the Dodgers and their 55,941 clamoring fans. He walked in one run before squirming from the jam with a 4-2 lead.

From then on he threw strikes. Oh, boy, did he ever. Moe equaled a series record by striking out six straight batters. In all, he fanned 11 batters, allowed only one hit for six and two-thirds innings, and hiked off the field with a 5-2 victory. The historic loser had finally become a heroic winner.

Drabowsky, who resides in Highland Park, Ill., and is a successful stock broker on Chicago's LaSalle Street, finished with an 88-105 record for regular-season play and was 1-0 in World Series action.

DICK DROTT

DROTT, RICHARD FRED
B. July 1, 1936, Cincinnati, Ohio.
BR TR 6'0" 185 lb.

Dick Drott, a 20-year-old rookie right-hander, was facing Willie Mays in an exhibition game in the dusty, old town of Alpine, Tex. Cub manager Bob Scheffing winked at his coaches and yelled from the dugout, "Knock him down, Dick."

Drott threw a fastball that almost knocked the buttons off Mays's jersey and then struck him out on a wide-breaking curve. "I never thought the kid would have the nerve to dust off the great Mays," said Scheffing. The brash, boyish-looking Drott went on to pitch a two-hitter and earned a spot on the Cubs' staff.

Drott, whose real name is Drottski, is of Russian descent. He began as a third baseman at age 9 with a kids' team in Cincinnati. When the regular pitcher suffered a broken finger, the manager, inspired by Drott's strong throwing arm, substituted Dick.

The Cubs signed Drott out of Western Hills High and assigned him to Cedar Rapids in 1954. There he won 5 and lost 7, but struck out 93 in 108 innings. He made the big leap to Scheffing's Los Angeles club in 1956 and set a Pacific Coast League record of 184 strikeouts, despite a plain 13-10 record.

Scheffing and Drott were now Cub rookies in 1957. It was the eighth inning of the opener at Wrigley Field. The Milwaukee Braves had a 4-1 bulge with runners on first and third and two out.

Scheffing summoned Drott to replace starter Bob Rush. He gave Drott a last second bit of instruction, "Remember, kid, this is Eddie Mathews. He's just another ballplayer trying to fatten his average. Get that ball over the plate and you'll be all right."

"Mathews? Just another batter?" sighed Drott. "I was nervous. My stomach wouldn't stand still. All those people in the stands. I said to myself, 'Boy, what a spot.' " Drott got the Braves' slugger to pop up to shortstop Ernie Banks and marched off the mound. It took one pitch for Drott to regain his poise and cockiness.

Rookie Cub pitcher Dick Drott struck out Hank Aaron four times in one game in 1957. He wound up with 15 strikeouts, beating the Braves at Wrigley Field.

Drott became the Cubs' new pinup against the same Braves on May 26, 1957, before a crowd of 32,127 at Wrigley Field. He was busy striking out everyone in the Braves' lineup. Hank Aaron, the 1956 National League batting champion, went down four times. The Cubs had held a 7-3 lead and Drott had 14 strikeouts going into the ninth inning.

Then Chuck Tanner got a windblown double and Del Crandall homered. Scheffing came out to remove Drott and the crowd booed. Scheffing let Drott continue. The next batter, Johnny Logan, backed away from a pitch and got a pop single. Again Scheffing trudged to the mound and again the crowd jeered.

The dangerous Bill Bruton was next up. Scheffing gave Drott one more chance. By the time Scheffing had returned to his dugout seat, Drott fanned Bruton on three straight fastballs to set a modern-day Cub record of 15 strikeouts.

Drott later came up with a 14-strikeout 4-0 shutout over the Giants and finished with a 15-11 record that included 170 whiffs. And it wasn't all hard work for the fun-loving rookie.

Late in the season, teammate Moe Drabowsky was hit by a pitched ball. When umpire Stan Landes showed little emotion, Moe tumbled to the ground. Drott then entered the scene, pushing a wheelchair. Drabowsky was awarded first base and Drott was thumbed out.

Drott went from a red-hot rookie to a sore-armed sophomore in 1958, winning only 7 and dropping 11. He never recovered, winning 2 games and losing 12 the next three seasons. The prospect was now a suspect.

The end came on Oct. 9, 1961, when Drott was selected by the Houston Colt .45s for $75,000 in the expansion draft. By this time, Drott's hummer was humdrum and he won only 3 games in two long seasons in Houston. One was a 1-0 victory over the Cubs.

Drott concluded with a 27-46 record. In a Cub uniform he was 24-34. Baseball, however, remained his first love. During the summer months Drott works with youngsters in Chicago parks as part of the city's Reach Out program. "I'd rather see boys join a baseball league than a street gang," said Drott, who enjoys the practice as much as the kids.

DON ELSTON

ELSTON, DONALD RAY
B. April 6, 1929, Campbellstown, Ohio.
BR TR 6'0" 170 lb.

Don Elston was a Cub relief pitcher whom they let get away early in his career, but were fortunate enough to repossess as he approached his prime. Elston was a product of the Cub farm system, starting out at Elizabethtown in 1948. Over the next four years he moved along to Janesville, Springfield, Ill., Sioux Falls, and Springfield, Mass., compiling records that were generally respectable but not especially eye-catching.

Late in the 1953 season Don was given a brief look with the Cubs, but lost his only decision, being ravaged for a 14.40 ERA in five innings. Obviously, his time had not yet come, so for the next two seasons, it was back to the Cub farm chain—Des Moines in 1954 and Los Angeles the following year. During the winter of 1955-56, Elston was swapped to the Dodgers for a thoroughly washed up Russ Meyer, whom the Cubs had earlier let go with his best years ahead of him.

The Dodgers had no immediate need of Elston, so they optioned him to St. Paul; otherwise, it might have been a typical Cub-Dodger trade of that era in which Brooklyn invariably got the better of the deal. By May 23, 1957—after brief service in Dodger blue—Elston was back in Cub pinstripes, in exchange for pitchers Vito Valentinetti and Jackie Collum. Don worked both as a starter and reliever that year, finishing with a deceptive 6-7 record in 145 innings, which would be the most of his major league career.

The Cubs were pinning their future hopes on starters Dick Drott and Moe Drabowsky, both of whom had enjoyed fine rookie seasons in 1957. But both came down with arm problems the following season, losing their effectiveness all but completely. As a result, Elston was called in for overtime bullpen duty, while another relief ace, Bill Henry, was obtained from Portland to help pick up the slack. Thanks to home run power and the pitching of Elston and Henry, the Cubs salvaged a semirespectable tie for fifth place with the Cardinals. Don, for his part, appeared in a league-leading 69 games to set a Cub record (since broken several times), while putting together a 9-8 record with 10 saves and a sparkling 2.88 ERA.

A nobody two years earlier, Don emerged as one of the top fireman in the league as the 1959 season opened. The Cubs again finished in a tie for fifth, helped along by Elston's bullpen artistry. Appearing in 65 games to again top the league, Don was 10-8 with 13 saves. For another feather in his cap, he was selected to the NL All-Star squad, although he did not pitch. The following year, with a Cub team that sank to seventh place, Don was 8-9, but still picked up another 11 saves.

Beginning in 1961 Elston's effectiveness began to diminish, and he was used less frequently. By 1963 his exploits became overshadowed by the stellar relief work of Lindy McDaniel, a recent acquisition from the Cardinals. Following a 2-5 log in 1964, Don called it quits. During his nine years in the majors, Elston was 49-54 (all with the Cubs) with a 3.69 ERA and 63 saves.

LEE WALLS

WALLS, RAY LEE JR.
B. Jan. 6, 1933, San Diego, Calif.
BR TR 6'3" 190 lb.

On May 1, 1957, the Cubs traded their popular double-play duet of second baseman Gene Baker and first sacker Dee Fondy to the Pirates for first baseman Dale Long and outfielder Lee Walls.

A product of the Pirate farm system, Walls was with the parent club briefly in 1952 before being sent down to the Hollywood Stars for more seasoning. Rejoining the Cubs in 1956, he batted .274 in 143 games his first full season.

Although his batting average fell to .237 in 1957, Lee became an immediate favorite with Wrigley Field fans. Nicknamed "Captain Midnight" because of his oversized, wire-rimmed glasses, the bespectacled Walls was not a particularly fast outfielder, but was a good judge of a flyball, seldom making a miscue.

On July 2, 1957, he became only the eighth player in Cub history to hit for the cycle, collecting a single, a double, a triple, and a home run in the same game. It was not enough, however, as the Reds beat the Cubs 8-6 in 10 innings.

In 1958 the Dodgers abandoned Brooklyn for the West Coast, making the Los Angeles Coliseum their home for the first four years. With its short left field line, the Coliseum was tailor-made for the right-handed Walls, especially when the Cubs came to town that April 24.

All Lee did was smash three homers and drive in eight runs as the Cubs made bums out of the Dodgers 15-2 in their highest scoring game of the year.

The immortal Gene Fodge went the distance for his first and only major league win.

For the season, Lee batted .304 with 24 home runs and 72 RBI. He was one of five Cub sluggers to belt 20 or more homers that year, the other four being Ernie Banks (47), Moose Moryn (26), Bobby Thomson (21), and Dale Long (20). The Cubs had 182 homers for the year, still the club record.

But 1958 turned out to be Lee's only season in the sun. The following year his batting average plummeted to .257 while his home run count sank to eight and his RBI output to 33. On Dec. 6, 1959, Walls was traded to Cincinnati with pitcher Bill Henry and outfielder Lou Jackson for outfielder Frank Thomas.

In the years that followed, Walls drifted from the Reds to the Phillies to the Dodgers, never regaining that rare form of the summer of '58. He retired in 1964, with a .262 batting average and 670 hits.

DALE LONG

LONG, RICHARD DALE
B. Feb. 6, 1926, Springfield, Mo.
BL TL 6'4" 205 lb.

Dale Long wrote his name into the record books in Long hand with somc Long strokcs. It was thc month of May in 1956 when the 29-year-old Pittsburgh Pirates' sophomore hit eight home runs in eight consecutive games, a mark never achieved even b.y Babe Ruth.

Long connected for his eighth homer off crafty Brooklyn Dodger righty Carl Erskine on May 28 at Forbes Field. "At first I didn't think it was going in," recalled Long. "I just put my head down and ran.

"I passed Bobby Bragan (Pirate manager) at third and just shook my head because it was hard to believe. But the big thing was what happened next."

After Long crossed the plate and disappeared into the dugout, the 32,221 fans wouldn't let the game continue until Long took a bow. He popped his head out of the dugout, doffed his cap, and waved.

It took the elongated Long a long time (12 years) to make that curtain call. He was 17 and had already served a one-year hitch in the navy. He was planning to return to high school in Green Bay, Wis., and earn his diploma. Then, within a week he had two offers.

The Green Bay Packers wanted him to sign a football contract and the Milwaukee Brewers were knocking on his door, asking if he was interested in baseball. "Football was my favorite sport," said Long. "But I thought I would have a longer career in baseball."

Dale signed with the Brewers in 1944 after being scouted thoroughly by a bird dog named Casey Stengel. He spent seven long seasons in the minor leagues before surfacing with the Pirates in 1951.

The first baseman-outfielder reported to spring camp and was the center of a noble experiment by General Manager Branch Rickey, who wanted to convert him into a left-handed catcher. The experiment fizzled. And after hitting .167 in 10 games, Long was sold to the St. Louis Browns, where he batted .238 before going back to the bush leagues.

Long's trouble was that he kept hitting Long outs to straight-away center. "I always swung late and nobody mentioned it to me," said Long. "Finally, I started swinging earlier and began pulling the ball to right." The result was 33 homers for New Orleans and 35 for Hollywood.

Long was back in the biggies to stay, starting in 1955. He batted .291 and displayed long ball prowess with 19 doubles, 13 triples, and 16 homers. Then followed his record-setting spree in '56 that saw him wind up the season with 27 homers and 91 RBI.

The next season Long and outfielder Lee Walls were dealt to the Cubs for first baseman Dee Fondy and second baseman Gene Baker. Of the four, Long had the best year, hitting .305 with 21 homers.

In 1958 Dale was part of a power quintet. The Cubs reached their homer peak with 182 and boasted five players with 20 or more. The quintet consisted of Ernie Banks 47, Moose Moryn 26, Walls 24, Bobby Thomson 21, and Long 20.

Rickey's dream of turning Long into the major league's only left-handed catcher came true on Aug. 20, 1958. Long was pressed into service with one out in the ninth inning when the Cubs ran out of catchers. His two putout stay behind the plate was without incident.

Long went into the dugout and emerged with mask and pads. He was forced to use his first baseman's mitt since no left-handed catcher's mitt was available. Statisticians had to go back 56 years to find another lefty catcher in the National League.

Dale Long was the first and only left-handed catcher in Cub history. He wore his first baseman's mitt behind the plate in a late-inning emergency in 1958 at Wrigley Field.

The broad-shouldered Long again slugged his way into the record books during the 1959 season when he hit back-to-back pinch homers in successive games. The Cubs sold Long to the Giants in 1960, and from there he was reunited with Stengel when he was waived to the Yankees.

The next stop was Washington for a two-year stint with the Senators. Then it was back to the Yankees. He closed out his career with 132 homers, 55 as a Cub. Lifetime, Long was a .267 hitter with 805 hits.

Long later traded his flannels for the blue serge suit of an umpire, but never reached the majors. He is currently living in North Adams, Mass.

Finally, for trivia buffs: Who were the eight pitchers Long tagged for his eight homers in successive games? They were: Jim Davis, Ray Crone, Warren Spahn, Herm Wehmeier, Lindy McDaniel, Ben Flowers, and Carl Erskine.

TONY TAYLOR

TAYLOR, ANTONIO SANCHEZ
B. Dec. 19, 1935, Central Alara, Cuba.
BR TR 5'9" 170 lb.

It was only a paragraph or two in the back pages of the sports section. The Cubs had selected a .217-hitting third baseman from the Giants chain in the winter draft of 1957.

His name was Antonio Sanchez Taylor and he played second fiddle to bonus baby Joey Amalfitano at Dallas. When the well-muscled Cuban reported to the Cubs for spring training, he was switched to second base, a position he had never played, not even in the sugar cane fields of Matanzas.

Taylor would come to bat, cross himself, kiss the tip of his bat—and nothing would happen. The shy rookie was batting only .160. He was lost in the vastness of Chicago. Taylor had a language problem and was homesick.

Then his roommate, Ernie Banks, took him to (of all places) a sportswriter's home for dinner. After cocktails and a steak dinner, the writer's wife served ice cream covered with green creme de menthe.

Taylor loved the dessert and asked what the green stuff was. "It's Notre Dame holy water," said Jim Enright, the rotund sportswriter. Tony loved it and had a second helping.

From mid-June to mid-July, Taylor hit solidly, sparkled afield, and became the Cubs' top basestealing threat since Kiki Cuyler. Although he finished with a modest .235 average, Taylor stole 21 bases and proved an excellent leadoff batter.

There was no sophomore jinx for Taylor, who sprinkled hits off his bat like holy water. He finished with a .280 average, on 93 runs scored, 175 hits, 30 doubles, 8 triples, and 8 homers. He had 23 steals. In addition, he was involved in one of baseball's weirdest homers.

In a game against the Giants at Wrigley Field, Taylor led off with a sharp liner over third base. The ball rolled past the Cub bullpen where Giants' left fielder Leon Wagner lost track of it.

The Cub pitchers leaped up and pretended to look for the ball under their bench. Their performance was so convincing that Wagner joined in the search. Taylor, meanwhile, rounded the bases for an inside-the-park homer.

Actually, the ball was lying some 20 feet farther down the line in the rain gutter down at the base of the left field wall. When Wagner retrieved the ball, Taylor was sitting in the Cub dugout.

Then came the bombshell. Taylor and catcher Cal Neeman were traded to the Phillies for pitcher Don Cardwell and first baseman Ed Bouchee on May 13, 1960. Taylor made no attempt to conceal his sadness over being torn away from Banks and the Cubs. He was heartbroken.

"At Wrigley Field, I like that place," said Taylor. "Play all daylight ball. It's best infield in league and fans very nice." But most of all, he missed Banks.

"I never make it without Ernie," sighed Taylor. "He tell me where to play hitter and how to make double play. At the plate, too, he help me. I get bad some times looking in dugout when swing at ball. Ernie never get angry. He remind me all the time to keep head still and eye on the ball."

At first it appeared as if the Cubs got the better of the deal. Cardwell pitched a no-hitter in his Cub debut. Taylor, meanwhile, was off to a slow start with the Phillies.

After a game one night in Connie Mack Stadium, Taylor returned to the clubhouse and found a package in his locker with a card reading: "Thought you might enjoy a little Notre Dame holy water. Drink it in good health." It was signed, "A Friend."

Somehow, Phillies' GM John Quinn had heard about the story and sent the package to Taylor. Quinn's ploy worked. Taylor became a sizzling Philly minion.

For the next 11 seasons, Taylor would come to bat, cross himself, kiss the tip of the bat in his inimitable style, and give any pitcher a tough out. He was traded to the Tigers in 1971, but returned to the Phillies two seasons later and was given a standing ovation upon his return.

Taylor, who later became a Phillies' coach, wound up with a .261 average, 2,007 hits, and 234 stolen bases. His career was Taylor-made with a little pat on the back from Banks and a sprinkle of "Notre Dame holy water."

BOB ANDERSON

ANDERSON, ROBERT CARL
B. Sept. 29, 1935, East Chicago, Ind.
BR TR 6'4½"
210 lb.

Bob Anderson never had a winning season in his seven years as a Cub. His career record was 36-46, and he was 33-45 in a Cub uniform. But the "Hammond Hummer" wasn't just another pitcher.

He is best remembered for standing on the mound and throwing snowballs in the Cubs' snowed-out 1959 opener, and he was one of the principal participants in the famed double-ball incident on June 30, 1959.

After the snow job, the towering blond right-hander came back the next day and shutout the Dodgers 7-0 at Wrigley Field. The Dodgers went on to win the World Series, while Andy had to be content with his lone major league shutout.

And, now, the double-ball incident. The Cubs were playing the Cardinals at Wrigley Field. Stan Musial was at bat with one out in the fourth inning.

Anderson ran the count to three balls and a strike and then delivered the pitch that set off the confusion. Andy's pitch either ticked Musial's bat or was a wild heave. Here, the fun began.

The ball bounced toward the screen. Cub catcher Sammy Taylor ignored it, thinking it hit Musial's bat for a foul ball. Plate umpire Vic Delmore, however, called it ball four and awarded Musial first base.

Anderson ambled to the plate, claiming it was a foul ball. Cub third baseman Alvin Dark rushed in to retrieve the ball, which had been fondled by the bat boy, who flipped it to field announcer Pat Pieper. Everyone got into the act.

Pieper dropped the ball like a hot potato and Dark scooped it up. Musial, meanwhile, broke for second base. At the same time, umpire Delmore pulled out another ball and handed it to Anderson.

Andy and Dark saw Musial streaking for second. They both fired in that direction. Anderson's throw was wild again and sailed over second baseman Tony Taylor's head into center field, while Dark's toss went to shortstop Ernie Banks, who tagged out the sliding Musial.

Musial ignored Ernie's tag. He got up and tried for third base. Center fielder Bobby Thomson retrieved the ball and casually lobbed it into the Cub dugout.

Play was stopped. Both dugouts emptied. Fingers waved in all directions. Umpire Delmore ruled Musial out at second base. Umpire Al Barlick ruled Musial safe at first base. They huddled and Musial was called out. (They didn't mention which base).

Cardinal manager Solly Hemus announced he was playing the game under protest, claiming the bat boy interfered with the ball when Musial was halfway to second base. Cub manager Bob Scheffing protested that the ball ticked Musial's bat and should be ruled a foul ball.

What about Musial? "I thought the ball was foul, but the guys in the dugout yelled and I ran to first base," said the Man, breaking out in an impish grin. "And when I saw Tony Taylor leap for the ball over his head, I ignored Banks's tag and headed for third base."

The result? Hemus dropped his protest after St. Louis went on to win 4-1. The National League dropped Delmore from its umpiring crew at the end of the season.

Anderson? He was dropped from the starting rotation. He was a relief pitcher the remainder of his Cub career, which concluded after the 1962 season when he was traded to the Tigers for third baseman Steve Boros.

And wouldn't you know it. Anderson had his lone winning season with Detroit in 1963. He was 3-1.

GLEN HOBBIE

HOBBIE, GLEN FREDERICK
B. April 24, 1936, Witt, Ill.
BR TR 6'2" 195 lb.

Approximately 50 miles south of Springfield there is an Illinois crossroads town named Witt. Even your favorite geography map may not show it. Pitcher Glen Hobbie put the tiny hamlet on the map.

The coal-mining town of some 1,165 was seldom out-Witted when it came to basketball. There hardly had been a year when there wasn't a Hobbie on the Witt High School team. There was one stretch of two decades (1936-1956) when there was a Hobbie in every basketball box score.

The Hobbie brothers—Earl, Kelvin, Roy, Kenny, Ray, Glen, and Dave—maintained the athletic feats at Witt High, with its average enrollment of 65. Glen, the second youngest of 10 Hobbie children, averaged 22.9 points as Witt won 69 of 75 games during his tenure.

"We didn't have a baseball team because there weren't enough kids," said Hobbie, who sported a blond crew-cut and had the angular looks of a basketball player. "I played American Legion ball and later pitched for the Hillsboro Cardinals, just 10 miles from Witt."

Hobbie attracted big league scouts when he won 15 straight for the semipro team, while winning 22 and losing only 2. The 6′2″ right-hander with the lantern jaw, protruding ears and busted-looking beak, was originally in the White Sox chain.

He was assigned to Superior (Wis.) in the Northern League in 1955, but hurt his back trying to fire his fastball on a cold, damp day. "I wasn't worth a darn for a year and a half," recalled Hobbie. "I couldn't even get the ball up to the plate."

After posting a 15-15 record at Memphis in 1957, his contract was purchased by the Cubs. He appeared in two games for the Cubs late in that season with no wins or losses.

At that time, the Cubs were heralding their young pitching staff, which included Moe Drabowsky, Dick Drott, and Bob Anderson. The long-necked Hobbie was just another longshot. But he received his chance as a regular starter on May 6, 1958.

Hobbie faced the Cincinnati Reds in the refrigerated atmosphere of Wrigley Field and turned in a heart-warming performance. He pitched his first shutout in pro ball, winning 4-0, and passed the crucial test by striking out Frank Robinson with the bases loaded in the eighth inning, breaking off a curve that dropped at least two feet.

Hobbie finished the season as the ace of a staff that had a deuce of a time winning. His 10 victories against 6 losses were a team high. The next year, Hobbie ranked with the best in the National League.

Hobbie got off to a solid start by pitching a one-hitter, beating the Cardinals 1-0 before 2,501 frigid fans at Wrigley Field on April 22, 1959. He had a perfect game until Stan Musial stepped to the plate with two out in the seventh inning.

With the count a ball and a strike, Hobbie threw a curve, low and away. Musial sliced the ball to left, just inside the foul line for a double. Glen gained some measure of revenge with two out in the ninth by inducing Musial to tap to the mound for the victory.

Hobbie wound up with 16 victories and 13 losses and pitched 10 complete games. He again won 16 in 1960, but led the league with 20 losses as the workhorse of a club that won only 60 games. He was also among the leaders with 16 complete games.

One of his triumphs came on his first major league homer on Aug. 25, 1960. It was a dramatic ninth-inning shot that sailed into the Wrigley Field bleachers off Vinegar Bend Mizell to beat the Pirates 2-1.

Hobbie's three-year record was 42-39 with a mediocre team. Then came his downfall early in the 1961 season. He had pitched against the Cardinals and, after driving home, discovered he couldn't get out of his car.

"I don't know what was wrong with my back," said Hobbie. "But it had me in a sweat and I didn't know which way to go." Hobbie had a pinched nerve and a protruding disc and was sidelined. When he returned he went to a herky-jerky motion and strained his shoulder.

For the next three seasons Hobbie was 19-37. To show how luckless he had become, Glen hit two homers in one game and didn't receive credit for the victory because the Cub relief crew couldn't hold the lead.

Hobbie was 0-3 when he was traded to St. Louis for veteran pitcher Lew Burdette on June 2, 1964. He wound up 1-2 at St. Louis, finishing his career with a 62-81 record. In a Cub uniform, Hobbie was 61-79.

LOU BOUDREAU

BOUDREAU, LOUIS
B. July 17, 1917, Harvey, Ill.
BR TR 5'11"
193 lb.

Over the past generation, Hall of Famer Lou Boudreau has become familiar to all Cub fans as their color man on WGN radio. In his playing days he was one of the AL's finest shortstops. On another occasion, he even managed the Cubs—for all they were worth.

Boudreau started in pro ball with Cedar Rapids in 1938 and appeared in one game for the Indians late in the season. After spending the first half of 1939 with Buffalo, Lou was back in Cleveland permanently. During his first full year he was not only the AL's leading shortstop but drove in 101 runs as well.

In April 1942 the 24-year-old Boudreau became the youngest manager in major league history when he was named Indian field boss. Two years later he was the AL batting champion with a .327 mark.

Lou's greatest triumph came in 1948 when his .355 average and 106 RBI led Cleveland to the world championship. For his efforts he was named MVP in the league.

Released by the Indians in November 1950, Boudreau signed with the Red Sox, where he finished his playing career two years later. Lifetime he was a .295 hitter with 1,779 hits and 68 homers.

After managing the Red Sox for three seasons and the A's for another three, Lou joined the late Jack Quinlan as the radio voice of the Cubs in 1958. After two years on the job, he became involved in another one of owner P. K. Wrigley's bizarre maneuvers.

For the third time in his career, Charlie Grimm had agreed to manage the Cubs in 1960. However, after they lost 11 of their first 17 games, Grimm decided he had had enough. So Charlie was moved behind the mike and Lou got stuck with the Cubs for the rest of the year. Burdened with the albatross of a talentless team, Boudreau could bring the team only 54 wins and 83 losses for a seventh place finish.

Then it was back to the radio booth, where he has been ever since. Over the years he was gained renown for such slogans as "That kid's got mustard on the ball;" "Those walks'll kill ya, Vince;" and "Mike Smit just knocked another one out of Wrigley Field."

SECTION FOUR 1961-1965 The College that Flunked

On Dec. 21, 1960, P.K. Wrigley pulled another one of his renowned surprises. He announced that henceforth the Cubs would no longer have a field manager but would be run by a system of eight rotating coaches. The original eight were Rip Collins, Charlie Grimm, Elvin Tappe, Goldie Holt, Vedie Himsl, Harry Craft, Bobby Adams, and Rube Walker. Others who floated in and out before the system was junked included Bob Kennedy, Buck O'Neill, Lou Klein, Charlie Metro, Al Dark, Freddie Martin, Mel Wright, and Mel Harder.

As anyone outside of the Cub brass could have predicted, the result was utter chaos. One head coach would tell a player to play his position one way; the next one would have him learn it a different way. The same applied to hitting and pitching.

Not unexpectedly, the Cubs again finished seventh in 1961 as head coaches rotated in and out on a revolving door basis, the position drifting from Himsl (10-21) to Craft (7-9) to Tappe (42-53). Billy Williams was voted Rookie of the Year and Ron Santo, Sophomore of the Year, while George Altman played like a coming superstar. Ernie Banks began to slow down at shortstop and was moved first to left field, without much success, and later to first base, where he remained for the rest of his career.

In 1962 the National League expanded to ten teams, putting new franchises in New York and Houston. For the Cubs, it was especially embarassing as the fledgling Colt .45s (later the Astros) beat them out for eighth place. It was the poorest record yet by a Cub team as they lost 103 games. Again, the head coach job revolved three times—Tappe (4-16), Klein (12-18), and Charlie Metro (43-69). The ultimate in futility came on June 5 when shortstop Andre Rodgers had a chance for an unassisted triple play against the Giants—and muffed it.

The sole promising newcomers were rookies Ken Hubbs and Lou Brock, the former being named Rookie of the Year.

The winter brought some significant changes. Bob Kennedy was named head coach while Robert Whitlow, a retired air force colonel, was hired as athletic director. Larry Jackson and Lindy McDaniel were obtained from the Cardinals to bolster an abominable pitching staff.

The coaches stopped spinning as, for all practical purposes, Kennedy was manager in all but title. The Cubs were the surprise of the National League, thanks to strong pitching, both on the front line and in the bullpen. They held second place until mid-July and even though they finally sank to seventh, their 82-80 record was the best by a Cub team in 17 years.

The bright hopes were given a tragic setback when Ken Hubbs was killed in a plane crash in February 1964. It left a pall of gloom on the team and rendered them weak up the middle. Worse yet, the pitching reverted to its previous form. Only Jackson and to a lesser extent Bob Buhl showed consistent effectiveness. Banks was still a dependable slugger while Williams and Santo enjoyed their first .300 seasons.

Left fielder Billy Williams and second baseman Ken Hubbs of the Cubs won back-to-back Rookie of the Year awards in 1961 and 1962.

Five players could not carry the load, however. The team played above .500 until early July, after which they finally slid back to eighth place.

In January 1965 Whitlow was dismissed and by mid-June Kennedy's head had rolled too. His replacement, the recycled Klein, had no better success. The reason the Cubs did not run out of gas this time is because they never had any to begin with—the longest winning streak was four games. Banks, Santo, and Williams remained a triple threat but beyond that the Cub attack was roughly equivalent to that of a cub scout pack. Submariner Ted Abernathy was a one-man bullpen, but little could be said for the starters. Fans saw a glimmer of sunshine in the arrival of second baseman Glenn Beckert and shortstop Don Kessinger, but once again the Cubs could only beat out the Mets and the Astros.

DON CARDWELL

CARDWELL, DONALD EUGENE
B. Dec. 7, 1935, Winston-Salem, N.C.
BR TR 6'4" 210 lb.

Storybook endings are common. Pitcher Don Cardwell applied a novel twist with a storybook beginning. He authored a no-hitter in his Cub debut.

On May 13, 1960, the Cubs acquired Cardwell and Ed Bouchee from the Philadelphia Phillies for Tony Taylor and Cal Neeman. Two days later, Cardwell faced the St. Louis Cardinals in the second game of a Sunday doubleheader at Wrigley Field.

The towering right-hander came within one pitch of a perfect game, although two spectacular outfield catches saved the no-hitter in the ninth inning.

The raw-boned side-armer walked Alex Grammas, the second batter to face him. After that he retired 26 in succession, seven via strikeouts. The crowd of 33,543 was on its feet as Cardwell strode to the mound for the ninth inning.

Carl Sawatski, a pudgy ex-Cub, pinch-hit for Hal Smith and took two quick strikes. Then he lashed a long drive to right field. The crowd groaned. But right fielder George Altman, who stands 6'4", leaped against the exit gate on the bend of the bleachers and grabbed the liner. One out.

George Crowe, who ruined a no-hitter for Warren Hacker of the Cubs with a ninth-inning pinch homer several years earlier, batted for pitcher Lindy McDaniel. Crowe worked the count to 2-1 and flied to Richie Ashburn in medium center. Two out.

Joe Cunningham, who was batting .324, was the only man blocking Cardwell's entrance to the Hall of Fame. Cunningham worked Cardwell to 3-1 and punched a hump-back liner to short left. The ball looked like it was going to drop in . . . but wait.

Walt "Moose" Moryn came thundering in and made a miraculous one-handed catch at his shoetops. Moryn clutched the ball and raced all the way to the infield. The Cubs won 4-0. It was the most dramatic debut by a newly traded player in the history of baseball.

Spectators poured onto the field. Some seemed intent on dismantling the 24-year-old hurler so they could take home a piece of him as a souvenir. It was a happy mob scene. No one was in a fighting mood. Veteran observers said it was the greatest demonstration since Gabby Hartnett's "Homer in the Gloamin' " in 1938.

"They pulled at my arm, banged me on the shoulders and everywhere," drawled Cardwell. "I'm half numb. If that's what you have to go through I don't know whether I want to pitch another no-hitter."

There was no encore for the snub-nosed, crew-cut pitcher, who finished the season with a 9-16 record, 8-14 with the Cubs. He did lead the team in strikeouts with 150 and showed power at the plate, hitting five homers.

There was one aspect that set Cardwell apart from other pitchers. Keen batters were detecting his pitches by the way he held the ball, so he developed the hidden-ball windup. When Cardwell would step on the rubber and begin his windup, he'd keep the ball in the glove.

He would then pump once with both arms going above his head and his right hand empty. At the top of the windup, Cardwell would take the ball out of his glove and come on through with the pitch.

It seemed to work. In 1961 Cardwell led the Cubs in every pitching department while compiling a 15-14 record. The Cubs won only 64 games that season. Cardwell thus accounted for almost one-quarter of the victories. He did fall off in the power department, slugging only three homers.

After a disappointing 7-16 record in 1962, Cardwell was traded with Altman and the legendary Moe Thacker to the St. Louis Cardinals for Larry Jackson, Lindy McDaniel, and Jimmy Schaffer. But he never got to wear a Cardinal uniform.

The Cards shuffled Cardwell to the Pittsburgh Pirates a month later in a deal involving Dick Groat. Cardwell stayed with the Pirates for four seasons before joining the New York Mets in 1967.

Country boy Cardwell seemed out of place in New York. He was the squarest-looking member of the Amazin' Mets, who swept past the Cubs in September to win the 1969 National League pennant and whip the Baltimore Orioles in the World Series.

Most of the Mets sprouted long hair, dressed in mod outfits, and were adorned in beads. Cardwell kept his crew cut and thought it was detrimental for a ballplayer to wear beads.

Cardwell closed out his career with the Atlanta Braves in 1970. His pitching log was 102 wins and 138 losses. He wound up with 15 homers. His Cub record was 30-44, but he'll always be remembered for his dramatic debut, hurling a no-hitter the first time he donned a Cub uniform.

GEORGE ALTMAN

ALTMAN, GEORGE LEE
B. March 20, 1933, Goldsboro, N.C.
BL TR 6'4" 200 lb.

Photographers were snapping pictures of the Cubs' window-breaking crew at their Mesa, Ariz., camp in 1959. From left to right they stood: Ernie Banks, 47 homers; Moose Moryn, 26; Lee Walls, 24; Bobby Thomson, 21; and Dale Long, 20.

Then something in the background diverted their attention. George Altman, a monstrous looking rookie, was taking batting practice. Altman, 6'4" and 200 pounds, took five swings. He rocketed the first four balls over the right field fence and hit the bottom of the clapboard fence on his fifth try.

Altman looked like a fellow who could muscle into the Cubs' home run row. In 1958 they had smashed 182 homers, a team record. It appeared the Cubs wouldn't be taking many rookies home with them. But they had to find room for Altman.

The spindly-legged Altman was an all-around athlete in Goldsboro, N.C., where he played baseball, football, basketball, and excelled in track. He earned a scholarship to Tennessee A&I, a hotbed of future Olympic track stars.

Following college Altman joined the Kansas City Monarchs, the reigning champs of Negro baseball. The Monarchs, who produced Gene Baker and Ernie Banks, sold Altman's contract to the Cubs in 1955.

After batting .263 for Burlington of the Three-I League, Altman's career was interrupted by two years of military service. He resumed baseball in 1958, batting .325 for Pueblo of the Western League.

The Cubs' manager Bob Scheffing, batting coach Rogers Hornsby, plus executives Charlie Grimm and John Holland, watched in awe as Altman tore into Cub pitching in spring training. They agreed he was a "real swisher" and a "prospect."

Altman, who could play the three outfield positions as well as first base, was platooned at the outset by Scheffing, but eventually wound up as the regular center fielder.

The long-legged rookie at first refused to bite at low pitches and was frequently called out on strikes. Hornsby taught Big George to golf the low pitches.

One low pitch wrecked the San Francisco Giants' fading hopes for a pennant. It happened in the bottom of the ninth inning on Sept. 22 at Wrigley Field.

The Giants were clinging to a 4-3 lead with two out and one on for the Cubs. Sam Jones, a 20-game winner, rushed into relief, tossed a knee-high pitch, and Altman golfed it into the seats for a 5-4 Cub victory.

Altman batted close to .300 the final two months of the season for a .245 average and 47 RBI. He displayed occasional power with 14 doubles, 4 triples, and 12 homers. But the 1960 season was something else.

After playing winter ball in Cuba, Altman became the first casualty of spring training. Preliminary diagnosis indicated it might be malaria. Extensive hospital tests later revealed the towering Altman was suffering from infectious mononucleosis. It sapped his energy and left him listless through much of the season. In addition, Big George was slowed by an ankle injury.

He was, however, one of the unsung heroes of Don Cardwell's no-hitter on May 15, 1960. Much was said about Moose Moryn's shoetop catch on the dead run with two out in the ninth inning that preserved Cardwell's no-hitter in his Cub debut.

But in that same inning, Cardinal pinch hitter Carl Sawatski led off with a towering drive deep to right field. Altman raced to the wall, brushed against the ivy vines, timed his leap perfectly, and with his long limbs grabbed the ball in the webbing of his glove.

As a semiregular, Altman finished with solid extra base power, delivering 16 doubles, 4 triples, and 13 homers, while hiking his average to .266.

The 1961 season provided big days for Big George. "You've got to be healthy to play this game," said Altman, who finally shook off mono and the nagging ankle.

He joined Banks and newcomers Billy Williams and Ron Santo as the Cubs' solid Big Four. Altman especially swung a torrid bat during June, collecting 10 homers. He was named to the All-Star team and responded with a pinch homer in his first plate appearance.

It was a vital homer, giving the National League a 3-1 lead in the eighth inning. The American League came back with two in the ninth to tie, but the National League prevailed 5-4 in extra innings.

When the season concluded, Altman had an eye-popping .560 slugging average and led the league with a dozen triples. In addition, he had 28 doubles, 27 homers, drove in 96 runs, and batted .303.

1962 was a season of uninterrupted progress for the gentle giant who boosted his average to .318, with 27 doubles, 5 triples, 22 homers, and 74 RBI.

The Cubs, however, were hurting for pitchers. Of their Big Four sluggers, Banks was Mr. Cub, and Santo and Williams were youngsters with unlimited potential. Altman was the most expendable.

He was the key player in a six-man off-season deal with the Cardinals, who sent Larry Jackson, their top starter; and Lindy McDaniel, their top reliever; plus catcher Jimmie Schaffer to the Cubs for Altman, no-hit pitcher Cardwell, and the storied catcher, Moe Thacker.

From a St. Louis viewpoint, Big George looked 12-feet tall. After all, Sportsman's Park had a short porch in right field. But Altman's 1963 average dropped 44 points to .274 and his homer total dwindled to 9. "I had my eyes on the wall—not the ball," said Altman.

The following season found Altman in a New York Mets' uniform. He was traded for pitcher Roger Craig. Big George didn't take much of a bite out of the Big Apple. His average was sliced to .230 in a season beset by injuries, including a dislocated shoulder.

That winter, Altman attended the Chicago Baseball Writers' Dinner and received a big ovation when he was introduced. That evening, head coach Bob Kennedy turned to GM Holland and said, "John, did you hear that hand Altman got? They like him here."

A few days later, the Cubs reacquired Altman for outfielder Billy Cowan. The next two seasons Altman was plagued by injuries and was mainly used as a spare outfielder and pinch hitter. He drew his Cub release early in the 1967 season. At age 34 Altman still thought he had a baseball future.

And he was right. He signed on with the Lotte Orions and became a legend in Japan through the next decade. Perhaps it was the rice or raw fish, but Altman hit .300 or better in six of his eight seasons in the Orient with a high of .351 in 1974. His career total of 205 homers is tops for a foreigner and his lifetime batting of .307 is third in Japanese baseball history.

Although he never lost his yen for Japanese ball, Altman returned to Chicago at age 42 and began a new career selling stocks and bonds for a LaSalle Street brokerage company.

As a major leaguer, George was a .269 lifetime batter with 832 hits and 101 homers.

DICK ELLSWORTH

ELLSWORTH, RICHARD CLARK
B. March 22, 1940, Lusk, Wyo.
BL TL 6'3½"
180 lb.

In the summer of 1958, a pencil-thin, stoop-shouldered left-handed pitcher went to the mound against the White Sox at Comiskey Park. He was a $50,000 Cub bonus baby, just five days out of Fresno (Calif.) High School.

The 18-year-old pitcher was obviously nervous, walking four batters in the first two innings. Cub pitching coach Fat Freddie Fitzsimmons called time, waddled to the mound, and confronted the raw recruit.

"Just make believe you're back in Fresno, facing high school kids," said Fitzsimmons. The crew-cut youngster managed a wan smile, settled down, and tossed a four-hitter as the Cubs won 1-0.

That marked the debut of Dick Ellsworth on June 16, 1958. Cub manager Bob Scheffing, elated over Ellsworth's poised performance in downing the White Sox, pegged him as a starter four days later.

It was a disaster. The Cincinnati Reds pounded Ellsworth for four hits, mixed in with three walks and shelled him from the mound in the third inning. The next day, the gawky rookie took his 0-1 record and 15.43 earned-run average to Fort Worth.

Ellsworth also found the Texas League wasn't comparable to American Legion ball, where he posted 110 victories against only 5 losses. At Fort Worth, Ellsworth was 1-7.

Nevertheless, the Cubs knew they had a sound prospect who possessed a sinking fastball, a good slider and curve. All that was lacking was control, experience, and perhaps a little more meat on his bones.

The following season Ellsworth was 10-14 at Forth Worth, but was more effective than his record indicated. He allowed only 139 hits in 197 innings and struck out 152. After winning two in a row and compiling an 0.86 ERA with Houston at the outset of the 1960 season, Ellsworth was recalled by the Cubs.

Lou Boudreau, the new Cub manager, greeted the towering lefty and sent him out to face the Pirates. Ellsworth set down Pittsburgh 5-1 for his first big league win. Control? He didn't walk a batter.

But pitchers don't compile winning records with losing ballclubs. Ellsworth's ledger read 26-45 in his first three seasons, including a 9-20 mark in 1962.

Then followed the 1963 season. In the opening series at Wrigley Field, Ellsworth stopped the Dodgers 2-0 on three hits. "After the game I thought . . . boy, that was a good one. If I can beat the Dodgers like this I should be able to beat other clubs, too." reasoned the maturing moundsman.

He just wound up and cut loose with that long left arm and that sinking fastball would nick the corner of the plate. He'd fire again and that big, breaking curve would bite off a bit of the inside corner.

The result? Ellsworth led the Cub staff in starts (37), completed games (19), innings pitched (291), strikeouts (185), shutouts (4), and his earned-run average of 2.10 was second only to Sandy Koufax, who was 1.88.

Included among Ellsworth's 22 victories (against 10 defeats) was a one-hitter against the Phillies on June 1. That lone hit was a cheapie. Wes Covington, a slew-footed slugger, laid down a drag bunt in the sixth inning and beat it out against an infield that was playing back.

Ellsworth earned the Comeback of the Year Award at the tender age of 23. Moreover, he became the first Cub left-hander to win 20 games since Hippo Vaughn in 1919.

That winter Ellsworth was named Chicago Player of the Year by the local writers. Joining him on the podium for a chat was a burly, 75-year-old whose leathery, weather-beaten face revealed the passage of baseball time. It was Hippo Vaughn. Flashbulbs popped as the pair posed.

What could Ellsworth do for an encore? Nothing. Somehow he reverted back to his old form the next three seasons, including a horrid 8-22 record in 1966. The Cubs finished last under Leo Durocher and the Lip took a back-up truck and unloaded Ellsworth in Philadelphia for pitcher Ray Culp.

After a dull 6-7 record at Philly, Ellsworth was dumped at Boston's Fenway Park, a graveyard for left-handed pitchers with its Green Monster left field wall that hovers only 315 feet from the plate.

Ellsworth whistled past the graveyard and posted a 16-7 record, thus becoming the first player to earn Comeback of the Year honors in both leagues. It was, however, his last glimmer in the limelight.

In the next four seasons, Ellsworth bounced from the Red Sox to the Indians and finally to the expansion Brewers, where he was 0-1 in 1971.

His record for 13 big league seasons was 115-137, including an 84-110 mark in Cub flannels. He will always be remembered as the scared high-school youngster who stopped the hated White Sox in his Chicago debut.

LOU BROCK

BROCK, LOUIS CLARK
B. June 18, 1939, El Dorado, Ark.
BL TL 5'11½"
170 lb.

"If you want to hit the bull's-eye you have to take a shot at it," said Cubs' owner P.K. Wrigley.

"We're taking more than a shot at the flag," said Cubs' general manager John Holland. "We're cutting loose wih both barrels."

"I believe the deal puts us in a much better position to make a run for the flag," said Cubs' head coach Bob Kennedy. "I think this is going to make us a little more respected."

The date was June 15, 1964. The Cubs had just completed a six-player trade with the St. Louis Cardinals. They obtained pitchers Ernie Broglio, Bobby Shantz, and outfielder Doug Clemens. In return the Cubs gave up pitchers Paul Toth, Jack Spring, and *outfielder Lou Brock.*

The two big names were Broglio and Brock. The Cardinals knew what they needed; the Cubs didn't. It was the worst trade in Cubs' history. That Blue Monday ranks alongside the A's 10-run inning against the Cubs in the 1929 World Series.

Louis Clark Brock went on to become baseball's greatest basestealer with a grand larceny total of 938, including a then record 118 in 1974. He led the Cardinals to three pennants and two World Series victories. He haunted the Cubs for the next 16 seasons. He even collected his 3,000th big league hit against the Cubs. That cinched his Hall of Fame entry.

And Broglio? One can't pitch very well with a sore arm? He spent two and one-half arduous seasons with the Cubs and won seven games.

Brock had a humble beginning. His father separated from his mother, leaving nine children. She earned their keep as a domestic. Life in Baton Rouge, La., was bleak for young Lou, who never knew skates or a bike, but received loving care from his mother, a religious woman.

Young Brock was the fleetest of athletes in high school and never hit under .450 on the baseball team. He wanted to quit school because he couldn't raise money for college tuition.

Brock wrote letters to Southern and Grambling, asking if they wanted anybody who could work his way through college. He was accepted at Southern after getting a job in the maintenance department as a janitor. He made the baseball team as a freshman and then looked to football.

"I showed up at practice one day," recalled Brock. "Me and all of my 165 pounds and looked around at all the other candidates. Every one was six inches taller and weighed at least 220 pounds. Right then I decided I was no football player."

Brock had scouts from 10 big league clubs following him. The Milwaukee Braves offered the most money. "But I looked at their outfield of Aaron, Bruton, and Covington and decided it was pretty solid.

"My chance of coming up fast looked better with the Cubs." Brock signed for a reported $30,000 and was shipped to St. Cloud of the Northern League in 1961.

Lou proved a real Brock buster at St. Cloud, leading the league with a .361 average. His 117 runs scored, 181 base hits, and 33 doubles were also league highs. In addition, he stole 38 bases. The Cubs brought up the 21-year-old youngster at the end of the season.

"I hit a homer my first time up at Southern University," recalled Brock. "And I homered in my first trip at St. Cloud." When he stepped to the plate for the first time at Wrigley Field, he singled to center. But the speedy center fielder failed in his next 10 trips and finished the season with an .091 average.

As a 1962 rookie, Lou hit .263, made a ton of mistakes, and led the league in anxiety. The Cubs switched him from center to right, where he had no fun in the sun. He had breathtaking speed and a fine throwing arm, but was a butcher on high flies and skidding grounders.

He was also held to 16 stolen bases, but displayed some extra base prowess with 27 doubles, 7 triples, and 9 homers. One of his homers was a historic blast.

The slender, shy Brock went to the plate with two on in the first inning against the New York Mets on June 17 at the Polo Grounds and cut at a high slider off Al Jackson.

The ball sailed over center fielder Richie Ashburn's head and kept going and going. It went over the big green partition in right center. The 470-foot blow was the first ball ever hit into those bleachers. Joe Adcock of the Braves hit one into the left side against the Giants' Jim Hearn in 1953.

Despite his occasional flashes of speed and power, many skeptics believed Brock was too green and needed more seasoning in the minors. It didn't help when the Cubs kept switching him from left to center to right to the bench during the 1963 season.

Although his development was slow, the Cardinals took notice on July 28, 1963, when he drove in five runs with two homers, a triple, and a sacrifice fly as the Cubs outlasted St. Louis 16-11. One of his homers was off *Broglio.*

Brock got off to a slow start in 1964. Then about the middle of May he decided to stop pulling the ball on inside pitches. Instead of tapping the ball to the infield, he started hitting line drives.

"More than anything, I think it was maturity," said Brock. "I lifted my average about 20 points the last two weeks I was with the Cubs." Somehow, they failed to notice. The June 15 trading deadline came . . . and Brock went.

Before heading for St. Louis, Brock scribbled a note to his Cub teammates and taped it over his dressing stall: "It's sort of hard to say farewell to a nice bunch of guys. I enjoyed every moment of it. So fellows, take care and the best of luck to each one of you—Lou."

He would steal 50 or more bases 12 straight seasons, including a magnificent 118 in 1974 to surpass the supposedly insurmountable 104 set by the Dodgers' Maury Wills in 1962. Then Brock chased and finally passed the ghost of Ty Cobb as the all-time base bandit, 938 to 892.

KEN HUBBS

HUBBS, KENNETH DOUGLAS
B. Dec. 23, 1941, Riverside, Calif.
D. Feb. 13, 1964, Provo, Utah.
BR TR 6'2" 175 lb.

The headline was horrifying: "CUB STAR HUBBS DEAD. Plane, Bodies Found In Utah Lake."

Ken Hubbs, the National League's Rookie of the Year in 1962, who played a record 78 games without an error at second base, was dead at 22. He and his lifelong friend, Dennis Doyle, 23, were found in the wreckage of a light plane in Utah Lake near Provo, Utah.

Hubbs and Doyle were on a return flight from Provo Airport to Morrow Field near their hometown of Colton, Calif., a 550-mile trip. Flying conditions were unfavorable when the single-engine red and white Cesna 172 took off at 11 a.m. on Thursday, Feb. 13, 1964.

Authorities said the temperature was one below zero, with snow flurries. Visibility was only three miles. Seconds after takeoff Ken's plane dived into the water and smashed into an ice-covered section of the lake 200 yards south of desolate Bird Island.

The bodies were recovered two days later. A helicopter was first to reach the crash site. A jeep posse reached it two hours later. One body was found in the cabin, the other outside. Hubbs had just received his pilot's license three weeks earlier.

Hubbs, second of five sons of Mr. and Mrs. Eustis Hubbs, was an all-around athlete. As a little leaguer he once hit four homers in a game and set a record with 17 consecutive hits. His Colton team went to the Little League World Series in Williamsport, Pa., and he carried them into the finals before they lost. He pitched them to victory in the semifinals and, as the shortstop, hit a homer and single in a losing cause the next day.

Hubbs, then 12, and his father stopped in Chicago en route to the Little League series. They went to Wrigley Field to see the Cubs, and Ernie Banks hit two homers, one out in the street in left and one in the center field bleachers.

"I remember Kenny saying to me 'Dad, wouldn't it be great if I could do something like that someday?' " recalled the elder Hubbs.

In high school, Ken was president of his senior class. Doyle was vice-president. Ken was also a four-letter man . . . shortstop in baseball, quarterback in football, playmaker in basketball, and a high jumper in track. One day during a lull in baseball, Hubbs joined the track workout "just for fun" and cleared the bar at 6′2″ with his baseball uniform on.

His father was his greatest fan, attending every athletic event even though he was confined to a wheelchair. His favorite tale was about Ken's exploits in a state basketball semifinal.

"Colton was down five points with only 27 seconds left," said the elder Hubbs. "First he stole the ball and sank a basket. As the other team brought the ball back, Ken was fouled. There were only nine seconds left. Ken sank the first free throw and Colton took time out.

"They still needed two points, so they decided to have Ken hit the backboard with Norm Housley going for the rebound. Housley got it, flipped the ball to Ken and he made the basket just as the gun sounded. That tied it and Colton won in overtime."

Young Hubbs was flooded with college scholarships, but baseball was in his blood. Baseball scouts were constantly knocking on the Hubbs' door until Ken became ill. He had four impacted wisdom teeth and was running a temperature.

Only one scout didn't give up. He was Gene Handley of the Cubs, who came over and helped with the ice packs. Hubbs then signed with the Cubs in the spring of 1959 for a modest bonus.

Kenny was converted to a second baseman in the minor leagues and two years later reported to the Cubs' spring training camp in Mesa, Ariz., at the tender age of 20. Young Hubbs was extremely nervous and recorded his feelings every week in his "Rookie Diary."

First week: "I don't know what to think out here. I'm wondering who will get the first chance? I'm a little anxious and nervous. I hope it's me."

Second week: "I got the first shot and now I have to hold it. I feel a lot better now. There's a little of the tension off, but there are other symptoms of pressure."

Third week: "I'm in good shape and ready to go. If I can keep myself from swinging at bad balls, I have no worries at all."

Fourth week: "I'm happy, but surprised. My stomach was acting up and I thought I had the flu. I didn't want to lose any time."

Fifth week: "The regular players have been very nice to me. I kind of feel at ease out there now."

Sixth week: (Hubbs appears a cinch to open the season at second base.) "I sleep a little sounder now that things are going well."

Hubbs was in the opening-day lineup in 1962 and nobody ever got him out of there. On June 13 he began a fielding streak that wiped out all records for perfection. Ken established major league records for second basemen by playing 78 consecutive games without an error. He handled 418 chances in a row without a boot.

It wasn't until Hubbs tied Red Schoendienst's National League mark by playing his 57th successive game Aug. 14 that the media picked up on his assault on the record books. Ken's next target was the major league record of 73 games and 414 chances by Bobby Doerr of the Boston Red Sox in 1948.

Cameras began to focus on the young rookie, who admitted he felt the tension as he was approaching the record. Finally, on Sept. 5 it was all over. Hubbs set the record—and then erred. It came in the eighth inning of the second game of a twi-night doubleheader in Cincinnati. Hubbs threw wildly past shortstop Andre Rodgers on an easy double-play grounder.

One of the curious aspects of Hubbs and his pursuit of the record is that he did it with an old, battered Jerry Lumpe glove that was torn in three places. He ordered a Chuck Cottier model with a deeper pocket, but stayed with the old one throughout the streak. "The new glove is still in its box," said Hubbs. "I probably will never use it now."

Meanwhile, everyone overlooked Ken's offensive contributions. In one doubleheader sweep over the Phillies he had eight hits in eight trips, going three-for-three in the opener and five-for-five in the nightcap.

When the season was over, Hubbs was named to the National League's all-fielding team, becoming the first rookie to win a Gold Glove Award since the trophies were established in 1957. Kenny was a cinch for Rookie of the Year honors, and when the votes were released, it was almost unanimous, with one writer opting for Donn Clendenon of the Pirates.

Hubbs encountered a "sophomore jinx" in 1963. His batting average dipped from .260 to .235, but he remained almost flawless afield. And he was still the sandy-haired youngster who considered a night out on the town, a movie and a malted.

It seemed as if the Cubs were set at second base for the next decade. That was all wiped out on that tragic morning on a desolate lake in Utah. Among the pallbearers were head coach Bob Kennedy, and teammates Ernie Banks, Ron Santo, Don Elston, Dick Ellsworth, and Glen Hobbie.

The Chicago writers announced that the Ken Hubbs Memorial Award for excellence and exemplary conduct on and off the field would be presented annually at their Diamond Dinner. The first recipient was Ernie Banks.

At the dinner in January 1965, Banks rose to the dais and accepted the award from Willie Mays of the Giants. Banks fought back the tears and said, "This award means more to me than any I've ever received. Kenny was the way people should be. Those of us who knew him admired and cherished him. I just hope my two sons turn out to be as fine a man as Ken Hubbs. . ."

In his sadly brief stay in the majors, Hubbs was a .247 batter with 310 hits.

BOB BUHL

BUHL, ROBERT RAY

B. Aug. 12, 1928, Saginaw, Mich.

BR TR 6'2" 180 lb.

It was a raw, windy afternoon at Wrigley Field on May 8, 1963. Bob Buhl stood with bat firmly in hand, staring soberly at Alvin McBean, the Pirates' pitcher.

Fearlessly accepting the challenge, McBean stretched and fired a fastball. Buhl cut at the offering and smashed a vicious wind-blown pop fly that eluded shortstop Ducky Schofield's grasp. The pop dropped for a fourth-inning hit, sending a Cub runner home.

Showing a brilliant burst of memory, Buhl pulled up at first base. It was his first hit in a Cub uniform, and his first since 1961. Buhl was 0-for-1962, going hitless in 70 at bats, a major league record. He finally connected after 88 futile attempts.

But Robert Ray Buhl was not paid to hit. He was a pitcher, and a good one, even if the Cubs latched on to him near the tail end of his career.

Buhl, a 6'2" right-hander with jet-black hair, blue-piercing eyes, a Kirk Douglas-cleft chin, and an ever-present five o'clock shadow, was signed by the Chicago White Sox prior to his graduation from high school in Saginaw, Mich.

The Sox were ordered to cut him loose immediately, and he was picked up by the Boston Braves as a free agent in 1946. After a brilliant 19-10 start at Madisonville, Buhl bounced about the bushes for three seasons with little success. He had a good hop on his fastball, but was held back by wildness.

His career was interrupted by the Korean conflict, where he served as a paratrooper, making 19 battle jumps. At the advanced age of 25, Buhl reported to the Braves' camp in 1953. The hairy-chested Buhl stood out among the other fuzzy-cheeked rookies and earned a spot on the roster.

Braves' manager Charlie Grimm, who managed Buhl at Dallas in 1950 when he compiled a mediocre 8-14 record, noticed the change in the hard-working pitcher. "He was a wild youngster then," said Grimm. "He's still a bit wild, but just enough to keep those batters honest."

Buhl never did get a chance to pitch in Boston. The franchise was shifted to Milwaukee in the waning days of spring training. The good burghers went wild over the Braves, making instant heroes out of Spahn, Mathews, Burdette, Bruton, Pafko, and the rest of the cast.

But Buhl remained in the background until mid-May when Grimm granted his first start. It was a frigid 30 degrees in Milwaukee when Buhl took to the mound against the hard-hitting New York Giants. He remained cool by tossing a two-hitter for an 8-1 victory. In fact, he had a one-hitter shutout until the ninth inning when the Giants pushed across their lone run on a sacrifice fly.

In his next start he shut out the Phillies 4-0 and soon settled into the rotation as part of the Braves' "Big Three" behind Warren Spahn and Lew Burdette. Buhl completed his rookie season with a 13-8 mark.

He had an 18-8 record in 1956 and came back to lead the

National League with a .720 percentage on 18 wins and 7 losses as the Braves won the 1957 pennant.

Buhl continued to produce for the Braves until they took inventory in 1962 and decided to discard him. His fastball had lost some zip and he never had much of a curve because of a stiff, muscular wrist that gave the ball more of a wrinkle than a spin.

The Braves swapped the 33-year-old veteran to the Cubs for Jack Curtis, a 25-year-old lefty, on April 30. The ex-paratrooper jumped right into action for the Cubs two days later.

They sent him to the mound against Sandy Koufax and the Dodgers in Los Angeles. After surrendering a first-inning homer to Wally Moon, Buhl pitched hitless ball until he was relieved in the seventh inning with a 2-1 lead. The Cubs held on to win 3-1. It was to be their last victory over Koufax for the next three and a half years.

Buhl finished as the ace of an inept staff with a 12-14 record. How did he win? He still had a slider, but mostly it was brute strength and determination. Facing Buhl was like wrestling with a bear for a couple of hours.

Buhl, along with Larry Jackson and Dick Ellsworth, gave the Cubs some semblance of a starting rotation during the mid-1960s. His best Cub season was 1964 when he was 15-14. And in 1963 he even got his batting average up to .108.

A Buhl-pitched game hardly took more than two hours. He was such an intense worker that he seldom wasted time on catcher's signals. He just kept pumping. But when Leo Durocher took over the Cubs, Buhl seemed to run out of gas.

Leo unloaded Buhl and Jackson to the Phillies on April 21, 1966, for outfielders John Herrnstein and Adolfo Phillips and a little-known rookie pitcher named Fergie Jenkins. Buhl departed with a 51-52 Cub record.

Buhl, who was dropped from the rotation by Durocher and asked to be traded, saw even less service with the Phillies. He posted a 6-8 mark in 1966 and then drew his release early the following season after getting into only three games.

Overall, Buhl won 166 games and lost 132, the bulk of his wins with the Braves.

LARRY JACKSON

JACKSON, LAWRENCE CURTIS
B. June 2, 1931, Nampa, Id.
BR TR 6'1½" 175 lb.

Back in 1952, when Harry Truman was in the White House and gasoline was 22 cents a gallon, a 21-year-old phenom with Fresno burned through the California League like a forest fire. He was Larry Jackson, who finished the year with 28 wins, just 4 losses, and 351 strikeouts.

Jackson, who had broken into the pros with Pocatello of the Pioneer League the year before, also made stops at Houston of the Texas League, Omaha of the Western League, and Rochester of the

International League before being called up to the Cardinals in 1955.

For the next eight years, he was a dependable pitcher, winning 101 games for the Redbirds. His best year in St. Louis came in 1960, when he won 18 and lost 13.

Larry came to the Cubs along with Lindy McDaniel and Jimmy Schaeffer in exchange for George Altman, Don Cardwell, and Moe Thacker on Oct. 17, 1962. As a Cub in 1963, Jackson pitched more effectively than ever, as witnessed by his 2.55 ERA, sixth best in the league. Yet due to a chronic lack of support, his record was only 14-18.

The Cubs could score only 29 times during his 18 losses and four times he was shut out, three of them by a 1-0 edge. Eight of his defeats were by one run, and he lost his last seven in a row.

But brighter days were ahead the following year as Larry bounced back to a 24-11 mark with a 3.14 ERA. His victory total was the most by a Cub hurler since Charlie Root won 26 in 1927.

On June 30, he came within inches of posting a no-hitter against the Reds at Wrigley Field. Pete Rose obtained the lone hit, a single in the seventh inning, and was the only Cincinnati batter to reach first base in the game. The Cubs had but two hits off Red pitcher Joey Jay, both by Jim Stewart, whose single in the sixth drove in Dick Bertell for the day's only run.

Finally, Jackson tied a major league record for pitchers that campaign by going the entire season without an error, accepting 109 chances flawlessly.

Unfortunately, the nonsupport jinx came back to haunt Larry in 1965 as his log plunged to 14-21. Even so, his four shutouts were high on the Cub staff. After losing his first two decisions in 1966, Jackson was traded to the Phillies with Bob Buhl for Fergie Jenkins, Adolfo Phillips, and John Herrnstein.

Jackson hung on with the Phillies for three years before retiring in 1968 with a lifetime 194-183 record. As a Cub, he was 52-52, which should have been a lot better. After leaving baseball, Larry returned to his native Idaho, where he became active in politics, including an unsuccessful attempt at the governorship.

LINDY MCDANIEL

MCDANIEL, LYNDALL DALE
B. Dec. 13, 1935, Hollis, Okla.
BR TR 6'3" 195 lb.

Could you picture Lindy McDaniel on the Gashouse Gang? Such players as Pepper Martin, Lippy Durocher, Frankie Frisch, Ducky Medwick, and Dizzy Dean were a hairy-chested bunch, hardly noted for gentle manners or delicate language.

McDaniel, didn't drink, didn't smoke, and didn't cuss. In addition, he carried a Bible. The gangling divinity student helped carry on the Cardinals' winning tradition as one of baseball's greatest relief pitchers. He was possibly the only preacher with a great knockdown pitch.

Lindy, the oldest of three pitching McDaniel brothers from

Hollis, Okla., was 19 when he reported to the Cardinals from Abilene Christian College on Sept. 2, 1955. He warmed up under the scrutiny of Cards' manager Harry Walker and was brought in from the bullpen to face the Cubs in a losing cause. The $50,000 bonus baby gave up a line drive homer to Walker Cooper.

Two weeks later, McDaniel was touched for a grand-slam homer by Ernie Banks. It was Mr. Cub's fifth slam of the season, setting a major league record. It looked like McDaniel didn't have a prayer as a big leaguer.

But Lindy was blessed with a fastball and a forkball. He became the ace of the Cardinal staff with a 15-9 record in 1957. He was soon joined by brother Von, another $50,000 bonus beauty, who pitched a two-hitter in his debut.

A third brother, Kerry Don, also signed for $50,000, and it appeared as if the Cardinals would havc Lindy, Von, and Kerry Don to match "Me and Paul," the old Dizzy and Daffy Dean combo of two decades earlier.

After winning seven games, Von developed a hitch in his delivery, which was followed by a sore arm. Kerry Don developed back trouble and never reached the big leagues. That left Lindy as the lone pitching McDaniel.

He slumped to a 5-7 record in 1958 and was switched to the bullpen. Lindy preferred going on relief. "For three innings I can really cut loose," said McDaniel. "I can stay keyed up. I never liked anticipating starts. It always made me nervous."

McDaniel immediately became the top relief specialist in the National League. He always answered the bell to put out a fire. "The other night the telephone rang in my hotel room and I jumped out of bed and started to warm up," chuckled Lindy.

McDaniel came to the Cubs on Oct. 17, 1962, along with pitcher Larry Jackson and catcher Jimmie Schaeffer for outfielder George Altman, pitcher Don Cardwell, and legendary catcher Moe Thacker. It was one of the better Cub trades as Jackson became their stopper and McDaniel their top reliever.

And McDaniel provided one of the most thrilling moments in recent Cub history. Wrigley Field was the scene. The Cubs and San Francisco Giants were tied 2-2 in the 10th inning on June 6, 1963.

The bases were loaded with one out for the Giants when McDaniel was summoned from the bullpen. Ed Bailey was the batter. Lindy ignored Bailey and fired the ball to second base to pick off an embarrassed Willie Mays. He then turned his sights toward Bailey and struck him out on a forkball that must have dropped three feet.

But that's not all. In the bottom of the inning, Lindy checked the bat rack and found one of Ron Santo's dirty, old discards. He worked the count to two balls and two strikes against crafty southpaw Billy Pierce, who then threw a belt-high curveball.

McDaniel slammed the pitch into the left field bleachers for a game-winning homer and trotted around the bases with a wide grin on his face. He was greeted at home plate by every Cub.

In his three seasons with the Cubs, McDaniel won 19 games and saved 39, including a league-leading 22 when he was named Fireman of the Year. Lindy was traded to the Giants after the 1965 season with outfielder Don Landrum for two little known rookies, pitcher Bill Hands and catcher Randy Hundley, who soon became a valued Cub battery.

McDaniel continued as an ace reliever with the Giants and New York Yankees before closing out his career with the Kansas City Royals in 1975. During his 20-year stay, McDaniel won 141 games and lost 119. He appeared in 987 games, second only to knuckleballer Hoyt Wilhelm's 1,070.

TED ABERNATHY

ABERNATHY, THEODORE WADE
B. March 6, 1933, Stanley, N.C.
BR TR 6'4" 210 lb.

Whenever submarine ball pitchers in Cub history are discussed, there is but one name that comes to mind—Ted Abernathy. In 1965 he was a one-man bullpen.

Ted made his professional debut in 1952 with Roanoke Rapids, where he won 20 games. Following a brief stop at Chattanooga and a year in the military service, Abernathy was given a try with the Washington Senators in 1955. Posting a 5-9 record, he was shipped to Louisville the following year. Brought back to Washington late in the season, he suffered an elbow injury that forced him to develop an underhand delivery.

Still, it took awhile for Ted's submarine to surface. In between look-sees at Washington, Abernathy spent the next several years drifting in and out of such minor league cities as Louisville, Chattanooga, Miami, Charlotte, Austin, Vancouver, Salt Lake City, and Jacksonville. Finally the Indians gave him a chance in 1963. He responded with a 7-2 mark and a 2.90 ERA. But after he slipped the following year he was sold to the Cubs on April 11, 1965.

Previously a nobody, Abernathy became the pitching sensation of Chicago almost overnight. Setting a major league record (since broken) with his 84 appearances, Abernathy fanned 104 batters with his submarine ball in just 136 innings. Although his record was only 4-6, he saved 31 games and had an ERA of 2.58. For his efforts, he was given the Fireman of the Year Award.

Then Leo Durocher was hired as Cub manager. Abernathy did not fit into Leo's rebuilding plans, so on May 28, 1966, he was traded to the Braves for Lee Thomas and Arnold Earley, whose combined Cub accomplishments were zilch. At the end of the season, Ted was drafted by the Reds.

Abernathy made a spectacular comeback in Cincinnati, winning Fireman of the Year honors again in 1967 with a 6-3 mark, 26 saves, and a phenominal 1.27 ERA. He followed this with another fine season in 1968.

On January 9, 1969, Ted returned to Chicago when he was traded to the Cubs for Clarence Jones, Ken Myette, and Bill Plummer. In the early part of the 1969 season, Ted and Phil Regan shared the mop-up chores and both were equally effective. But from midseason on, Durocher went almost exclusively with Regan, while Abernathy sat on the bench. By the end of the year Regan was getting bombed as Abernathy continued to be ignored. He finished the year at 4-3 with a 3.18 ERA.

Due to personality clashes between Abernathy and Durocher, Ted was traded to the Cardinals for infielder Phil Gagliano on May 29, 1970. A month later the Redbirds traded him to the Royals for pitcher Chris Zachary. Ted finished his career at Kansas City, retiring after the 1972 season.

He was 63-69 lifetime with 148 saves and a 3.46 ERA.

SECTION FIVE 1966-1972 From "Dig Durocher" to "Dump Durocher"

On Oct. 25, 1965, the predictably unpredictable Cub owner, P. K. Wrigley, gave Cub fans another bolt of lightning when he announced that Leo Durocher—the complete antithesis of the staid Cub image—was to be the new field manager. *The Sporting News* described it as "a revival meeting in the Windy City."

Returning to managing for the first time in a decade, Durocher vowed to get rid of the country club atmosphere and lay down the law to "safety first" players. Declaring that the Cubs had the nucleus of a good team, Leo said, "This is not an eighth place ball club." He was right. The Cubs finished tenth in 1966, tying the club record with 103 losses.

There was hope in spite of it all. Thanks to Durocher's insistance, catcher Randy Hundley and pitcher Bill Hands were obtained from the Giants, and pitcher Fergie Jenkins from the Phillies. Under the guidance of coach Pete Reiser, Glenn Beckert and Don Kessinger became respectable at bat, while improving defensively. Rookie pitcher Ken Holtzman showed promise and the Cubs played .500 ball (15-15) the last month of the year.

By 1967 most of the so-called deadwood of the 1965 club had been chopped away, leaving only the dependables and unproven youngsters. Even so, few if any scribes were willing to rate the Cubs any higher than eighth. They ended up eating their words. The Cubs bolted all the way to third place for their first upper berth finish in 21 years. Led by Jenkins's 20 wins, the pitching improved vastly while the tightened-up defense gave the Cubs the league's best-fielding honors for the first time since their last pennant in 1945. Signs reading "Durocher for Mayor" began popping up in the Wrigley Field stands as Cub fans came out of the woodwork after two decades of hibernation.

The Cubs at last were being touted as a factor in the pennant race. Unfortunately, it looked like business as usual when the team got off to a poor start in 1968. At one point the team was held scoreless for 48 consecutive innings to tie the major league record. But the

The Chicago Cubs, 1969

Cubs built up steam in the second half, again capturing third place as the infield of Santo, Kessinger, Beckert, and Banks remained tops in the National League. Additional strength came from the emergence of Bill Hands as a reliable starter, and the acquisition of Jim Hickman and relief ace Phil Regan from the Dodgers. Meanwhile, Wrigley Field paid attendance crossed the million mark for the first time since 1952.

Then came euphoria. For most of the year, 1969 was the kind of season every Cub fan dreamed about. It was the year of Willie Smith's game-winning homer on opening day . . . Ron Santo clicking his heels after every home victory . . . Dick Selma leading the yellow-helmeted Bleacher Bums in cheers . . . Durocher saying, "How 'bout another Slitz, fellas" . . . the "Hey Hey Holy Mackerel" song . . . the free Cub photos in the supermarkets . . . Ken Holtzman's no-hitter . . . a (then) club record 1,674,993 home attendance.

The Cubs were the leaders of the pack from day one, building up an 8½-game lead by mid-August. Then the Mets came out of nowhere to charge into the pennant while the Cubs collapsed, finishing eight games behind New York. The dream had become a nightmare, and things would never be the same.

The 1970 Cubs belted 179 home runs—three shy of the club record, but could do no better than a tie for second, in spite of Hickman and Billy Williams enjoying their greatest seasons. The Cubs picked up such seasoned veterans as Johnny Callison, Joe Pepitone, and Milt Pappas in hope of finding the finishing touch, but to no avail.

An 11-game winning streak early in the year was obliterated by a 12-game losing spree a month later. The infield was slowing down at the corners and the bullpen had fallen apart. Some writers began suggesting that Durocher should retire. More ominously, the unity that had characterized Leo's early years was rapidly disintegrating.

By 1971 relations between Durocher and many of the players had so deteriorated that the coaches served as intermediaries. The year of Ernie Banks's 500th homer was also the season of the dugout mutiny. While clubhouse lawyers all but demanded that Leo be sent to the guillotine, Wrigley put an ad in the papers saying, "The 'Dump Durocher' clique might as well give up."

The Cubs finished in a tie for third. Leo was back the following year, but not for long. On July 24, with the team two games above .500, Whitey Lockman took over the reins and the Cubs climbed to second place by season's end. A few years later, Durocher would write in his autobiography that his greatest regret was being unable to bring a championship to Wrigley Field.

LEO DUROCHER

DUROCHER, LEO ERNEST
B. July 27, 1905, West Springfield, Mass.
BR TR 5′10″
160 lb.

Leo "the Lip" Durocher spent 50 flamboyant years in baseball. He was pugnacious, bombastic, and full of con. He was always in the middle of the game's magic moments.

The Yankees? He was one of Babe Ruth's roommates and was dubbed "The All-American Out" by the Bambino, who watched Leo's woeful batting stroke.

The Cardinals? He was captain of the 1934 Gashouse Gang that included the charismatic Dizzy Dean, Pepper Martin, Frankie Frisch, a pennant, and a garbage-strewn World Series victory over the Detroit Tigers.

The Dodgers? He led "Dem Bums" to the beanball wars and the 1941 pennant, and was around when Jackie Robinson broke the color line.

The Giants? He managed the team that produced Bobby Thomson's famous home run that won the 1951 pennant. He served as a father figure for Willie Mays, who made that magnificent catch to help sweep the Indians in the 1954 World Series.

The Cubs? Yes, even the Cubbies. The ivy-covered walls of Wrigley Field rumbled for six and one-half seismatic seasons as the brash and dapper skipper led them from last place to second, kept them over a million attendance—but never got them a pennant.

Durocher took over Mr. Philip Knight Wrigley's staid ballclub in 1966 and generated excitement and controversy. There was the Don Young affair, the trip to Camp Ojibwa, the collapse of 1969, the 1971 clubhouse meeting that produced a near mutiny, and a letter from P.K.

After all the dust had cleared, Durocher's overall record at the Cubs' helm was just a tinge over .500. His Cubs won 535 games and lost 526. When he departed, Cub fans missed the noise, the rhubarbs, the bitterness—and the fun.

Leo Ernest Durocher was born in West Springfield, Mass., and was a feisty little tyke. His father took much pleasure in him, but Leo admitted, "I was such a rotten son." His mother always called him Leo. "It was the sportswriters that labeled me 'the Lip,' not mom," declared Durocher.

At 16 Durocher worked in tobacco fields for $6 a day. He decided then to become a ballplayer, starting out at Hartford in the Eastern League. At that time, his hero was shortstop Rabbit Maranville, who also hailed from Springfield. Leo, too, was a shortstop. And like Maranville, he couldn't hit, but was impressive afield.

Durocher caught the eye of a Yankee scout and was brought up to the big leagues in 1925, getting to bat once as a pinch hitter and failing to connect. It wasn't until 1928 that he rejoined the Yankees as a utility infielder, hitting a surprise .270.

Yankee manager Miller Huggins liked the youngster and roomed him with Babe Ruth. The Babe winced when he saw Durocher swing the bat, and took him to dinner and made him eat scallions because they "were the greatest cure for a batting slump." In return,

Durocher used to help Ruth to bed when the Babe went on an alcoholic bender.

But even the Babe couldn't tolerate Durocher's constant popping off. When Huggins died, Durocher's exit from the Yankees was inevitable. He was claimed on waivers by the Cincinnati Reds in 1930.

When Durocher's batting average sagged to .217, the Reds traded him to the Cardinals in a six-player deal that included pitcher Paul Derringer. It was a steal for Cincy. But Durocher had found a home.

The Cards' regular shortstop, Charley Gelbert, was hurt in a hunting accident, and the Cards were desperate. It was Durocher who tagged his Cardinal teammates "The Gashouse Gang."

It all started when pitcher Dizzy Dean bragged the Cardinals could win the pennant in any league. Durocher nodded and replied, "They wouldn't allow us in the American League because we're a bunch of gashouse players." The team thus became "The Gashouse Gang."

Frankie Frisch saw Leo as a threat to his job security as Cardinal manager and finally found an excuse to peddle him after the 1937 season when Durocher's average plummeted to .203.

Would you believe a .203 hitter commanded four players in return? The Brooklyn Dodgers gave up infielders Jim Bucher and Jersey Joe Stripp, outfielder John Cooney, and pitcher Roy Henshaw on Oct. 4, 1937, to acquire one self-centered, ruthless, charming egotist who could field with the best.

It didn't take long for Durocher to take charge of the Dodgers. He replaced Burleigh Grimes in 1939 and made the team a contender. Every day was a three-ring circus at Ebbets Field. Leo was "fired" constantly by Larry MacPhail, who ran the club like a stone-aged George Steinbrenner.

Then there were the beanball and duster battles. Many involved the Cubs. One Cub pitcher, Hi Bithorn, even threw the ball at Leo in the dugout, while another, Claude Passeau, had his uniform ripped off trying to get at Durocher during a free-for-all. In another rhubarb, Cub shortstop Len Merullo knocked out some of Dodger baserunner Dixie Walker's teeth.

While the Cubs seemed to win the battles, the Dodgers (and Leo) seemed to win the wars. Brooklyn won the 1941 pennant with a roster of ex-Cubbies, including Dolph Camilli, Hugh Casey, Curt Davis, Larry French, Augie Galan, Billy Herman, Kirby Higbe, and Babe Phelps. The Cubs finished sixth that season.

It was during that era Durocher, ever the flip Lip, entered *Bartlett's Quotations* with his stinging remark: "Nice guys finish last." In full context, Durocher said, "Take a look at Mel Ott's New York Giants. All nice guys. They'll finish last. Nice guys. Finish last."

In 1947 Durocher wasn't around to finish anywhere. He was suspended for the season by new baseball commissioner Happy Chandler for associating with so-called gamblers. What really happened was never fully revealed, but Chandler vaguely cited "unpleasant incidents" that caused the banishment.

Leo spent the season watching Burt Shotton lead the Dodgers, with Jackie Robinson breaking the color line, to a pennant. "That was *my* team," moaned Durocher.

The next year Durocher returned, but he lasted only until a midseason switch. Shotton resumed command of the Dodgers and Durocher moved to Coogan's Bluff. It was bad guy Durocher replacing nice guy Mel Ott at the Giants' helm.

The Giants, led by Johnny Mize's 51 homers, hit a record 221 home runs, but finished only fourth in 1947. "This ain't my kind of team," said Durocher, who grabbed a back-up truck and unloaded most of the sluggers. In one deal he sent Sid Gordon and Willard Marshall to the Boston Braves for the double-play duo of Al Dark and Eddie Stanky, his former Dodger clone.

But there was one missing ingredient, a center fielder. That superstar descended upon him in 1951 with the coming of Willie Mays. "I always said Mays was the best ballplayer I ever saw," beamed the Lip with brassy assertiveness. "One Mays in a lifetime has to be a rarity for any manager."

Durocher's Giants trailed the Dodgers by 13½ games in mid-August, and then won 37-of-44 games to tie Brooklyn, forcing a three-game pennant playoff. The Giants won it all on Bobby Thomson's historic homer, but bowed to the Yankees in the World Series.

The next two years were painful for Durocher. Mays went into the army, and the Dodgers' Boys of Summer won two straight pennants. Worst of all, Leo was now on the receiving end of a famous baseball quotation. The remarks came during the waning days of the 1953 pennant race. They were made by Dodger manager Charley Dressen, a former Durocher crony, who uttered, "The Giants is dead." It was not grammatical, but it was correct. Leo's Giants finished fifth in 1953.

But Willie came marching home the next season and Leo finally had a World Series winner. They swept the Indians four straight, highlighted by the pinch-hitting of Dusty Rhodes and the miracle catch by Mays. After finishing third in 1955, Durocher joined NBC as a TV color commentator on the "Game of The Week."

He returned to baseball as a coach for the LA Dodgers in 1961. Surprisingly, Durocher lasted four seasons under manager Walter Alston. Indeed, they were baseball's odd couple. Durocher, always noisy, dapper, and a Hollywood-type hunch player, seemed miscast as an underling to the quiet, conservative, rustic Alston.

The media expected the pair to clash, with Durocher second-guessing every Alston maneuver. It never happened. But Leo was anxiously awaiting to be unleashed again as top dog.

The opportunity came in 1966, when Cub owner P. K. Wrigley abandoned his doomed-to-failure College of Coaches. "I'm the manager," was Durocher's first declaration as he tugged on his Cub cap for the flashing cameras. The Cubs, in another futile season, had finished eighth. "This ain't no eighth-place ballclub," roared the Lion. He was right. They finished 10th under Durocher in 1966.

Nevertheless, it was a progressive 10th. Suddenly, the Cubs outsmarted the other clubs in player trades. And Durocher had a hot hand in all the deals. Three trades helped turn around the team.

The Cubs acquired the rookie battery of Bill Hands and Randy Hundley from the Giants; they stripped the Phillies of pitcher Fergie Jenkins and center fielder Adolfo Phillips; and they relieved the Dodgers of reliever Phil Regan and slugger Jim Hickman, giving little of value in the three big transactions.

Durocher paired youngsters Glenn Beckert and Don Kessinger at the keystone, nurtured a skinny southpaw named Ken Holtzman, and took Jenkins out of the bullpen. Combined with holdover sluggers Ernie Banks, Billy Williams, and Ron Santo, the Cubs climbed from a 59-103 record in 1966 to an 87-74 mark and third place in 1967.

Durocher was putting all the pieces together. And the ballclub was on a honeymoon with Leo. The fans sensed this was a team on the move. The Bleacher Bums, a yellow hard-hatted cheering section in the left field bleachers, was making itself heard. Excitement and fun had returned to Wrigley Field.

With Durocher instilling confidence, the Cubs were now for real. Although they again finished third in 1968 with an 84-78 record, everyone eyed the upward surge. Could 1969 be the year?

In the opener, Willie Smith hit a three-run pinch homer in the 11th inning to beat the Phillies. That movie script victory sparked a fan frenzy that would accompany the team all year.

The players had absolute faith in every Durocher maneuver and bolted out of the gate, winning seven of their first eight games. There was now a genuine love affair between the fans and their Cubbies. Pennant fever swept Chicago.

Leo was lionized throughout the city. The team looked like a sure winner. It carried into July. Then followed the first hint of disaster. The Cubs were five games ahead of the surprising New York Mets when the teams met at Shea Stadium on July 8.

Jenkins, the Cubs' ace right-hander went into the ninth inning with a 3-1 lead before a packed house. Rookie center fielder Don Young misplayed a looping flyball into a double and then shied away from another fly ball. The end result was a 4-3 Met upset.

Durocher and Santo blew up. "If a man can't catch two fly balls, you don't deserve to win," bellowed Durocher, who had a penchant for making bad things worse. "That was bush. Strictly bush."

If anything, that one contest instilled some new-found confidence in the Mets. Then followed another "incident." Durocher went AWOL and visited his stepson at a summer camp in Eagle River, Wis. For trivia buffs, the name of the camp was Ojibwa.

The local sportswriters, who had begun sparring and feuding with Durocher, had a field day. But when Leo apologized to

Wrigley, all was forgiven and it was back to the heated pennant race.

The Cubs rolled into August enjoying an 8½-game lead over the Cardinals. The Mets were in third. A no-hitter by Holtzman later that month helped swell the rising tide of pennant fever.

Then came September. The Cubs lost 11-of-12, while the Mets won 10 in a row. It was all over. It was an unpleasant experience that haunted the Cubs for the next decade.

Forgotten was the Cubs 92-70 record, their best since the 1945 pennant winner. Forgotten was their attendance of 1,674,993, surpassing the old mark set by the 1929 storied crew of Wilson, Hornsby, Grimm, and all that gang.

Who was to blame? Wrigley blamed the collapse on too many off-the-field activities, pursuing the extra buck. But most blamed Durocher for not resting his regulars during the dog days of summer. The heat of playing daylight ball at Wrigley Field had taken its toll.

"It was a composite slump," growled the Lion. "The hitting, the pitching, the fielding all went bad. If we had only played .500 ball. The Mets kept winning, winning, winning . . ."

Durocher added more firepower for 1970 with sluggers Joe Pepitone and Johnny Callison and a fourth starter in Milt Pappas. The Cubs finished ahead of the Mets, but again were bridesmaids. This time it was the Pirates who surged ahead in the September stretch. Although their record dropped to 84-78, there were few open incidents or blowups.

But there was much smoldering behind the scenes between Durocher and his veteran players as the 1971 season wore on. Leo became more withdrawn. The feuding and turmoil reached its peak during a clubhouse meeting on Aug. 23. Leo literally tore into Santo, Pepitone, and Pappas, while the writers tore into Durocher for his handling of the ballclub.

A "Dump Durocher" clique had developed. Buttons were issued: "Leo Must Go" and "Leo Must Stay" and sales were about equal. Wrigley, obviously prodded by the press, responded in a unique way.

He advertised in all four Chicago papers, backing Durocher and slapping down the players (with the exception of Banks). The Cubs went into a deep slumber following Wrigley's ad and finished tied for third with the Mets at 83-79.

Durocher finally stepped aside on July 24, 1972. The Cubs were 46-44. The open grumbling was over. Whitey Lockman, Durocher's successor, rallied the club to a second-place finish.

A month later, Durocher reappeared as manager of the Houston Astros. He applied the old carn and hype by billing center fielder Cesar Cedeno as a "young Willie Mays."

Leo soon soured on Cedeno, and the Astros soured on Leo. He resigned on Oct. 1, 1973. His managerial record was 2,019 won and 1,709 lost. Not bad for a .247 hitter who left you snarling.

It was rumored that a Japanese team wanted Durocher's

managerial services. He refused the honor. It would have been appropriate to say, "Nice guys finish in Taiheiyo."

BILLY WILLIAMS

WILLIAMS, BILLY LEO
B. June 15, 1938, Whistler, Ala.
BL TR 6'1" 175 lb.

Cubs' batting instructor Rogers Hornsby leaned against the batting cage under the boiling sun in Mesa, Ariz. His steel-gray eyes were peering at a lean and lithsome left-hander, lashing at fastballs from a pitching machine.

Hornsby, perhaps the greatest right-handed batter of all-time, stood there transfixed at Billy Williams, who was cracking the ball solidly. At the end of his turn, Williams started to leave the cage. "Stay in there," bellowed Hornsby, "hit a few more."

The Rajah watched the sweet-swinger take his stance at the plate. He noticed the quick hands, the whiplash wrists. As the ball reached the plate Hornsby took note of Williams uncoiling like a cobra striking or a steel trap suddenly snapping shut.

After about 10 minutes, the laconic Hornsby said "OK, Williams, that's enough." He walked away without smiling.

A sportswriters confronted Williams, and shouted, "Hey, kid. Nice going."

"Why?" asked the puzzled rookie.

"He liked you, that's what. Hornsby liked you. He said you had a nice swing."

Hornsby told the Cub management to keep Williams and a young third baseman named Ron Santo and get rid of the rest.

That moment gave Williams the needed confidence. He was no longer the skinny youth who had learned to hit by swinging a broom handle at pop corks in a little whistle stop called Whistler, Ala., a sawdust town outside of Mobile.

Williams, the youngest of five children of Frank and Jesse Mary Williams, used to spend much of his time swimming during the lazy days of summer down at Eight Mile Creek.

His first introduction to a baseball bat was a painful experience when he was eight. His sister Vera was swinging him around by the hand when he ran into a bat his brother Adolph was swinging. It split his lip wide open.

Despite the bloody lip, baseball was in Billy's blood. His father had played first base with a semipro outfit, and Billy followed his brothers Franklin, Clyde, and Adolph, playing sandlot ball with the Mobile Black Bears.

Ivy Griffin, a scout for the Cubs, went to Mobile to look over Hank Aaron's younger brother Tommie. He looked over Tommie, but saw something he liked about Billy's swing and concentrated instead on the green youngster. Franklin, meanwhile, had been signed by the Pittsburgh Pirates organization and told them about his kid brother.

The Pirates were about to offer Billy a $1,000 bonus, but were too late. Griffin had signed Billy, giving his dad a cigar and Billy a $25 bus ticket to Ponca City, Okla.

It was the first time the 18-year-old Williams had been away from home. He got off the bus and stood in the terminal in a daze. He was met by a middle-aged black named Mr. Reed, who took him to his home. The year was 1956 and only white ballplayers were allowed at the hotel.

Williams was no immediate smash at Class D Ponca City. He fell down chasing the first fly ball in his direction and appeared in only 13 games, getting four singles in 17 trips. He enjoyed Mrs. Reed's home cooking in Ponca City, but road trips were something else. The team traveled in station wagons and when they stopped at restaurants, Billy was left behind in the car. Sometimes his teammates forgot to bring him sandwiches.

In his second season at Ponca City, Billy batted .310, hit 17 homers, and drove in 95 runs. And it was only a 127-game schedule. From there he moved up the ladder to Pueblo, Burlington, and finally to San Antonio in 1959, where he teamed with Santo.

Suddenly, Billy's stomach started acting up. The blistering Texas heat made it feel worse than ever. Williams jumped the club in June, hopping a train and heading home. He spent a week fishing, relaxing, and swimming in his favorite spot at Eight Mile Creek.

Buck O'Neill, a scout and coach who has meant a great deal to the Cubs, was dispatched to bring him back alive. With the aid of Billy's father, Buck accomplished the mission.

"I was discouraged, I don't know why," said Williams. "I was young. I just felt like quitting, that's all. But Buck and my dad told me baseball was good for me, and I listened." The stomach problem was disclosed to be an ulcer.

After going on a proper diet, Billy wound up hitting .318 at San Antonio. He moved up to Ft. Worth and tore up the league, batting .476 in five games. Williams then received a call from the Cubs and was told to report to Wrigley Field. He arrived on Aug. 6, and was told by manager Bob Scheffing he would bat third in the lineup and play left field.

The Cubs were facing Jim Owens of the Philadelphia Phillies. Tony Taylor opened with a single and Jim Marshall sent him to third with another hit. That brought up the sinewy rookie, who stepped to the plate, spit in the air and took a swipe at the saliva with his bat. Perhaps some great expectorations would come from that habit.

Williams then slapped at the ball and was thrown out at first, Taylor scoring on the play. At least, he drove in a run in his first major league at bat. But mostly it was a look-see trial. "I would look out there and see the other guys playing," said Williams. He got into 18 games and batted only .152.

The Cubs didn't want Williams rusting on the bench. They sent him to Triple A Houston in 1960 where he had an up and down season. He went down, chasing a low liner in Louisville and suffered a shoulder injury. Then he fell into a slump, his average dropping to .150. Buffs' manager Enos Slaughter kept him in the lineup, but sent an SOS to the Cubs, who sent Hornsby to Houston. Williams had developed a hitch in his swing and was getting nothing but popups and strikeouts. Billy was also holding the bat straight up while waiting for the pitch. Hornsby instructed him to tilt it back . . . cocked and ready. "I kept at it and started hitting again," said Williams.

The Rajah stayed on and watched Williams from the stands. Billy would turn in Hornsby's direction and the old master would point toward his eyes, meaning, "Keep your eyes on the ball."

Hornsby then wired the Cubs: "Suggest you bring up Williams. Best hitter on team."

One of the Cub officials called Hornsby and said, "He's better than anyone else down there, huh?"

Hornsby shot back, "He's better than anyone up there."

Williams kept hitting line shots and wound up batting .323 with 26 homers and 80 RBI. He joined the Cubs in late August and displayed more poise and confidence. In a game against the Dodgers at the vast Coliseum, manager Lou Boudreau summoned Williams to hit against fastballing Stan Williams. Billy connected on a 1-1 count and met a fastball for a game-winning homer. It was the first of his 426 big league homers.

Then followed mass confusion. Cub owner P. K. Wrigley had a brainstorm. He did away with a manager and instituted a rotating coaching system in 1961. A normal manager would have placed Williams in left field and would go about worrying about the other positions. But, no.

The confused rookie was a pawn in the so-called College of Coaches. He was benched by one, restored to the lineup by another, and was switched around the outfield. Never a polished fielder, Billy misjudged a few fly balls and was labeled a defensive risk. In addition, his batting average fell to .143.

It wasn't until the middle of June, with some front-office interference by Cub GM John Holland, that Williams was restored to the lineup. He celebrated his birthday on June 15 by hitting a grand-slam homer in a 12-6 rout of the Giants at Candlestick Park. He then went on a binge with 10 hits in his next 19 trips and improved steadily afield. Williams was a regular at last.

Williams finished with a .278 average. He had 20 doubles, 7 triples, 25 homers, scored 75 runs, and drove in 86. That was good enough to beat out Joe Torre of the Braves for National League Rookie of the Year honors.

In addition, his 25 homers bettered the Cubs' previous first-year mark of 19 set in 1954 by Ernie Banks. Williams joined Banks, Santo, and George Altman as the team's fearsome foursome. Banks cranked 29 homers, Altman 27, and Santo 23, giving the quartet 104. But alas, the team lacked pitching, speed, and was weak up the middle. The Cubs had no manager and wound up with a 64-90 record.

"I believe he's going to win the batting championship and he'll rank as one of the greatest in the game," predicted Banks. "He's got that confidence and that is more than half the battle at the plate."

Sophomore jinx? Forget it. Billy boosted his average to .298, hit 22 homers, and batted home 98 runs in 1962. And he remained modest and unassuming. His locker flanked Banks and Santo and he was overshadowed by the pair. Williams didn't go for flashy cars or fancy clothes. He remained a small-town lad.

When the season would end, Williams would head back to Alabama and go fishing on the Mobile River. "When I fish I can think about things . . . such as how some of those pitchers got me out," said Williams. "While I wait for some fish to bite, I figured out how some of those pitchers got me on the hook."

The 1963 season was a significant one for Williams. On Sept. 22, 1963, Williams went hitless in five at bats. But little did he suspect he would play the next 1,116 without missing a game.

Billy Williams resembled Ted Williams at the outset of the 1964 season. He tore the league apart in the merry month of May, batting a blistering .455 with 51 hits. That earned Billy a berth on the All-Star team.

As usual, his big moment went unnoticed. Billy poled a long homer off pitcher John Wyatt, but someone pushed the wrong button and that long blast wasn't seen by the TV audience. It was the first run in a 7-4 National League victory.

And when Williams hit his 100th career homer, it was "Ernie Banks Day." Billy finally reached the coveted .300 mark, finishing the season with a .312 average. In addition, his 33 homers tied him with Bill Nicholson for the club record for a left-handed swinger.

In 1965 Williams, Banks and Santo really tampered with the pitchers. The three combined for 315 RBI with Williams getting 108; Banks, 106; and Santo, 101. Williams even tampered with Dodger pitching great Sandy Koufax.

Sandy the Dandy tossed a perfect game against the Cubs in Los Angeles on Sept. 9, striking out 14 batters. Williams had two strikeouts and a fly out. Cub pitcher, Bob Hendley, meanwhile allowed only one hit in the 1-0 defeat.

Koufax and Hendley hooked up again five days later at Wrigley Field. The game was scoreless going into the sixth inning. Williams and Cub second baseman Glenn Beckert were in the on-deck circle. Billy turned to Glenn and said, "Beck, I think I've got it figured out. You get on base and we'll have a couple of runs."

Beckert then walked and Williams followed with a homer, the Cubs winning 2-1 for their first triumph over Koufax in three years. "The first three times up he started me off with a fastball," said Williams. "He threw it in the same place. I didn't get the bat all the way around, so I went with it a little bit and hit it to left field."

Billy finished the season topping the Cubs in every offensive category. He had 115 runs scored, 203 hits, 365 total bases, 39 doubles, 6 triples, 34 homers, 108 RBI, and a .315 average. His 34 homers broke his tie with Nicholson.

The 1966 season brought on Leo Durocher as Cub manager. Durocher started cleaning out the deadwood, but left Billy in the outfield and forgot about him. "He's got a picture-perfect swing," snapped Leo. "Why should I tamper with him?"

The Cubs were on the upward trend with Durocher, who penciled the name Williams in the lineup every game. Billy eventually passed Richie Ashburn's record of 694 consecutive games for an outfielder. When he appeared in his 718th game, he moved ahead of Banks as the all-time Cub iron man.

Durocher excused Williams from all pregame practice and ordered him to stay away from the ballpark until about 45 minutes before game time. "I'm interested in conserving his energy," snapped Durocher. "Why waste it running around in the humid heat two hours before the game?"

Williams responded with some big games for Leo. He collected six hits in nine trips in one doubleheader against the Cardinals, hitting for the cycle with a single, double, triple, and homer in the second game on July 17, 1966.

Perhaps his biggest binge was in September 1968 when he collected 10 hits in 14 at bats against the Phillies and Mets, including five homers in two games to tie a major league record.

Williams carried his batting spree into the fabled 1969 season. After Willie Smith won the Cub opener with an extra-inning homer, Williams pounded out four successive doubles to clobber the Phillies 11-3 in the second game. The Cubs then went into orbit, winning 32 of their first 48 games.

Williams was nearing Stan Musial's National League record of 895 consecutive games. June 29 was designated "Billy Williams Day" at Wrigley Field. A crowd of 41,060 shoe-horned its way into the old ivy-vined ballpark to see Williams tie and surpass The Man in a doubleheader against the Cardinals.

Fergie Jenkins and Bob Gibson were hooked in a scoreless duel until Williams doubled and was singled home by Banks. Willie Smith added a two-run homer and the Cubs won the opener. Williams had tied Musial.

Between games, Billy sheepishly headed for home plate with his wife and four daughters. He was nervous and choked up when he received a car, a pool table, and other gifts. Then he was presented with a rod and reel from the writers and a motorboat from his teammates. Ah, fishing!

In the second contest, Banks hit a three-run homer, Santo had a homer and drove in five runs. And Williams? He had two singles, a double, and a triple.

All he needed was a homer to hit for the cycle again. Billy swung from the heels and struck out. Still, the crowd rose and gave him a thundering ovation. The National League iron man title was his.

Cub pennant fever spread into August. Besides his timely hitting, Williams was almost flawless afield. His catch against the vines on Aug. 19 saved Ken Holtzman's no-hitter. It came in the seventh inning against the Braves' Hank Aaron at Wrigley Field.

Hank hammered a towering fly that looked like a Waveland Avenue wallop. Instead, the wind caught hold of it. Williams, with his back against the vines at the curvature of the left field wall, timed his leap and grabbed the ball for the game-saver.

Later came the turnabout. The Cubs went sour in September and the Mets surged past them into first place. Williams was one of the few Cubs who didn't fall apart. In a Sept. 5 game against the Pirates, the Cubs lost 9-2. Williams had two homers and two doubles, the only four hits off Pittsburgh pitcher Steve Blass.

The 1970 season saw the end of Billy's consecutive-game string. On April 30 he reached the 1,000-game milestone in Atlanta. The scoreboard flashed "Congratulations, Billy" as Williams doffed his cap. Only two players (Lou Gehrig, 2,130 and Everett Scott, 1,307, both American Leaguers) topped the 1,000 mark.

The end game came on Sept. 3 against the Phillies at Wrigley Field. Durocher scratched Billy's name from the lineup. For trivia buffs, Williams was replaced in left field by the redoubtable Cleo James.

The crowd kept chanting, "We want Billy," as Fergie Jenkins, Billy's roommate, downed the Phillies 7-2. The tension and strain was over. "It was my decision, not Durocher's," said Williams.

The feat failed to grab the headlines. On that day, Vince Lombardi, the coach who built the Green Bay Packers into a legend, had died of cancer.

That season was Billy's best offensively. He led the league in total bases with 373, tied Pete Rose for first in base hits with 205, finished second to Johnny Bench in homers (45 to 42) and runs batted in (148 to 129), and his 137 runs scored were the most in the league since Chuck Klein had 152 in 1932. In addition, Williams batted a career high .322.

Billy started the 1971 season off with a bang, breaking up another Gibson-Jenkins pitching duel with a 10th-inning homer for a 2-1 victory at Wrigley Field. But his average "tumbled" to .301.

He atoned for that by winning his first batting title in 1972 with a .333 average. His best effort was eight-for-eight in a doubleheader against Houston. He also slugged .606, the highest for a Cub since the heyday of Ernie Banks.

It was Williams, not Banks or Santo,who became the first Cub to sign a $100,000 contract. He was also the first Cub to sport a mustache since Bobby Lowe in 1903.

Whitey Lockman, the new Cub manager, experimented with Williams at first base. At best it could be said he gave it a noble try. The iron man was showing a bit of rust. His average dipped to the .280s.

The Cubs, meanwhile, were shipping out their name players. Williams was sent to the Oakland A's on Oct. 23, 1974, for pitchers Darold Knowles, Bob Locker, and a young second baseman named Manny Trillo. The trade was advantageous for both sides. The Cubs plugged an infield gap with Trillo, while Williams sipped his first champagne as the A's won a division title in 1975. But he no longer was Billy the Kid. After batting .244 and .211, Williams drew his A's release.

He returned to the Cubs for a short time as a batting instructor.

In his splendid career, Williams batted .290, with 2,711 hits, 426 home runs, and 1,475 RBI.

RON SANTO

SANTO, RONALD EDWARD
B. Feb. 25, 1940, Seattle, Wash.
BR TR 6'0" 190 lb.

The Cubs have had many colorful and outstanding performers at third base—Ed Williamson, Heinie Zimmerman, Stan Hack, Bill Madlock, and more. None, however, handled the hot corner more tenaciously than Ron Santo during the 1960s and early '70s.

A Pacific Coast native, Ron was the product of an Italian-American father and a Swedish-American mother. In his playing days, he often kidded, "I'm half-Italian, half-Swede, and all American."

As a youth at Seattle's Franklin High School, Santo excelled at baseball and football and had a burning desire for victory. Emotional and occasionally explosive, he would sometimes rearrange locker doors with his fists after tough losses. During one summer, he was batboy for the Seattle Rainiers of the Pacific Coast League.

Santo had also caught the eye of Dave Kosher, an unofficial Cub talent scout. Upon graduation from high school in 1959, Ron was signed to a Cub contract. He joined the team with the loyalty of a bulldog. Optioned to the Cubs' Texas League farm club in San Antonio, he responded with a .327 average and 87 RBI. This earned him a ticket to the Cubs' Double A club in Houston the following spring.

During the winter, however, the Cubs had dealt away their aging third baseman, Al Dark, leaving a major gap in the infield. None of the replacements proved satisfactory. So with less than a year and a half of minor league training, Santo was ordered to the parent club.

It was June 26, 1960. Although exhausted from a lack of sleep after a last minute flight from Houston to Pittsburgh, Ron collected three hits and drove in five runs as the Cubs took two from the Pirates, 7-6 and 7-5. When he pulled into second base with a double, Pirate shortstop Dick Groat said, "You have a good swing, kid. Stay in there. You oughta be around a long time."

Sporting a flat-top haircut with slicked back fenders on the sides, Santo made an immediate hit with the leather-jacketed teenaged "greasers," who dominated the Wrigley Field bleachers during the late '50s and early '60s. More importantly, the third base job was his for keeps, and he protected it with his life. In 95 games he batted .251, drove home 44 runs, and was voted Chicago Rookie of the Year by the local baseball writers.

Sophomore jinx? Not for Santo. In 1961 he upped his totals to

.284, 23 homers, and 83 RBI, earning him the National League Sophomore of the Year honors. With his aggressive, take-charge attitude, Ron quickly earned the respect of everyone.

Following a subpar 1962 season Santo came back in '63 to gain full-fledged stardom, which he credited to learning to hit to right field as well as left. Leading the club in batting with a .297 average, he also led in RBI with 99 and tied Billy Williams with 25 home runs.

Ron was selected to the All-Star team for the first time, and was named National League Player of the Month in June. During game one of a Memorial Day doubleheader, Santo, often kidded for his slowness afoot, even pulled a successful double steal with Williams. For the contest, Ron was five-for-six and scored twice as the Cubs slammed the door on the Mets 12-0, thanks to a 10-run fourth inning.

With Santo's coming of age, the team responded accordingly, winning 23 more games in 1963 than in the year previous. Their 82-80 record was the best by a Cub team since 1946.

The Cubs slipped back to eighth place in 1964, but Santo enjoyed the best overall season of his career.

Although he finished several notches down in the MVP Award voting to fellow third baseman Ken Boyer, Ron outdid the St. Louis superstar in nearly every category—batting, .313 to .295; doubles, 33 to 30; triples, 13 to 10; home runs, 30 to 24; putouts at third base, 156 to 131; assists, 367 to 337; fewer errors, 20 to 24; and fielding average, .963 to .951. Boyer exceeded Santo only in RBI, 119 to 114; and runs scored, 100 to 94. In addition, Ron homered at least once in every park in the league. Ken, nevertheless, had the advantage of playing with a world championship team.

With his first Gold Glove Award to his credit, Santo had established himself as the third baseman of the future. Diving after smashes that no one else would wave a finger at, Ron and his pinstriped Cub uniform looked like they had been through six months of trench warfare by the fourth inning of every game.

His specialty was the bare-handed spear of a hard bounder, charging in like a bull and firing to first for the out. During his spare time, Ron had opened a pizzeria in Park Ridge. After heroic Cub victories, he would frequently pick up the tab for the entire house.

In 1965 Santo was named Cub captain at age 25, the youngest Cub player so named. By July 12 he was carrying his heroics to the national level. The scene was the All-Star Game at Metropolitan Stadium in Bloomington, Minn., as Ron's seventh-inning single drove Willie Mays across the plate for the winning run in a 6-5 National League win. Although Ron did not match his 1964 totals, he still came through with a .285 average, 33 homers, and 101 RBI, thanks to a strong second half.

That winter, Leo Durocher was hired as Cub manager, thereby scrapping the unsuccessful College of Coaches. Santo was wild with enthusiasm. "It's the greatest thing that's ever happened to me, and the most exciting. He's got me so steamed up with great expectations, I can hardly sleep nights thinking of getting to camp.

"Put me on record. I'm a Leo Durocher-type ballplayer . . .

"What are we? Well, for one thing we're first division for sure. And if we get a good start, we're not going to settle for just that. We'll settle for nothing less than just plain first . . . because if once we get our teeth into first, they're going to have to kill us to get us out of there."

Although the Cubs finished 10th in 1966, Santo had the kind of year that first place teams are made of . . . when the rest of the team follows in the right footsteps. Batting .312, he stroked 30 homers, drove in 94 Cubs, and set a 20th century club high by hitting safely in 28 consecutive games from May 31 through July 4.

In fact, the few games the Cubs did win were largely due to Ron's clutch hitting. The Braves were in town May 28, and the score was tied 5-5 in the bottom of the 12th. With two men on, Santo jacked one out of the park for a sudden-death 8-5 victory. The following day he performed an encore by homering in the bottom of the 10th to provide a 3-2 edge over Atlanta. It was that way all year.

The 1967 season, however, was something else. The Cubs soared all the way to third to crash out of the second division for the first time in 21 years as placards reading "Durocher for Mayor" began popping up in Wrigley Field. Once again, captain Ron led the charge with a .300 average, 31 homers, 98 RBI, and 107 runs scored.

Ron's glove was slicker than ever also. He established a record with 393 assists at third base, since broken by Mike Schmidt of the Phillies in 1974 with 404. His best day came May 9 as he slapped five straight singles off Giant pitching to lead the Cubs to a 10-2 win at Chicago.

Although the Cubs pulled in third again in '68, Santo limped home with a .246 average, his worst in six years. Still he won his fifth straight Gold Glove Award. After that came the memorable season that would have been better off forgotten.

Sparked by seven victories in their first eight games, the Cubs of 1969 pulled into an early lead and increased it steadily. Santo batted .395 in the month of June. Suddenly, Wrigley Field was the place to be seen, even for lakefront trendies who knew nothing about baseball.

After one 10-inning win over the Pirates on a Jim Hickman homer, Santo clicked his heels three times on his way to the Wrigley Field clubhouse. Although Eastern writers bad-mouthed it as "bush," the victory dance was a hit with euphoric Cub fans, and it became part of Ron's routine whenever the Cubs won.

Shortly afterward occurred an incident that should have been quickly forgotten, but instead did much to damage Santo's reputation. Center fielder Don Young missed two easy fly balls July 8 in a 4-3, ninth-inning loss to the Mets. Durocher fumed and so did Santo. "Young was just thinking of himself," Ron complained.

"He got his head down, worrying about his batting average and not about winning the game. All right, he can keep his head down, and he can keep on going right out of sight for all I care. We don't need that sort of thing."

In a moment of anger, Ron had said things he did not mean.

Although Santo made a public apology the following day, a handful of thick-headed boobirds never let him live it down, making him their scapegoat for the rest of his career. Worse yet, the Cubs fell apart, losing the pennant to the hated upstart Mets by eight games.

Although Santo finished at .289 with 29 homers and 123 RBI—a career high—it was small consolation after the September swoon. There was no more heel-clicking at the end of this bittersweet year.

The following year was more of the same. The Cubs won 11 straight during April and May, only to lose 12 in a row a couple of weeks later, and ultimately finished second again. Santo, who dropped to .267, still led the club in RBI with 114 and in game-winning RBI with 17, a fact that his critics conveniently lost sight of.

In September, when the club was struggling to keep afloat, Ron came through with a .375 mark. The greatest day of his career had come July 6, in a doubleheader against Montreal. In the first game his two-run homer provided the margin in a 3-2 triumph. In the nightcap he knocked both a grand slam and a two-run blast, driving in eight runs to power the Cubs to a 14-2 victory.

By now Santo was slowing up a bit at third. Fans began to joke about his "pizza belly." Relations with Leo Durocher had cooled to an off-again, on-again state, but the extent of the split was exaggerated by Durocher's enemies in the press.

Aug. 28, 1971, was set aside as Ron Santo Day at Wrigley Field. Shortly after, it was revealed that Ron had been a lifelong diabetic. Santo arranged for the proceeds to go to the Diabetic Association of Chicago. The outing was a financial success with 34,988 on hand at the park, but the Braves put a damper on the affair by nipping the Cubs 4-3.

From that point on, the personal milestones came with ease. Santo's 300th career home run came Sept. 21 as rookie Burt Hooton blanked the Mets 3-0. Ron celebrated his 2,000th hit Aug. 26, 1972, a three-run homer that propelled the Cubs to a 10-9 win over the Giants. Santo upped his average to .302 in 1972, but the longed-for Cub pennant remained elusive. In spite of a strong second half, the Cubs finished second, 11 games behind the division champion Pirates.

The soft-spoken Whitey Lockman had replaced the fiery Durocher as Cub field boss, but in 1973 the frustrations went from bad to worse. From first place and a 4½-game lead July 10, the Cubs tumbled to fifth place as owner P. K. Wrigley announced that he would "back up the truck."

Santo, who refused to pull up roots from Chicago, was traded to the White Sox. Reduced to the role of a part-time second baseman, Santo batted only .221 in 1974. Calling it quits while he was ahead, Santo retired with 2,254 hits, a .277 average, and 342 home runs. As a third baseman, he led the league in assists seven consecutive years, putouts seven seasons (six consecutive) and double plays six times.

Through smart business investments—namely oil and insurance—Ron had become a millionaire on his own. He will always be remembered as one of the Cubs' all-time gutsiest players.

DON KESSINGER

KESSINGER, DONALD EULON
B. July 17, 1942, Forrest City, Ark.
BB TR 6'1" 170 lb.

Back in 1948 the Cubs thought they had the next Marty Marion in shortstop Ron Smalley. They were wrong. However, 20 years later they had Marion in the person of Don Kessinger, whose road to stardom was not an easy one.

An all-conference baseball and basketball star at the University of Mississippi, the slender Kessinger signed with the Cubs upon his graduation in 1964. He was placed in Fort Worth, where he batted a paltry .236 in 77 games. The Cubs brought him up to Chicago at the end of the year for a brief trial, but were unimpressed, so it was back to Texas the following spring.

The Cubs began the 1965 season with Roberto Pena at shortstop, but after Pena made 17 errors in his first 51 games, Kessinger was hastily recalled under the principle of "any port in a storm." Nervous and uneasy, he committed nine errors in his first 11 contests.

Although Don made history by participating in three triple plays, he finished the season with 28 errors, a .201 batting average, and only 14 runs driven in. It was hardly an indication of great things to come.

In 1966 Leo Durocher was appointed Cub manager, and along with him came Pete Reiser as batting coach. Reiser took Kessinger under his wing and taught him to become a switch-hitter. "That saved my career," said Don, after jacking his batting average up to .274. Meanwhile, the infield of Ron Santo at third, Kessinger at short, Glenn Beckert at second, and Ernie Banks at first was molding into one of the greatest in Cub history.

As Don's defensive skills improved, the team soared to third place in 1967. For the first time in 22 years, the Cubs led the National League in fielding. Both performances were repeated in '68.

By now Don was covering ground as if it were going out of style, leading the league in assists (573), double plays (97), and total chances per game (5.5). Occasionally, he helped win games with his bat also. On Aug. 11 he gathered five hits in seven trips as the Cubs gained a second wind to take the Reds 8-5 in 15 innings.

The 1969 season appeared to be the year of the Cub. Kessinger hit well over .300 into midseason, setting a big league seasonal high by fielding 54 consecutive games at short without an error (since broken). He reached base in each of the Cubs' first 41 games, and the entire Cub infield was selected for the All-Star team.

But as the team went, so did Kessinger, regardless of cause and effect relationship. Worn out from overwork and uptight from pressure by the surging Mets, Don slid to a .273 mark by the year's sour end as the Cubs dropped to second behind the New York usurpers.

Even so, he paced the club with 38 doubles and 109 runs scored. Furthermore, his glove was stickier than ever. He topped the league in every defensive category: percentage (.976), games (157), fewest errors (20), total chances (828), putouts (266), assists (542), and double plays (101).

To prove it was no fluke, he repeated the following season with his second straight Gold Glove Award. Thanks to competent base running, his 14 triples in 1970 were the most by a Cub player since Phil Cavarretta had 15 in 1944. But he would have swapped it all for a Cub pennant as the team again pulled in second.

Although the Cubs were beginning to show signs of age in 1971 as they dropped to third place, it was a season of personal milestones for the Cub shortstop. On June 17 Don became only the 62nd player in National League history to pick up six hits in a game, collecting a double and scoring three times, including the game winner, as the Cubs sneaked by the Cardinals 7-6 in 10 innings. Not since 1937, when Frank Demaree pulled it off, had a Cub collected six hits in a single contest.

On Aug. 21 he appeared in his 1,000th major league game. By coincidence, it was Glenn Beckert's millenium game also. Aug. 31 was another memorable day. Kessinger went five-for-six and drove home the winning run to beat the Expos 7-6 in 10 innings. Sept. 22 was the occasion of his 1,000th career hit.

In the summer of 1972 Kess found himself on the National League All-Star team for the fifth consecutive year. That July 24 Whitey Lockman replaced Leo Durocher as Cub manager. Leo's hard line approach had inspired some players to the ultimate, while rubbing others the wrong way, Kessinger included.

Don later admitted that he had been on the verge of stomach ulcers. After the change of chiefs, the Cubs rallied to finish a strong second. Don's batting percentage reached his earlier high of .274.

In 1973 the Cubs were hoping for their last hurrah, but the frustration went from bad to worse. Leading the league with a 46-31 record on June 29, the Cubs ran out of gas completely, finishing in fifth, seven games below .500.

It was then that owner Phil Wrigley, convinced that the team could no longer win, with Durocher or without, began the rummage sale. The following year, the Cubs finished dead last. Kessinger was their only representative on the All-Star squad.

By 1975 Don was the last survivor of the near-great 1969 Cub roster. His infield partners were now Andy Thornton at first,

Manny Trillo at second, and Bill Madlock at third. That year witnessed another milestone for Kessinger as he surpassed Joe Tinker's record for most games played at shortstop in a Cub uniform.

Nevertheless, Kessinger's head was soon on the chopping block too. On Dec. 28, 1975, he was traded to the Cardinals for pitcher Mike Garman, in another classic example of the Cubs giving up more than they received.

Now on the decline, Don lasted a season and a half with St. Louis before being sold to the White Sox on Aug. 20, 1977. The year after, still playing regularly, he was one of the few bright spots on an otherwise lackluster Sox defense.

Don was named White Sox manager in 1979, but he did not like the job and resigned before the season ended. The team had won 46 and lost 60. Upon his resignation, Kessinger retired as a player also.

In his career, Don was a .252 hitter with 1,931 hits. Never known for his power, he had a home run output of 14. However, his 1,618 games at shortstop set a Cub record, which is likely to be around for quite awhile.

GLENN BECKERT

BECKERT, GLENN ALFRED
B. Oct. 12, 1940, Pittsburgh, Pa.
BR TR 6'1" 190 lb.

The Chicago baseball writers held their annual Diamond Dinner at the Palmer House in the winter of 1966 and the main attractions were Mickey Mantle and Sandy Koufax. Also on the dais were Leo Durocher, the new manager of the Cubs, and Eddie Stanky, who was making his White Sox managerial debut.

All were in midseason form. But the quip of the evening belonged to Glenn Beckert, a Cub second baseman who was accepting the Chicago Rookie of the Year Award. "It's very seldom a .240 hitter gets to the speaker's table," said Beckert. "But Mr. Durocher's here, so I'm not alone."

Stanky turned to Durocher and whispered, "This boy must have a five-year contract. Can you imagine me saying that to you when we were with the Dodgers?"

Leo just beamed. He was new to the Cubs, but he had a gut feeling the team was set at second base. From that night on, Beckert probably was Durocher's favorite Cub. He was his kind of player.

As a youngster, Beckert was always small. "I'll bet I didn't weigh more than 140 pounds when I graduated high school," said Beckert. Nevertheless, he was all-city in baseball and basketball at Pittsburgh's Perry High.

He quickly added height and weight when he entered Allegheny College and gained recognition as an outstanding shortstop under coach Mike Garbark, who was a Cub backup catcher to Gabby Hartnett in 1938.

Beckert, now 6'1" and 190 pounds, attracted many scouts and

accepted an invitation to work out at Yankee Stadium, all expenses paid. He turned down a Yankees' bonus offer because he promised his father he would finish college. When he returned to school, he received a shock. He was ruled ineligible in sports for accepting expenses from the Yankees.

Beckert stayed in college and graduated in 1961 with a degree in political science. He then accepted an $8,000 bonus from the Boston Red Sox. After hitting .280 at Waterloo, Beckert was thrown into the minor league draft because the Red Sox felt they had a better prospect at shortstop named Rico Petrocelli.

In December 1962 the Cubs claimed Beckert in the draft for a paltry $8,000. Glenn spent the next two seasons in the minors, hitting .288 at Wenatchee and .277 at Salt Lake City. Then tragedy struck.

Ken Hubbs, the Cubs' fine young second baseman, was killed in a private plane crash. Beckert was hustled to the winter instructional league to learn to make the pivot and to fill Ken's shoes.

By the start of 1965 Beckert was the Cubs' second baseman. In his first major league at bat he faced fireballing Bob Gibson of the St. Louis Cardinals and struck out on three pitches. He performed creditably afield, but his hitting was lamentable. His average kept sliding lower and lower as he tried harder and harder.

In mid-August his average was down to .219. "I was swinging too hard," recalled Beckert. "Then I stopped thinking about home runs." He worked to control his swing. He choked up on the bat two inches, started to make more contact, and began punching the ball to all fields. The result? He hit safety in 18 of the team's last 20 games and added 20 points to his average.

Beckert also benefited by the arrival of a raw, rangy shortstop from Dallas-Ft. Worth in midseason. His name was Don Kessinger. A new double-play combination was born.

Through the years the Cubs thrived on famed double-play combos. There were Tinker and Evers, followed by Herman and Jurges, then Banks and Baker, and now Kessinger and Beckert. "They are going to play and I'm going to give them every possible opportunity to play together," said Durocher.

For the next eight seasons, Beckert and Kessinger covered the Cubs' keystone. Kessinger would bat leadoff with Beckert second. Then would follow sluggers Billy Williams, Ron Santo, and Ernie Banks.

The two even combined for a baseball rarity. They both played their 1,000th major league game the same day—Aug. 21, 1971.

Although the teenaged female fans thought Beckert looked like Paul Newman with his baby-blue eyes, opposing pitchers eyed him differently. They found him to be the toughest hitter to strike out in either league. In 1965 he struck out only 36 times in 656 at bats. But that was only the beginning.

Beckert led the league in fewest strikeouts the next five seasons, highlighted by the 1968 season when he went to the plate 643 times and fanned 20 times for a phenomenal average of one strikeout every 32.15 trips.

In addition, Beckert was the leading streak hitter on the club. Three times he hit safely in 20 or more consecutive games. His top total was a 27-game string in 1968. Between his streaks and strikes, Beckert was also a student of the bat stroke.

In a game against the Phillies on July 16, 1968, Beckert singled home the lead run in the sixth inning. Then in the eighth inning, he singled, stole second, and scored the go-ahead run on Santo's single. But the Phillies battled back to tie the score.

Finally, in the 12th inning, Al Spangler walked and Adolfo Phillips ran for him. Beckert twice tried, unsuccessfully, to bunt the runner along. Then he noticed the third baseman creeping in. Beckert faked a bunt, then slashed the ball past him and brought Phillips chugging home with the winning run.

When Beckert got on the team bus after the game, the rest of the club gave him an ovation. "He'll beat you so many ways, running, hitting, fielding, stealing a base," said Durocher. "He's a hustler. He battles the heart out of you. You may get him out, but he'll never stop battling you. Never. He'll knock down a house to win."

Cubs double-play combo Glenn Beckert and Don Kessinger both played their 1,000th game on the same day.

Beckert kept flirting with the coveted .300 batting average, but never attained it until the 1971 season. He was batting a brisk .342 when a thumb injury cut his season a month short. It happened on Sept. 3 in St. Louis. He ruptured tendons in his right thumb diving for a ball. He was knocked out of action and finished third behind Joe Torre and Ralph Garr for the batting crown.

Beckert's .342 average was the highest by a Cub second baseman since Rogers Hornsby hit .380 in 1929.

The Pittsburgh Kid also had something extra. Players call it guts. He went down several times in smashing pileups and he always seemed to be getting hit by big guys.

In 1965 he was hipped at home plate by Joe Torre, the Braves' 230-pound catcher, and sent sprawling. When Beckert tried to crawl back toward the plate, Torre accidentally spiked his hand while falling on him. The next day Glenn was a mess, but he played.

In another incident, muscular slugger Richie Allen of the Phillies jolted Beckert as Glenn attempted to pick up a slow-rolling grounder. Both fell in a heap. Beckert held the ball. Allen was out. And Beckert remained in the game.

Then there was a tension-packed 1-0 Cub victory over the Cardinals on April 16, 1969. In the seventh inning, Mike Shannon of the Cards plowed into Beckert at second base. Glenn was waiting with the ball, but Shannon tried to bowl him over and jar the ball loose. Beckert was slammed in the face and was carried off the field on a stretcher.

Shannon angrily threw his helmet as the partisan St. Louis crowd booed their own hometown product. Beckert was hospitalized overnight for observation, but returned to the lineup the next day sporting facial bruises and a cut lip.

Over the years, Beckert gained much-deserved honors. He was named the National League's All-Star second baseman four years in a row, starting in 1968. He won the Gold Glove Award in 1971 as the top fielding second baseman.

Durocher was supplanted as manager by Whitey Lockman in midseason 1972 after some stormy battles with his players. Beckert was not one of them. "I had my best years under Leo," said Beckert. "I can't criticize him."

Injuries began to take their toll on Beckert, who developed knee problems and an arthritic ankle. His batting average dropped along with his playing time the next two seasons.

The Cubs began to sweep out the old Durocher-era gang. Gone were pitchers Ken Holtzman, Bill Hands, and Fergie Jenkins, plus Banks, Santo, Williams, and the others.

Beckert was traded to the San Diego Padres for young outfielder Jerry Morales on Nov. 12, 1973. It was an advantageous deal for the Cubs. Morales became the Cubs' regular right fielder, while Beckert pounded the pines for the Padres. He bowed out with a .375 average, but that was only for nine games in 1975.

Beckert, who was called Bruno by his Cub teammates, had a career batting average of .283 while collecting 1,473 hits. His 243 strikeouts in 5,208 at bats averaged out to a strikeout every 21.3 trips.

KEN HOLTZMAN

HOLTZMAN, KENNETH DALE
B. Nov. 3, 1945, St. Louis, Mo.
BR TL 6'2" 185 lb.

When Ken Holtzman was a Cub rookie he was billed as the "Next Koufax." While his career wasn't as dandy as Sandy's, Holtzman did grab some limelight with two no-hitters, an unbeaten season, and four World Series triumphs.

In addition, Holtzman beat Koufax in their lone head-on duel, coming within three outs of a no-hitter. "I don't want to be the second Sandy Koufax," said the wiry left-hander. "I just want to be the first Ken Holtzman."

Young Ken, who possessed a live fastball, a sweeping curve, and a fine changeup, began pitching at age seven in the St. Louis suburb of University City. As a product of the Khoury League, Holtzman compiled a fantastic nine-season record.

He won 255 games and lost only 5—200 of those victories were shutouts and 50 were no-hitters. His record at University City High was 31-3 and he was selected by the big league scouts as the No. 1 college left-hander while at the University of Illinois.

Holtzman was picked by the Cubs in the fourth round of the 1965 draft and received an estimated $65,000 bonus. He was quickly brought up after fanning 114 batters in 86 minor league innings.

He was summoned from the bullpen to face the Giants late in the 1965 season. His first major league pitch was belted out of Wrigley Field by Jim Ray Hart. And the next batter, Tom Haller, slammed a long fly to center field. "I knew then I'd have to work hard to make the team," gulped the 20-year-old recruit.

But the Cubs were thin on pitching and manager Leo Durocher needed stiff competition for his gin rummy games. Holtzman got his first major league start on April 24, 1966. It was before a packed house at Dodger Stadium. His pitching opponent was Don Drysdale.

The boyish-looking Holtzman overcame the tension and pitched six shutout innings to beat the world champions 2-0. Durocher sent him to the clubhouse to lie down and rest as sinkerballer Ted Abernathy held the Dodgers to two hits in the remaining three innings.

It was another of those miserable seasons for the Cubs, who finished 10th in the 10-team league. Holtzman wound up as the Cubs' leading pitcher with 11 wins and 16 losses.

All season, Holtzman had been hoping to pitch against Koufax. It was like the young gunslinger trying to knock off the No. 1 guy. Holtzman got his chance in the Sunday finale of a four-game Cub-Dodger series. Saturday was the Jewish solemn day of Yom Kippur and neither was in uniform.

An hour before game time on Sunday Durocher and Holtzman sat across a foot locker, playing gin rummy in the clubhouse. Leo's mouth was working like a steam pump. "I needled him to make him mad," said Durocher, whose psychological tactics worked.

Holtzman went out and blitzed Koufax 2-1 before a surprised crowd of 21,659. Koufax allowed only four hits, but Holtzman was sharper. He went into the ninth inning with a no-hitter. Ground singles up the middle by Ducky Schofield and Maury Wills, sandwiched around a walk, broke up the no-hit bid. Durocher gave Holtzman a bonus—the four bucks he owed him from their card game.

The Cubs and Holtzman got off to a quick start in 1967. Ken won four in a row before being notified that his Illinois National Guard unit was to embark on a six-month tour of duty. The Cubs gave Holtzman a 20-gun salute, beating the Dodgers 20-3 at Wrigley Field on May 21. Holtzman thus departed for Fort Polk, La., with a 5-0 record.

Pvt. Holtzman was soon transferred to Fort Sam Houston, Tex. The Cubs learned that their prize lefty might be available for weekend passes and dispatched scout Elvin Tappe, a former catcher, to work out with Holtzman during off-duty hours.

Following a two-month layoff Holtzman returned on Aug. 13 and defeated the Phillies 6-2 before a jammed house of 32,750 at Wrigley Field. He was granted three more weekend passes, won all three games, and finished the season with a 9-0 record.

The 1968 season was a bit disappointing for Holtzman. He was only 11-14. The military had a hand again, taking him away from the team 10 times. Still, in one 10-day span he pitched three successive shutouts.

Then came bittersweet 1969. The Cubs made their big pennant

push and Holtzman won 17 games. But their big guns of August soon turned to September mourn. When the dust of battle had cleared, the New York Mets held the pennant aloft while the Cubs waved the flag of surrender.

Holtzman, however, had his big day on Aug. 20, 1969. He pitched a no-hitter as 41,033 shoehorned into Wrigley Field. He was helped by a number of scintillating plays and a 16 mph wind blowing in from center field.

Ron Santo's two-run homer off Phil Niekro established an early lead for the Cubs. From then on all attention was focused on Holtzman, who rolled on, inning after inning without allowing a hit.

In the sixth inning Hank Aaron, baseball's quickest wrists, lashed his bat against an inside fastball. "I thought it was going right out of the city," sighed Holtzman. Aaron broke into his home run trot. Then halfway to second he stopped.

The wind was blowing the ball back. Cub left fielder Billy Williams, his back brushing the left field well wall, reached to glove the baseball. It preserved the shutout, the no-hitter, and sent Aaron back to the dugout muttering to himself.

There was more suspense upcoming. The last batter standing between Holtzman and eternal fame was Aaron again. It was now two out and a full count on Aaron. Holtzman whipped across a fastball, about knee high, and Aaron cracked a sharp grounder to second baseman Glenn Beckert, who threw him out. Before the ball got to first base, Holtzman was swarmed under by jubilant Cubs. Oddly, in that 3-0 triumph, Holtzman failed to fan a single batter.

The 1970 season was an instant replay. Holtzman again won 17, but the Cubs came up short again, bowing this time to the Pirates. Grumbling became widespread between Durocher and his players. Holtzman no longer was Durocher's pet partner for gin rummy. He did pitch a one-hitter against the Giants at San Francisco. Kenny held the Giants hitless until one out in the eighth inning when the light-hitting Hal Lanier slapped a clean single to center. There was little tension as the Cubs romped 15-0.

Holtzman fell entirely out of favor the following season, winning only 9 and dropping 15. Durocher even bypassed Holtzman in the late season pitching rotation. But there was one bright spot—another no-hitter.

It came on June 3, 1971, at Cincinnati's Riverfront Stadium. Holtzman found a worthy pitching opponent in Gary Nolan, who allowed an unearned run in the third inning before losing 1-0.

As in the first no-hitter, Holtzman was aided by a fine play in the outfield. The little-known Brock Davis raced into right center to haul down George Foster's long drive in the seventh inning. Holtzman was strongest at the finish, striking out three of the last four batters, including the dangerous Lee May for the final out. Even Durocher was delighted. He wrapped his arms around Holtzman, who was tired and shocked.

It was no shock when Holtzman was traded to the Oakland A's for outfielder Rick Monday on Nov. 29, 1971. Kenny was finally on a winner. The A's, with a cast of unforgettable stars such as Reggie Jackson, Catfish Hunter, Vida Blue, Joe Rudi, Rollie Fingers, and Sal Bando, fought and snarled their way to three straight World Series triumphs from 1972 through '74.

Holtzman won 19, 20, and 19 and registered four series victories. In addition, he batted .667 and .500 in the last two series, clubbing three doubles and a homer.

The A's failed to win a pennant in 1975 and Holtzman failed by one pitch of his third no-hitter at Oakland on June 8. He just missed with two out and two strikes on Tom Veryzer, who ripped the ball beyond the reach of center fielder Billy North's desperate lunge. Kenny settled for a one-hit, 4-0 victory over the Tigers. Despite winning 18 games that season, Holtzman was unhappy with A's owner Charles O. Finley. The two constantly hassled over contract negotiations and Holtzman wanted out. He got his wish on April 2, 1976. Holtzman was sent to the Orioles along with Jackson for Don Baylor and Mike Torrez.

His stay in Baltimore was short. Two months later he was part of a 10-player deal with the New York Yankees. Holtzman found little happiness in Yankee pinstripes. He was used sparingly by manager Billy Martin and didn't pitch a single inning in the World Series of 1976 or '77.

There was an obvious coolness between Martin and Holtzman that was never revealed. The end came on June 10, 1978, when Holtzman was shipped back to the Cubs for a player to be named later. That player turned out to be relief pitcher Ron Davis. So much for Cub deals.

Anyway, Holtzman was unleashed from the Yankee doghouse and even welcomed the return to Wrigley Field, where he once moaned, "I hate this ballpark. It stinks. I don't ever want to pitch here again or anywhere else for the Cubs."

Holtzman's first assignment was a relief chore against the Reds at Cincinnati. He relieved Rick Reuschel in the late innings and earned a save by inducing the dangerous George Foster to ground out for the final out.

Holtzman, however, was at the end of his string. He was an occasional starter and retired at the conclusion of the 1979 season with a 174-150 record, nine more wins than the storied Koufax—but 85 more losses. His Cub record was 80-81.

BILL HANDS

HANDS, WILLIAM ALFRED
B. May 6, 1940, Rutherford, N.J.
BR TR 6'2" 185 lb.

Along with Fergie Jenkins and Ken Holtzman, pitcher Bill Hands was one of the Cubs big three that helped make them pennant contenders during the late 1960s and early '70s.

Signed by the Giants upon graduation from high school, Hands entered the Frisco farm chain in 1959, bumping along the minor league trail from Hastings to Fresno to Eugene to Springfield to Tacoma, back to Springfield, and back to Tacoma before finally hitting the parent club late in 1965. He lost his only two decisions.

That autumn there was a revival meeting in Chicago as P. K. Wrigley announced the hiring of the fiery Leo Durocher as the Cubs' new manager. Upon Leo the Lip's insistence, the Cubs traded Lindy McDaniel and Don Landrum to the Giants for Hands and catcher Randy Hundley on Dec. 2, 1965.

In his first year at Wrigley's friendly confines, Bill hardly looked like the answer to the Cubs' problems, finishing with a soggy 8-13 record and a 4.58 ERA. To make it more embarrassing, he failed to complete a single start.

Nevertheless, Durocher refused to give up on him, saying "Our scouts rated him as a can't miss prospect, and I'm sure they're right." In 1967, with the Cubs zooming to third place from the cellar, Bill was used mostly in long relief, posting a 7-8 season, which belied the effectiveness of his pitching. His 2.46 ERA was tops on the Cub staff, and he hurled his first career shutout.

As the Cubs continued their upward surge, so did Hands. With another third slot finish in '68, thanks to a strong second half, Hands matured as a pitcher, winning 16 and losing 10. His ERA was 2.88 while his four shutouts led the staff. With his fastball beginning to blaze, Bill reached a career high by fanning 12 Mets on May 5. Moreover, he developed remarkable control, walking only 36 batters in 259 innings.

In May, when Hands was 4-0, he was named Cub Player of the Month. During his rest days Bill became the clubhouse chess champion, defeating nearly all of his teammates.

Then came 1969, the year the Cubs won the pennant—almost. Working 300 innings, Bill contributed 20 victories and 14 losses. Although Fergie Jenkins won 21 and whiffed 273 batters, Hands was, in many ways, more effective. His 2.49 ERA was lowest among Cub pitchers, but more importantly, Hands was the jinx breaker of the team, halting losing streaks four times. When the team withered with the autumn leaves of September, Bill was the only starter still winning games on a regular basis. The Cubs had dropped eight straight when Bill stopped the Cardinals 5-1 on Sept. 12. Then the club lost three more before he clipped Montreal 5-4 in his next outing.

Earlier in the year, Hands snapped two five game losing streaks, beating Montreal 2-0 on June 20, and the hated Mets 6-2 on July 10. When he won his 20th game by beating the Pirates 3-1 on Sept. 28, he broke an 11-game Cub losing streak at Forbes Field that dated back to July 15, 1968. Bill's reward was being named Chicago Player of the Year by the Chicago baseball writers.

The following year, hampered by muscle spasms in his pitching arm, Bill slipped a bit, posting an 18-15 log as his ERA ballooned to 3.70. Against the pennant winning Big Red Machine from Cincinnati, however, he was 4-0. The 1971 campaign was a disaster for Hands as his total fell to 12-18, much of it due to poor support.

He enjoyed a comeback of sorts in '72, winning 11 and dropping 8, while trimming his ERA down to 2.99. That season he came his closest to pitching a no-hit game, holding the Expos to a solitary safety in a 3-0 victory Aug. 3. But Bill no longer possessed the stamina he once had, going only 189 innings.

That winter he, Joe Decker, and Bob Maneely were swapped to the Twins for Dave LaRoche, who went on to win nine games for the Cubs over two years.

Hands, though, had left his best years behind him as a Cub. After an unsuccessful season and a half in Minnesota, he was sent to the Texas Rangers, where he hung up his glove after the 1975 season.

Lifetime, Bill was 111-110 with a 3.35 ERA. As a Cub, Hands was 92-86.

RANDY HUNDLEY

HUNDLEY, CECIL RANDOLPH
B. June 1, 1942, Martinsville, Va.
BR TR 5'11"
170 lb.

Cecil Randolph Hundley is a name you normally would associate with the British diplomatic corps. This Hundley headed the Cubs' catching corps and ranked among baseball's iron men until his knees caved in.

Randy Hundley, a prematurely balding blond with long thin dark sideburns and flashing teeth, was lovingly called "the Rebel." The Martinsville (Va.) native had a drawl so deep you would think it came from his shoes. Fans in the left field bleachers at Wrigley Field would wave the Confederate flag when Hundley strode to the plate.

Hundley was originally signed by the San Francisco Giants as an 18-year-old catcher out of Bassett (Va.) High School, where he batted better than .500. The Giants were then on a bonus spree and Hundley signed for $90,000 in June 1960.

Randy knocked about the minors for several seasons without much progress. Giants' manager Herman Franks looked unfavorably on Hundley because "he's a one-handed catcher."

"My dad was a semipro catcher and he taught me to protect my hand that way," replied Hundley.

The Giants "unloaded" Hundley and pitcher Bill Hands to the Cubs on Dec. 2, 1965, for reliever Lindy McDaniel and outfielder Don Landrum. After the trade, Franks, a former catcher and .199 career hitter, said, "Hundley can catch, he can throw, and he can run, but he can't hit me if I walk in front of him."

The deal was engineered by new Cub manager Leo Durocher, who indicated Hundley would be his No. 1 catcher. Leo liked the way Hundley agitated the batters and the umpires behind the plate. "I want a catcher who hollers," growled the Lion.

It didn't take Hundley long to do his schtick. In the Cubs' first visit to Atlanta, Hundley stuck his bat in catcher Joe Torre's glove and Torre was charged with interference. Braves' manager Bobby Bragan yelled that Hundley did it deliberately. As an old-time catcher under Durocher, Bragan added, "I think it was a smart play."

Durocher just winked at the dastardly deed and said he didn't believe a rookie "kid" would do such a thing. Asked if he did it on purpose, Randy replied, "Yes."

He did it a month later, with Houston catcher John Bateman the victim, and it led to the winning run.

The umpires soon took notice of the brash rookie, who never swore, but knew how to needle them. "He's a good catcher and a lousy umpire," said one of the arbiters after spending a long afternoon with Randy making the calls behind the plate.

Hundley immediately became the Cubs' take-charge guy. Riding the bus after a tough loss, Hundley scolded the losing pitcher. "What was on your mind today?" drawled Randy. "You sure didn't have your mind on pitching." Durocher sat in the front of the bus and beamed.

"He makes this team look like a ballclub," said Durocher. "He's a professional behind the plate and everything seems to click more smoothly when he's catching."

Hundley surprised even Leo with his hitting. Coach Pete Reiser opened his stance. He drew marks in the batting cage for his feet and Randy started making contact.

On May 19, 1966, Hundley had a double and a triple in a 7-1 victory over the Astros. He even stole home. It probably was the first theft of home by a Cub catcher since the heyday of Johnny Kling at the turn of the century. Hundley did it by studying the time-consuming windup of Houston reliever Gary Kroll.

A month later, Hundley hit his first big league grand slam off Dodgers' ace Don Drysdale. When the season ended Hundley had 19 homers, the most by a Cub catcher since Gabby Hartnett hit 22 in 1934. He also chipped in with 63 RBI.

But it was his solid catching that drew the raves. He caught 149 games, a record for a rookie catcher, and he was named to the all-rookie team. However, there was one drawback. The long hot summer took its toll. The lean and hungry Hundley dropped 17 pounds off his 170-pound frame.

The following season the Cubs jumped from last to third and Hundley was a vital factor. He set a league record with only four errors and four passed balls in 152 games behind the plate and won the Gold Glove as the outstanding catcher.

Durocher called Hundley his quarterback. "Leo feels I should take charge out there," said Hundley. "As catcher, everything is in front of me and I can see all the plays develop. I like it because I'm in the game every moment."

Hundley was the only catcher in either league to catch both ends of doubleheaders. "It doesn't help if I sit on the bench and rest," said Hundley. "I feel funny there and it tires me out if I'm not playing," he added after his 12th-inning single beat the Dodgers on Sept. 7, 1967.

The Cubs moved up to second in 1968 with Hundley catching a major league record 160 games. Leo just couldn't remove him from the lineup. "His indispensable quality is fierce, aggressive leadership on the field. He advises, praises, scolds, and browbeats the pitchers and hollers at the infielders to keep them alert," said Durocher.

Hundley became the first backstop to catch 150 or more games three years in a row. As the Cubs made their pennant push in 1969, Randy caught 151 games and hit 18 homers, but was dog-tired in the dog days of the season.

As the backbone of the ballclub, Hundley caught 612 of 624 games in four seasons. Then it happened. Carl Taylor, a 212-pound Cardinals' outfielder collided with Hundley at the plate on April 21, 1970. As usual, Hundley held his ground and prevented Taylor from scoring.

But Randy suffered torn cartilage in his left knee that required surgery. He was sidelined until Aug. 3, missing 89 games. "He's the one guy we can't compensate for," moaned Leo, whose pennant hopes went with Hundley's injury.

The hex struck again during spring training. Hundley hurt his right knee in a routine rundown play. He stumbled, chasing an Angels' baserunner back to third. As he lay sprawled in the dirt, he let out a cry of anguish. "Oh, my knee, my knee." He was carried off the field.

It was diagnosed as a severe sprain and the knee was placed in a cast. Hundley missed the Cub opener and sat restlessly through the first month of the season. He kept pestering Durocher to let him play. Leo relented and Randy returned on May 12.

He played flawlessly afield and even got a single, but reinjured the knee three days later and was sidelined for two weeks. The Rebel returned again on May 27, wearing a special knee brace and said he was available for pinch-hitting.

He got his wish, stepping to the plate as a pinch hitter, he hit a pop fly and went down in a heap. Blood and fluid flowed from the knee and he was carted off the field on a stretcher.

This time it was diagnosed as a torn cruciate ligament. Randy was placed on the disabled list and underwent surgery on June 3. But that wasn't all. He suffered an acute gall bladder attack and other postoperative complications. There was swelling, inflamation, and bleeding of the knee.

For awhile he was on the "critical list" and one hospital spokesman said, "We almost lost him." A tube was inserted in his nose and a splint on his knee. His weight was down to 145 pounds. He looked gaunt. He missed all but nine games in 1971.

It was disastrous for the Cubs. Durocher began to lose his grip on the team. As one of the cooler heads, Hundley was highly respected among the players. He might have been able to hold the club together.

Hundley returned in 1972 with his $1 million brain and two 98 cent knees. Tape covered his legs from hip to ankle. He had more wrappings than King Tut.

Hundley was hobbling and living with pain. He ached every time he went into a crouch and every time he legged it to first. But he took the field on April 16, 1972, against the Philadelphia Phillies.

It was a raw, windy, frostbitten spring day. For nine innings he crouched and called the signals as Cub rookie Burt Hooton delivered his baffling knuckle curve.

A no-hitter. It was the floppy-haired rookie's day. It was also the balding veteran's day, as Hundley singled home two runs in the 4-0 victory.

Hundley was also behind the plate when Milt Pappas came within a pitch of a perfect game late in the season against the San Diego Padres. Pappas walked a batter and settled for a no-hitter. Hundley delivered two hits in the 8-0 triumph.

In between the no-hitters, Randy didn't do much hitting. His average sank to .218 and his power was cut to five homers. By 1973 Hundley was no longer the iron man, hitting only .226 and catching infrequently.

On Dec. 6, 1973, Hundley was traded to the Minnesota Twins for George Mitterwald, a catcher five years younger with two good knees.

The Rebel refused to knock the Cubs. "It's a class organization," said Hundley. "I'm proud to be part of it for eight years. Chicago is a great city. I'm just disappointed we didn't win a pennant."

After a disappointing season with the Twins, Hundley was placed on waivers. He was picked up by the Padres as a spare catcher and played sparingly before being released.

In 1976 Hundley returned to his adopted city. He was back in Cub flannels as a player-coach. The Confederate flag waved in the bleachers, but the Rebel could not reach it.

He caught only 13 games that season and two the next before becoming a full-time coach. His manager? Herman Franks, the chap who thought he was a bush leaguer.

Hundley, who batted .240 with 80 homers and 372 RBI as a Cub, now conducts off-season baseball camps for those who want to play against former big leaguers.

FERGIE JENKINS

JENKINS, FERGUSON ARTHUR
B. Dec. 13, 1943, Chatham, Ontario, Canada
BR TR 6'5" 205 lb.

Who has been the most durable iron man of the Cubs' pitching corps in the postwar era? There can be only one answer—the tall black Canadian, Fergie Jenkins. Gangling, stoop-shouldered and overpowering, Fergie performed feats unheard of in Wrigley Field since the milk and honey days of the 1920s and '30s.

A product of the Phillies' system, Jenkins received his minor league practice at Miami, Buffalo, Arkansas, and Chattanooga.

After Fergie bounced around four years in the sticks, generally pitching in relief, the Phillies brought him up late in 1965. He won two out of three decisions, but was generally unnoticed.

On April 21, 1966, the Cubs traded pitchers Bob Buhl and Larry Jackson to Philly for Jenkins, outfielder Adolfo Phillips, and first baseman John Herrnstein. Fergie's debut a few days later was a sensational one. He belted a home run and shut out the Dodgers for six innings to win 2-0.

Regardless, he still considered himself a bullpen artist. It was only through the incessant prodding of manager Leo Durocher and pitching coach Joe Becker that he entered the starting rotation late in August. Finishing with a 6-8 record, he already displayed a fearsome fastball and a deceptive slider, fanning 148 batters in 182 innings.

The year 1967 was the blossoming time both for the youthful Cub team and for Jenkins. For the first time in 21 years, the Cubs broke into the first division with a third place finish, thanks partially to Fergie's 20-13 record and 2.80 ERA. Displaying masterful control and stamina, he led the league with 20 complete games, while his 236 strikeouts set a 20th century high for a Cub pitcher, eclipsing the 225 recorded by Long Tom Hughes in the distant epoch of 1901. In fact, no Cub hurler had fanned more than 200 men since 1909, when Orval Overall had done the trick.

Like all fastballers, however, Fergie often served the gopher ball, especially in the early innings, and this singular weakness was frequently his downfall. Other than that, his work left no reason for complaint.

The next season was one of both triumph and frustration. Shaving his ERA down to 2.63, Jenkins once again won 20 games to become the first Cub pitcher to pick up 20 wins two years in a row since Lon Warneke during the Great Depression.

In addition, he surpassed his own strikeout record by upping the count to 260, while his 308 innings pitched represented the first time a Cub went over 300 frames since Charlie Root in 1927. On July 27 he fanned 13 Dodgers. But he could have easily won 25 or more games with the proper support, as five of his 15 losses were by the frustrating 1-0 margin.

The sweet spring and sour autumn came in 1969. After the first 90 games, the Cubs were 56-34 to lead the league. Jenkins was at the head of the pack with 12-6. But the Cubs slumped to second and their ace slipped with them. Fergie finished at 21-15, losing most of his starts in the disastrous September.

Even so, he again raised his strikeout total to 273, while his seven shutouts were tops by a Cub since Hiram Bithorn had the same number in 1943. With the club finishing second again the following year, Fergie lifted his victory count to 22 while striking out 274, which remains both his career high and the club record.

But it was the 1971 season that belonged to Fergie more than any other. Appearing in his second All-Star Game (he had previously pitched in the '67 contest), he won 24 games to pace the league while losing only 13. Jenkins also led in complete games (30), and innings pitched (325), tied for the lead in starts (39), and was second in strikeouts with 263.

In addition to this, he was 6-0 against the Phillies, pitched two two-hitters, two three-hitters, two four-hitters, and set a personal high for strikeouts in one game with 14. Better than ever with his bat, Fergie socked six homers and collected 20 RBI. To cap it all off, he was voted winner of the National League Cy Young Award, the first Cub so honored.

Jenkins continued to mow down the opposition in '72 as he made his third All-Star appearance. He was also named to *The Sporting News* All-Star team, hurled 11 consecutive complete games, and pitched the first one-hitter of his career, a 4-0 masterpiece over the Phillies at Veterans Stadium July 27. When he notched his 20th victory with a 4-3 win at Philadelphia Sept. 8, he became one of only three Cub pitchers to win 20 or more games for six consecutive seasons. The other two were Clark Griffith (1894-99) and Mordecai Brown (1906-11).

When Fergie expressed pride at joining this elite group that included such fairly recent stalwarts as Robin Roberts and Warren Spahn, the press misquoted him as saying "I'm in a class by myself now," making him look like an egomaniac.

Sooner or later Jenkins was due to have an off year, and in 1973 it happened. His record tapered off to 14-16, his ERA ballooned to 3.89, while his strikeout count dwindled to 170. Worse yet, he finished only seven of his starts, which was anything but typical. The Cubs, panicking and unloading players *en masse*, swapped him to the Texas Rangers for infielders Vic Harris and Bill Madlock.

It was a deal that Cub fans will always view with mixed emotions. While Madlock soon became the best batter in the league, Jenkins was far from washed up. Deep in the heart of Texas, he bounced back with a 25-12 mark in 1974, the best of his career.

However, following a so-so year the season after, Jenkins was traded to the Red Sox, who traded him back to the Rangers after a two-year stay in Boston that was largely disappointing. With the Rangers, Fergie again relocated the groove, putting together an 18-8 record in 1978 and a 16-14 mark the following campaign, before age began to catch up on him.

The Cubs, meanwhile, had been purchased by the Chicago Tribune Company, which promised to "build new traditions." Upon seeing Jenkins's name on the free agent list in November 1981, the team's management promptly signed him.

Returning to the scene of his former glory, Jenkins emerged as the ace of an otherwise shoddy Cub pitching staff in 1982. After being 8-13 at one point, Fergie rallied late in the year to finish at 14-15, leading Cub starters in innings pitched (217), strikeouts (134), and ERA (3.15). With any kind of support, he could have picked up several more wins. Strikeout number 3,000 came May 25 in a 2-1 loss to the Padres at San Diego.

Gambling on Jenkins to retain his effectiveness in spite of his advancing years, the Cubs were disappointed. The Fergie of 1983 was not the Fergie of 1982, much less of 1971. His record dropped to 6-9 with a 4.30 ERA. His only complete game was a shutout over the Cardinals June 10 that brought back memories of the Jenkins of old.

Released by the Cubs in the spring of 1984, Jenkins retired to his native Canada. He finished his major league career with 284 wins, 226 losses, 3,192 strikeouts, and a 3.34 ERA. If he had ever played for a New York team, he would probably be a cinch for the Hall of Fame.

ADOLFO PHILLIPS

PHILLIPS, ADOLFO EMILIO LOPEZ
B. Dec. 16, 1941, Bethania, Panama
BR TR 6'1" 175 lb.

Ole! Adolfo, Ole! One player turned Wrigley Field into a bullring after the Cubs gored the New York Mets 5-3 and 18-10 in a doubleheader on June 11, 1967.

His name was Adolfo Emilio Lopez Phillips and he had the bull by the horns after hitting four homers and two singles and driving in seven runs.

Adolfo could have worn a cape as he accepted the bravos from the senors and senoritas while the Mets paraded pitchers from the bullpen to the slaughter.

Phillips, a frail-looking center fielder from Panama, had a homer and a single, made a diving somersault catch, and ran wild on the basepaths in the first game.

He was part of a double steal and then attempted to steal home. Phillips was out in a cloud of dust and laid there in a daze. He was helped to his feet and dusted off by none other than Cub manager Leo Durocher.

Durocher and Phillips were the Cubs' odd couple. "We very good friends," said Phillips in his halting English. "We play cards and laugh and joke. We slap each other on the back, like pals."

"He could be the next Willie Mays," Durocher often boasted.

In the second game Phillips could even have made Mays envious. He hit a three-run homer to put the Cubs ahead. When he returned to center field he was greeted by shouts of "Ole! Ole!." He responded by crossing his arms over his head in triumph.

In his next turn at bat, Phillips cracked a two-run homer. By this time the shouts of "Ole! Ole!" reverberated throughout the bleachers. Adolfo revealed the ham in him by doffing his cap and bowing. The only thing missing was a shower of flowers.

When he strode to the plate for the third time, even the staid box seat patrons joined the chorus. Adolfo connected for another homer and rounded the bases like a proud matador.

What could he do for an encore? Everyone was standing in anticipation as Mighty Adolfo went up to bat again. He leveled his bat, swung, and dropped a single into left field.

Upon returning to center field, he was greeted by silence. He had let his followers down. Adolfo shrugged his shoulders and flexed his muscles. Suddenly, there was a crescendo, "Ole! Adolfo, Ole!" They liked singles hitters, too.

But the moment on center stage was brief. Phillips was tabbed as a comer after being obtained from the Philadelphia Phillies along with pitcher Fergie Jenkins and first baseman John Herrnstein for veteran pitchers Bob Buhl and Larry Jackson on April 21, 1966.

Phillips was installed in center field by Durocher and he displayed the rare combination of speed and power. His 32 stolen bases were the most by a Cub since the heyday of Kiki Cuyler.

After three seasons of near stardom, Phillips was ready for the Cubs' 1969 pennant push. But it wasn't to be. Adolfo broke his right wrist during spring training and was replaced by Don Young, another enigmatic figure in Cub history.

Durocher grew impatient. Leo insisted other Cubs were playing hurt and the two had different versions of how to hustle. Adolfo, a moody and sensitive player, sought pats and received brickbats from his manager.

Always prone to injury and frequently hit by pitches, Phillips started falling away from strikes on the inside corner. There were no more card games or laughs. "Leo stopped talking to me. He just walks past me and never says anything," lamented Adolfo.

And then came the moment. Phillips was shunted to the lowly Montreal Expos for infielder Paul Popovich on June 12, 1969. Phillips was stunned. He shook hands with his old teammates. Durocher extended his hand, but Phillips refused. "I no shake hands with that man," said Phillips.

There were no plaudits in Montreal and there was little for his palate. "Good restaurants in Chicago. I like red beans and rice. There is no Latino soul food in Montreal," sighed Adolfo.

In the Cubs next meeting with the Expos there was a melee on the field. Phillips sought out Durocher, and Leo, then 64, was ready to take on Adolfo. But they were restrained by teammates.

The Expos sent Phillips to Winnipeg in 1971. He made a brief return with the Cleveland Indians in 1972, but failed to get a hit in seven at bats. Adolfo was through at age 29.

From there he drifted to the Mexican League and then faded from the scene a puzzled, bitter young man.

In his eight big league seasons, Phillips was a .247 hitter with 463 hits and 59 homers.

JIM HICKMAN

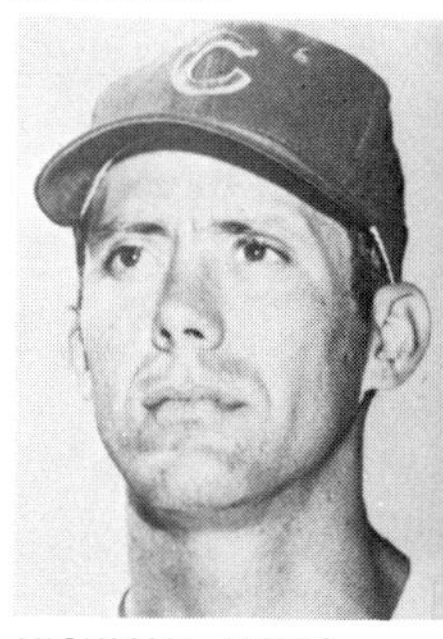

HICKMAN, JAMES LUCIOUS
B. May 10, 1937, Henning, Tenn.
BR TR 6'4" 205 lb.

If there was ever an unexpected hero in Cub history, it was Jim Hickman. A near-nothing for a dozen years, he emerged as an overnight hero when least expected. But that is getting ahead of the story.

Originally signed by the Cardinal organization in 1956 when he was a 19-year-old Tennessean with a mountain drawl, Hickman bounced around the St. Louis farm chain for six years. He was scarcely noticed by the parent organization.

In 1962 he was drafted by the expansion New York Mets, which in itself looked like the kiss of death. During the five years he toiled with Clown Prince Casey Stengel's clowns, Jim displayed fair power, but never hit over .257 in a season. He also developed a reputation as a mediocre fielder and an easy batter to strike out.

After one season with the Dodgers, Jim came to the Cubs along with pitcher Phil Regan on April 23, 1968, in exchange for Ted Savage and Jim Ellis. Immediately optioned to Tacoma, he seriously considered quitting baseball.

However, at the end of May, Hickman was called to Chicago. He looked like a wasted investment at first, batting a paltry .223 in 75 games. The following season began just as poorly, and by Aug. 1, 1969, his batting average had sunk to .216. Nevertheless, manager Leo Durocher refused to give up on him.

Then came Jim's resurrection from the dead. While the league-leading Cubs began to tire in the August heat, the soft-spoken Hickman came off the bench to bat .301 for the month with 10 homers and 25 RBI.

However, Jim could not carry the team on his shoulders as they finished second to the Mets, a sour end to what might have been a storybook season. But Hickman, finishing with a .237 average and 21 homers, was making genuine headlines for the first time in his career.

In 1970 Hickman picked up where he had left off. Displaying a hot bat with a smooth, level swing, he hit .315, smashed 32 home runs, drove in 115 runs, and scored 102. Jim's 13 game-winning RBI were second only to Ron Santo's 17, while his 17-game hitting streak was tops on the club.

His biggest thrill came in the All-Star Game at Cincinnati's new Riverfront Stadium, July 14, when he drove in Pete Rose with a game-winning single to give the National League a 5-4 12-inning victory.

Following that super season, Jim received previously undreamed of accolades. Chicago sportswriters gave him the Chicago Headline of the Year Award, while *The Sporting News* named him Comeback Player of the Year. Back down home, he was honored as Tennessee Pro Athlete of the Year. In two short years, Jim Hickman had gone from a nobody to a bona fide star.

If 1970 was the year to remember, '71 was a season to forget. Hampered with stomach ulcers and a bout with pneumonia, Hickman missed nearly a month of the season. His average fell to .256, although he still managed to hit 19 home runs.

This was also the year of the infamous "clubhouse rebellion" against manager Leo Durocher. While the clubhouse lawyers and dugout radicals thundered for revolution, "Gentleman Jim" preferred to do his speaking with his bat, coming through with timely hits in spite of his ailments. A staunch supporter of Durocher, Hickman was on nonspeaking terms with several of his teammates by the end of the season.

But the wounds healed the following year, and Jim came back with a .272 average, 17 homers and 64 RBI. April 28, 1972, was one of the greatest days of his career. On that damp, overcast Friday afternoon, Hickman drove six runners across the plate with two homers and a double, as the Cubs outlasted the Reds 10-8 at Wrigley Field.

By 1973 Jim was slowing down as advancing years dropped his batting average to only .244 in 201 trips to the plate. Hickman was traded to the Cardinals for pitcher Scipio Spinks the following spring. He served as a part-time outfielder before retiring at the end of the '74 season.

Lifetime, he was a .252 batter with 1,002 hits and 159 home runs. As a Cub, however, Jim was .267 with 97 homers. Since leaving baseball, he has returned to his native Tennessee to pursue the life of a prosperous gentleman farmer.

PHIL REGAN

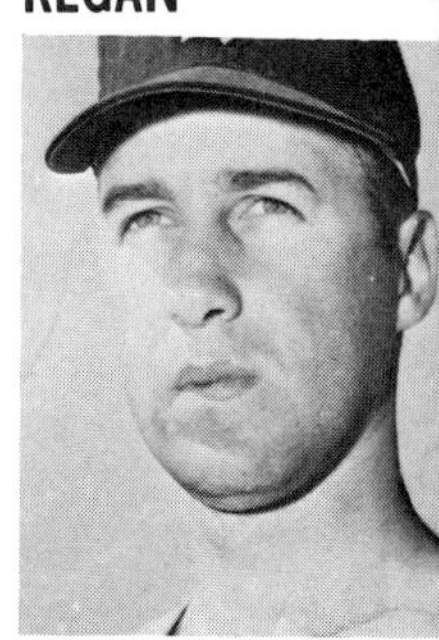

REGAN, PHILLIP RAYMOND
B. April 6, 1937, Otsego, Mich.
BR TR 6'3" 200 lb.

Did he or didn't he? That was the question so often asked as to whether or not Cub relief ace Phil Regan was a practitioner of contemporary baseball's most verboten strategy, the spitball. Only the pitcher himself knew for sure.

For Regan, the road to becoming a bullpen king was long and tedious. Signed by the Tigers in 1956, Regan spent close to five years in the Detroit farm chain before making it up to the Tigers late in 1960. Over the next five seasons, Regan occasionally showed flashes of brilliance as a Tiger starter, but was unable to attain consistency. His yearly won-lost marks ranged from 15-9 to 0-4, while his ERAs ran the gamut from 3.86 to 5.25. By mid-1965, the Tigers were about ready to call it quits with Phil. They optioned him to Syracuse. During the off-season he was picked up by the ever-alert Dodgers.

Once he donned the Dodger blue, Regan enjoyed a rebirth that was nothing short of miraculous. Converted to the bullpen by the crafty Walt Alston, Regan responded with 14 wins, only one loss, 21 saves, a 1.62 ERA, the Comeback Player of the Year Award, and Fireman of the Year honors, as the Dodgers won the pennant. His late-inning snatchings earned him the nickname "the Vulture."

But after Regan slipped to 6-9 with only six saves the following campaign, the Dodgers began thinking that he was only a one-year wonder. On April 23, 1968, Regan and Jim Hickman were swapped to the Cubs for Ted Savage and Jim Ellis, in what turned out to be a steal of a deal for Chicago. Hickman would later rise to unprecedented heights, while Regan picked up where he had left off in '66.

Time after time he pulled games out of the fire, including credit for both wins in a double victory over the Pirates July 7. In the meantime, ominous rumors began floating around that Phil was doctoring the ball with "greasy kid stuff." One story even had a tube of Vaseline falling out of Regan's pocket as he slid into base.

The controversy reached a crescendo Aug. 18, during the first game of a doubleheader with the visiting Reds. Shortly after Phil entered the game in the seventh inning, plate umpire Chris Pelekoudas stalked out to the mound and inspected Regan's cap and glove, claiming he detected a foreign substance.

Later, Pelekoudas charged Phil with throwing three illegal pitches. He nullified a fly ball and a strikeout, and he changed a strike call to a ball. Finally, third base umpire Shag Crawford, the senior man on the crew, grabbed a towel and wiped Regan's brow. It was the biggest Wrigley Field rhubarb since Andy Pafko's disputed catch, as 30,942 booing, jeering, and hissing fans littered the field with debris.

"I didn't start umpiring yesterday," said Pelekoudas. "I've been an umpire for 20 years and I know an illegal pitch when I see one."

To this, Regan retorted, "I don't see how they can say that any ball that sinks is a spitter."

By the time the game was over Randy Hundley, Al Spangler, and manager Leo Durocher had been given the heave-ho, but Regan, surprisingly, remained in the game.

Leo, never one to avoid a confrontation, remarked, "If he was using an illegal pitch, then why didn't they throw him out of the game?" Ironically, the hubbub had no bearing in the outcome of the game. The Cubs were already behind 2-1 when Regan took the mound, and there was no scoring by either side for the rest of the contest.

Regardless of his umpire problems, Regan went on to a banner season. By the end of the year he was 12-5 (with 10 wins as a Cub) with 25 saves (21 for Chicago) and a sparkling 2.19 ERA. The result was another Fireman of the Year Award.

As the 1969 season unfolded, Regan continued to dominate the Cub relief corps. With the Cubs sailing along at the head of the National League fleet, the Regan mop-up became part of the daily routine. After the first 106 games, Phil had appeared in 49 of them, with 11 wins and 10 saves on his ledger.

The winds of September, however, spelled Armageddon for the Cubs' pennant bid. Perhaps nothing personified the swan song of the '69 Cubs as did the demise of Phil Regan. Although he finished with a 12-6 record and 17 saves, thanks mainly to his pre-September effectiveness, his ERA inflated to 3.70. Instead of putting out the fires, Phil was now getting burned himself.

Leo Durocher's critics claimed that he had overworked Regan while underworking submariner Ted Abernathy.

Others said it was because the umps were on the lookout for the spitter. Still others viewed it simply as a case of National League batters catching onto Regan's tricks. Whatever the reason, Regan would never again be an effective reliever. In 1970 he fell to 5-9 with a 4.74 ERA. The year after, it was more of the same as

Durocher became afraid to use his bullpen. The 1971 campaign witnessed 75 complete games by Cub hurlers, tops in the league and a postwar Cub high.

Regan soon drifted into oblivion. After a handful of appearances in '72, he was given his release. Signing with the White Sox, he failed to stick there, either, and by August his big league days were over.

He retired with a 96-81 record, including 92 saves and a 3.84 ERA.

WILLIE SMITH

SMITH, WILLIE
B. Feb. 11, 1939,
Anniston, Ala.
BL TL 6'0" 182 lb.

The Cubs were involved in a tight game. Manager Leo Durocher scanned the dugout and barked, "Tell Willie Smith to grab a bat. I want him to pinch-hit."

"You can't do that, skipper," replied outfielder Jim Hickman. "You traded him last season." Yes, Willie Smith was gone . . . but not forgotten.

Wonderful Willie provided the Cubs' punch in the pinch. It was his homer that sent an opening day crowd of 40,796 at Wrigley Field home delirious. The date was April 8, 1969.

The Phillies and Cubs had exchanged the lead five times. It was now 6-5 Phillies in the bottom of the 11th inning. Randy Hundley singled with one out and Durocher sent Smith to bat for Hickman. While swinging in the on-deck circle, Smith hit himself in the hip with the bat. It really stung.

Several minutes later, Smitty stung the ball, drilling it high and deep into the right field bleachers for a 7-6 Cub victory.

Smith, a reformed pitcher, played first base and outfield for the Cubs after being acquired on waivers from the Indians midway through the 1968 season. Earlier, he had pitched for the Tigers and was a .300-hitting regular outfielder with the Angels.

But as a Cub, Smitty's dittys were pinch hits. In three seasons his 26 pinch hits drove in 26 runs. Four were pinch homers, one short of the Cub record held by Ernie Banks. Overall, Smith hit 19 Cub homers.

Smith closed out his career with the Reds in 1971 and somehow lost his touch in the clutch, failing to deliver a hit in 20 at bats.

Willie was a lifetime .248 hitter with 410 hits. As a pitcher, he was 2-4.

DON YOUNG

YOUNG, DONALD WAYNE
B. Oct. 18, 1945,
Houston, Tex.
BR TR 6'2" 185 lb.

Bespectacled Don Young's stint with the Cubs was brief, but will be long remembered. Young was the central figure in one of the club's most gnawing defeats.

Signed originally by the Cardinals, Young was acquired by the Cubs. But after collecting only two hits in 35 at bats in 1965, Young drifted back to the minors.

When Cub center fielder Adolfo Phillips broke a bone in his right hand during spring training of 1969, Young was back with the Cubs. He was in center field as the Cubs and Mets met before 55,096 at Shea Stadium on July 8, 1969.

The two clubs were locked in a heated battle for first place in the National League's East Division. Going into the ninth inning the Cubs led 3-1 on Fergie Jenkins's one-hitter.

Pinch batter Ken Boswell opened by sending a soft fly to short center. Young started slowly for the ball and it fell safely for a gift double. One out later, Donn Clendenon drove a shot to deep left-center. Young made a long run, had the ball in his glove, and then let it trickle out. It was ruled a double.

The Mets went on to win and there was no laughter in the Cubs' clubhouse. Cub manager Leo Durocher started popping off about "that kid in center field."

"Two little fly balls," roared the Lion. "He watches one and lets the other drop."

Ron Santo, the Cubs' fiery third baseman and team captain, went into a tirade and berated the defenseless Young, who sat transfixed and silent.

Strangely, the Cub fans' bitterness turned from Young to the duo of Durocher and Santo.

Young batted .239 with six homers and 27 RBI that season and had a career average of .218. He drifted from the scene after 1969. But he will be long remembered in Cub history, perhaps with a bit of resentment and sentiment.

DICK SELMA

SELMA, RICHARD JAY
B. Nov. 4, 1943, Santa Ana, Calif.
BR TR 5'11" 180 lb.

Pitcher Dick Selma was a zany Wrigley Field phenomenon. His cheerleading spread from the left field bleachers to the whole ballpark. It was the giddy summer of 1969 and the Cubs were the hottest ballclub in the big leagues.

Selma would stand up in the bullpen, wave a towel, and point his finger at the sky. Then he would draw circles in the air while the crowd would let loose with piercing screeches.

Dick would then jump in the air and bring his right forefinger down, pointing straight at the ground. This was a signal for the avid "Bleacher Bums" to burst into a song that sounded like the humming of a million bees. All that was missing were the pom-pons.

Richard Jay Selma was a right-handed pitcher with the zaniness attributed to left-handers. He spent only six months of a 10-year major league career in a Chicago uniform, but will probably be best remembered as a Cub.

The hard-throwing native Californian attended Fresno High, the same school that produced pitchers Jim Maloney, Dick Ellsworth, and Tom Seaver. He received a reported $20,000 bonus to sign with the Mets in 1963.

The fun-loving hurler was named Rookie of the Year in the California League after striking out 221 batters in 185 innings with a 2.58 ERA and a 12-6 record at Salinas.

Two years later he was a full-fledged Met. After four seasons Selma had a mediocre 17-21 record. He was selected by the Padres in the 1969 expansion draft.

Selma spent less than a month as a Padre, posting a 2-2 mark. The Cubs obtained him in a three-for-one deal that sent pitchers Joe Niekro, Gary Ross, and infielder Francisco Libran to San Diego.

The Cubs had a starting trio of Fergie Jenkins, Bill Hands, and Ken Holtzman. Selma became the fourth wheel, reeling off seven victories against only one loss and igniting the fans with his cheerleading.

When the Cubs went into their September slump, Selma played a key role. On Sept. 11 he was the losing pitcher in a crucial game against the Phillies in Philadelphia.

His errant throw from the mound to third base on a pickoff play sailed way into left field, allowing a run to score. The Cubs lost 4-3, their eighth in a row.

Selma finished the season with a 10-8 record and wound up in Durocher's doghouse. He was traded to the Phillies with outfielder Oscar Gamble for outfielder Johnny Callison on Nov. 17.

But Selma's affection for Cub fans remained intact. On April 14, 1970, the Phillies opened the season at Wrigley Field against the Cubs.

Dick raced out to the bleachers where he was showered with coins. After the game, a 5-4 Cub victory, Selma joined the gang in Ray's Bleachers. He spilled $8 worth of silver on the bar and ordered, "Drink up, when it's gone you're on your own again."

Selma bounced around the majors until 1974, going from the Phillies to the Angels to the Brewers, finishing with a 42-54 record.

To the fans in the bleachers the name Dick Selma always brings back pleasant memories. To them he will always be a Cub.

MILT PAPPAS

PAPPAS, MILTON STEVEN
B. May 11, 1939, Detroit, Mich.
BR TR 6'3" 190 lb.

"Your attention, ladies and gentlemen. Have your pencils and scorecards ready. Now pitching for the Cubs, Miltiades Stergios Papastedgios."

For boxscore brevity it was necessary to take that name and slice it down to Milton Steven Pappas, the Greek with the sometimes Golden Arm.

Milt Pappas came close to carving baseball immortality on Sept. 2, 1972. He was one pitch away from a perfect game against San Diego at Wrigley Field. He retired the first 26 Padres, then walked a batter on a full count. He got the next hitter to salvage a no-hitter.

That climaxed a career that began on Beechwood Ave. in Detroit where Milt's father, a Greek immigrant, opened a confectionary store. Despite his fondness for candy, young Miltie threw no lollipops on the mound and was signed as a fuzzy-cheeked 18-year-old by the Baltimore Orioles.

After pitching only three games for Knoxville of the Sally League, Pappas joined the Oriole's "Kiddy Korps" in 1957. Baltimore had four starters (Steve Barber, Jerry Walker, Jack Fisher, and Milt Pappas) all 21 or younger.

Of that quartet, Pappas proved the best, compiling a 110-70 record in eight seasons. Then everything went downhill. He opened two restaurants in Baltimore without success. The first burned to the ground and the second folded after Milt's partner killed himself.

Then followed the famed Frank Robinson trade. Robby and Pappas were the principal players involved in the four-man trade with the Cincinnati Reds on Dec. 9, 1965.

Robinson won the 1966 Triple Crown, batting .316 with 49 homers and 122 RBI, leading Baltimore to a World Series sweep over the Los Angeles Dodgers. He topped off the season as a unanimous selection for Most Valuable Player Award.

That didn't sit too well in Cincy. At that rate, Pappas would have to win 25 games for the Reds to keep pace. Unfortunately, the Reds finished fifth and Pappas's popularity sank with a 12-11 record.

Pappas escaped Cincy with a 30-29 record in two and one-half lonely seasons. He was dealt to Atlanta where he became a borderline (18-20) pitcher. The Cubs acquired Pappas on June 26, 1970, for $75,000 and outfielder Jimmie Hall. It was apparent at the outset that Pappas preferred Wrigley's gum to Atlanta's grits.

Pappas had a 2-2 record, a reputation of not being able to go nine innings, and was said to be a clubhouse lawyer. Manager Leo Durocher cleaned the slate and installed him in the rotation alongside Fergie Jenkins, Bill Hands, and Ken Holtzman.

Pappas responded with 10 victories down the stretch and then chalked up 17 triumphs in 1971, topping his previous high of 16 with the Orioles. But Milt saved his best for 1972.

He started slowly with a 6-7 record and then reeled off 11 wins in a row, including his near-perfecto on Sept. 2. It was a dank and overcast day when Pappas set out to earn his niche against the Padres.

His first close call came in the fifth inning when Nate Colbert smashed a one-hopper deep in the hole at short. Cub shortstop Don Kessinger made a clean pickup on the grass, which was slick because of morning rains. Kessinger planted his foot on the dirt and then threw, Colbert was out by a half step.

Pappas got his turn in the eighth inning. Derrel Thomas hit a ground smash back to Pappas, who fell down, scrambled to his feet, and made a frantic throw to first baseman Jim Hickman. Thomas was out by a whisker.

The "heart stopper" came in the ninth inning. Leadoff batter

John Jeter hit a routine fly ball to left-center. Center fielder Bill North came in for the ball but slipped and fell on the wet turf. Suddenly, left fielder Billy Williams appeared and made the catch.

The "heart breaker" came with two out in the inning. Pinch batter Larry Stahl swung and missed the first pitch. The next was wide for a ball. He then swung and missed for strike two and the crowd was on its feet. One more pitch and Pappas would have a perfect game.

It was not to be. The next three pitches were outside and Stahl drew a walk. The third and fourth balls to Stahl were fairly close to the strike zone and Pappas was hoping for a borderline call. But umpire Bruce Froemming said, "They weren't there."

It was almost anticlimatic when pinch hitter Gary Jestadt hit a routine popup, which second baseman Carmen Fanzone handled easily, squeezing the ball in his glove. The Cubs won 8-0 with Pappas settling for a no-hitter.

But it was to be his last hurrah. Pappas struggled through a 7-12 season in 1973 and was released at the conclusion of the year. His National League log was 99-90, thus missing by one victory being one of a handful of pitchers with 100 wins in each league.

One victory and one pitch short for Miltiades Stergios Papastedgios, who finished his career with 209 wins, 164 losses and a 3.40 ERA. He is the only pitcher to chalk up 200 big league wins without ever winning 20 in a season.

JOE PEPITONE

PEPITONE, JOSEPH ANTHONY
B. Oct. 9, 1940, Brooklyn, N.Y.
BL TL 6'2"
185 lb.

The Cubs were part of the Pepi Generation. Joe Pepitone brought his mod touch to a staid ballclub in the early 1970s. He was adored by the public and an enigma to management. In essence, the free-spirited slugger was a shameful waste of baseball talent.

Brooklyn-born Pepitone grew up in a neighborhood that fostered teen gangs. But in reality, he wasn't a wild youngster. His first love was stickball, the local street version of baseball. He was a "four-sewer player," meaning he could hit a ball to the fourth sewer from where he was standing.

Brooklyn was then Dodger country, yet young Pepi was a fan of the hated Yankees. He would venture to Ebbets Field to cheer for the Dodger opponents.

Pepitone played high school ball and was captain of his team. He was then set back by a shooting incident. "A kid brought a gun to class with him," recalled Pepitone. "It was the last period and I was walking back to my home room to get my jacket.

"He was standing in a group of guys, and just kidding around. He pulled this .38 caliber police revolver and jumped out and shot me. He didn't know it was loaded.

"I spent 12 days in the hospital. I was in surgery for about seven hours. The bullet missed my heart by a quarter of an inch, went through some fatty tissue, and came out my back. It missed my spine by a quarter of an inch."

Pepitone recovered and received bonus offers from the Dodgers and the Yankees. Although the Dodgers offered more, he signed with the Yankees in 1958. After four years in the minors, Pepitone joined the Yankees in 1962.

These were the pennant-winning Yankees of Mantle, Maris, and Berra, and Pepitone fit in. In jest, Mantle once said, "Hey, rookie, shine my shoes."

"Go shine 'em yourself," yelled Pepitone. "I'm a Yankee now, just like you are. I'm part of the ballclub."

In 1963 Pepitone supplanted Bill Skowron at first base and over the years developed into a power hitter, taking advantage of the short porch at Yankee Stadium for 166 homers.

The young man with the "bedroom eyes" and prominent nose was one of the first players to grow long hair and long sideburns. And the Yankees never bugged him about it. Then one day he went AWOL, was fined $500, and suspended. "I'm the only guy besides Ruth who was ever suspended by the Yankees," said Pepitone. "Babe Ruth and me."

The Yankees put up with Ruth's antics, but not Pepitone's. They dealt him to Houston for outfielder Curt Blefary in the winter of 1970. The Astros were naut for Pepi, who jumped the club in midseason.

Pepi was placed on waivers and the Cubs grabbed him for cash and a player to be named later (Roger Metzger). Then the honeymoon began. "I love it in Chicago," beamed Pepitone. "I'm a big city boy. When I wake up in the morning, I like to see big buildings. I didn't like it in Houston because all I could see was flat land."

A black limousine, complete with a chauffeur, a pad in the Executive House, female admirers. The town was his. Pepi paraded into the Cub clubhouse, attired in bell-bottoms, an open-necked shirt, and a vest, plus a hair-dryer.

Pepitone and his hairpiece made their debut at Wrigley Field on Aug. 11, 1970. He collected a pair of doubles in a 4-1 win over the Giants before 33,931 adoring fans. "Having a big crowd like this rooting for you makes you want to play," sighed Pepitone. "It's beautiful."

And it seemed as if Pepi was in the middle of every Cub victory. His two-run homer helped Fergie Jenkins beat the Dodgers. His ninth-inning homer helped Bill Hands beat the Padres.

Besides driving home 30 runs in his first 29 games, Pepi played a solid center field and kept the Cubs loose. Pepitone even threatened to buy Cub manager Leo Durocher a hairpiece.

When he wasn't playing ball, Pepitone was the toast of Rush Street. He was sort of a roadshow version of Broadway Joe Namath. He also took up fishing aboard majestic yachts off Lake Michigan. "In Brooklyn, I would grab a pole, some string, open a sewer lid and catch a rat," grinned Pepi, who finished with 27 homers.

The Cubs switched Pepitone to first base in 1971 and he batted over .300 for the first time in his career, checking in with a .307 mark. "I don't care if he has hair down to his ankles," said Durocher. "He's a helluva guy."

Pepi's only trouble early that season was with the law. Once after leaving a Rush Street night spot, he was tagged out by the police and charged with driving without license plates and with displaying an expired driver's license. He posted a $25 bond and left the station, saying, "You guys must be Sox fans."

Division and Rush soon became Pepitown as he opened "Joe Pepitone's Thing," a basement bar for swingers, would-be swingers, assorted youths with casual swaggers, and singles mixers.

Even the Establishment found his watering hole the "in place." Mrs. P. K. Wrigley, son William, and daughter-in-law Joan wended their way to be seen on the scene. But not Cubs' owner P. K. Wrigley.

Late in the season, Pepi was among the ringleaders in a "Dump Durocher" rebellion, which was squelched by Wrigley.

The next spring Pepitone got off to a slow start and baseball's famous dropout quit the Cubs on May 1, saying he no longer loved the game and that he was bothered by gastritis. When Pepi decided to walk out and devote full time to his cocktail lounge, he was hitting a dismal .120.

But the dropout dropped in again a month later, saying in jest that his mother "missed her $100-per-week check." Actually, Pepi's mom did come to Chicago and made it plain that he'd better return to baseball.

Durocher didn't lay out a red carpet. "If he thinks he can come in here and step right in and get his job back, he's mistaken," roared the Lion. "First, he'll have to prove to me that he's in shape."

Under the rules, once a player is placed on the voluntary retired list he isn't eligible to return before 60 days. Pepitone worked his way back to shape, but there was a coolness toward him when he returned July 1.

He wore his bushy black wig and his mod clothes and tried to act the clown in the clubhouse. But there was no spontaneous enjoyment of his antics. He was tolerated, but that was all.

Pepitone got his batting average up to .262, but his homer total dropped to eight. Durocher, meanwhile, departed, or was pushed out later that season in favor of Whitey Lockman.

Pepitone received an offer to play ball in Japan, but he rejected the offers and stayed with the Cubs.

Joe quit clowning and sought the Cubs' acceptance. He was hitting .268 and was third on the club with 18 RBI when he was traded to the Atlanta Braves for cash and minor league prospect Andre Thornton on May 18, 1973.

But after playing only three games in Atlanta, Pepitone quit the Braves and left for Japan. Pepi-san was a hero in his Japanese debut, driving in the winning run with a single as the Yakult Atoms nipped the Yomiuri Giants 2-1 in Tokyo.

After 14 games, Pepitone was batting .143. Then he made an unexpected (to the Japanese) exit, leaving for New York, never to return. The Japanese had one word for Pepitone, "Bush."

Pepi owed back taxes and was paying alimony on his broken marriages. He opened a restaurant in Brooklyn, but only his friends from the neighborhood came in to free load. Business was bad. The place burned down. He posed for a nudie magazine. He joined a softball team.

Pepitone then collaborated on a book *Joe, You Could Have Made Us Proud.* It was a heart-breaking peek into the mind of a troubled man.

But the Pepi story is not over. He remarried and discarded his mod duds in favor of a suit, with a shirt and tie. The hair is cut shorter. And he's back with the Yankees as a minor league batting instructor. Quite probably, he is at peace with himself.

During his major league days, Pepitone was a .258 batter with 219 homers and 721 RBI.

SECTION SIX 1973-1980 Feats of Futility

Following the Cubs' strong finish in 1972, hopes were high for the new season, especially among the anti-Durocher faction, who had finally gotten rid of their scapegoat.

In early 1973 it looked as if the Cubs were being resurrected. Rick Monday made them solid in center field for the first time since Andy Pafko's day, while Jose Cardenal in right provided some much needed speed and colorful antics. Great deeds were expected from youthful pitchers Burt Hooton and Rick Reuschel.

At the start of July the Cubs were 46-31, holding first place by eight games. Then came a collapse that dwarfed 1969 as the team tumbled to fifth place, seven games under .500. The front line was simply worn out from advancing age.

P. K. Wrigley promised to "back up the truck," and back it up he did. By the following spring Santo, Beckert, Hundley, Pappas, and Hickman had all been dispatched by one means or another. As could have been easily predicted, the Cubs of 1974 dropped to last in the NL East.

Exactly two years after he had replaced Durocher, Whitey Lockman was himself replaced by Jim Marshall, whose luck was no better. Bill Madlock, the new third baseman, was the only youngster of any promise. Over the winter, stalwart Billy Williams was dealt to the A's.

In 1975 the Cubs started off like a rocket, then fizzled in June, eventually settling in fifth place. They had a dependable new second baseman in Manny Trillo while Madlock created a sensation with his league-leading .354 average, the highest by a Cub in 30 years. As had been the case so many times in the past, lack of pitching was the team's downfall. Reuschel continued to lose the heartbreakers while Bill Bonham and Ray Burris were inconsistent at best. The last member of the 1969 squad, Don Kessinger, was traded after the season.

The Cubs "celebrated" their 100th anniversary in 1976 by finishing fourth with an identical record to the year before. In many ways the season was an instant replay of 1975—Madlock won the batting crown, Cardenal was the top Cub basestealer, and Monday the main home run threat.

That winter brought more of what critics called "cosmetic changes." Former head coach Bob Kennedy was named general manager while somber-faced Herman Franks was hired as the new field boss. Madlock and Monday demanded substantial pay hikes and were promptly sent packing. Bobby Murcer, whom the Cubs picked from the Giants for Madlock, ended up getting a fatter contract than Bill had wanted. On April 12, 1977, the enigmatic Phil Wrigley died at age 82, leaving the team to his son, William Wrigley, Jr.

Although the Madlock deal was questionable, the Monday trade turned out to be a good one. Shortstop Ivan DeJesus combined with Trillo to form a popular "Latin connection" in the heart of the infield. Bill Buckner, who also came from the Dodgers with DeJesus, became the most consistent Cub hitter in several years.

Suddenly, the Cubs were winning ball games, zooming to 47-22 at one point.

The main reason was Bruce Sutter. Virtually unnoticed outside of Chicago the previous year, the young fireman was suddenly the terror of the league with his "split-fingered" fastball, a pitch that defied definition as well as batters.

But as Sutter went so went the team. After he was sidelined in August, the team collapsed, eventually finishing fourth with an 81-81 record.

In 1978 the Cubs edged up to third place but it was a pyrrhic victory as they slipped below .500. In spite of the acquisition of slugger Dave Kingman, the Cubs' home run total of 72 was their lowest since 1947.

The following season was dominated by Kingman's 48 homers and Sutter's 37 saves. Although the team played competent ball for much of the season, it was the same old story—fifth place. Herman Franks resigned with a week to go in the season, being replaced by Joe Amalfitano, for the time being.

In 1980 Preston Gomez was hired as the new manager. With neither leadership nor morale, the Cubs were listless all season, finishing last. Gomez did not even last the year, being replaced by Amalfitano after 90 games. Fans were becoming increasingly critical of the Wrigley regime, as many felt that the younger Wrigley looked upon the team as no more than a hobby, if not an outright burden.

BURT HOOTON

HOOTON, BURT CARLTON
B. Feb. 7, 1950, Greenville, Tex.
BR TR 6'1" 210 lb.

Burt Hooton sat in front of his TV set and dozed off. "My thoughts sorta carried me away. I envisioned myself pitching a no-hitter," drawled the curly-haired blond. "Then I fell asleep and the first thing I saw in my dream was the ball jumping off my bat for a homer."

The following day (April 15, 1972) was cold and rainy, with a raw, biting wind blowing in from the north. Hooton went to the mound for the Cubs against the Philadelphia Phillies at Wrigley Field.

Hooton fulfilled his dream by pitching a no-hitter, beating the Phillies 4-0, but he never did hit that homer.

Hooton, making only his fourth major league start, burst onto the scene boasting a trick pitch called the knuckle-curve. The chunky right-hander with the Texas twang called his pitch the "thang." It's a cross between a curve and knuckler and has the effects of a dry spitter.

"I started fooling around with the knuckle-curve when I was 14, pitching in the Corpus Christi Pony League," recalled Hooton, who went on to pitch four no-hitters in high school ball. "Baseball was my favorite sport. I was too chicken to play football," added Hooton.

When Hooton was fresh out of Corpus Christi High, he was selected by the New York Mets, but parental persuasion for a college education won out. Hooton took his knuckle-curve to the University of Texas, where he set several records, while being named All-American three straight years.

As a Longhorn, Hooton tossed two more no-hitters, compiling a 35-3 record with 384 strikeouts and only 69 walks in 283 innings. He represented the United States in the World Amateur Baseball Tournament in South America in 1970 and fired a no-hitter against Cuba, the eventual champion.

The Cubs had the second choice in the secondary phase of the 1971 draft, which consisted of players who had been drafted by other clubs, but had not signed. They waited patiently as the Washington Senators took Pete Broberg, a fastballing pitcher off the Dartmouth campus.

The Cubs then went into a rush act for Hooton. They selected him on Wednesday, June 10 in New York, rushed him to Chicago, and signed him for boxcar figures, presumably a $100,000 bonus, the following day. He joined the club that Sunday, watched his teammates for nine days and then drew his first starting assignment against the St. Louis Cardinals at Wrigley Field.

For the benefit of trivia buffs, Lou Brock was the first batter he faced. Brock went down swinging, but Hooton lasted only three innings and was not involved in the decision. The Cubs then shipped their young phenom to Tacoma of the Pacific Coast League.

Tacoma catcher Ken Rudolph was awed by Hooton's knuckle-curve. "It looks like a super sinker," said Rudolph. "It has a top spin on it and it goes down—it drops a foot and a half. He throws it so hard it looks like a spitball, but you can see the rotation on it, so you know it isn't."

Hooton was only 7-4 at Tacoma, but had three shutouts and a 1.68 ERA, and he struck out 135 batters in 102 innings.

Moreover, he struck out 16 Spokane batters and then broke a Coast League record that had stood since 1905 when he fanned 19 Eugene (Ore.) batters. The Spokane manager was Tom Lasorda, who kept that game indelible in his mind.

The 21-year-old hot-shot was recalled by the Cubs and started against the Mets in the second game of a twi-nighter in New York's Shea Stadium. For six and one-third innings he dazzled the crowd of 21,302 by holding the Mets hitless. He finished with 15 strikeouts and eventually won 3-2.

As usual there still were some skeptics about any quick predictions of stardom for the Cub rookie, but, at least, the Met batters were convinced. He encored his performance the following week at Wrigley Field, tossing a two-hitter, beating the Mets and Tom Seaver 3-0 on Ron Santo's 300th homer.

"Damn, that's some kind of curveball that kid's got," said Cub manager Leo Durocher. "The only man I ever saw who had one as good was Tommy Bridges. I mean a real hard curve."

Durocher now had his pitching rotation set for the 1972 season. He named Fergie Jenkins, Bill Hands, Milt Pappas, and the new hotshot, Hooton. After Jenkins dropped the opener, Durocher picked Hooton as his second starter.

Leo wasn't around to witness the no-hitter. He had the sniffles and remained at home, riveted to his TV set, turning over the reins to coach Pete Reiser.

Hooton's no-hitter wasn't exactly a gem. He walked seven batters and came close to losing it in the seventh inning when Greg Luzinski got all of a fastball and bashed it high and deep to left-center.

The ball probably would have bounced onto Waveland Avenue, but the howling north wind brought the ball back in the park, enabling center fielder Rick Monday to make the catch in front of the 368 foot sign.

"I watched Monday back up to the wall and I kept thinking, 'blow in wind. . . . Come on Rick . . . atta boy,' " said Hooton.

Luzinski again stood between Hooton and the "Hall" with two out in the ninth inning. Burt fired a knuckle-curve for a strike, then another. The frigid fans stood in anticipation as Luzinski came out swinging on the next pitch and Hooton was swallowed by his teammates.

Did success spoil Hooton? Did complacency set in? Did the youngster begin thinking, "Maybe this isn't going to be so tough?" Anyway, Hooton did little to distinguish himself as a Cub after that no-hitter.

There were a few games where Cub fans could savor. One came on Sept. 16, 1972, when Hooton's grand slam off Seaver helped lead to an 18-5 romp over the Mets at Wrigley Field.

But, to put it mildly, Hooton was a bust as a Cub. He followed an 11-14 rookie season with two more losing seasons (14-17 in 1973 and 7-11 in 1974) and was dropped from the rotation, shunted to the bullpen, and was even used in mop-up situations.

Sometimes his knuckle-curve acted more like a nickel-curve. And the extra flab didn't help him on the slab. Whether it was due to being out of condition, poor coaching, or poor attitude, he was of little use to them.

At the outset of the 1975 season, Hooton was 0-2 with an 8.18 earned run average. Finally, on May 2, 1975, Hooton was traded to the Los Angeles Dodgers for pitchers Geoff Zahn and Eddie Solomon.

Outfielder Rick Monday once rescued an American flag in Dodger Stadium and later won a National League flag for the Dodgers. But in between he did his best slugging for the Cubs.

Monday, a product of the Santa Monica (Calif.) sandlots, played with the Dodgers' summer rookie team in 1964 and was set to sign a $20,000 bonus with Los Angeles. His mother had the pen in her hand when she decided she wanted Rick to have a college education first.

"I was only 17 and she didn't think I was mature enough," said the articulate Monday. "I was put in touch with Bobby Winkles, the Arizona State coach, and he gave me a scholarship."

About 70 to 100 tried out for the team and from that group emerged what possibly was the greatest array of college talent ever assembled. In addition to Monday, there were outfielder Reggie Jackson, third baseman Sal Bando, and catcher Duffy Dyer.

In Monday's sophomore season, Arizona State won the NCAA championship with a 54-8 record. Major league scouts flocked to see the team in action and all focused their attention on the loose-limbed left-handed slugger.

Rick was the Sun Devils' leading hitter with a .380 average. He had driven in 45 runs and 31 of his 63 hits were for extra bases, including 10 doubles, 12 triples, and 9 homers.

Charles O. Finley, whose A's were then based in Kansas City, had the first selection in baseball's first free agent draft of human flesh. The so-called "grab bag" came about because the owners consistently violated their own bonus rules, cheated on each other, and couldn't trust each other.

There were 600 youngsters eligible and Monday was the first choice. He signed with Finley's A's for a $104,000 bonus in 1965. After a short stint in the minors, where he had moderate success, Rick reported to the A's in the closing days of the 1966 season.

Monday had driven all night from Mobile to KC with teammate Sal Bando and arrived early in the morning. "We were so tired," recalled Monday.

In his tapered A's uniform, Monday appeared gaunt. His straight blond hair stuck out the sides of his cap like straw shoots. Veteran Jim Pagliaroni labeled the boyish-looking recruit "Ricky Blue Eyes."

"I played that first day, too," said Monday. "Was I scared?" Well, I should have had a rope to tie my knees together. They were shaking. I went to bat against Jim Lonborg of the Red Sox and took a third strike."

Monday went to bat 14 times before he finally singled off the Orioles' Jim Palmer. He wound up with 4 hits in 41 at bats for a sensational batting average of .098.

Finley, who moved his A's to Oakland in 1968, was building a dynasty with the Sun Devils' trio of Monday, Bando, and Jackson, plus such standouts as Catfish Hunter, Bert Campaneris, and Vida Blue among others.

But as the A's moved closer to the top, Monday became less of a factor. There were no qualms about his hustle or defensive ability. He hit more for distance than average and was a frequent strikeout victim. A's manager Dick Williams soon benched Monday against all left-handed pitchers.

In addition, Monday was in and out of the lineup due to military

MONDAY, ROBERT JAMES
B. Nov. 20, 1945, Batesville, Ark.
BL TL 6'3" 195 lb.

commitments. When his average plummeted to .245 in 1971 from a .290 the previous season, Rick was traded to the Cubs for southpaw Ken Holtzman.

It was a big break for Holtzman. He leaped from Cub manager Leo Durocher's doghouse to a penthouse as the A's went on to win three straight World Series. Somehow, Monday justified the trade. He easily was the Cubs' best center fielder since Andy Pafko.

Monday arrived at the tailend of the Durocher era. The Cubs started unloading their many veterans, but Monday was a fixture for the future. Although his average was only .249, Rick displayed extra base power and stole a dozen bases. His biggest day was May 16, 1972, when he stroked three successive homers in an 8-1 victory over the Phillies at Veterans Stadium.

Monday, who was moved to the leadoff spot by new manager Whitey Lockman, found the homer range in 1973 by hiking his total to 26, high on the Cubs. Perhaps his most satisfying homer came on June 8 in Cincinnati.

Reds' manager Sparky Anderson was quoted in a story saying the Cubs were a collection of aging stars, with little speed and little hope. Lockman tacked the clipping on the bulletin board and Monday took notice.

There were two outs and a man on with the Reds leading 5-4 in the late innings. Monday tore into lefty Tom Hall's first pitch and ripped the ball into the right field bleachers for a 6-5 victory.

Besides contributing with the glove and bat, Monday was an alert baserunner. He won one game for the Cubs with a mad dash from second base to home plate on a deep flyout. It came in the eighth inning against the Montreal Expos on April 11, 1975, at Wrigley Field.

Monday was perched on second after singling and moving up on a grounder. Pete LaCock then drove the ball deep to rookie Gary Carter, a catcher playing right field.

After Carter flagged down the ball, Monday tagged and kept churning. He rounded third at full speed, made a head-first slide, and beat the throw home for a 2-1 victory.

Undoubtedly his finest moment was on April 25, 1976, in a losing cause at Dodger Stadium. It was the 100th anniversary of the Cubs' first game.

The dramatic moment came in the fourth inning when he snatched an American flag from two men who tried to set it afire. "I saw those two clowns come on the field," said Monday. "But I didn't know what they were doing. Then I saw them spread the flag like a picnic blanket and attempt to set it afire."

He swooped in behind the apparent protestors and carried the flag out of danger. The message board flashed: "Rick Monday . . . You Made A Great Play." . . . The crowd gave him a standing ovation.

Monday had three hits, scored two and drove in one, but the Cubs failed to rally 'round the flag and dropped a 5-4 decision to the Dodgers in 10 innings.

The 1976 season was Monday's best and his last as a Cub. He led the team with 32 homers, and was rewarded by being shipped to the Dodgers with reliever Mike Garman for first baseman Bill Buckner, shortstop Ivan DeJesus, and minor league pitcher Jeff Albert.

DeJesus filled the hole at shortstop, while Buckner consistently was around the .300 mark and won a Cub batting title. Monday, meanwhile, was handed the center field spot, but a back injury, a heel problem, and other assorted ouches kept him on the sidelines much of the time. The Dodgers kept winning without much of a contribution from Monday until Oct. 19, 1981.

The Dodgers and Expos were tied at two games apiece going into the deciding playoff game for the National League pennant. It was a typical October day in Montreal. Snow was forecast.

The weatherman was wrong. It rained that morning, leaving a chill, damp afternoon, hardly conducive to the summer game. But by midafternoon the sun even made a brief appearance.

The Dodgers and rookie sensation Fernando Valenzuela and the Expos, with ex-Cub Ray Burris, were locked in a 1-1 duel for eight innings. Steve Rogers, the Expos' pitching ace had replaced Burris in the ninth inning.

Rogers disposed of the first two Dodgers, but Monday disposed of Rogers and the Expos, belting a fastball deep into right-center field.

"I knew I hit the ball well," said Monday. "But I couldn't see it because of the glare." The ball cleared the fence for a game-winning homer. The Dodgers won 2-1 and clinched the pennant. It was a Dodger blue Monday with Rick supplying the Monday punch.

Despite his heroics, Monday remained a semiregular until his retirement in midseason 1984. He closed his career with 241 homers, 106 in a Cub uniform. Rick will best be remembered as the player who saved one flag and won another.

JOSE CARDENAL

CARDENAL, JOSE DOMEC ROSARIO
B. Oct. 7, 1943, Matanzas, Cuba
BR TR 5'10" 150 lb.

The Cubs have had a long heritage of zany performers. One of the main characters preserving this time-honored tradition through the 1970s was the wiry outfield speedster, Jose Cardenal.

Before coming to Chicago, Cardenal had been a well-traveled performer. Following minor league training in El Paso, Eugene, and Tacoma, Jose was brought up for a cup of coffee with the Giants early in 1963. He made his way into only nine games before it was back to El Paso, where he belted Texas League pitching for a .312 average and 36 homers. The next year Jose spent another season in Tacoma before being called back to San Francisco late in the race. In November 1964 he was swapped to the Angels for Jack Hiatt.

During the next three seasons, Jose played regularly for California, reaching a high of .276 in 1966. Still, many observers looked upon him as more of a clown than a serious athlete, so he was traded to the Indians. At Cleveland in 1968 and '69, he perfected his basestealing skills, with 40 and 36.

Traded to the Cardinals in 1970, Jose had his best season yet, batting .293. But that did not prevent him from being sent to the Milwaukee Brewers midway through the following season. After nine years in the majors, he had yet to find his proper niche and develop long-term consistency as a player.

On Dec. 3, 1971, the Cubs traded Jim Colborn, Earl Stephenson, and Brock Davis to the Brewers for Cardenal. It was the turning point in his career.

Jose came to Chicago with a reputation as a "hot dog," and he lived up to it, but he was a likable "hot dog." In Wrigley Field he finally found a happy home. He became the hero of the local Latino population.

He did juggling acts for the bleacherites during practice, and he played the violin in the clubhouse to entertain his teammates. He once missed batting practice because the crickets had allegedly kept him awake all night. Another time, Cardenal cancelled out because his eyelid was stuck shut—so he claimed, anyway. After that, the Cubs' motto became "Jose, can you see?" He drove to the park in flashy sports cars and went in for snowmobiling during the winter.

But whatever his quirks, Jose paid instant dividends on the diamond, batting .291 in '72 and resurrecting the lost art of basestealing at Wrigley Field with 25 swipes. His 1,000th career hit came June 13, in a 4-3 loss to the Padres.

Moreover, Cub owner P. K. Wrigley had taken a special liking to Cardenal, who in turn played his heart out. In 1973, with the aging Cub team dropping to fifth place, Jose came up with his first .300 season, batting .303 to pace the club. It earned him the Chicago Player of the Year award from the local sportswriters. He had become a master at stretching singles into doubles, and could deliver the homers when the occasion called for it. He followed suit in '74 with a .293 average and 72 RBI, one of the few redeeming achievements of a last place Cub squad.

The 1975 season was by far Jose's best. Reaching career highs of 182 hits and a .317 batting clip—eighth high in the league—Cardenal made the switch from right field to left with no problems. He scored 85 runs while his 34 stolen bases were the most by a Cub player since Kiki Cuyler pilfered 37 in 1930, a faded memory to most Cub fans. With the veteran Billy Williams having been dispatched to Oakland for his final fling, Jose was now easily the most popular player on the team.

The sensitive Cardenal loved the approbation of Cub fans and seldom let them down. His greatest heroics came May 2, 1976, as he collected six hits (four singles, a double, and a home run) and drove in four runs, including the game winner, as the Cubs outlasted the Giants 6-5 in 14 innings at Candlestick Park.

It was another productive year for Jose. He missed the coveted

.300 mark by only a fraction of a point and again topped the club in steals with 23.

Jose's first five years with the Cubs had been his most productive stretch in baseball. But on April 12, 1977, the greatest benefactor of his career, Phil Wrigley, died at age 82. Cardenal, one of the few players who attended the funeral, expressed his opinion that the entire team should have been there.

Additional complications soon arose. Bob Kennedy, the Cubs' new general manager, had openly disliked Jose when he had previously been his upstairs boss in St. Louis, and his opinion had not changed.

Herman Franks, the new Cub field manager, shared Kennedy's views, and Cardenal found himself on the bench just as often as not. To worsen matters still more, Jose suffered a knee injury, putting him on the disabled list for several weeks. Unhappy and unhealthy, he slipped to .239 in 226 trips. That fall he was dealt to the Phillies for pitcher Manny Seoane.

Jose had left his heart in Chicago and once again became a baseball drifter. He spent about a year and a half with the Phils and a year with the Mets before winding up with the Royals at the end of 1980.

Lifetime, Jose was a .275 hitter with 1,913 hits, 138 homers, and 329 stolen bases. In spite of his travels, Cardenal is seldom remembered as a Cardinal, but always as a Cub.

RICK REUSCHEL

REUSCHEL, RICKY EUGENE
B. May 16, 1949, Quincy, Ill.
BR TR 6'3"
225–245 lb.

Hey, fatso! When ya goin' to lose weight?" Rick Reuschel stands on the mound and ignores the jibes from the stands. Reuschel is big and beefy with a Bunyanesque body that belies his baby face. But he is an athlete.

The date is June 29, 1974. The scene is Montreal's Jarry Park. Reuschel and the Cubs are leading the Expos 2-1 in the last of the ninth with one out and a runner on first.

There's a pop bunt. Reuschel shoots off the mound for the ball that is no higher than his round tummy. The ball is just about to hit the first base chalk line. Reuschel makes a swimmer's dive, catches it, and flips to first base from a prone position for a double play.

The Cubs win 2-1. Expos' fans watch unbelieving, then rise for an ovation. Who needs the slim, trim type? The Cubbies will accept Reuschel for what he is—a whale of a pitcher.

For awhile the Cubs had two Reuschels, Rick and Paul. And they made baseball history by becoming the first brothers to combine on a shutout victory, beating the Los Angeles Dodgers 7-0 on Aug. 21, 1975, at Wrigley Field.

Rick was pitching a five-hitter when a blister on his pitching finger became raw and tender. He departed with one out and one on in the seventh inning. Paul ambled in with his equally ample belly and pitched one-hit ball the rest of the way.

Not even the Deans, the Perrys, or the Niekros can make that brotherly boast.

The Reuschels were raised on a farm in Camp Point, Ill., near Quincy. Mom and pop Reuschel have eight children, seven boys and a girl. Paul and Rick rank third and fourth in age. Both are husky six-footers who haven't missed many meals.

"When he was Little League age I used to have to beg him to play with me," said Paul. "He'd rather play cowboys and Indians, stuff like that." Rick didn't get serious about baseball until he entered Western Illinois University in Macomb.

Paul had gone to Western and was the pitcher on the baseball team. He set several school records, among them the most victories and strikeouts. "You know what happened then," added Paul. "Rick broke all my records."

In 1969 Rick led Western Illinois to the Illinois Intercollegiate Athletic Conference championship with a 10-0 record and a 1.29 earned-run average. He was then signed by Cubs' scout Elvin Tappe in the third round of the June 1970 free agent draft. Tappe had earlier tapped older brother Paul.

Rick, however, rose faster than Paul. He was 9-2 with Huron of the Northern League in 1970 and 8-4 with San Antonio of the Texas League in 1971. He was promoted to the Cubs from Wichita in June 1972 after leading the American Association in everything, including a 9-2 record and 1.33 ERA.

The round, ruddy-faced rookie made his big league debut on June 19 against the Giants at Wrigley Field. Cub manager Leo Durocher blinked when Rick tripped over the pitching rubber on his first delivery. Rick regained his composure and struck out Bobby Bonds, the only batter he faced.

He recorded his first victory against the Giants the following day, relieving Burt Hooton in the third inning. Rick gave up two runs on five hits over the last six innings as the Cubs, paced by batterymate Randy Hundley's grand-slam homer, romped 15-8.

Reuschel also did his bit at the plate. He hit a pop-fly double in his first big league at bat, driving in a run during a five-run Cub fourth inning. "I saw the ball plop down and just lay there," recalled Rick. "So I kept going." He made it to second by sliding under the tag. That made Durocher blink again. Rick also got a single in the eighth to go two for three.

"His slider and fastball were really moving," said Hundley. "The fastball dips almost a foot when it reaches the plate."

"I'm not hesitating about starting him against any team," added Durocher. "And he can have all the strawberry shortcakes and pork chops he wants."

The big farm boy made his first start on June 27, 1972, and made it look as easy as pitching hay through a barn door. He threw only 92 pitches, allowing six hits in an 11-1 romp over the Philadelphia Phillies.

Reuschel remained stoic during those days of Cub upheavals. Durocher was soon gone, replaced by Whitey Lockman, a slender manager who issued an ultimatum, demanding that Rick get down to 220 pounds.

His Cub teammates came to Rick's defense. "He isn't fat," said one. "He's just a big guy—big boned, big frame." Lockman then asked if Reuschel had any favorite foods? Rick replied, "I like everything."

Reuschel wound up his rookie season with a 10-8 record and stepped in as the stopper of the staff, recording a 14-15 record with a woeful ballclub, the following season.

In 1974 brother Paul joined the Cubs. One look and it was obvious they were brothers. Paul was an inch taller at 6′4″, but seemed a mite trimmer. And he wore glasses.

Shortstop Don Kessinger wanted to know, "Who's prettier?" Catcher George Mitterwald looked at them and shook his head. He was stumped. Then he took off each man's cap. When he noticed Paul's balding head, Mitterwald said, "That one," and he pointed at Rick.

Rick Reuschel and Paul Reuschel were the only brothers ever to combine on a shutout. The two portly Cub pitchers beat the Dodgers 7-0 at Wrigley Field.

The Reuschels, however, did not emerge as a famed brother duo. Paul, pitching exclusively in relief, always remained on the fringe, winning 12 and dropping 11 in parts of four seasons. He was dropped from the team midway through the 1978 season. Paul was acquired by the Cleveland Indians where he closed out his career in 1979.

Rick, meanwhile, was pounds the best of the Cub pitchers. He even became a 20-game winner, compiling a 20-10 record in 1977. Undoubtedly, his best remembered victory that season came in relief.

The Cubs and Cincinnati Reds were engaged in a slugfest at Wrigley Field on July 28. Eleven homers sailed out of the park. The Reds led five times and the Cubs bounced back five times.

The Cubs had run out of pitchers and summoned Reuschel from the bullpen with the score tied 15-15 in the 13th inning. Rick set down the Reds in order in the top of the inning.

The first two Cub batters went out. They had exhausted all their pinch hitters and Reuschel had to bat for himself. He obliged by stroking a single up the middle. When Steve Ontiveros singled, Reuschel chugged to third, making it with a hook slide.

Then the crowd of 32,155 rose to its feet as the little-known and seldom-used Davey Rosello chopped a grounder between shortstop and third base. Reuschel trotted home as the ball skipped by into left field for a hit and a 16-15 triumph.

Reuschel always saved his best performances for the dog days of August. In August 1977 he was 5-0 and came back the following August with a 7-0 mark. While Rick remained consistent, the team was inconsistent.

It was an era of change for the Cubs. Players were coming and going through the swinging door. Reuschel remained unflappable.

Reuschel was one of few who bled Cub blue. "I'm too old to be moving around," said Reuschel. "I want to win a pennant like everyone else, but I want to win it here."

Rick resided in nearby Arlington Heights and purchased a farm in southern Wisconsin. He cared for his team. He cared when Bruce Sutter was traded and Larry Biittner left because the Cubs could not or would not meet their salary demands.

Then it happened to Reuschel. Rick was traded to the New York Yankees on June 12, 1981, in a deal so complicated it took 14 months to complete.

The Cubs reportedly received $400,000 plus pitchers Doug Bird and Mike Griffin and infielder Pat Tabler. That wasn't the end of the deal. In the months to come the Cubs also surrendered pitchers Bill Caudill and Jay Howell.

Reuschel finally was with a winner. The big ample belly in the Big Apple. Most players would have been elated. The Yankees tore up his contract for a fatter one.

Reuschel got to pitch in a World Series. But his Yankee record was only 4-4 and he developed arm trouble, forcing him to miss the entire 1982 season.

After drawing his release, Reuschel signed a conditional contract with the Cubs. Rick was 3-4 with Quad Cities before he was brought up to the parent club near the conclusion of the season and posted a 1-1 record.

The 1984 season was one of mixed emotions for the big guy. The Cubs were finally a winner, but Rick spent much of it on the disabled list with assorted injuries. He did manage a 5-5 record while pitching in tough luck. He dropped a 1-0 heartbreaker to Houston and 2-1 in 10 innings to Montreal.

Reuschel wasn't eligible for postseason play and when he entered the free agent grab bag, he was ignored by the Cubs. Reuschel signed with the Pirates. He was sent to Hawaii in 1985.

It was a shame because the Chubby Cubbie beefed up a scrawny pitching staff for more than a decade, winning 135 and losing 127. His 1,367 strikeouts rank him third behind Fergie Jenkins and Charlie Root on the all-time Cub list.

RAY BURRIS

BURRIS, BERTRAM RAY
B. Aug. 22, 1950, Idabel, Okla.
BR TR 6'5" 200 lb.

Ray Burris was a Cub moundsman of the 1970s who never fulfilled his early promise. As of this writing, he is still active.

Ray was signed by the Cubs as their 17th round selection in the 1972 free agent draft, following his graduation from Southwestern State College of Waterford, Okla. After spending the '72 season in Midland, Burris spent the next two years commuting from Chicago to Wichita. Appearing mostly in relief, he won four and dropped six in a Cub uniform.

Assigned to the starting staff in 1975, Ray hurled his first major league shutout, a 6-0 four-hitter versus the Braves, on May 26. He finished the season with an impressive 15-10 ledger for a Cub team that finished tied for fifth. His ERA, however, was a not so impressive 4.12.

In 1976 Burris started off slowly and remained that way well into July, posting a 4-11 mark at that point. Then he turned things around, winning 11 of his last 13 decisions, including his last five in a row, to finish at 15-13. He trimmed his ERA to 3.11, led the club in shutouts with four, and was 6-1 in August, when he was voted National League Pitcher of the Month. For a time, it looked as if the Cubs had another Fergie Jenkins.

But the euphoria turned out to be fleeting. Burris won 14 the following year but lost 16 as his ERA expanded to 4.72. It was also in that season that he was involved in one of the most bizarre incidents in baseball history.

The Cubs were in New York's Shea Stadium for a night game on July 13. Ray was on the mound with the Cubs leading 2-1 in the sixth inning when a blackout engulfed the area, at 9:28 p.m. (Eastern time), leaving 30,000 fans (and 10 million other New Yorkers) stranded in the darkness. With Mets' board chairman M. Donald Grant conferring with plate umpire Harry Wendelstedt, the game was in limbo until 10:40 p.m., when it was officially suspended.

The blackout had its humorous aspects. Cub outfielder Jerry Morales remarked, "No wonder I struck out twice." All the police could say was "We're waiting for orders." The contest was finally completed Sept. 16 as Burris waited patiently to earn the credit for a 5-2 Cub win.

In 1978 things went from bad to worse as Ray slipped to 7-13. He then announced that he had become a born-again Christian. Unfortunately, his pitching did not enjoy a corresponding rebirth. On May 23, 1979, Burris was traded to the Yankees for pitcher Dick Tidrow.

Burris has since drifted from the Yanks to the Mets to the Expos to the A's and, in 1985, to the Brewers. Although Ray put in a creditable season for Oakland last year (13-10, 3.15 ERA), he has yet to regain the effectiveness of late 1976.

Lifetime, he is 93-114.

WHITEY LOCKMAN

LOCKMAN, CARROLL WALTER
B. July 25, 1926, Lowell, N.C.
BL TR 6'1"
175 lb.

If Leo Durocher was Leo the Lip, then Whitey Lockman was Whitey Lockjaw. During his six and a half seasons as Cub manager, the fiery, flamboyant Durocher thrived on turmoil. Lockman, his successor, was not one to rant or rave or kick over water coolers.

That's the way P. K. Wrigley wanted it when calm Whitey replaced angry Leo as manager on July 25, 1972. Yet, the radical transition wasn't all that good. It wasn't altogether Lockman's fault that the excitement was gone. He just inherited an aging ballclub.

The Cubs went from contender to pretender under Lockman's two seasons at the helm. They lacked fire. There was no dash or sparkle about them. They just plugged along at a .500 pace.

When the straw-thatched Lockman was replaced by Jim Marshall midway through the 1974 season he left behind a 157-162 won-lost ledger.

Carroll Walter Lockman was born in Lowell, N.C., on July 25, 1926, the son of a textile mill overseer. He was the youngest of five children. "My father died when I was eight months old," said Lockman.

Lockman broke into the New York Giants lineup on July 5, 1945. He hit a home run in his first time at bat off George Dockins, a St. Louis Cardinals' left-hander.

He had a .341 average for 32 games before entering the army the following month. Whitey didn't rejoin the Giants until 1947 and broke his ankle during spring training. He got into only two games that season, hitting .500 with one hit in two trips.

Lockman remained an outfielder until the 1951 season when he was switched to first base to make room for a young phenom named Willie Mays. That was the year of the "Miracle of Coogan's Bluff" and Lockman played a big role.

During his 15-year big league career, Lockman collected 1,658 hits with 114 homers and a .279 batting average. He spent the next four years as Giants' coach and landed his first managerial job, guiding Dallas-Ft. Worth to a second-place finish in 1965.

When Durocher took over as Cub manager in 1966, he summoned his old "buddy" as third base coach. Whitey then flitted about the Cub organization the next few seasons in such roles as manager at Tacoma and player development supervisor.

Lockman was the obvious choice as Durocher's successor, receiving the news on his 46th birthday. They still called him Whitey, but the hair was now the color of October straw, pale yellow. His face had deep furrowed lines.

The tension and bickering among the players vanished under Lockman. But so did the fun. Gone was pitcher Dick Selma, waving a towel and egging on the left field bleacher bums. Gone was Ron Santo, clicking his heels. Gone was Joe Pepitone.

Also departing were such favorites as Fergie Jenkins, Jim Hickman, Glenn Beckert, Randy Hundley, Ken Holtzman, Milt Pappas, and Bill Hands. Ernie Banks and his home run wand were in mothballs.

The Cubs took on the image of their manager. It was the blond leading the bland. They finished second to the Pirates in 1972, dropped to fifth in 1973 and wound up sixth in 1974 with Marshall replacing Lockman at the All-Star break.

Lockman headed for cover upstairs as vice-president. He is now a scout for the Montreal Expos.

It was the final game of the 1976 season. The Cubs, as usual, were hopelessly out of the pennant chase. But they had one glimmer of salvaging the sad season. He was Bill Madlock, a chunky third baseman, who seemed shorter than his announced 5′11″ and heavier than his reported 180 pounds.

Madlock, who had won the batting title with a .354 mark the previous season, was attempting to retain his crown against Cincinnati outfielder Ken Griffey. Going into the final day, Griffey was batting .337 with Madlock in pursuit at .333. Reds' manager Sparky Anderson wanted Madlock to do the chasing, so he decided to let Griffey sit out the game.

Madlock was mugged the previous week in New York's fashionable Waldorf-Astoria Hotel and had been in and out of the lineup with a few bruises. He was still hurting when he faced the Montreal Expos at Wrigley Field.

In the first inning Madlock laid down a perfect bunt and beat it out for a hit. He had trimmed Griffey's margin to two percentage points, .337 to .335. The Cubs scored a pile of runs and the heavy-bearded Madlock got a chance to bat in the second inning.

He hit a slow roller down the third base line and beat the throw for another hit. It was now Griffey .337 and Madlock .336. His next plate appearance was in the fourth inning and he hit the first pitch with his short, sweet stroke over the second baseman's head for a solid single. Bill had tied Griffey at .337.

Madlock's big moment came in the sixth inning. The Cubs were comfortably ahead and Madlock received a standing ovation from the slim crowd of some 7,000. It sounded like 70,000 as he laced a line single to left field. Bill had overtaken Griffey .339 to .337.

Madlock's exploits apparently reached Cincinnati where the Reds were playing the Atlanta Braves. Griffey was hustled into the game as a pinch hitter and struck out. It was now Madlock .339 and Griffey .336.

Cub manager Jim Marshall then decided to let Griffey do the chasing. After going four-for-four, Madlock was taken out for pinch batter Rob Sperring in the eighth inning. Imagine, taking out a .339 hitter for a .258 hitter. Sperring, incidentally, added to the fun by getting a hit.

Madlock's reward for winning two straight batting titles? He was shunted to the San Francisco Giants, along with Sperring, for Bobby Murcer, Steve Ontiveros, and the aptly named Andy Muhlstock.

Some guys get no respect, and Madlock tops that category. He was the 268th selection when the St. Louis Cardinals chose him in the 12th round of the 1968 free agent draft. Madlock, an all-around athlete at Eisenhower High School in Decatur, Ill., spurned the Cards' offer in favor of attending storied Keokuk (Iowa) Junior College.

But Madlock finally succumbed to pro baseball. He was the 99th player picked in the secondary draft the following season, signing with the Washington Senators. The Senators soon deserted

BILL MADLOCK

MADLOCK, BILL, JR.
B. Jan. 12, 1951, Memphis, Tenn.
BR TR 5′11″
180 lb.

Washington, shifting their franchise to the Dallas-Ft. Worth area and emerging as the Texas Rangers.

Madlock, meanwhile, was submerged in the minors, wandering from Geneva, N.Y.; Pittsfield, Mass.; Denver; back to Pittsfield; and winding up at Spokane, Wash.; in 1973. There he hit .338 and finished second for the Pacific Coast League batting title.

Bill was called up by the Rangers in September and hit .351 in 21 games. As a reward he was a "throw-in" as part of a package that sent teammate Vic Harris to the Cubs for six-time 20-game winner Fergie Jenkins.

The Cubs coveted Harris as a basestealing second baseman. Madlock, however, faced more pressure. He was replacing Ron Santo, a 14-year veteran at third base who was dealt to the crosstown White Sox in a five-player trade. "Santo has his job to do and I have mine," said Madlock.

He turned in quite a job, leading the Cubs in hitting with a .313 mark, despite being sidelined one month with a severe ankle injury. That was only a prelude to some explosive exploits in the 1975 season.

A typical Madlock day at the plate? Try June 3, 1975, against the Giants at Wrigley Field. With the Giants leading 5-4, Madlock led off the ninth inning with a homer onto the left field catwalk. In the 10th inning his run-scoring double off the right-center field wall clinched a 6-5 victory.

Typically, too, he wasn't selected as the starting third baseman for the National League in the All-Star Game. That honor went to Ron Cey of the Los Angeles Dodgers. But Bill was around at the finish. His two-run single in the ninth inning gave the National League a 6-3 victory and earned Madlock co-MVP honors with New York Mets pitcher Jon Matlack.

In addition, Madlock went six-for-six against the Mets on July 26, a triple and five singles, to help him finish 22 points ahead of the Cards' Ted Simmons for the batting title.

After retaining his title in 1976 with his final-day heroics, Madlock boasted a three-year Cub batting average of .336, a mark topped only by Rogers Hornsby's .350 in Cub annals.

It was the era of free agents and Madlock wanted a bigger slice of the pie. He sought a five-year contract in the neighborhood of $1 million. The Cubs offered him crumbs and then moved him out of the neighborhood.

He was banished to the Giants on Feb. 11, 1977, by new Cub general manager Bob Kennedy, who then surprised all by giving the newly acquired Murcer, a player of lesser talent than Madlock, a fatter contract.

Madlock's batting crowns were gone with the cold, swirling winds of San Francisco's Candlestick Park. His average dipped to .302 and .309 the next two seasons.

He was then rescued by Pittsburgh in midseason 1980 and helped the Pirates to the NL pennant. Madlock capped the season by batting .375 as the Pirates beat the Baltimore Orioles in the World Series.

Madlock was one of the few benefactors of the strike-shortened 1981 season. He won his third batting title with a .341 average. After "dropping" to .319 in 1982, Madlock notched his fourth batting title with a .323 average in 1983.

Billy wasn't as fortunate last season. He suffered an elbow injury and his stroke went sour, dipping to .253 before he underwent surgery in midseason.

But the unkindest cut had come when the Cubs cut him adrift. Chalk up another donkey trade for the Cubs. And whatever became of Andy Muhlstock?

JERRY MORALES

MORALES, JULIO REUBEN
B. Feb. 18, 1949, Yabucoa, P.R.
BR TR 5'10" 175 lb.

Jerry Morales was recently on his second tour of duty with the Cubs. First signed by the Mets' organization, Morales made his debut at age 17 with Marion of the Appalachian League in 1966.

In the years that followed, he made stops in such never-to-be-forgotten places as Winter Haven, Raleigh, Durham, and Visalia. On Oct. 12, 1968, Jerry was selected by the expansion San Diego Padres in the draft. And where did they send him? Promptly to Elmira of the Eastern League.

Although Morales had not been especially impressive in the minor leagues, the fledgling Padres needed all the help they could get, so Jerry was called up to the big time late in 1969.

He made his way into 19 games but batted just .195 and found himself optioned to Salt Lake City in 1970. Then it was back to San Diego briefly, then out to Hawaii for more seasoning. Not until September of 1971 was Morales back in the majors for keeps.

During the next two campaigns, Morales appeared on a semiregular basis as a Padre, reaching .281 in 122 games in 1973. Still, he was unable to crack the lineup on an every day level.

On Nov. 12, 1973, the Cubs sent their aging second baseman, Glenn Beckert, to the Padres for Morales. Beckert's best years were behind him, so the deal worked out well for the Cubs, who were rebuilding for the umpteenth time.

Given the starting position in left field, Jerry responded by hitting .273, clouting 15 home runs, and driving in 82 runs to pace the club. With Jose Cardenal and Rick Monday, the trio gave the Cubs a highly respected defensive outfield, one of the few highlights of a last place team. On May 22, 1974, Jerry smashed two homers against the Mets, driving in six runs in a 9-6 Cub win.

Over the next three seasons, Morales remained a valuable member of the Cub lineup, batting .270, .274, and .290. Batting in the clean-up position, he drove home 91 runs to lead the club in 1975, and hit 16 homers the following year for a career high. Continuing to be a hero against the Mets, he smacked two homers and drove in four runs in a 5-4 victory before an opening day throng of 44,818 on April 13, 1976.

Although Jerry had the highest batting average of his career in 1977, he did not fit into the plans of the new Cub manager, Herman Franks. That winter, he was dispatched to the Cardinals with Steve Swisher for catcher Dave Rader and outfielder Hector Cruz, whom general manager Bob Kennedy seemed to imagine would be the next Joe DiMaggio, which he was not.

As for Morales, he was not the same after leaving the Cubs, whatever the reason. He played a year with the Cardinals, one with the Tigers, and another with the Yankees, with his highest batting average being .254 as a part-timer in New York.

By 1981 Jerry was back in a Cub uniform, thanks to the free agent draft. In a strike-shortened season, he hit .286 in 84 games. He spent most of the 1982 campaign with the Cubs' Iowa Triple A team, but returned late in the season, batting .284 and knocking home 30 runs on just 33 hits. Again used sparingly in 1983, Morales batted just .195 and drew his release at the end of the season. Jerry was a lifetime .260 hitter with 1,173 hits and 95 homers.

MANNY TRILLO

TRILLO, JESUS MANUEL
B. Dec. 25, 1950, Edo Monagas, Venezuela
BR TR 6'1" 150 lb.

Wolves were howling at the Cubs' door when they acquired Manny Trillo. And many were howling in laughter when they dealt him away. The slim native of Venezuela was never fully appreciated in a Cub uniform.

Trillo, tall, dark with a boyish, sly grin, gave the Cubs four seasons of artistic play at second base, something they lacked before his arrival and after his departure.

There must be something in the Venezuelan air or water that grows such, smooth, fluid infielders as Chico Carrasquel, Luis Aparicio, Dave Concepcion, and Manny Trillo.

Signed originally by the Philadelphia Phillies in 1968, Trillo's minor league credentials were as slim as he is trim. "Trillo can't hit. . . . He has no strength," read some of the scouting reports. He was written off as a big league prospect.

Manny proved them wrong. After hitting .302 at Des Moines in 1972 and .312 at Tucson the following season, Trillo became the center of attention during the 1973 World Series.

He was brought up to the Oakland A's near the end of the season and batted .250 in 17 games. But he was ineligible for the series.

A's owner Charles O. Finley, in a pique, fired second baseman Mike Andrews for his two errors at second base and sent him home. Finley wanted to put Trillo in uniform.

This ploy irked other teammates and Andrews was reinstated by Commissioner Bowie Kuhn. Trillo thus became a household name without donning a uniform.

Trillo, the man on Finley's wanted list, was found wanting. He was shipped back to the bushes in 1974. His name didn't crop up again until Oct. 23, 1974, when he was sent to the Cubs in a three-for-one deal. He was accompanied to Chicago with relievers Darold Knowles and Bob Locker. In return the A's received long-time Cub hero Billy Williams.

The consensus of opinion was that the Cubs were victims of a heist. Some typical comments: "Worst Cub trade since the Lou Brock for Ernie Broglio deal," and "How stupid can the Cubs be, giving up a player of Williams' caliber for three guys nobody knows."

The lone dissenter was Cubs' general manager John Holland, the victim of the Brock debacle. "Trillo is the key man," said Holland. "We needed a second baseman and we think we got one who can field with anyone."

Holland was right. After second baseman Glenn Beckert ran out of gas in 1973, the Cubs' keystone brigade of 1974 resembled the Keystone Kops with such comics as Vic Harris, Rob Sperring, Billy Grabarkewitz, Ron Dunn, and Matt Alexander on the beat.

Trillo took charge in 1975 and stopped all that traffic. It helped with veteran Don Kessinger at shortstop as a double-play partner. "He's one of the easiest guys I've worked with," said Kessinger. "He doesn't have a good arm. He has a great arm."

Cincinnati Reds' manager Sparky Anderson proclaimed Trillo's arm "the best I've ever seen. Bill Mazeroski had a quicker arm, but not as strong," said Sparky.

Cub broadcaster Lou Boudreau, a Hall of Fame shortstop, also praised Trillo. "Joe Gordon's the best I've ever seen," said Boudreau. "Manny's right up there with Joe."

There was a bit of hot dog in Trillo's repertoire that irked batters going down the line to first base. Manny would scoop up the ball, hesitate until the runner got close to the base, and then whip the ball with a quick sidearm motion. It agitated the runners, but Cub fans ate up his act.

Manny's hitting proved a bonus. Although he batted .248, Trillo proved tough in the clutch, driving in 70 runs. It was the most by a Cub second baseman since Don Johnson drove in 71 in 1944.

Trillo's average dipped to .239 and he had 59 RBI in 1975, but he tightened the defense with 527 assists and took part in 111 double plays.

In 1976 Trillo teamed well with shortstop Ivan DeJesus as the "Latin Connection." They were a busy double-play combo with both topping the league in assists. Trillo had 467 and DeJesus 595.

Then followed what was supposed to be Trillo's big year. He led the league in hitting at .362 in mid-June. His main hitting rival was outfielder Dave Parker of the Pittsburgh Pirates.

The 6′5″, 250-pound Parker came to Wrigley Field and crossed bats with the 150-pound Trillo in a photo. Parker looked like he could devour Trillo for breakfast.

While Parker continued to eat up National League pitching and eventually win the batting title at .338, Trillo slipped badly and finished with a .280 mark. Manny was a prime example of a player wilting in day games under the hot sun at Wrigley Field. In addition, Trillo played all winter in Venezuela. It took its toll on the frail athlete.

Despite his nosedives at the plate, Trillo continued to make the spectacular plays afield. The DeJesus-Trillo tandem was now the best in the league. In 1978 they teamed for 1,036 assists, tops in the majors.

It was ironic that Trillo had not garnered any Gold Glove Awards. The whole Wrigley organization was low key. The deadbeats failed to drumbeat the talented Trillo. The Cubs weren't manic over Manny.

Meanwhile, the Philadelphia Phillies were climbing in the standings. They lacked only a second baseman to put them over the top. They eyed Trillo. They dangled three benchwarmers and the Cubs' GM Bob Kennedy fell into the trap.

After haggling all winter the trade was consummated on Feb. 23, 1979. The Cubs received second baseman Ted Sizemore, outfielder Jerry Martin, and catcher Barry Foote, plus minor league pitchers Derek Botelho and Henry Mack for the coveted Trillo. The Cubs even threw in outfielder Greg Gross and catcher Dave Rader.

Surprisingly, the Chicago media and Cub fans hailed the trade, citing Trillo's midseason fadeouts at the plate. Martin, Foote, and Sizemore became instant Cub regulars.

But the Cubs sank from the pennant chase and the three were dispersed in trades. Trillo, meanwhile, thrived on the Astro-Turf carpet at Veterans Stadium.

He was the hero of the storied 1980 championship playoff against the Houston Astros, batting a rousing .381, and he earned a World Series ring as the Phillies downed the Kansas City Royals in six games.

The Gold Glove Awards he deserved as a Cub also came his way. The Phillies knew when to get on the Gold standard. Trillo was acknowledged as the best fielding second baseman in 1979, 1980, 1981, and 1982.

He then became a many-traveled Trillo, bouncing from the Cleveland Indians, to the Montreal Expos, to the San Francisco Giants, spending much of his time on the disabled list.

STEVE STONE

STONE, STEVEN MICHAEL
B. July 14, 1947, Cleveland, Ohio
BR TR 5'10" 175 lb.

Steven Michael Stone was a player of many facets—all turned on. Picture him a poet, a ping pong prodigy, a pitcher, and a proud possessor of the national pastime's Cy Young Award.

In addition, the chunky, curly-coiffured Clevelander was a collegian at Kent State, a chess connoisseur, and a creative chef.

Steve's parents were rabid Indians' fans and his mother envisioned her son as another Koufax. "Of course, there's only one Sandy Koufax," said Stone, who brushed off Brush High School batters with an 0.46 ERA as a junior. He also turned the tables on his prep rivals as a ping pong champ.

Steve played Little League and American Legion ball and once pitched both ends of a legion doubleheader. On the sandlots he posted a 23-1 record for a Cleveland amateur team.

At Kent State University, Stone formed a formidable battery with former Yankee catcher Thurman Munson, who perished in a crash landing in 1979 while piloting his private plane.

Stone was captain of the Kent State team and was All Mid-American Conference. He graduated with degrees in history and government in 1969, thus missing the tragic anti-Vietnam demonstrations by a few months. "A girl who was our fraternity sweetheart was killed by the Ohio National Guard. So the event is bitterly etched in my memory," said Stone.

Steve then signed with the Giants and traveled the farmhand trail through their system from Fresno to Amarillo to Phoenix to Frisco. As he traveled, Stone took up chess, but couldn't find suitable opponents, so he turned to poetry.

Two of his works, "Friend" and "Memories," were published in Los Angeles, San Francisco, and Cleveland papers. The short-fellowed flinger was thus renowned as a poet who could throw it.

After no decisions in his first three big league starts in 1971, Stone came up with a five-hit shutout over the Pirates and wound up with a 5-9 season. He was 6-8 the following year, but lowered his earned-run average to 2.98 from his 4.14 rookie season.

The former chess master then made another move. He was used as a pawn with outfielder Ken Henderson in a deal for White Sox pitcher Tom Bradley on Nov. 29, 1972. His White Sox stint was brief, only one season, where he posted a 6-11 mark.

He did have one memorable game, the season finale, when he retired 24 batters in a row and struck out a dozen for a 10-inning, 1-0 victory over the A's.

Then followed a blockbuster deal with the crosstown Cubs on Dec. 11, 1973. Cub hero Ron Santo was shunted to the South Side for the Sox quartet of catcher Steve Swisher, and pitchers Ken Frailing, Jim Kremmel, and Stone.

Stone, who spent the winter working over a hot stove as part-owner in a Chicago restaurant chain, cooked a winning recipe for the Cubs, feasting on an early 5-0 season mark.

Stone wound up with an 8-6 record. The following season he became a regular in the Cub rotation, registering a dozen victories, that included triumphs over such biggies as Steve Rogers, Tom Seaver, Jerry Koosman, J. R. Richard, and Phil Niekro.

Shoulder miseries kept Steve on the disabled list through much of the 1976 season, limiting him to a 3-6 mark. He then became the first Cub to declare himself a free agent and was signed by the White Sox on Nov. 24. He departed with a three-year Cub log of 23-20.

He was signed by Bill Veeck for a bargain-basement contract of $60,000 and responded with a 15-12 record as the Sox became the "South Side Hit Men" and made a good run at the division title.

After a 12-12 season in 1978, Stone became baseball's first player to opt for free agency a second time.

There were chuckles when the pitching-rich Baltimore Orioles made their first entry into the free agent market by signing Stone to a $200,000-plus contract. He had lost more games than he had won and had a history of arm trouble.

Stone made an 11-7 contribution as the Orioles won the 1979 pennant. Steve even got into his first World Series, but was tagged for four hits and two runs in two innings as Baltimore lost in seven games to the Pirates.

In 1980 Steve suddenly fulfilled his mother's prophecy. Wearing Koufax's No. 32 jersey, Stone went into the season with a 78-79 record. Surprisingly, he blossomed into the major league's winningest pitcher, setting an Orioles' record with 25 victories in one season. Stone, who had never won more than 15 in a season, now won 14 in a row.

And guess who was on the mound at the start of the All-Star Game at Dodger Stadium? Mixing curves with a much-maligned fastball, Stone hurled three perfect innings, striking out three batters.

At the conclusion of the season Stone had a 25-7 record, good enough to edge the A's Mike Norris for the coveted AL Cy Young Award, 100 to 91. What could he do for an encore?

There were no extra bows in 1982. Arm trouble plummeted his record to 4-7 and he announced his retirement, concluding with a 107-90 career record.

He spent part of the 1982 season as a color commentator on ABC telecasts and drew excellent reviews. Stone now does commentary of Cubs' games on WGN TV with Harry Caray. He has also opened a restaurant in Scottsdale, Ariz., and another in Lake Tahoe.

GEORGE MITTERWALD

MITTERWALD, GEORGE EUGENE
B. June 7, 1947, Berkeley, Calif.
BR TR 6'2" 205 lb.

Which Cub would be best suited for a United Nations post? George Mitterwald? The Baron is of German-French-Austrian-Scottish-Portuguese descent. And he was part-catcher.

Mitterwald resembled Cub catcher Gabby Hartnett in one aspect. Both were slow afoot. But the Baron did have one super-sensational afternoon against the Pittsburgh Pirates at Wrigley Field. The date was April 17, 1974.

On that wind-swept Wednesday, Mitterwald smashed three homers, one a grand slam, had a double, drew a bases-loaded walk, and drove in eight runs as the Cubbies romped 18-9.

It was only his seventh day in a Cub uniform, having come over from the Minnesota Twins on Dec. 6, 1973, for catcher Randy Hundley. The deal wasn't popular with Cub fans, even though the Rebel had two damaged knees and the Baron was pronounced healthy.

Mitterwald had failed to drive in a single run in the Cubs' first six games. He had missed two games with a stomach ailment and was sporting a black eye, the result of a wild Ken Frailing warmup pitch. In addition, Mitterwald was suffering from sinuses that day.

"Something like that comes along once in a lifetime," said Mitterwald. "When you have a day like that you have to cherish it and remember it because it isn't likely to happen again."

The first homer off starter Jerry Reuss came in the first inning with the bases loaded and sailed over the left field wall onto Waveland Avenue. It was the one he stopped to watch. "I felt that one," he smiled. "I knew it was out."

The second homer came with a man on in the second inning and landed on the green in center field. After drawing a bases-loaded walk in the fourth inning, Mighty Mitty muscled his third homer to right center in the sixth.

The stage was set for the eighth inning and Mitterwald's final plate appearance. "The guys on the bench were kidding," recalled Mitterwald. "They said, 'get another homer and you'll have a super day.'

"On the way to the plate, manager Whitey Lockman told me, 'Don't get a single.' I didn't. I swung hard, but all I could get was a double to left-center."

Lockman removed Mitterwald for pinch runner Matt Alexander. As he trotted to the dugout Mitterwald received a standing ovation from the 15,560 fans.

What did George do for an encore? Well, he suffered a knee injury, lost his first string job to the weak-hitting Steve Swisher, and played only 78 games, hitting .251 with 7 homers and 28 RBI.

Mitterwald was in and out for the next three seasons, hitting .220, .215, and .238. When he sought a pay boost, the Cubs' GM Bob Kennedy objected.

George entered the free agent draft and drew scant attention. He finally signed with the lowly Seattle Mariners but was released in midseason. The kindly Kennedy then took Mitterwald back on his own terms—as a bullpen warmup catcher.

STEVE SWISHER

SWISHER, STEVEN EUGENE
B Aug. 9, 1951, Parkersburg, W. Va.
BR TR 6'2" 205 lb.

It was the summer of 1976. Cincinnati Reds' manager Sparky Anderson had a problem. He was filling out the National League roster for the annual All-Star Game. The rules state that every club must be represented. That meant he was forced to take a Cub player.

Sparky scratched his silver-thatched mane and scribbled a name: Steven Eugene Swisher. Wow. Steve Swisher—All-Star catcher.

Johnny Bench and Bob Boone handled the catching chores in a 7-1 victory, so Swisher was safely tucked away in the bullpen.

Steve Swisher was one of those "can't miss" prospects who rapidly evolved into a "can't hit" suspect. At Parkersburg (W. Va.)

High, the strong, young shortstop batted a robust .462. Swisher was switched to catcher at Ohio University.

The White Sox made Swisher their No. 1 draft pick on June 5, 1973, stating "he is the big, strong catcher we needed." They assigned him to Knoxville where he knocked the ball for a .211 average.

Swisher then became part of a White Sox package with pitchers Steve Stone, Ken Frailing, and Jim Kremmel in a four-for-one deal for Cub third baseman Ron Santo on Dec. 11, 1973.

Swisher was dispatched to Wichita where he pounded the pill for a .196 average in 52 games. He was now ready for the Cubs. He hit his first big league homer on June 28, 1974, against the Expos at Montreal and his first (and only) grand slam off Barry Lersch of the Cardinals on Sept. 20. But when the season concluded, Swisher was holding up the league with a .214 mark.

After going 0-for-17 at the outset of the 1975 season, he was sent to Wichita to regain his confidence. After waving the wand for a .284 Wichita average it was back to .213 woe in Cub flannels.

But 1976 was going to be different. Cub batting instructor Lew Fonseca worked hours, days, weeks with the swinging Swisher. His finest day as a Cubbie came on April 17 against the Phillies at Wrigley Field.

Steve hit a solo homer in the second inning and an RBI-single in the third as the Cubs jumped to a 12-1 lead. But Mike Schmidt came back with three homers and the Phillies led 15-13 in the ninth. Yes, the wind was blowing out.

With two out and two on in the bottom of the ninth, Staunch Steve sent the game into overtime with a two-run single. Three hits and four RBI in one game for our hero. But Schmidt did his bit with a two-run homer in the 10th for an 18-16 Philly win.

Nevertheless, Swisher continued swishing away. In his first 40 games Swisher hit safely in 30 of them for a .322 average. In one hot streak Swisher collected 11 hits in 18 at bats, including five in succession.

He was batting .394 against Sparky Anderson's world champion Reds. Swisher made Sparky's eyes sparkle at All-Star time and was the lone Cub selected.

Then it was back to below normal. Swisher's average plunged deeper, finishing with a .236 mark. There was less of the same in 1977. He pounded the pines more than the pill for a pulsating .190 average.

Swisher's Cub connection was severed on Dec. 8, 1977, when he was dealt to the Cards with outfielder Jerry Morales for catcher Dave Rader and outfielder Heity Cruz.

Who is the only player to hit three homers in his Cub debut? Hack Wilson? Ernie Banks? Dave Kingman? Naw. It was Rufus James Marshall.

JIM MARSHALL

MARSHALL, RUFUS JAMES
B. May 25, 1932, Danville, Ill.
BL TL 6′1″ 190 lb.

Jim Marshall, who bears a close resemblance to actor Gene Hackman, hails from Danville, Ill., which is also Hackman's hometown.

The Marshall family left Danville and settled in Compton, Calif., when Jim was a youngster. When Jim was 18, Johnny Wooden was trying to recruit him for basketball at UCLA, and Brick Owens sought his signature for the Oakland Oaks ballclub.

Marshall picked baseball and spent nine long seasons in the minor leagues as a first baseman, hitting 202 homers. His contract was purchased by the Chicago White Sox after he hit 30 homers and drove in 102 runs with Vancouver of the Pacific Coast League in 1957.

The eager rookie never got to play for the Sox. He was traded to the Baltimore Orioles with pitcher Jack Harshman and outfielder Larry Doby for pitcher Ray Moore, outfielder Tito Francona, and infielder-outfielder Billy Goodman on Dec. 3.

Marshall's stay with the Orioles was brief. After hitting only .215 in 81 games, Marshall was sold to the Cubs on Aug. 23, 1958. The next day he reported to manager Bob Scheffing and broke in with a bang, hitting two homers in the first game and another in the second as the Cubs split a doubleheader with the Phillies. He batted .272 with five homers in the remaining 26 games.

The following season, Marshall shuttled from first base to the outfield as a part-timer. He managed to collect 11 homers and 40 RBI, while hitting .252.

The journeyman then took many journeys. He was traded to the Boston Red Sox in 1960, followed by stopovers with the San Francisco Giants, New York Mets, and the Pittsburgh Pirates.

After closing out his big league career in 1962, Marshall accepted an offer to play with the Chunichi Dragons in the Japan Central League and remained for three years, hitting 78 homers.

Marshall was then ready to return home and become a manager. He sought out Cubs' GM John Holland and agreed to start at the bottom. There was no team lower than Lodi in the California League. Then he moved up the ladder to San Antonio, Tacoma, and Wichita before he rejoined the Cubs as third base coach in 1974.

The season was only half over when Marshall took over the Cub reins, replacing Whitey Lockman on July 24, 1974. During his tenure he earned the sobriquet of "Captain Hook" for his propensity to remove pitchers quickly.

"You can't afford to let the other team get too far ahead," said Marshall, who had the nucleus of a fair starting crew with Rick Reuschel, Bill Bonham, Steve Stone, Burt Hooton, and Ray Burris. Most of those hurlers enjoyed greater success when they moved on to other clubs.

Under the Marshall Plan the Cubs did show some progress, moving from sixth to fifth to fourth. But when Bob Kennedy was named Cubs' general manager, he brought in Herman Franks as manager and Marshall was out.

In his two and one-half seasons, Marshall's overall record was 175 victories and 218 losses.

Marshall spent the 1981 season as a coach in Japan.

LARRY BIITTNER

BIITTNER, LARRY DAVID
B. July 27, 1946, Ft. Dodge, Ia.
BL TL 6'2" 205 lb.

One of the most underrated of recent Cub players, Larry Biittner was a dependable utility outfielder-first baseman with the Cubs from 1976 through '80.

Biittner, who gained his minor league experience in Savannah, Pittsfield, and Denver, made his big time debut with the Washington Senators in 1970. Remaining with the team when they became the Texas Rangers two years later, Biittner did not hit higher than .259 and was traded to the Expos after the '73 season.

He spent most of the following season in Memphis, not seeing action in Montreal until late in the schedule. In 1975, however, Larry had a fine season for the Expos, batting .315 in 121 games.

Off to a poor start the season after, Biittner and Steve Renko were swapped to the Cubs for Andre Thornton on May 17, 1976. Still off-key, Biittner finished the year a .237 part-timer.

In spite of this, he was given a starting position in left field the next year, while sometimes subbing for Bill Buckner at first base. The outcome was the best overall performance of his career. Batting .298, he attained personal highs with 147 hits, 28 doubles, 12 homers, 74 runs scored, and 62 RBI—not spectacular, perhaps, but certainly gratifying.

On May 17, Larry, Steve Ontiveros, and Gene Clines homered in the third inning. In the fifth Biittner, Jerry Morales, and Bobby Murcer connected for consecutive homers as the Cubs racked the Padres 23-6. It was the only time the Cubs had three homers in an inning twice, thanks partially to Larry.

On another occasion, he even "pitched," so to speak. It was the first match of an Independence Day doubleheader at Wrigley Field and hopelessly out of reach. Biittner took to the mound for one and one-third innings, fanned three of his former teammates, but served three gopher balls and gave up six runs, all of them earned. Final score: Expos 19, Cubs 3.

April 14, 1978, was something else, however. A record opening day crowd of 45,777 jammed its way through the Wrigley Field turnstiles on a dark and dreary Friday afternoon. The Cubs and Pirates were deadlocked at four apiece when Larry led off the ninth. He promptly stroked Jim Bibby's first offering into the left field bleachers to give the Cubs and their throng a heartwarming 5-4 win.

With Dave Kingman as the Cubs' new left fielder, Biittner saw less action that season, but developed into their best bench man. He was 11-for-33 as a pinch hitter, driving in 12 runs in that capacity. The following year, with a .290 average overall, he was

12-for-37 as a pinch hitter, knocking home 11 runs.

Following an off season in 1980, Biittner entered the free agent market and signed with the Reds, where he was used only sparingly in the strike-shortened 1981 season. The next year he batted .310 as a substitute. After serving as a part-timer for Texas in 1983, Larry drew his release. He left the majors a .273 lifetime hitter with 861 hits and 29 homers.

BRUCE SUTTER

SUTTER, HOWARD BRUCE
B. Jan. 8, 1953, Lancaster, Pa.
BR TR 6'2" 190 lb.

Sunday, May 9, 1976, was Mother's Day. The wind was blowing out and the Reds were blowing out the Cubs. Cincinnati's Big Red Machine had rocketed six homers out of Wrigley Field and was leading the pitch-poor Cubs 14-2 after eight innings.

It was safe to bring in a raw recruit who had arrived the previous day from the bushes. The rookie right-hander held the Reds scoreless in the ninth inning and even struck out a batter. The newcomer was Bruce Sutter.

Little did the Cubs or their fans know that they had a diamond in the rough, for a jewel like Sutter comes along once in a lifetime.

The blue-eyed, shaggy-haired reliever possesses what is called a split-fingered fastball. He grips the ball between his fingers like a forkball and after releasing it, the ball drops and the batter gets that sinking feeling. Batters either beat the ball into the ground or miss it completely.

Sutter quarterbacked the football squad, captained the basketball team, and, of course, pitched while being named the outstanding athlete at Donegal High School in Mt. Joy, Pa. In addition, he played semipro ball for something called Hippey's Raiders.

He was signed to a pro contract for a whopping $500 bonus by Cub scout Ralph DiLullo in the fall of 1972. He was sent to the Arizona Instructional League where he posted a 3-0 record with an 0.90 ERA and 7 saves. At that stage young Sutter depended on a blazing fastball.

Then his elbow popped. There was cartilage damage. Young Sutter went home for an operation. His ulnar nerve was rerouted and his fastball took another route. It was gone. His career was in jeopardy.

In filing a report to the parent organization, minor league manager Walt Dixon said, "When Sutter is ready for the big leagues, that will be the day the Communists take over."

Fred Martin, a grizzled, wizened roving pitching instructor, who was surprisingly kept in the low minors by the slow-thinking Cub brass, took Sutter aside and showed him a pitch of his own. It was Freddie's trick pitch that did the trick.

The split-fingered fastball appeared to be an optical illusion the way the ball dropped. Batters just went through the swing. Sutter tied for the lead in saves with 13 at Midland, Tex., in 1975 and was promoted to Wichita, where he was 2-1 before joining the Cubs.

Sutter helped patch the league's worst bullpen, replacing the redoubtable Oscar Zamora as relief ace. Catcher George Mitterwald was the first Cub to take notice of Sutter's repertoire. "He looks unbelievable to me," sighed the Baron. "I never saw a ball drop like that."

Rival batters and managers were equally impressed. "He's unreal," said outfielder Ellis Valentine of the Montreal Expos after fanning on three pitches—low, lower, and lowest.

"He's magnificent. Just magnificent," added manager Sparky Anderson of the Reds, whose praise was echoed by other big league pilots.

Cub fans also joined in. When Sutter would saunter from the bullpen, the Wrigley Field organist would strike up the TV commercial, and the fans would follow with "Plop Plop, Fizz Fizz . . . Oh What A Relief He Is."

When the 1976 season concluded Sutter had 10 saves and 6 victories and was named Chicago Rookie of the Year. He allowed only 63 hits in 83 innings, with 73 strikeouts and 26 walks. His 2.71 ERA was lowest on the Cubs.

That was only the beginning. Sutter was nearly unbeatable early in the 1977 season as the Cubs led the National League for 69 days. But overwork caused a swelling, which formed a knot under his right shoulder blade, and Sutter went on the disabled list.

Without Sutter the Cubs completely collapsed. At one juncture they were 25 games above .500. By the time Sutter returned they were hopelessly out of the race. Never had a team relied so heavily on one player.

The knot on the backside finally subsided. Sutter returned in the final month. On Sept. 9 the Cubs and Expos were tied 2-2 after seven innings. Sutter was summoned from the bullpen for the eighth inning. Did he have the old magic?

Just ask the Expos. Brucie struck out Warren Cromartie, Andre Dawson, and Tony Perez. And in the ninth inning, he threw the minimum *nine* pitches, fanning Ellis Valentine, Gary Carter, and Larry Parrish. The Cubs scored a run in the 10th inning and Sutter was a 3-2 winner.

After that contest, Expos' manager Dick Williams joined the Sutter fan club. Williams, who managed relief ace Rollie Ringers during their heyday with the Oakland A's, said, "I've been hearing about Sutter. And he's the best I've seen. He challenges you. He says 'OK, baby, here it is. Try and hit it.' "

When the season concluded Sutter finished second to Fingers among the league's firemen with 31 saves and 7 victories. His earned-run average? It was 1.35. Control? He issued only 23 walks and 7 were intentional. And he had more strikeouts (129) than innings pitched (107).

Sutter wasn't that effective in 1978, but he received more national attention with his first All-Star Game appearance. He entered the contest in the eighth inning with the score tied 3-3. The scheduled batters for the American League were George Brett, Jim Rice, and Dwight Evans.

After Brett bounced out, Rice took three swipes with his bat and was bug-eyed. After striking out he stood in the batter's box, stared at his bat in disbelief, and then glared at Sutter. Evans also went fishing and got the hook. The National League scored four runs in the bottom of the inning and Sutter, wearing a Cub uniform, got the win.

Sutter, who grew a grubby beard for an even more menacing appearance, finally beat out Fingers for the Fireman's Award in 1979, tying a National League record with 37 saves. He again was the winning pitcher in the All-Star Game, ending the 7-6 squeaker by striking out Rick Burleson.

How important was Sutter to a mediocre Cub team? The Cubbies won only 80 games. Sutter's 37 saves, plus 6 victories adds to 43. Thus, he had a hand, or a split-finger, in more than half their victories. He was named Cy Young Award winner as the league's best pitcher.

Cub minor league manager Walt Dixon once stated, "The day Bruce Sutter makes the major leagues will be the day the Communists take over."

Following that prestigious award, naturally, comes a financial reward. But Sutter was a Cub. Owner Bill Wrigley, troubled by inheritance taxes and an impending divorce, offered Sutter a $350,000 contract.

Sutter asked for $700,000. His case went to arbitration. Under the rules an arbitrator must choose one figure or the other. Tom Christenson, a Cub fan and New York University law professor, heard the case and decided in Sutter's favor. As soon as Wrigley heard the verdict, he gulped. Sutter's Cub days were numbered.

Sutter wondered how the fans would accept him. As the highest paid player in Cub history (before Rick Sutcliffe), he feared the cheers for his deeds would give way to hoots for his greed. The opposite was true. He remained a big favorite.

And when the All-Star Game rolled around, there was Sutter, again on the mound for the National League. He pitched hitless ball in the last two innings, fanning Lance Parrish for the final out, earning a save in the 4-2 win.

Although Sutter had 5 victories and 28 saves, his strikeout total (76) failed for the first time in four seasons to exceed his innings pitched (102). And his earned-run average of 2.65 was not suitable for a Sutter.

The split-fingered flinger and the Cubs finally split on Dec. 9, 1980. Sutter, who had gone through thin and thin for the Cubs, a team with no immediate past and an uncertain future, was dealt to the Cards for three players—Ken Reitz, Tye Waller, and a youngster named Leon "Bull" Durham.

The Cards came forth with cash, offering Sutter $3.5 million for four years, plus incentives that made him a million-a-year-pitcher. "No one has done what Sutter has during the time he has been in the big leagues," said Cardinals' GM-manager Whitey Herzog.

"No one has allowed that few hits per innings pitched (371 in 492) that many strikeouts (512), that many saves (133)."

With Sutter in the bullpen, St. Louis vaulted from pretender to contender to champion. It was disheartening to Cub fans, watching Sutter pitch hitless ball to save another All-Star Game, stand defiantly on the mound for the final outs of the 1982 World Series triumph over the Milwaukee Braves, and finally, tie Dan Quisenberry for the all-time record of 45 saves in a season in 1984. He did it all in four seasons while wearing a uniform with two Redbirds perched on a bat.

But wait. There was one brief encounter of the exhilarating kind. It happened on June 23, 1984, at Wrigley Field before a packed house of 38,079.

The Cards had led 7-1 after two innings and 9-3 after five and one-half. Sutter entered like a Darth Vader with St. Louis ahead 9-8 in the ninth. He surrendered a homer to a rising star named Ryne Sandberg for a 9-9 tie.

In the 10th inning, the Cards again led 11-9. Sutter walked Bob Dernier on a full count, bringing up Luke Skywalker, oops, Sandberg again. It was a Star Wars attraction, with Sandberg sending Sutter's serve into the bleachers for a 11-11 tie. The Cubs went on to win 12-11 that inning on Dave Owen's bases-loaded hit.

Imagine, two homers off Sutter, back-to-back. Perhaps the guy *is* human. "I made two bad pitches . . . and both went out of the park," lamented Sutter.

At the conclusion of the season, the Atlanta Braves made their pitch and landed Sutter for six seasons for a reported $10 million. Imagine, $10 million for a guy on relief.

BOB KENNEDY

KENNEDY, ROBERT DANIEL
B. Aug. 18, 1920, Chicago, Ill.
BR TR 6'2" 193 lb.

Bob Kennedy was the first product of the White Sox farm system. And he was a home-grown product. "I was born and raised on Chicago's South Side," said Kennedy, "a White Sox fan to the bone." Nevertheless, for good or bad, Kennedy will be remembered long for his affiliation with the Cubs.

In 1936 when Bob was throwing touchdown passes for De LaSalle High School, his father wanted him to fill a varsity suit at Notre Dame. His Uncle Bob was a baseball fan and contacted Sox scout Billy Webb.

He bragged about the youngster who pitched four no-hitters in American Legion competition, played solid third base, and could hit. Webb signed Kennedy, who eventually wound up at Longview, Tex.

It was opening night at Longview in 1938 and Al Schacht, baseball's celebrated clown, did his pregame pantomime. Then a real clown took over. Rookie Kennedy made five errors and struck out three times—twice with the bases loaded. In the ninth inning he tripped over the bag and the ball sailed over his head while the winning run scored.

Kennedy slammed his locker shut. "No more baseball for me," he said. "I'm going back to Chicago."

"Everyone has a bad night now and then," said Schacht. "Sleep it off. You'll feel like playing ball in the morning."

Kennedy did. He smacked three doubles the next afternoon.

The handsome, husky Irishman made his Sox debut in the final days of the 1939 season. He played the final three games and collected two hits in eight trips. In 1940 Kennedy was among the top rookies, batting .252, with 153 hits and 52 RBI. He gained recognition for his rifle-like throws and was known as "the man with the slingshot arm."

Kennedy's hitting fell off the next two seasons. He shared third base with Dario Lodigiani. Then came the war. Kennedy was publicly inducted as a navy air cadet in special ceremonies between games of a Comiskey Park doubleheader with Cleveland on Aug. 9, 1942.

The marines became a great equalizer. As flight instructor to Ted Williams, Kennedy, who hit .206 in 1941, made Williams, a .406 hitter that same season, stand at attention.

After three years in combat as a Corsair fighter pilot, Kennedy emerged as a captain. He returned to baseball, found Floyd "The Blotter" Baker firmly holding third base and was shifted to the outfield. Then came his big break. Kennedy was traded to the Indians for outfielder Fat Pat Seerey on June 2, 1948. The Indians went on to win the pennant, while the Sox finished last.

Kennedy batted .302 in 66 games and also singled home a run in his first World Series at bat in the second game against the Braves in Boston. The Indians won the series in six games and Bob batted .500. (He struck out in his other at bat).

At age 32, Kennedy was recalled by the marines for active duty in the Korean conflict. When he returned he bounced around the majors, going from Cleveland to Baltimore to a second hitch with the White Sox. From there, it was on to Detroit, the White Sox again, and finally, the Dodgers in their final season in Brooklyn in 1957. In his 16-year career, Kennedy hit .254 with 63 homers and 443 RBI.

Kennedy served three years as a scout with the Indians and helped in the signing of pitchers Sam McDowell and Tommy John. He was given his first managerial job by General Manager Herman Franks at Salt Lake City in 1962.

Kennedy was then hired to serve in the Cubs' College of Coaches for the 1963 season. The team had gone through two years of frustration and discord under its system of rotating coaches. Kennedy stepped in and ended the coaching merry-go-round.

A dozen coaches reported to the Mesa (Ariz.) camp that spring and the 42-year-old Kennedy took command as head coach. "I wouldn't have taken the job if I wasn't going to be the head man," said Kennedy.

To many, Kennedy came off as a cold fish. He wasn't much for interviews or small talk and seldom hung around the dugout for chit-chat, but he played sound percentage baseball.

He instilled confidence by using a fairly set pitching rotation of Larry Jackson, Bob Buhl, and Dick Ellsworth, and a set batting order, blending veteran Ernie Banks with youngsters Billy Williams, Ron Santo, Ken Hubbs, and Lou Brock. The quartet, surprisingly, was developed in the Cub farm system. The result was an 82-80 record, the team's best since 1946.

But the 1964 season was something else. Second baseman Hubbs perished in a plane crash prior to spring training, and Brock, the speedy base bandit, was sent to St. Louis in a six-player trade. Brock and Cardinal pitcher Ernie Broglio were the big names in the transaction.

It was the worst trade in Cub history. Brock hit .348 and led the Cardinals to the pennant, while the sore-armed Broglio won a mere seven games in Cub flannels. It was a trade that was to haunt the Cubs for the next 16 years.

General Manager John Holland took the brunt of the heat for the debacle, but Kennedy was also at fault. He kept shifting Brock around the outfield, and at times, benched him in favor of Don Landrum.

The Cubs remained in a tailspin in the 1965 season. Holland (with orders from owner P. K. Wrigley) reportedly gave Kennedy an ultimatum: either step up into the club's front office as an administrative assistant or be fired. Kennedy stepped up. He was replaced as field boss by Lou Klein on June 15 (a year after the Brock trade) and quietly departed from the scene at the conclusion of the season.

Kennedy joined the Dodgers' front office in 1966, was hired as a Braves coach in 1967, and even became a full-fledged "manager" with Charlie Finley's A's in 1968. It was the A's first season in Oakland (Finley abandoned Kansas City) and their best since Connie Mack's A's of 1952 in Philly. Despite their 82-80 record, Kennedy was given the heave-ho the final day of the season.

Bouncing Bob next bobbed up in St. Louis as the Cardinals' director of personnel and player development. Then came the big surprise. He was summoned to Wrigley's office in 1976 and emerged as general manager. His first move was to select Herman Franks as manager.

His first trade was his best. He dispatched outfielder Rick Monday and pitcher Mike Garman to the Dodgers for first baseman Bill Buckner and the little-known shortstop, Ivan DeJesus.

The first step backwards was the mysterious case of Cub third baseman Bill Madlock, a two-time batting champion, who was demanding a five-year deal at $200,000 per season. Kennedy unloaded Madlock to the Giants in a five-player swap that brought outfielder Bobby Murcer and his rocking chair to Chicago.

P. K. Wrigley had passed on and his son William, the third generation Wrigley, took command. It was now the era of free agents. The Cubs, however, remained stagnant. Their lone venture, signing enigmatic slugger Dave Kingman, had mixed results.

Kennedy was of the old school. His Marine Corps temperament was not conducive to dealing with the new generation players and their obnoxious agents. His most puzzling move came when he sent speed demons Rodney Scott and Jerry White to the Montreal Expos for outfielder Sam Mejias. Scott and White gave the Expos much-needed speed, while Mejias batted .182 for the Cubs.

Perhaps his worst move was breaking up the league's best double-play combo of DeJesus and Trillo. Kennedy received three malcontents from the Phillies for Trillo and two others.

The final straw was the trading of ace relief pitcher Bruce Sutter to the Cardinals. Sutter went to arbitration and wound up with a $700,000 contract. That was too rich for the Cubs; Sutter was gone. And although the Cubs did receive the promising Leon Durham, how many teams trade a reliever of Sutter's stature?

Kennedy cleaned out his desk and handed in his resignation on May 22. He felt it best to leave for the good of the team and recommended Franks as his successor. Kennedy was then hired as a superscout with the Houston Astros.

Kennedy's son Terry is a catcher with the San Diego Padres.

HERMAN FRANKS

FRANKS, HERMAN LOUIS
B. Jan. 4, 1914, Price, Utah.
BR TR 5'10½"
187–250 lb.

He sits in his flannel undershirt, puffing on a huge cigar in the manager's office at Wrigley Field. At his feet is a sawdust-filled box into which he spits tobacco juice.

His aim isn't too accurate. His undershirt is brown-flecked. His floppy socks are soaked with tobacco stains. The not-so-jolly fat man pats his ample tummy. He dons his warmup jacket and sunglasses and waddles to the batting cage.

A night's stubble covers his unsmiling face. The thick-set ominous figure greets reporters. He listens to their questions as a stream of tobacco juice escapes from his clenched teeth.

His patience is exhausted and he replies, "Now, that's a stupid question." Then he adds. "What else would you like to know?" End of interview.

Gruff and garroulous, Franks produced results.

Who else but Franks could handle such diverse personalities as Dave Kingman, Bill Buckner, Bobby Murcer, Barry Foote, Ted Sizemore, Jose Cardenal, Mike Vail, and Jerry Martin, and finish with a 238-241 record in three Cub seasons. Only three games under .500 with those malcontents.

Franks, who actually weighed 187 during his playing career, attended the University of Utah and then set out to play minor league ball in 1932. He had a brief cup of coffee with the Cardinals in 1939 before catching on as a third-string catcher with Leo Durocher's Brooklyn Dodgers.

Herman's lifetime batting average was a glittering .199. But the selective service isn't that selective and took Franks into the army after Pearl Harbor.

Durocher waited four long years for hefty Herman to return. When he did, Leo shipped Franks to Montreal. Herman worked his way back to the big leagues with Connie Mack's Philadelphia A's in 1947 and '48 and then rejoined Leo as a coach with the New York Giants in 1949. Franks remained Leo's loyal second banana with the Giants through the 1955 season.

After he left the Giants, Franks became general manager of the Salt Lake City ballclub and hired Bob Kennedy as his manager. It was the start of a crony system that carried into the Cubs in later years.

But first, Franks was summoned to the San Francisco Giants as a heal to mend all wounded heels. Alvin Dark was fired as Giant manager because he couldn't mold a unit out of a team split three ways among American blacks, Latins, and whites.

The Giants were bulging with talent. Willie Mays, Juan Marichal, Orlando Cepeda, Willie McCovey, and Gaylord Perry were a few of the working hands. Franks stepped into a hot spot in 1965 and he cooled it. In addition, Herman took the financially troubled Mays and made him solvent.

The benevolent Franks even showed a soft spot. "You have to treat players as individuals," said Franks. "Some you give a pat on the back and others a kick in the butt." He even showed some results in the standings, finishing second four years in a row.

But his victory total kept sliding each season. He won 95, then 93, then 91, then 88, and then was given the heave-ho, not to return until he was summoned by Durocher as a Cub coach, late in the 1970 season.

"He'll build a fire under some of those guys," said Durocher. "He'll needle and bark, get them steamed up and agitated, and it might push them a little farther."

It was reported that Franks called Cub outfielder Billy Williams aside and convinced him to sit it out after 1,117 consecutive games to conserve his energy and lengthen his career.

Herman's Cub coaching career was brief. His next appearance was as manager. When Bob Kennedy was named general manager in December 1976, his first act was to bring back the Beast. The Cubs' Odd Couple put together a solid team on the field for the 1977 season.

Shortstop Ivan DeJesus and first baseman Bill Buckner were obtained from the Dodgers for outfielder Rick Monday. His next maneuver was made in spite and eventually backfired. Two-time batting champ Bill Madlock was shipped to the Giants for third baseman Steve Ontiveros and his Hairline Creations, and outfielder Bobby Murcer and his rocking chair.

DeJesus and second baseman Manny Trillo, though not getting the proper hype as the league's best double-play duo, plus the timely hitting of Buckner, Ontiveros, Jerry Morales, and Larry Biittner, and Murcer's most welcome 27 homers, gave the Cubs a presentable lineup.

But it was with the pitching that Franks showed his most savvy. Rick Reuschel suddenly developed into a 20-game winner and reliever Bruce Sutter, used only in the late innings when the Cubs were tied or ahead, was devastating.

The result? The Cubs got off to a fast start, grabbing an 8½-game lead and even shot to 25 games above .500. But Sutter suffered a midseason injury and the Cubs proved vulnerable. They limped home with an 81-81 record.

It was then decided to enter the free agent market in 1978 for some much-needed power. Dave Kingman was available. It seems that a Dave Kingman is always available.

Owner Bill Wrigley, Kennedy, and Franks courted Kong, who signed a fat bonus contract. One of the bonuses offered was an extra stipend if Kingman could break Hack Wilson's Cub RBI record. Kingman grabbed the pen and signed. Then he gulped when he discovered Wilson's RBI record was 190.

Kingman's 28 homers and his strange adulation from the fans came in handy because Murcer's homer production tumbled to 9. Buckner stung the ball at .324 and rookie pitchers Mike Krukow and Dennis Lamp were uncovered. But somehow, the tobacco-stained Cubbies collapsed in the stretch and finished third at 79-83.

A housecleaning was in order for 1979. And it was Kennedy and Franks who were taken to the cleaners. They gift-wrapped Trillo and two others to the Phillies for three benchwarmers who might as well have been named Moe, Larry, and Curly.

It was a chaotic season. One that Franks didn't even survive. Murcer and his rocking chair were gone by midseason. Franks was gone with one week left. "I've had it up to here," yelled Herman, spraying tobacco in all directions. "Some of the players are actually crazy."

The Cubs were 80-82 when Franks was replaced by loyal coach Joey Amalfitano. Was Herman never to be seen again? Heck no. When the Cubs completely unraveled in May 1981, Kennedy quit under fire. Wrigley needed a general manager. He brought back Franks.

There were other rumblings. The baseball strike was impending, which was no surprise. The sale of the Cubs from the Wrigley empire to the Tribune empire, was, well, no surprise either.

Franks presided over both. And when Dallas Green took over the Cubs, Franks thus represented the last link of the old tradition, walking into the sunset, squirting tobacco juice in all directions.

BILL BUCKNER

BUCKNER, WILLIAM JOSEPH
B. Dec. 14, 1949, Vallejo, Calif.
BL TL 6′ 185 lb.

The hair is long and snaggy. The brows are fierce and bushy. The mustache is thick and droopy. The temperament is hair-trigger. Somehow, the eyes are warm and friendly.

But the most notable characteristic of this macho-handsome ballplayer is his walk. He hobbles about on a grotesque, damaged left ankle that suggests pain with every stride.

Playing baseball on one leg, Bill Buckner is better than most players on two. Buckner hustles without the hoopla of a Pete Rose because he was a winner on a chronic loser.

Buckner probably was the most popular, unpopular player in Chicago. Billy Buck was respected, but not idolized by Cub fans, a la Ernie Banks. When Dallas Green took over as general manager of the team, it was evident that the gamer would eventually become a goner. After several seasons, Buckner was deported to Boston for pitcher Dennis Eckersley and minor league catcher Mike Brumley.

In his controversial 7½-year hitch, Billy Buck ranks among the all-time Cubs. His 1,136 hits in 3,788 trips is good for a .300 average, placing him among only 17 Cub players in the .300 plateau in 108 seasons.

Many detractors claim that Buckner remained a true-blue Dodger during his stormy stay with the Cubs. He was signed by the Dodgers after terms at Southern Cal and Arizona State.

It is hard to imagine, but the limping lefty was a superb wide receiver at Napa (Calif.) High School, being named to the Coaches' All-American team his junior and senior seasons as well as being chosen to the Northern California Football Hall of Fame. In baseball he hit .667 as a junior and .529 as a senior.

He reported to Ogden of the Pioneer League in June 1968, joining a cast that included Steve Garvey, Bobby Valentine, and Tom Paciorek among others. His first manager was Tom Lasorda. Buckner was the best of the rookie class, topping Garvey for the batting title .344 to .338.

Buckner, Garvey, Lasorda, and all that gang advanced to Albuquerque in the Dodger chain. Garvey, then a third baseman, outhit Buckner .373 to .307. When they reached the majors, both were frustrated.

Garvey, a failure at third base, was switched to first base to keep his hot bat in the lineup. With little chance to play, Buckner was sent down to Spokane, where he batted .335.

When he returned the intense competitor grumbled about manager Walt Alston's inability to field a set lineup. As a platooned player Buckner couldn't keep his temper under control. At first he threw an occasional bat or helmet or kicked the water cooler.

In San Francisco he advanced on Juan Marichal with a bat in hand because he thought the veteran Giants' pitcher was throwing at him. In St. Louis he attempted to rip first base out of the ground after bouncing out on a routine play.

When Lasorda joined the coaching staff in 1973, Buckner more or less settled down. In addition, Alston found a regular spot in left field for the fiery first baseman.

The Dodgers won the pennant in 1974 and Buckner was a big contributor with 182 hits and a .314 batting average. But Buckner was the goat of the World Series.

The Oakland A's were leading 3-2 after seven innings of the sixth game. Buckner led off the eighth inning with a routine single to right-center. Center fielder Billy North let the bouncing ball skip over his glove. Buckner dashed for second base, ignored third base coach Lasorda's stop signal, and kept going.

Right fielder Reggie Jackson tracked down the ball and threw to second baseman Dick Green, who relayed the ball to third baseman Sal Bando. Sal blocked the bag, waited for Buckner's arrival and applied the tag.

Buckner looked up in amazement as he saw umpire Bill Kunkel's out signal. He had ignored the old baseball axiom that you never make the first out of an inning at third base or home plate.

Two subsequent fly balls and a wild pitch and the Dodgers would have tied the score. Reliever Rollie Fingers closed the door and the A's won the series. "I thought I had a good shot," nodded the numb Buckner.

There was more misery to follow. Buckner tore apart his left ankle sliding into second base against the Giants at Dodger Stadium on April 18, 1975. He was placed on the disabled list and underwent surgery that September.

Somehow, the belligerent Buckner rebounded in 1976, batting .301 with 193 hits. He even stole 28 bases. But that limp was evident and he underwent surgery again in October to have bone chips removed.

The Dodgers, knowing Buckner would never be the same, parceled him wih the little-known shortstop Ivan DeJesus to the Cubs for center fielder Rick Monday and reliever Mike Garman on Jan. 11, 1977.

It was new Cub general manager Bob Kennedy's first major trade—and his best. DeJesus became a regular and Buckner, though obviously disillusioned and disgruntled, became a Chicago fixture.

Buckner missed 40 games, most of them early in the season. He could run straight ahead, but would pull up in pain when he attempted turns. His main enjoyment was batting a strong .370 against the Dodgers.

Billy Buck and his black bat were waiting when the Dodgers paid their first visit to Wrigley Field on June 6, 1977. He was two-for-three, drove in a run and showed up his old mates when he bunted in the seventh inning. When the pitcher messed up the play, he rounded first and half-limping, belly-flopped into second. He fell shy of the bag, but bounced and rolled safely into second.

The gimpy Buckner was then pulled for a pinch runner. After the 3-1 Cub win, Dodger skipper Lasorda sent word to the clubhouse that he still regarded him as a son.

"Bull," replied Cub manager Herman Franks. "Lasorda

unloaded him because he could barely walk. I'm his daddy now." It was the start of a good relationship that turned to hatred between Franks and Buckner.

On Aug. 19, Buckner went four-for-five wih two homers and five RBI in a 6-2 win against the Dodgers. The following day he was three-for-four with one homer and three RBI as the Cubs won 5-4. "I get excited playing the Dodgers," said Buckner. "Yes, it's sort of a revenge thing."

But Buckner missed the winning. The Cubs led the division, then went into their annual swoon. Through it all, Buckner hit a personal high in homers with 11, drove in 60 runs, and batted .284.

Although a series of muscle pulls limited Buckner to 117 games in 1978, it was quite an eventful season. He finished second to Pittsburgh's Dave Parker in batting with a .324 average and continued to bombard his former LA teammates, collecting 20 hits in 50 trips for a .400 average.

He also went seven-for-seven against the Mets on June 23-24, winding up with a .429 average against the New Yorkers. The Cubs were a surprise third in the NL East and Billy Buck was chosen Chicago Player of the Year by local writers. In addition, he was named Most Popular Professional Athlete in a poll of fans by Sports Phone.

But the 1979 season was long and arduous for the high-strung athlete. His average tumbled to .284 and he took a back seat to slugger Dave Kingman, who chased the 50-homer mark and fell short with 48.

A perfect example was the May 17 slugfest against the Phillies at Wrigley Field. Buckner hit a grand slammer and drove in seven runs, but was overshadowed by three king-sized Kingman homers. The Phillies, who blew a 21-9 lead, finally won 23-22 on a homer by Mike Schmidt.

The season ended bitterly. The Cubs went into a typical late-season spin and Franks singled out Buckner among the constant "whiners" who drove him crazy. Buckner demanded equal time on TV prior to a Cub game, but the tension remained even though Franks resigned.

The bitter Buckner was offensive to rival pitchers and the Cub organization in 1980. He won the batting title with a .323 average and fanned only 18 times in 614 trips for an astounding ratio of once every 34.1 appearances.

In a public statement he criticized the Cubs for their indifference to winning, adding "I didn't say anything the others weren't thinking. I just feel the club has gone backwards a bit." A bit? The team finished dead last. It was the first indication that Buckner wanted to be traded.

The Cubs unloaded Kingman and pitchers Bruce Sutter and Rick Reuschel, leaving Buckner as the lone big-named rostered player for 1981. During the strike-shortened season, the Wrigley family sold the team to the Tribune Co.

Through all the turmoil Buckner batted a solid .311 and drove in 75 runs in only 106 games. New GM Green assured Cub fans that the popular Buckner would be retained.

Nevertheless, Buckner didn't fit in. He had a shoving match with new manager Lee Elia, but also took out his frustrations on opposing pitchers, lashing out 201 hits, driving home 105 runs, and batting .306.

Buckner continued to beef throughout the 1983 season. Most of it was aimed at the weather or Wrigley Field. It was either too cold or too hot. The grass was too high. He also resented being switched to left field and being removed from the third spot in the batting order.

Green vowed that Buckner would be his top trading priority in the winter meetngs. But he found no takers. For better or worse, Buckner was still a Cubbie.

When the 1984 season opened, Buckner was pounding the pines. New manager Jim Frey moved outfielder Leon Durham to first base and reduced Buckner's role to pinch-hitting.

On May 25 the chains were finally removed and the freed fire-eater fled to Fenway. Buckner collected his 2,000th career hit in a Red Sox uniform and wound up the season with a .278 average. The Cubs won the division title. Perhaps they could have used his competitive fire in their playoff against the Padres.

IVAN DE JESUS

DE JESUS, IVAN
B. Jan. 9, 1953, Santurce, Puerto Rico
BR TR 5'11" 175 lb.

Ivan DeJesus came to the Cubs as a throw-in in a trade and ended up a star. The date was Jan. 11, 1977, when the Cubs sent Rick Monday and Mike Garman to the Dodgers for Bill Buckner, Jeff Albert, and DeJesus. But that's getting ahead of the story.

Ivan was signed to his first professional contract by the Dodgers in 1969. He was still a fuzzy-faced high school kid. He broke into the minors with the class A Daytona Beach team in 1970, and for four years alternated between there and Bakersfield.

Finally, in 1974 DeJesus was promoted to the Dodgers' Triple A club at Albuquerque. After hitting .298, he was given a chance with the parent club at the end of the year. The next two seasons followed the same pattern. By the end of 1976, he had but 131 major league at bats, coupled with an anemic .183.

Then came the trade to Chicago. Although it was Buckner the Cubs were after, DeJesus paid immediate and long-term dividends also. Filling the shortstop gap left vacant by Don Kessinger's departure, he combined with Manny Trillo to form a Latin duo that performed like clockwork. He also showed skill on the basepaths, topping the club with 24 stolen bases.

In 1978 Ivan raised his average to .278, led the league in runs scored with 104, and set the club pace in total bases with 219. In addition to this, his 41 stolen bases tied the record for a Cub shortstop set by Joe Tinker back in the tintype days of 1904.

The following year Ivan upped his average to .283 and drove in 52 runs. These are still his career highs. However, Manny Trillo had been dealt to the Phillies in a steal for Philadelphia, which many felt had affected Ivan's morale. He had lost a good friend whom he could talk with in Spanish.

DeJesus slipped to .259 in 1980, but on April 22 he enjoyed the kind of day that most players only dream of. He homered in the first, doubled in the third, singled in the fourth, and tripled in the fifth, thus becoming only the ninth player in Cub history to hit for the cycle, and the first since Billy Williams and Randy Hundley in 1966. For the game, Ivan was five-for-six with two runs scored and two RBI as the Cubs beat the Cardinals 16-12 on Barry Foote's grand-slam homer in the bottom of the ninth.

Ivan also enjoyed his finest season defensively in 1980, committing only 24 errors in 782 chances. Finally, his 44 stolen bases set a high for a Cub shortstop. But the spirit of the whole team was low, DeJesus included.

Disaster struck the following year. In a season reduced to 106 games by a lengthy players' strike, Ivan fell to a horrendous .194, driving home only 13 runs. To many, it appeared that he wanted to be traded.

When the new Cub management took over in the autumn of 1981, DeJesus did not fit into their plans. On Jan. 27, 1982, he was traded to the Phillies for infielder Ryne Sandberg and veteran shortstop Larry Bowa, who became Ivan's replacement.

DeJesus has not since recaptured the magic of his first four years in Cub pinstripes. With the Phillies he has raised his average a bit, reaching .255 in 1984, but has slowed down both afield and on the basepaths.

A minor controversy surfaced late in 1982 when the press quoted Cub catcher Jody Davis as saying that DeJesus had been intentionally allowing Latin players to slide in safely at second base when they should have been out. DeJesus denied the allegation, and the matter quietly died thereafter.

In 1983 Ivan collected his 1,000th career hit and his first World Series ring. Unfortunately, he was one of the goats in the series as the Orioles clipped the Phillies in five games. Batting an anemic .125, he collected only two hits and committed a costly error. Through 1984, DeJesus is a .255 lifetime batter with 1,146 hits.

BOBBY MURCER

MURCER, BOBBY RAY
B. May 20, 1946, Oklahoma City, Okla.
BL TR 5'11"
180 lb.

Give Bobby Murcer a rocking chair and a short porch and he's satisfied. With the Cubs, Murcer rocked with ease in his chair, but seldom got rolling when his swings only reached the warning track at Wrigley Field.

Murcer, a moon-faced Sooner with bright blue eyes and high cheek bones, was compared with Mickey Mantle when he reached the big leagues at age 19 in 1965. Both were from Oklahoma. Both were signed by scout Tom Greenwade. And both were shortstops in the minor leagues.

Murcer was given Mantle's old locker at Yankee Stadium and he succeeded Mickey in center field. But his development was delayed by two years (1967-68) in military service. Eventually Bobby matured into one of the league's finest hitters and outfielders.

From 1969 through '73 Murcer walloped 129 homers with a high of 33 in 1972. Moreover, he batted .331 in 1971 and was undoubtedly the Yankees' newest slugging idol.

He even outdid Mantle on June 24, 1970, when he hit four successive homers in a doubleheader against the Detroit Tigers at Yankee Stadium. After he hit his fourth homer (there was a walk between No. 2 and No. 3) Murcer lifted his cap and waved to the crowd a la Babe Ruth.

In 1974 he was rewarded with a $120,000 contract, passing the Babe, Lou Gehrig, Joe DiMaggio, and Mantle as the highest paid Yankee of all time. But then he lost his ballpark.

The city of New York decided to renovate Yankee Stadium. It was decided the Yankees would share Shea Stadium with the Mets for the next two seasons. Murcer's left-handed batting stroke was ideal for the 296-foot short porch in the Bronx.

Bobby kept swinging, but his drives didn't carry in straightaway right field at Shea Stadium. The result? Murcer's homer production plummeted to 10 in 1974.

With his stock tumbling on the market, Murcer was traded for Bonds. Outfielder Bobby Bonds, like Murcer, was chasing a ghost on the opposite coast. Murcer had his Mantle, while Bonds had his Willie Mays. Having placed unreasonable pressures on both, the Yankees and Giants made a logical exchange on Oct. 22, 1974.

Murcer didn't take to the swirling wind at San Francisco's Candlestick Park and had two ordinary seasons in Giant livery. In addition to the short right field foul lines, Murcer missed the crowd adulation and excitement of New York.

He did, however, maintain his sense of humor. Playing in a park where the seagulls outnumbered the patrons, Murcer remarked that the kidnapped Patty Hearst could have been held captive in the upper stands without anyone taking note.

Meanwhile, Bob Kennedy, the Cubs' new general manager, was having contract problems with third baseman Bill Madlock, who was coming off two straight batting titles. Rather than give in, Kennedy gave Madlock to the Giants for Murcer in a five-player deal on Feb. 11, 1977.

Then came the shocker. Kennedy gave Murcer, coming off a .259 season, a fatter contract than the .339-hitting Madlock was demanding. Moreover, it was a five-year pact, making Murcer the highest paid in Cub history.

"I'll hit more homers than Madlock," boasted Bobby, who moved his rocking chair into the Wrigley Field clubhouse. Murcer filled the role of left-handed slugger, hitting 27 homers and driving in 89 runs. He was among the most popular players.

But the Cubs, who led the league for 69 days and at one juncture were 25 games above .500, collapsed in the stretch and finished fourth with an 81-81 record.

In 1978 Murcer collapsed. His homer production fell to nine with most of his best shots being caught at the warning track. It must be remembered that the dimensions down the right field wall at Wrigley Field are 353 feet, the longest in the major leagues.

Murcer, who laughed about the seagulls in San Francisco, began feeling the wrath of the boobirds in Chicago. After all, he topped the Cub payroll and contributed less than Bruce Sutter, Bill Buckner, Dave Kingman, Rick Reuschel, and others.

In addition to not producing the long ball in the clutch, Murcer played it safe in right field when he approached the ivy-covered wall or when it came to take a dive for sinking liners.

It seemed as if he saved his best for the road. One such occasion was on April 29, 1979, when the Cubs were in Atlanta. The Braves were leading 5-0 going into the ninth inning.

Kingman opened with a single and Steve Ontiveros walked. But pinch hitters Jerry Martin and Gene Clines popped out. One out to go. Ted Sizemore drew a walk to load the bases and Tim Blackwell singled home a pair to make it 5-2 Braves.

Pinch hitter Larry Biittner kept the rally alive by singling home Sizemore. It was now 5-3 Braves. Murcer stepped in against reliever Gene Garber and ran the count to a ball and a strike.

Murcer then rocketed a three-run homer over the right field fence to put the Cubs ahead 6-5. Sutter mopped up the Braves in the bottom of the ninth and Murcer was the chain-lightning hero of the quickest Cub comeback in almost two decades.

But Murcer's days as the Cubs rocker feller were numbered. The team started slicing the payroll and Murcer was the first one cut. He was sent back to the Yankees on June 11 for a minor league pitcher with the lyrical name of Paul Semall. In his two and a half seasons with the Cubs, Murcer connected for only 43 homers.

The chemistry between Murcer and his adoring Yankee fans was still there, although Bobby's role was reduced to pinch-hitting. He again received standing ovations when he propelled the pellet over the short porch in his beloved Yankee Stadium. It's too bad that ballparks aren't portable.

Bobby finished with 252 homers after the 1983 season and joined the Yankees' broadcasting team. You could say he became a rocker-socker.

PRESTON GOMEZ

GOMEZ, PEDRO MARTINEZ
B. April 20, 1923, Central Preston, Cuba
BR TR 5'11" 170 lb.

Herman Franks had resigned as Cub manager after the 1979 season and the local papers conducted polls to sound out the readers on a successor. The most popular choices were Billy Martin and Whitey Herzog.

One name never mentioned was Preston Gomez. He got the job. He didn't even last until August. His Cub managerial record was 38-52. Exit Preston Gomez.

Gomez was recognized as a strict disciplinarian. He wanted to build a ballclub on tight pitching and solid defense. Above all, he stressed speed. He inherited a club so clumsy and slow afoot that most players tripped over the foul lines.

Only two players possessed speed, shortstop Ivan DeJesus and center fielder Miguel Dilone. In Gomez's first move he insisted on getting rid of Dilone, who was dispatched to the Cleveland Indians for a paltry $35,000. Dilone went on to bat .341 and set an Indians' record with 61 stolen bases. So much for stressing speed.

Gomez actually was christened Pedro. He was born in a little sugar mill town named Central Preston, and he became known as "Preston" in the Cuban press. Gomez, an infielder in the Cuban leagues, reached the big leagues in 1944 with the Washington Senators. At that time there was no minimum baseball wage and Nats' owner Clark Griffith imported many Cubans at little cost.

Preston got into eight games and batted .286 on two hits in seven trips. From there, he beat around the bushes for the next 21 seasons as a player, coach, and manager.

Gomez was manager of the Havana club when Fidel Castro rose to power. There were more submachine guns than bats in the ballpark when Gomez's Havana Cubans of the International League met Gene Mauch's Minneapolis Millers of the American Association in the 1959 Junior World Series.

"We'd take our batting practice," recalled Gomez, "and race to the dugout as fast as we could. Guns were going all over the place. Then the doors in center field would open and out would come Castro.

"He'd have soldiers all around him with submachine guns and rifles and grenade belts. Then he'd throw out the first ball and sit on the bench next to me. The soldiers would sit in the dugout, too.

"Once in a while he'd lean over and say, 'Mr. Gomez, I think your pitcher is tired.' I'd have to say, 'Yes, you certainly are right about that.' And I'd have to get my pitcher out of there."

Gomez found it more relaxing as a coach under Walt Alston of the Dodgers. He spent three seasons at LA, before he was picked by general manager Buzzie Bavasi to manage the new franchise in San Diego in 1969.

It was a quiet summer for Gomez. His Padres finished last with a 52-110 record. There was more of the same until July 22, 1970, when Gomez lifted pitcher Clay Kirby for a pinch hitter although the youngster had hurled eight hitless innings.

The Padres were trailing the New York Mets 1-0 with Kirby the third scheduled hitter in the bottom of the eighth. The strategy backfired. Padre pinch hitter Clarence Gaston failed to get a hit, and the Mets jumped on reliever Jack Baldshun for three hits and two runs in the ninth inning for a 3-0 victory.

"I never hesitated to take him out," said Gomez. "I don't play for the fans. I knew they would be upset. I play to win." The fans did not take Gomez's decision as calmly. They greeted the announcement that Gaston was pinch-hitting for Kirby with catcalls and boos that continued long after the game.

Preston's Padres didn't have a prayer. The park was populated by wayward sea gulls and the team remained in the cellar throughout the 1970 and '71 seasons. Gomez was replaced by Don Zimmer on April 27, 1972. Gomez's managerial record in San Diego was 180 wins, 316 defeats.

"That job made me a better baseball man," said Gomez. "You learn by getting beat and frustrated." Gomez was without baseball employment for the first time in 26 years.

He joined the Houston Astros as a coach under Leo Durocher in 1973. He was Leo's personal choice as successor the following season. Preston finally had a .500 ballclub as the Astros finished fourth with an 81-81 record, but again he was foiled by a no-hitter.

Decisions. Decisions. It was the bottom of the eighth inning in Houston on Sept. 4, 1974, and Gomez's Astros were trailing Cincinnati 2-1 and the pitcher was due to bat. Time for a pinch hitter, right?

Wrong, declared the 8,024 fans, who made the Astrodome ring with boos when Gomez sent up Tommy Helms to bat in place of Don Wilson. The fans figured Wilson ought to get a chance to pitch the third no-hitter of his career, win or lose.

"I get paid for winning the ball game, not the no-hitter," said Gomez. When Helms grounded out, the booing became louder. "The fans didn't bother me," added Gomez. Reliever Mike Cosgrove then gave up the Reds' first hit, a single by Tony Perez in the ninth inning and Cincy went on to win 2-1.

After getting off to a 47-80 start, Gomez was lifted for manager Bill Virdon. He then returned to the coaching lines, with the St. Louis Cardinals in 1976 and the Dodgers in 1978 and '79.

The Cubs set about for a manager in 1980. The price tags on Martin and Herzog were too steep. They wanted someone at bargain basement prices for their bargain basement ballclub. Gomez took over a disgruntled outfit and it remained that way throughout his short tenure. At least, he didn't have to worry about taking out a no-hit pitcher.

Gomez is now back on the coaching lines with the California Angels.

Dave Kingman is an enigmatic home run slugger who has yet to attain his full potential. At one time, he had a chance to become the next Ernie Banks, Ron Santo, or Billy Williams, only to leave town in a tumult of jeers and hisses.

DAVE KINGMAN

KINGMAN, DAVID ARTHUR
B. Dec. 21, 1948, Pendleton, Ore.
BR TR 6'6" 210 lb.

Although Kingman starred in athletics at Mount Prospect High School only a few miles from Chicago, he apparently was overlooked by the Cub scouting staff. Instead, he signed with the California Angels, but was later drafted by the Giant organization after attending the University of Southern California.

Following two seasons of minor league training at Amarillo and Phoenix, Dave was brought up by the Giants late in 1971. In his first big league game, he belted a grand slam off Dave Giusti of the Pirates, and two more homers off Dock Ellis the next day. It was a promising debut for Kingman, who finished the remainder of the season with a .278 average, six home runs, and 24 RBI. The next season, he knocked 29 homers and drove 83 runs across the plate. On the negative side, however, he batted only .225 while fanning 140 times.

There could be no doubt of Kingman's power when he connected. The combination of his gargantuan physique and prodigious blasts earned him the pseudonym "King Kong." Unfortunately, he did not connect often enough. Furthermore, as a defensive outfielder, Kong looked about as graceful as the Frankenstein monster.

During the next two seasons it was much of the same thing—potential galore but no consistency. By 1975 the Giants had soured on Kingman and sold him to the Mets.

In his first year at the Big Apple, Kingman upped his home run count to 37 and his RBI count to 88. When the 1976 season unfolded, it finally looked as if Kong were beginning to tap his full resources. At midseason, he had 32 homers, tops in the league, while his 72 RBI were second. He then suffered a severe hand injury and could manage only five more homers and 14 additional RBI for the year, while batting .238.

Then came the disastrous 1977 season, in which Kingman appeared in four uniforms. Starting out with the Mets, he went to the Padres and then to the Angels before winding up with the Yankees. On Nov. 30 he signed with the Cubs as a free agent, in what Bob Kennedy thought would be the biggest steal since the Yankees captured Babe Ruth.

Upon coming to Chicago, Kingman had worn out his welcome everywhere he had been. Among the charges leveled at him were that he was moody, a loner, hostile to writers, and just out for himself rather than the team.

He had yet to hit over .238 in a full season. Nevertheless, the power-needy Cubs were willing to gamble, and Kingman was given a hero's welcome before he even swung a bat.

He soon began swinging and swung well. Under the tutelage of Cub batting instructor Lew Fonseca, Kingman raised his average to .266. Despite being sidelined with a pulled hamstring that cost him 43 games, he still topped the club in home runs with 28 and RBI with 79.

He delivered in the clutch, too, especially in a grueling match with the Dodgers at Los Angeles May 14. First he put an end to

Doug Rau's shutout with a two run homer in the sixth, narrowing the Dodger lead to 3-2. One inning later, he drove home Ivan DeJesus on a force to give the Cubs a 4-3 edge.

But the battling Dodgers came back, leading 7-5 in the ninth with one out to go. Kong promptly kept the Cubs alive with a 430-foot blast to knot up the score, after which came a long, scoreless hiatus. Finally, in the 15th inning, he dealt the killing blow with homer number three, a three-run punch to knock out the Dodgers 10-7.

That game was only a sneak preview of Kingman's marvelous feats to come in 1979. Getting off to a hot start, Kong was now receiving thunderous ovations every time he came to bat in Wrigley Field. On May 17 he belted three homers in a losing cause, as the Phillies out-pummeled the Cubs 23-22 in the highest scoring game in 57 years.

During June, he rocketed 12 baseballs over the fence, the most by a Cub in one month since Ernie Banks socked a dozen in June 1960.

However, the most pleasing clout came the 23rd of the following month, when his bottom-of-ninth blast with a man on gave the Cubs a 2-1 victory over the Reds with the sun going down at Clark and Addison. Earlier, the Cubs had edged Cincy 9-8 in 18 innings, in a game that had been started May 10, but was called because of darkness.

The rampaging Dave was far from finished. On July 27 he smashed a pair of homers to pace the Cubs to a 4-2 victory over the Mets. The next day he sent three more into orbit. Although the Mets beat the Cubs 6-4, Dave's five homers in two games tied a major league record first set by Cub legend Cap Anson back in 1884 and tied by several others, including Billy Williams in 1968.

By the end of the year, Kingman had set personal highs with a .288 average, 153 hits, 97 runs scored, and 115 RBI. His 48 home runs, top in either league, were second high in Cub history to Hack Wilson's 56 in 1930.

He was named Chicago Player of the Year by the local chapter of the Baseball Writers Association of America, and he received the Babe Ruth Crown from the Baltimore Professional Players Association.

At that point Kingman had Chicago in the palm of his hand, but the goodwill soon evaporated. The first ominous sign came the following spring when he dumped a bucket of ice water over the head of sportswriter Don Friske at Mesa, Ariz., for no apparent reason. Kingman then began writing (or signing his name to) a baseball column for the *Chicago Tribune*. The column was so verbose it was practically unreadable. These incidents earned him the sarcastic wrath of *Sun-Times* columnist Mike Royko, who named him "Ding Dong."

Even so, fans were willing to forgive and forget, particularly on April 19, 1980. Behind 9-1 after five and a half innings, the Cubs rallied to defeat the Mets 12-9, thanks largely to Kingman's two-run bell-ringer in the sixth and his grand slammer in the eighth—after New York had intentionally walked Bill Buckner to get at Dave.

Thereafter, things plummeted at breakneck speed. Out of the lineup with a shoulder injury, Kong—or was it "Dong"—often skipped going to the park to give his teammates moral support, preferring instead to loaf on his yacht in Lake Michigan.

The clincher came Aug. 7, when Kingman went AWOL on his own tee-shirt day. The demoralized Cubs, in the process, sank to the cellar.

In fairness, Kingman's statistics were still impressive considering how seldom he was in uniform. He hit .278 with 18 homers and 57 RBI in 81 games.

On Feb. 28, 1981, the fallen "angel" was traded to the Mets for Steve Henderson. Cub outfielder Scot Thompson was quoted as saying, "I think the Mets got gypped."

Meanwhile, Kingman had started an ice cream parlor on Chicago's North Side, which opened on opening day. To rub salt into an old wound, he labeled the washrooms "press rooms."

Although "Kingman's Landing" was smartly decorated with reasonable prices, there were usually more employees around than customers. After six months, it was a thing of the past. But then again, what did "Ding Dong" expect after the way he had thumbed his nose at Chicago fans?

As of this writing, Kingman is still sending horsehides into outer space, although during most seasons his batting average has regressed to its pre-Cub level. During his second honeymoon with the Mets, he stroked 37 homers in 1982 to lead the league, while driving in 99 runs with a .204 average. In 1983 his stats dropped to .198 with 13 homers and 29 RBI.

Released by New York, Dave went to Oakland. Declaring himself reformed, he showed it—for the time being at least—by hitting .268 in 1984 with 35 homers and 118 RBI.

Through last season, Kingman is a .238 lifetime hitter with 1,316 hits, 377 homers, and 1,025 RBI.

JOEY AMALFITANO

AMALFITANO, JOHN JOSEPH
B. Jan. 23, 1934, San Pedro, Calif.
BR TR 5'11"
175 lb.

Joey Amalfitano started at the top and worked his way down. He was a bonus baby when the New York Giants swept the Cleveland Indians in the 1954 World Series and managed the forlorn Cubs through the strike-torn 1981 season.

Pal Joey was part of the Giants' duo of "Jingles and Jangles." Jingles was pitcher Paul Giel, who came out of the University of Minnesota, while Jangles was Amalfitano, a high school hotshot infielder out of San Pedro, Calif. Each received bonuses of $50,000 for signing.

Under the bonus rule of that time, Amalfitano and Giel had to spend their first two seasons with the parent club instead of being farmed out. That meant they received $11,147 each for watching

Willie Mays make his spectacular World Series catch off the bat of Cleveland's Vic Wertz.

Amalfitano got into nine games that season. Manager Leo Durocher didn't let him appear at bat until the final week. Joey went hitless in five trips. "I never said anything," recalled Amalfitano. "In fact, I was so quiet I don't think many people knew I was there."

Amalfitano hit .277 and .255 as an irregular regular for the Giants in 1960 and '61, playing all four infield positions. He went to Houston in the expansion draft, hit .237, and was reacquired by the Giants, who soon shipped him to Tacoma.

After Ken Hubbs died, the Cubs were caught short at second base and snapped Joey up for the $20,000 waiver price. Amalfitano, now a pudgy 30, was just another utility player until his big moment on June 12, 1964, at Wrigley Field.

Shortstop Andre Rodgers was out with a bruised instep and second baseman Jimmy Stewart shifted to short. Joey got a start at second. A couple of Bobs, Veale for the Pirates and Buhl for the Cubs, were locked in a scoreless duel until the bottom of the sixth inning.

The Cubs put two runs across and had the bases loaded with big names (Billy Williams, Ron Santo, and Ernie Banks) when Amalfitano stepped up to face ace reliever Elroy Face.

Face threw a forkball and Joey swung at the first pitch. "I saw left fielder Jerry Lynch going back to the wall . . . saw it up and out of there," sighed Amalfitano. A grand-slam homer, the first and only of his 10-year career. The Cubs won 7-1.

"My folks are touring Italy, visiting their folks," added Amalfitano. "By the time they get word of my grand slam, I'll probably be back on the bench."

Joey remained a part-time player for two seasons and turned to coaching when Leo Durocher was hired as manager in 1966. "All those years on the bench, there was a lot to watch," said Amalfitano. "I wasn't asleep. I wasn't idle. I was always watching and learning. I sat next to Leo and took note of his strategical moves."

For the next decade, Amalfitano remained a coach with the Cubs, Giants, and San Diego Padres. He rejoined the Cubs in 1978 under Franks and replaced him as interim manager the final week of the 1979 season, compiling a 2-5 record.

Although Amalfitano was popular and respected by the players, he was not in the running for Cub manager in 1980. The fans preferred either Billy Martin or Whitey Herzog. The job went to Preston Gomez.

Amalfitano was asked to stay on as third base coach. He buried his ego and accepted. Gomez didn't last the season. The job fell into Joey's lap in mid-July. The Cubs staggered home last, winning 26 and dropping 46 under Amalfitano.

By now, it was a job nobody wanted. When the 1981 season rolled around, the club was depleted of most of its talent through trading blunders by General Manager Bob Kennedy and penny-pinching by owner William Wrigley.

Gone were relief ace Bruce Sutter and slugger Dave Kingman. The club stumbled out of the starting gate losing 12-of-13. They had the worst record in the big leagues, 15-37, when the players went on strike June 12. While other teams muttered, it was almost a welcome relief for the Cubs.

Meanwhile, Kennedy resigned and was replaced by Franks. Wrigley sold controlling interest to the Tribune Company. There was hope for the future. But would Joey be a part of it?

When the season resumed on Aug. 10, the Cubs showed a little spunk and almost played .500 ball, winning 23 and dropping 26.

But when Phillies' manager Dallas Green was appointed vice president and general manager, Amalfitano was swept out in a thorough housecleaning.

Joey then joined the Cincinnati Reds and then the Los Angeles Dodgers as a third base coach.

SECTION SEVEN
1981-1985 The Green Machine

The 1981 season opened with the aura of a wake. The players' union threatened a strike and the Cubs looked no better than they did the previous year. If anything, the team was in worse shape, having traded Bruce Sutter to the Cardinals.

From the beginning the Cubs played as if they were whipped before they even took the field. The fans groaned even more when their most reliable starter, Rick Reuschel, was dealt to the Yankees.

On June 12 the players in both leagues walked out over the issue of free agency. This turned out to be a mercy killing for the Cubs, who were already hopelessly buried at the bottom of the National League East. Although Cub fans hated to be without baseball, many were breathing sighs of relief.

Then came bigger news—on June 16 William Wrigley announced the sale of the Cubs to the Chicago Tribune Company, thus ending 65 years of Wrigley affiliation. The general opinion in North Side taverns was, "This is the best thing since Prohibition was repealed."

When the season was resumed on August 10 following the strike settlement, the Cubs continued on their path to the basement, after which Joey Amalfitano was relieved of his managerial duties.

In October Phillie GM Dallas Green was hired as the Cubs' new general manager. Bringing some players and executives with him from Philadelphia, Green vowed to "build a new tradition." He started by hiring former Cub utility man Lee Elia as field manager.

At the outset of 1982 the new tradition looked like the old tradition as the Cubs wallowed in the National League mudhole. Then came a surprising turnabout. The Cubs won 33 of their last 55 games to finish in fifth place with a 73-89 record. The bullpen of Lee Smith, Mike Proly, and Bill Campbell emerged as one of the best in the league, while a resurrected Fergie Jenkins won 14 games. Youngsters Ryne Sandberg, Jody Davis, and Leon Durham all displayed promise. For the last two months of the season, the Cubs had the second best record in the National League. Still, fans were leary of the shaky starting staff.

In the spring of 1983 Elia proudly stated that the Cubs were capable of playing .500 ball. But when the team started off sluggishly, he vented his frustration upon the fans. He called them unemployable unmentionables—although in less diplomatic language.

Although Elia made a public apology, a sour tone was set for the rest of the year. Once again the lack of dependable starters was the team's Achilles' heel. At one point the Cubs were up to 39-40 but the bullpen soon began to crumble from overwork. Administrative Assistant Charlie Fox took Elia's place as interim manager, but it was too late to reverse the downward trend. The Cubs again finished fifth, but with two fewer victories than the year before. The ".500 ball club" was 20 games under.

At the close of the season Fox was moved upstairs and replaced by Jim Frey, who had a winning record in his brief managerial stay with the Royals, leading them to the pennant in 1980.

Nevertheless, there was no reason for Cub fans to be optimistic when the 1984 season began. The team's 7-20 spring training record was the worst in the majors. Fans and experts alike could not envision anything higher than a fifth place finish. It looked like another long, sorrowful season.

Then came the unexpected—helped by some shrewd trades, the Cubs started winning. The acquisitions by Green of Rick Sutcliffe and Dennis Eckersley braced the shaky pitching staff. New left fielder Gary "Sarge" Matthews gave the Cubs a dependable clutch bat as well as leadership. Still, the general mood was that it was too good to be true.

By All-Star time, everyone was anticipating the annual fizzle, but the Cubs of Jim Frey and Dallas Green kept on winning, even on crucial road trips. Skeptics began to convert when the team took the lead, surging past the New York Mets, whose unforeseen resurrection paralleled the rise of the Cubs.

By mid-September the Cubs were nine and one-half games ahead of the Mets, who had all but conceded defeat. A five-game losing streak made Cub fans nervous, but when Sutcliffe slammed the door on the Pirates 4-1 at Pittsburgh September 24, the champagne flowed. The Cubs had won the Eastern Division championship. A record 2,107,665 fans poured through the turnstiles.

Another miracle team, the San Diego Padres, had taken the Western Division championship. When the Cubs took the first two playoff games at Wrigley Field, long-suffering fans could almost taste the first pennant in 39 years. But such was not to be. The Padres took the next three on their own turf to win it all.

At the start of 1985, the Cubs' lineup was the same as '84 with one exception; Shawon Dunston took over at shortstop from Larry Bowa. The team's pitching corps was solidified by the return of their chief starting pitchers and the acquisition of reliever Ray Fontenot from the Yankees. The Cubs also welcomed Brian Dayett, Chris Speier, and Lary Sorensen. The Cubs got off to a winning start in '85, battling toward the championship.

The Chicago Cubs, 1984 National League East Division Champions

With permission of the Chicago Cubs

DALLAS GREEN

GREEN, GEORGE DALLAS
B. Aug. 4, 1934, Newport, Del.
BL TR 6'5½"
210 lb.

Jimmy Piersall hammered a hanging curve for his 100th career homer and ran the bases backwards. Pete Rose found the ideal pitch to unload the lone grand-slammer of his career. In both instances, the pitcher was Dallas Green.

The rangy right-hander became a 20-game winner, but it took him eight years. Toiling for the Phillies, Senators, and Mets during the 1960s, Green compiled a 20-22 lifetime record. Thus, adversity was nothing new for the wavy-haired wunderkind.

Dallas Green is a winner. Like a surprising number of other baseball executives whose playing careers were less than spectacular, Green proved to be outstanding as a manager and in the front office. His Phillie minions were staked to their lone World Series title feast under Green's thumb in 1980. And before he managed, Green served as the Phillies' farm director, producing a bumper crop.

When the Cubs moved from the Wrigley Building to the Tribune Tower, Green came on to rid the team of its losing image. "I'm not here to win friends," drawled Dallas. "I'm here to win ball games."

Like John Wayne he showed true grit by turning goners into gamers. When he finished mopping up, only three players (Leon Durham, Lee Smith and Jody Davis) remained.

"Every trade we made, we were criticized," said Green. "Especially during the early days." Cub fans howled when shortstop Ivan DeJesus was swapped for shortstop Larry Bowa. But a throw-in was a kid named Ryne Sandberg.

Add Rick Sutcliffe, Steve Trout, Bob Dernier, Gary Matthews, Keith Moreland, Ron Cey, Dennis Eckersley, Scott Sanderson, and a steady hired-hand named Jim Frey and you have a National League East champ. From last to first in three seasons!

It was Green who put all the pieces of the puzzle in place. But Dallas wants the big prize—a World Series winner at Wrigley Field.

LEE SMITH

SMITH, LEE ARTHUR
B. Dec. 4, 1957, Jamestown, La.
BR TR 6'6"
235 lb.

There's no guessing game in the Wrigley Field bleachers. Fans can close their eyes and just listen to the ball pop into the catcher's mitt. Anyone can tell it's awesome Lee Smith firing blue smoke from the mound in relief for the Cubs.

The 6'6", 235-pounder brings no trickery to his relief work as did Bruce Sutter with his split-fingered fastball. Smith just rears back and dares the batters to hit his heat.

Smith built his powerful body by milking cows, slopping hogs, and carrying firewood on his family's farm in Louisiana. He built his reputation as a basketball and baseball star at Castor (La.) High School.

He won 15 in a row and then lost his final game, a one-hitter, at Castor. That performance alone had him mentally prepared for his future as a Cub. Smith was scouted by Buck O'Neill of the Cubs, who two decades earlier signed Ernie Banks.

But Smith wanted a college education and envisioned himself bouncing a basketball in the NBA. He sought out former Braves' slugger Joe Adcock, who resides in nearby Coushatta, La. Adcock advised him to get a college education and go for baseball afterwards.

In addition, a physician told Smith he wouldn't last more than two seasons in the NBA because of his "jumper's knees." It seemed that Smith had grown so fast that he didn't have much cartilage left in his knees.

Smith attended Northwestern Louisiana and was selected by the Cubs in the second round of the 1975 draft. But his climb to the majors was strewn with too many minor league losses.

While at Midland in the Texas League, Smith was introduced to relief pitching by manager Randy Hundley, the Cubs' former Rebel with a cause. Randy, a thinking man's catcher, wanted Smitty to concentrate on every batter.

Hundley brought Smith into a game with the bases loaded and one out and told him not to let anyone score. "I struck out the two guys and it turned my career around," said Smith.

In spring training the next season, Hundley was catching Smith. "We were fooling around on the sidelines and I started throwing sidearm," revealed Smith. Hundley asked Smith to throw sidearm in a game and a new career blossomed.

He was promoted to Wichita of the American Association in 1980. There he had 63 strikeouts in 90 innings and saved 15 games. Smith was brought up to the Cubs late in the season and he showed the right stuff, fanning 17 in 22 innings and winning two games.

The strike-shortened 1981 season was almost a total loss for Smith and the Cubs. Although Smith struck out 50 in 67 innings, he earned only one save and had a 3-6 record.

By the time 1982 rolled around, the Cubs were under new ownership and Lee was just another guy named Smith as far as Dallas Green and Lee Elia were concerned.

Somehow, Smith showed enough to stick, but was in and out as a starter and reliever. It wasn't until July that Elia turned Smith loose exclusively in the bullpen.

From July 8 on, Smith appeared in 35 games and allowed only four earned runs for a 0.96 ERA and 15 of his 17 saves. He retired an amazing 19 straight batters in one stretch from Aug. 18 to Sept. 7, with eight of them strikeout victims.

He was 0-4 as a starter and 2-5 overall with a 2.69 ERA. In addition, Smith hit a homer on July 5, striking the right field foul pole in Atlanta off veteran knuckler Phil Niekro. It was also his first big league hit.

The affable, gentlemanly giant was gaining recognition around the league as a premier reliever. Such hitters as Pete Rose and Mike Schmidt of the Phillies and Al Oliver of the Expos started tossing accolades.

Best of all, Smitty was recognized as a genuine talent by Dallas Green, even though Lee wasn't weaned in the Phillies' farm system. Smith was now deemed a suitable successor to Sutter.

The 1983 season saw Smitty surpass Sutter in saves 29 to 21. Lee's total topped the National League, as did his stingy 1.65 ERA. But his 103 innings pitched weren't enough for him to qualify for the ERA title.

His 91 strikeouts ranked him second among bullpen artists to the Phillies' Al Holland, who had 100. Somehow, Smith still had trouble winning clutch games, as attested by his 4-10 won-lost record.

But he was good enough to make the National League squad for the annual All-Star Game at Comiskey Park. The American League finally burst out of its slumber, ending its 11-game losing streak by shelling the National League 13-3.

Lee pitched one inning, gave up two runs, one unearned, but salvaged some respect for the Cubs. The highlight of the evening as far as Cub fans were concerned, was the moment Smith encountered Ron Kittle, the White Sox rookie wunderkind.

Suddenly, in the eighth inning it was Cubs versus the White Sox. Kittle at the plate and Smitty on the mound. All eyes were focused on the pair. The crescendo of the crowd was deafening.

It was strength against strength as Smitty fired a fastball and Kittle went fishing for strike three. Smitty had Kittle over a kettle.

Lee picked up where he left off in 1984. Although his earned-run average ballooned to 3.65, he won 9 and dropped 7, while saving 33 games, only four shy of Sutter's Cub record.

In one contest, on Aug. 2, the Cubs were leading 3-2 in the ninth inning with the Montreal Expos. Runners stood on first and third with one out.

Pete Rose slammed a line drive up the middle. The ball bounced off Smith's shoulder and shortstop Dave Owens caught it in midair and threw to first for a game-ending double play. That game came to be known as the "immaculate deflection" and proved that somebody up there liked the Cubs.

But the Padres prayed harder and Smith didn't escape unscathed in the National League playoffs when the pesky Steve Garvey poked Lee's smokeball for a game-winning homer to tie the ill-fated series at two games each.

Despite Garvey's crucial clout, the flame-throwing fireman is a fixture for the Cubs' future.

JODY DAVIS

DAVIS, JODY RICHARD
B. Nov. 12, 1956, Gainsville, Ga.
BR TR 6'4"
192 lb.

"Jo-dee! Jo-dee! Jo-dee!" The crescendo reached its peak in the sixth inning as 32,403 fans, jammed into Wrigley Field, shouted for a carrot-topped catcher to kiss one out of the park.

Ron Cey was walked intentionally to load the bases on Sept. 14, 1984, when Jody Davis selected a warclub and strode to the plate to face Mets' pitcher Brent Gaff.

"I heard the people screaming and I got the chills," said Davis. "It really got the adrenalin going. But when you're up there with the bases loaded, you try to put the crowd out of your mind and concentrate on what you're doing."

Gaff let loose with a fastball and Davis drove the first pitch into the left-center field bleachers for a grand-slam homer. That blow helped lift the Cubs and Rick Sutcliffe to a 7-1 victory and put them eight and one-half games ahead of the Mets in the National League East race.

As he churned the bases, the fans chanted, "Jo-dee! Jo-dee! Jo-dee!" They didn't stop until Davis returned to the dugout, came out, and doffed his cap. Late heroics were getting to be a habit with the popular Davis.

Perhaps his most dramatic homer of the season occurred on May 12 against Houston at the Astrodome, which is hardly a homer haven. The Cubs were trailing 4-2 with two out and two on in the top of the ninth.

Jody appeared as a pinch hitter against reliever Frank DiPino. He hit a 3-0 pitch over the center field fence for a 5-4 Cub triumph. Only this time he was greeted by deafening silence.

Davis could be the mainstay of the Cubs' catching corps for the next decade. But he almost died once after spilling pints of blood from a stomach hemorrhage.

It happened in 1980 at the St. Louis Cardinals' spring training camp in St. Petersburg, Fla. "I thought I had the flu or something," said the tall Georgian.

Davis went into the Cards' clubhouse and vomited blood in a garbage can. Teammate Ken Reitz rushed to the rescue.

"I just saw this big guy vomiting. At first it was old, dried blood. But after a while he was pumping the fresh, red stuff," said Reitz, who summoned the paramedics and helped lift Davis onto a stretcher and into an ambulance. Ken also donated blood.

Davis took 31 pints of blood before the surgeons found the ruptured blood vessel. Jody was hospitalized one month and spent two more at home. In the process he lost 50 pounds.

Jody returned late in June and played only 13 games at Springfield, Ill., batting only .167. The Cardinals left him unprotected in the draft, and he was purchased for $25,000 by the Cubs on Dec. 8, 1980.

The strong-armed young catcher was originally drafted by the Mets in 1976 after starring in high school and American Legion ball. In one legion game, Jody hit three homers, one a grand slam, and drove in eight runs. He was twice voted Most Valuable Player at Gainsville's North Hall High School, where he also lettered in basketball.

Davis reported to Marion of the Appalachian League in 1976, but batted only .232. It wasn't until 1979 that Davis blossomed into a hitter, batting .296 with 21 homers and 91 RBI at Jackson of the Texas League. His batting instructor at that time was Phil Cavarretta, the old Cub favorite.

The Mets, however, were touting John Stearns as their backstop of the future and Davis was sent to the Cardinals organization for pitcher Ray Searage.

Jody never saw a big league ballpark until he arrived at Wrigley Field at the outset of the 1981 season. He spent much of the early part in the bullpen as third stringer behind Tim Blackwell and Barry Foote.

The Cubs were sleep-walking at the start of the season and Blackwell and Foote did their bit. Foote went 0-for-22 and was shipped to the Yankees. The walrus-mustached Blackwell fared a little better, but Davis remained a spectator.

It wasn't until June 5 that manager Joey Amalfitano realized the Cubs had nothing to lose by giving Davis a good shot. Jody got three hits in a victory over the Dodgers and the Cubs won four of five with Davis behind the plate.

It took a midseason strike to stop Jody. When play resumed in August, Davis was the Cubs' No. 1 catcher. He was a take-charge guy, ordering the pitchers to throw more inside pitches. "You can't survive in this league by pitching outside and down the middle," insisted the rifle-armed receiver.

Davis finished with a .256 average, 4 homers, and 21 RBI. During the winter he was named Chicago Rookie of the Year by the local writers.

But he was just another face when the Cubs assembled for spring training in 1982. The team had a new general manager, Dallas Green, a new manager, Lee Elia, and a new catcher, Keith Moreland, all from the Phillies.

With those odds the job was automatically handed to Moreland, who started off with a hot bat and a cold glove. Baserunners were taking liberties with Moreland. Despite his .382 average Keith was hurting the team on defense.

Elia finally moved Moreland to the outfield and reluctantly handed the job back to Jody, who celebrated with a game-breaking homer against the Astros on May 9 at Wrigley Field.

The score was tied 3-3 in the bottom of the ninth. The Cubs had two runners aboard with two out and a full count on Davis. Reliever Randy Moffitt fired a fastball and Jody "hit the hell out of it," said Elia. The ball sailed onto Waveland Avenue for a 6-3 victory.

The Cubs seemed more complete with Davis behind the plate. Although he wound up with a .261 average and chased pitches that were a bit low and outside, Davis displayed some extra base power with 20 doubles and a dozen homers to go with 52 RBI.

Davis progressed as a batter in 1983. He stopped trying to pull outside pitches and learned to stroke the ball to right field. But his 23 passed balls were disturbing.

It wasn't disturbing, though, to hear "Jo-dee! Jo-dee! Jo-dee!" That was popularized during a three-game series against the Cardinals that drew 116,107 fans to Wrigley Field in mid-June. That's when Davis stroked three homers and drove in 10 runs. Among his blows was his first grand slam in the fourth inning off Bob Forsch on June 12.

Jody's 24 homers tied Ron Cey for the team leadership. In addition, he had 31 doubles and 84 RBI and upped his average to .271. His homer total was the most by a Cub catcher since the heyday of Gabby Hartnett.

Davis cut his passed ball total to nine in 1984 and set a personal high of 94 RBI, the most by a Cub catcher since Gabby (who else?) drove in 122 in 1930. In addition, Davis collected 19 homers.

Best of all, Davis provided a memorable moment for Cub fans when pitcher Rick Sutcliffe blew a third strike past Pittsburgh's Joe Orsulak in the ninth inning on Sept. 24 at Three Rivers Stadium.

Davis held the ball aloft and clutched Sutcliffe. Baseball's redheaded battery had led the Cub charge to the National League East Division title. Entering 1985, Davis is a .262 lifetime hitter with 427 hits and 59 homers.

LEON DURHAM

DURHAM, LEON
B. July 31, 1957,
Cincinnati, Ohio
BL TL 6'2"
210 lb.

Leon "Bull" Durham seems destined to be one of the keys to future Cub hopes. While he has yet to attain the status of a full-fledged star, he is headed in that direction. In spite of his nickname, he is not known to be a tobacco chewer.

In high school Leon played baseball, basketball, and football, earning letters in all three. As a hitter, he batted .385 and was 11-3 on the pitcher's rubber his senior year. This caught the attention of the ever-vigilant St. Louis Cardinals' scouting staff, who signed him in the June 1976 free agent draft. He was dispatched to the Cardinals' rookie team in Sarasota, Fla., where he remained the rest of the season.

During the next two years, Durham polished his skills at Gastonia, St. Petersburg, and Arkansas. By 1979 he was ready for the Cardinals' Triple A team in Springfield, Ill., of the American Association. He came through with a .310 average, 23 homers, and 88 RBI to earn Rookie of The Year honors.

The Bull started the 1980 season with Springfield, but was soon called up to the Cardinals. There he batted .271 in 96 games, singling off Met pitcher Mark Bomback in his major league debut.

Meanwhile, the Cubs had a problem on their hands in the person of Bruce Sutter, the bullpen ace. After an arbitrator had ruled in

Sutter's favor during contract negotiations the previous spring, the Wrigley organization did not want to hold his $700,000 contract any longer than necessary, so up he went on the trading block.

General Manager Bob Kennedy had his eyes on Durham, and went to St. Louis hoping to use Sutter as his ace in the hole. But Card front office boss Whitey Herzog, playing on Kennedy's twin anxieties to unload Sutter and grab Durham, apparently maneuvered him into taking Ken Reitz, an over-the-hill third baseman, and Tye Waller, a second-stringer—along with Leon—in exchange for Sutter. So instead of returning to Chicago with a full house, Kennedy went home with what looked like a handful of deuces.

Reitz lasted one year in a Cub jersey while Waller remained a bench-warmer. Durham, however, has been paying dividends. In the 1981 season, hampered by a player's strike, Durham batted .290 in 87 games, led the club in stolen bases with 25, triples with 6, and tied Bill Buckner for the home run lead with 10.

The following year Leon began charging after pitches like a bull in a china shop, finishing with a solid .312 average in his first complete season, tops on the Cubs and third in the league. Moreover, he paced the team with 7 triples and 22 home runs while his 33 doubles, 90 RBI, and 9 game-winning hits were second to Buckner. Durham's fielding continued to improve, and he did not suffer a prolonged slump all year.

Following Bull's splendid display in 1982, there were great expectations. Unfortunately, Bull saw action in only 100 games in 1983. His batting average dropped to .258 as he was bothered with hamstring and shoulder problems all year. Most of his 12 homers and 55 RBI came early in the season. A healthy Bull could have made the difference in many a Cub loss.

In the spring of 1984 it was decided to move Leon to where he would be least likely to get injured—first base. When Durham took over at that position, Wrigley Field fans received him with a resounding chorus of boos. They chanted "We want Buckner," for the star who had been the fixture at first for seven years. The jeers turned into cheers, however, when Bull led the Cub charge through the early months of the season. And Buckner was soon a memory, being traded to Boston for pitcher Dennis Eckersley.

The Bull gored National League hurlers in May, ripping them for a .351 average, nine homers, and 34 RBI, earning him Player of the Month honors. On May 8 he became the first Cub player since Dave Kingman in 1979 to homer in four straight games, collecting a single and a homer to drive in four runs as the Cubs outslugged the Giants 10-7 at Wrigley Field.

But the most dramatic act came at St. Louis on June 10. It was the top of the ninth as the Cubs nursed a 1-0 lead with the bases loaded. Leon was at third with Jody Davis at second and Larry Bowa at first. Suddenly, while the Cardinals were bird napping, Bull broke for the plate—and made it! With all eyes on Durham, Davis stole third and Bowa took second. It was the Cubs' first triple steal in so long that nobody could (and still cannot) remember when it last happened.

Although the Cubs' rally was squelched afterward, they held on to win 2-0. After the game, Cardinal manager Whitey Herzog said, "The Cubs are the best team I've seen."

Just as Leon appeared to be approaching super stardom, his old nemesis came back to haunt him at Wrigley Field on June 24. He jammed his right shoulder while diving back to first base to avoid a pickoff. The following day he was placed on the 15-day disabled list.

At the time of his mishap, Durham was batting .308 with 12 homers and 52 RBI. When he returned to the lineup after the All-Star break, his second half was somewhat of a letdown as his average tailed off to .279. Even so, Bull's 23 homers and 96 RBI marked career highs and were second on the Cubs to Ron Cey.

In the pennant playoffs against the Padres, Durham emerged as both a hero and a goat. In the second game, October 3, he played a sparkling defense to help preserve a 4-2 Cub victory at Wrigley Field, giving Chicago a 2-0 series lead. At San Diego, October 6, he powered a game-tying home run in a contest that the Cubs went on to lose 7-5, to tie up the series at two apiece.

Then came the tragic finale on the following day. The game began promisingly enough when Leon's two-run homer gave the Cubs a 2-0 lead in the first inning. Another by Jody Davis made it 3-0 in the second.

By the bottom of the seventh, the Cub lead had been whittled to 3-2. With one out and Carmelo Martinez at second, Tim Flannery's grounder went through Durham's legs like water through a sieve, enabling Martinez to score, tying the game. San Diego rallied to take a 6-3 lead and shut out the Cubs the rest of the way, winning the game and dashing Chicago's pennant hopes. "The ball stayed down. It didn't come up," said Durham at the Cubs' wake. "I make that play 200 times in a row." Ironically, it was only his eighth error of the year.

Bull's many 1984 accomplishments should not be forgotten. Were it not for his hot bat keeping the Cubs solvent in the early part of the season, they might never have made it to the playoffs. Entering 1985, Durham is a lifetime .285 hitter with 564 hits, 75 home runs, and 318 RBI.

MEL HALL

HALL, MELVIN JR.
B. Sept. 16, 1960, Lyons, N.Y.
BL TL 6'1" 185 lb.

A baseball purist watching outfielder Mel Hall would be bowled over. He's so bowlegged that he looks like he should be roping steers instead of steering roping line drives.

And that batting stance. There's no trace of a sweet-swinging Billy Williams. His stance, at one time, was so exaggerated that it appeared he was facing the catcher, not the pitcher. It has been modified, but still looks peculiar.

Hall is a diamond in the rough. His outfielding is spectacular, but unpolished. His baserunning resembles the old Babe Herman comedy-tragedies. At bat, he bails out against southpaw pitchers. But the raw talent is there.

For instance, Hall made a catch in St. Louis in the late innings on Sept. 26, 1982, that would've made Willie Mays take notice. Mel was playing shallow center when Lonnie Smith of the Cardinals pumped a ball bound for extra bases into right-center field.

Hall raced back at full speed and made an over-the-shoulder catch near the wall. Lonnie Smith kept running, thinking he had a possible inside-the-park homer. When he saw the ump signal out, Lonnie was aghast and turned his head toward the outfield in disbelief. Too bad it wasn't a clutch moment in the World Series. It would've rated with the memorable catches.

Melvin Hall, Jr., came from a baseball family. His dad, Melvin, Sr., was a minor leaguer. A cousin, Oscar Bennett, was an infielder in the A's organization.

As a youngster, Hall played Little League, Babe Ruth, and American Legion ball and was a standout at Port Byron (N.Y.) High, where he also dabbled in football and basketball. He was the Cubs' second selection in the June 1978 free agent draft.

Hall proved he had big league possibilities following an outstanding 1981 season at Midland when he batted .319 and led the Texas League in runs scored with 98 and base hits with 170. In addition, Hall hit 34 doubles, 24 homers, and drove in 95 runs.

He was promoted to the Cubs late in the season and hit a homer in his first game on Sept. 13 against Scott Sanderson of the Expos. But that was his lone hit in 11 trips.

Then it was back to the bushes. Hall tore apart American Association pitching and was named Rookie of the Year at Iowa where he scored 116 runs, collected 165 hits, had 34 doubles and 32 homers, drove in 125, and batted .329.

This time he was ready for the biggies. In a late season trial, Hall batted .263 with five extra base blows among his 21 hits. Mel opened the 1983 season with six hits in 15 trips, but suffered a broken left thumb on April 19 in Cincy and was on the disabled list until May 31, missing 41 games.

Hall made up for lost time by hitting safely in 16 of 19 games, including a hot spree from June 12 to June 21 when he lashed out 15 hits in 43 trips. By then, most of the media's attention was focused on Mets' rookie Darryl Strawberry.

But Mel couldn't be ignored as the big gun of August. He was named Player of the Month, batting .333 on 30 hits in 90 at bats with nine homers and 17 RBI. He had one incredible spree, Aug. 19-31, when he rocketed five homers in 11 at bats, including his first grand slammer off knuckler Phil Niekro of the Braves.

He was switched to third in the batting order, replacing a disgruntled Bill Buckner, who insisted rightfully that the spot was reserved for contact hitters. Buckner had only 30 strikeouts to Hall's 106 and had 626 at bats to Hall's 410.

In addition, all 17 of Hall's homers were off right-handed pitchers. But Hall proved himself a comer with his .283 average, some 26 points higher than Strawberry's .257. Yet guess who was the runaway winner as Rookie of the Year? It was the guy from the Big Apple who took the plum.

Nor was Hall the apple of new Cub manager Jim Frey's eye. After watching Mel butcher some balls during spring training, Frey decided the Cubs' biggest need was a pure center fielder for the 1984 season.

In the final week of spring training the Cubs traded with the Phillies for left fielder Gary Matthews and center fielder Bobby Dernier.

Hall was switched to right field where he was platooned with Keith Moreland. The ploy tightened the Cub outfield defense, but made for some disgruntled players.

The situation was solved somewhat on June 13. Hall was part of a seven-player package that parceled pitcher Rick Sutcliffe to the Cubs.

The transaction was clouded when Hall and minor league outfielder Joe Carter had failed to clear National League waivers. It wasn't until June 19 that Hall officially became a member of the Cleveland Indians. He was shifted to left field and was platooned again.

LEE ELIA

ELIA, LEE CONSTANTINE
B. July 16, 1937, Philadelphia, Pa.
BR TR 5'11" 180 lb.

Notre Dame's Knute Rockne was famed for his "Win One For The Gipper" speech. Lee Elia of the Cubs also gained renown for his clubhouse oratory.

Elia was seething after his 1983 Cubs got off to a 0-6 start. On May 1, following a rain-shortened loss to the Dodgers, he exploded with expletives deleted. The black-browed, craggy-faced manager, whose five o'clock shadow appears about noon, defended his inoffensive team against the "real" enemy—the poor, downtrodden Cub fan.

In his blistering speech, Elia assaulted the fans with salty language that would make sailors and bartenders blush. He addressed the fans as unemployed unmentionables.

Tapes of his tirade became collectors' items. Somehow, General Manager Dallas Green saved Elia's thin skin, convincing the hierarchy to retain his volatile manager.

The Cubs rallied after Elia's explosion. They even got to within one game of the .500 mark, but soon fell back into their losing pattern. Elia departed on Aug. 22 with a 54-69 record.

Nicknamed the "Banty Rooster" by his minor league teammates, Elia had spent seven long seasons in the bushes before being rescued by White Sox manager Eddie Stanky in 1966. Stanky and Elia are native Philadelphians.

"He's from Kensington and I'm from around 12th and Girard,"

noted Elia. Before he arrived at spring training some of Elia's buddies said, "Hey, don't forget to tell him you're from Philly, too." "Yeah, so is Ben Franklin and he ain't on this club." replied Elia.

Stanky sent the stocky shortstop back to Indianapolis, where he had hit 29 homers the previous season. But on June 1, Sox shortstop Ron Hansen suffered a slipped disc and was out for the season. Elia answered the distress signal and hurried out to Yankee Stadium.

"What a place to start my first major league game," said the 28-year-old rookie, who got a hit and was robbed of another and lost his shakes.

Elia lacked the range required of a big league shortstop and batted only .205 in 80 games. He hit 3 homers and drove in 22 runs, but was shipped back to Indy in 1967. In midseason Elia was traded for shortstop Jimmy Stewart and wound up in the Cubs' farm system at Tacoma, Wash.

Elia was no ball of fire at Tacoma either. But he did manage to escape from a fire at the Claypool Hotel in Indy. The entire Tacoma ballclub was in the hotel. Elia tied sheets together and went out the window. He fell the last 15 feet, but wasn't hurt.

After the fall he ascended to the Cubs. But there was little room at the top. Glenn Beckert was anchored at second base, Don Kessinger at shortstop, and Ron Santo at third base. Elia spent most of the 1968 season as a denizen of the dugout.

There was one moment of glory for him. It happened on an oppressively hot day in muggy St. Louis, Sunday, Aug. 4. The temperature climbed to 93 degrees as a crowd of 47,443 gathered at Busch Memorial Stadium for the unveiling of a Stan Musial statue and a game between the Cardinals and the Cubs.

It was to be a pitching match between Bob Gibson of the first-place Cardinals and Fergie Jenkins of the second-place Cubs. Four hours later, Musial, Gibson, and Jenkins were upstaged by the seldom-used Elia.

Gibson and Jenkins, who must have dropped 25 pounds between them on this sultry afternoon, were no longer on the scene for the 13th inning of this 5-5 struggle.

Randy Hundley opened the 13th with a single off southpaw Joe Hoerner and was sacrificed to second. After Al Spangler struck out, Cub manager Durocher scanned his bench for somebody, anybody to hit for pitcher Jack Lamabe.

Durocher had already used five pitchers, four pinch hitters and two pinch runners. Elia was his last resort. The rusty recruit took a strike, a ball, fouled off two pitches, then lined a single to left, scoring Hundley. Joe Niekro, the Cubs' sixth pitcher, retired the Cardinals in the bottom of the 13th for a 6-5 victory.

It was Elia's second base hit and first RBI of the season, lifting his average from .071 to .133. "I couldn't have saved it for a better occasion," Elia said. "All I was trying to do was protect the plate with two strikes on me. I just wanted to make contact."

"It's true. I had no other choice," Durocher said. "Just say I didn't pick a boy to do a man's job."

For the season, the former Delaware University student batted .176 with 3 hits in 17 trips to the plate. After the 1968 season, Elia beat around the bushes until quitting in 1973. His career big league average was .181.

Lee hooked on as a manager in the Phillies' chain and spent the off-season as a school teacher in Leavittown, Pa. His ballclubs always finished first, second, or third, and he earned a promotion as the Phillies' third base coach under Dallas Green in 1980.

When Green was named Cubs' general manager in 1981, Elia was his surprise selection as manager. The pair inherited a spiritless, talent-depleted team. They found no quick remedy and made their own mistakes along the way.

The Cubs got off to a sluggish start and Elia suffered through a 13-game losing streak, tying a club record. Elia even got into a shoving match with his first baseman, Bill Buckner. It appeared to be another dismal summer of discontent.

Elia's Cub attack was often one-dimensional. Rookie Ryne Sandberg would get on base with either Buckner or Leon Durham driving him home. Then they would be blanked for a couple more innings. Somehow, Elia made the most of what he had.

Ancient Fergie Jenkins was the best of a horrendous starting staff. Lee Smith was the lone dependable bullpen stopper. Elia made a truce with Buckner and the Cubs surged past the Mets into fifth place.

They even avoided 90 defeats, finishing with a 73-89 record. But 1983 was just another bleep season for Elia and another manager, Charlie Fox, was sworn in.

KEITH MORELAND

MORELAND, BOBBY KEITH
B. May 2, 1954, Dallas, Tex.
BR TR 6'0" 200 lb.

Keith Moreland has been the Cubs' regular right fielder since 1982. Breaking into the pros with Spartanburg in 1975, Moreland also saw service in Penninsula, Reading, and Oklahoma City in the Phillies' farm chain. At the end of the 1978 season he was brought up to the Phillies, but failed to get a hit in his only two trips to the plate. The following year it was back to Oklahoma City, where he batted .302, tied for the league lead in doubles with 34, hit 20 home runs, and knocked home 109 runs.

Keith was then recalled to Philadelphia, and this time it looked as if he were ready for the majors. Playing 62 games in 1980, he batted .314. However, when he dropped to .255 the next season, the Phillies soured on him.

On Dec. 8, 1981, the Cubs traded Mike Krukow and cash to the Phillies for Moreland, and pitchers Dickie Noles and Dan Larson. Keith was the Cubs' springtime wonder in early 1982, batting .356 through May 21 with eight homers and 33 RBI. At one point he hit safely in 18 of 19 games, and on May 7 he hit two homers while driving home seven runs in a 12-6 triumph over Houston.

His fielding, however, was something else. Stationed in the catcher's box at the outset, he uncorked throws that brought back memories of Roy Smalley. By mid-May he had relocated to right field. His bat soon went silent, as he finished at .261 with 15 homers and 68 RBI.

In 1983 Moreland was a far more consistent hitter. Hovering near the .300 level the entire season, Keith finished with a .302 mark to lead the team while upping his homer count to 16 and his RBI to 70. His 11 game-winning RBI were tied with Ron Çey for the club lead.

Despite his impressive showing, Moreland had no guarantee of a job the following spring. When outfielders Gary Matthews and Bobby Dernier were virtually stolen from the Phillies, the regular patrol was Matthews in left, Dernier in center, Mel Hall in right, and Moreland wherever there was an empty spot in the lineup.

During the early part of the season Keith was on the bench just as often as he was on the field. Several times he asked to be traded. After Hall was traded to Cleveland June 13, Moreland was again the regular right fielder, but he had only 29 RBI at the season's halfway point.

In the meantime, the Cubs of 1984 had developed a pattern of producing a new superhero every month. In May it was first baseman Bull Durham; the following month Ryne Sandberg reached unprecedented heights. Starting in July, pitcher Rick Sutcliffe emerged as an overpowering stopper.

In August it was Moreland's turn to rise to the occasion. Some of the other Cubs—Durham, Dernier, Davis—were beginning to wear out in the heat, but Keith, who had seen far less action, became the Cubs' "gun of August."

From Aug. 1 through Aug. 8, he went 18-for-34 for a .529 average with four homers, 15 RBI, four game-winning hits, and two game-tying hits. Game-winner number one was a grand-slam homer that provided the margin in a 4-3 victory over Montreal Aug. 5, with the Wrigley Field fans giving Keith a standing ovation. The bat he used, incidentally, was one he had borrowed from Sandberg.

Then the Mets, trailing the Cubs by only half a game, arrived in Chicago for a crucial four game series. The first contest saw Moreland collect the game-winner in a 9-3 romp. In the second game, the opener of an Aug. 7 doubleheader, his three-run homer was the catalyst for a six-run fifth inning in an 8-6 Cub win. After tremorous chants of "Keith, Keith" from the standing-room-only crowd, he emerged from the dugout waving his cap in acknowledgment. After the game he said, "I just don't know how to handle that sometimes. I mean, I don't want to be showing anybody up on their (the Mets') team, but you do want to thank the fans."

The nightcap was highlighted by a bench-clearing brawl when Moreland was hit on the thigh by a pitch from Met starter Ed Lynch. Keith charged the mound, roll-blocked Lynch, and the fight was on. "I just went out there to get my point across," said Moreland. "It's part of the game of baseball. I have no hard feelings against anybody." Gary Matthews added, "The Mets can't intimidate us. We don't have the big head. But they're not budging us from the dish either."

Although Keith went hitless in the second game, the Cubs were far from intimidated, winning 8-4. And Moreland struck back with a vengeance Aug. 8, going three-for-four with four RBI, including the game-winning single in a four-run seventh inning rally to give the Cubs a 7-6 comeback victory. As the New Yorkers limped out of town four and a half games behind, the *Chicago Tribune* sports headline was "Mets Go 0-for-Chicago." Manager Jim Frey remarked, "We've all seen players get hot like that. Ryne Sandberg carried us earlier. But Moreland got a big hit every time we needed it this week."

Keith was clearly the man of the hour as the demoralized Mets never again seriously challenged the Cubs' lead. Moreland, meanwhile, remained as hot as the weather. He was the hero again Aug. 11 when his ninth inning single in a 2-1 victory over Montreal was his fifth game-winning RBI in the last 12 games. On Aug. 28 he drove in six runs in a doubleheader sweep of Cincinnati with a three-run homer and a triple in game one, and two doubles and a single in the nightcap. The identical 5-2 wins gave the Cubs a five and a half game edge over the Mets, and Keith finished with a .360 average for August with five homers, 32 RBI, and eight game-winning hits, earning him the National League Player of the Month honors.

Although Moreland cooled off in September, he still finished with a .279 average, 16 homers to tie his personal best, and a career high 80 RBI, most of them in key situations. His 11 game-winning hits were third on the club to Gary Matthews's 19 and Bull Durham's 14.

In the playoffs Keith batted .333, but with no especially significant hits, as the Padres defeated the Cubs in five games. He did, however, give Cub fans an unforgettable thrill in the championship opener.

The Padres had the bases loaded with two out in the fourth inning when Carmelo Martinez slapped a sinking liner over Ryne Sandberg's head. Moreland charged in, dived, and picked the ball off the tops of the Wrigley Field grass blades. Had Keith missed it, he could well have ended up a goat, but he did not, and the Cubs went on to win 13-0.

Entering 1985, Keith is a lifetime .283 hitter with 541 hits, 57 homers and 292 RBI.

Dickie Noles had a brief but largely uneventful tenure as a Cub pitcher. In 1982 he posted a 10-13 record, his best to date.

DICKIE NOLES

NOLES, DICKIE RAY
B. Nov. 19, 1956, Charlotte, N.C.
BR TR 6'2"
190 lb.

Originally signed by the Phillies' organization, Noles bounced around in their farm chain for nearly five years before being called up in mid-1979. Over the next three years he commuted between Philadelphia, Reading, and Oklahoma City, winning six and losing 10 in the majors.

On Dec. 8, 1981, Dickie and Keith Moreland were traded to the Cubs for pitchers Mike Krukow and Dan Larson. His finest outing came on April 28, 1982, when he held the Reds to one hit in a 6-0 victory. The lone safety was a single by Eddie Milner, who would also spoil Chuck Rainey's no-hit bid in 1983.

As his record sagged to 5-10 in 1983, Noles spent much of the season undergoing alcohol rehabilitation. On July 2, 1984, he was swapped to Texas for player to be named later. In his two and a half seasons with the Cubs, Dickie was 17-25.

GARY WOODS

WOODS, GARY LEE
B. July 20, 1953, Santa Barbara, Calif.
BR TR 6'2"
190 lb.

During the past three seasons, Gary Woods has been a useful utility outfielder for the Cubs. At one time, he appeared doomed to be a minor league lifer.

Gary began his career with Lewiston of the Northwestern League in 1973 and made stops at Burlington, Birmingham and Tucson before getting a try with Oakland late in 1976. The following year he split the season between the Blue Jays and Toledo. He served briefly with Toronto again in 1978 but failed to stick.

Then it was off to Charleston and back to Tucson before resurfacing in the majors with Houston late in 1980. He spent all of the following season with the Astros, but was on the bench most of the time.

Woods became a Cub on Dec. 9, 1981, in exchange for outfielder Jim Tracy. In 1982 he had the best season of his career so far, getting into 117 games and batting .269. His fielding average was a slick 1.000.

Since that time Gary has been used more sparingly. In 1984 he batted only .235 but came through with seven pinch hits, second on the team to Richie Hebner. Entering 1985, Woods is a .243 hitter with 231 hits and 13 homers.

LARRY BOWA

BOWA, LAWRENCE ROBERT
B. Dec. 6, 1945, Sacramento, Calif.
BB TR 5'10"
155 lb.

Although Larry Bowa is of Polish descent, he was once carried on a list of outstanding American athletes of Italian ancestry. He has been the Cubs' shortstop since 1982, with uneven success.

Bowa began his career with Spartanburg of the Western Carolina League in 1966, batting .312 and playing 26 consecutive errorless games at shortstop. From there he moved up the ladder to San Diego, Bakersfield, Reading, and finally Eugene (Ore.) of the Pacific Coast League, the Phillies' Triple A team. After batting .287

at Eugene in 1969, Bowa was deemed ready for Philadelphia.

Larry was given the Phillies' starting job at shortstop in 1970 and he never relinquished it. He immediately gained a reputation as a stereotyped "good field, no hit" shortstop.

In 1971 he set a major league record for highest fielding average (.9869) and fewest errors (11) by a shortstop, only to see them wiped out by the Tigers' Eddie Brinkman the following year. In 1972 Bowa himself lowered his error count to nine and lifted his fielding average to .9874, both of which remain the National League standards. It was in that year also that he won his first of two Gold Glove Awards.

In the seasons that followed, Larry continued to be a smooth fielder while improving his batting skills, reaching a career high of .305 in 1975. He also proved himself a clever baserunner, stealing 39 bases in 1974, the year he was the starting shortstop on the National League All-Star squad.

Critics, however, regarded Bowa as an Astroturf hitter, whose average was fattened by the bounce of ersatz grass. They further maintained that his high fielding averages and miniscule boot totals were due to lack of range as much as fielding skill. One thing is certain, the Phillie brass was obviously satisfied with his work and he kept his job.

On Jan. 27, 1982, the Cubs traded Ivan DeJesus to the Phillies for Bowa and infielder Ryne Sandberg. Although Sandberg proved to be a worthy investment, some could see no logic in replacing the 29-year-old DeJesus with a Bowa who was pushing 37.

With the Cubs floundering miserably and Bowa hitting only .186 by June 8, he became the object of many a jeer and catcall from fans who longed for DeJesus. Larry then turned things around. He ended up batting .360 for the month of June.

However, it was a roller coaster thereafter, and he finished at .246. His 29 RBI were the lowest among the starting lineup and he had but one game-winning RBI. He had also slowed down at shortstop and was no longer a basestealing threat.

In 1983 Larry raised his batting average to .267, collected hit No. 2,000 of his major league career, and led the league in fielding average for the seventh time. Appointed team captain, he shared a title once held by such hallowed names as Charlie Grimm, Phil Cavarretta, and Ron Santo.

Captain or not, Bowa was clearly the weakest link at the plate in the Cub chain as the 1984 season unfolded. Time after time he came to the plate with runners on base and failed to drive them in, prompting cynical fans to label him "the constrictor." At one stretch he came to bat 130 times without driving home a run. He had but two RBI after June 30. More and more frequently, he found himself benched in favor of Dave Owen and Tom Veryzer.

On July 18 Bowa asked the Cubs to "play me or release me." Later, in regard to Jim Frey, he said, "He doesn't like me, so he doesn't play me." Frey replied, "He's not producing, that's all."

The situation reached its nadir at Wrigley Field August 3. Having spotted the Expos a 5-0 lead, the Cubs had rallied for two in the sixth, two in the seventh, and so far one in the eighth to knot up the score. Larry was at bat with the bases loaded and the squeeze play on. Unfortunately, Bowa missed on the bunt attempt, causing Keith Moreland to be cut down at the plate. Then, he bounced out to the pitcher to end the inning.

Worse was yet to come. In the top of the ninth, with the bases loaded and one out, Dan Driessen grounded a tailor-made double-play ball to Ryne Sandberg, who flipped to Bowa. Larry stepped on second for the force, then failed to get the ball from his glove as Max Venable crossed the plate with what became the winning run in a 6-5 heartbreaker.

Larry finished the season with a .224 average, no homers, and 17 RBI. In fairness, Larry's savvy was a big help. His experience and maturity provided psychological stability to a team largely composed of youths. Entering 1985, he is a .261 lifetime batter with 2,141 hits and 313 stolen bases. He has 15 career home runs.

RYNE SANDBERG

SANDBERG, RYNE DEE
B. Sept. 18, 1959, Spokane, Wash.
BR TR 6′1″ 190 lb.

It was Saturday, June 23, 1984, as the Cubs took on the Cardinals before a packed house at Wrigley Field. Cub fans all but slashed their wrists when the Cardinals took a 7-1 lead after two innings and a 9-3 margin after five and a half. But the Cubs clawed back like grizzly bears to chop the lead to 9-8.

That was the score when Ryne Sandberg came to the plate with three hits already under his belt, leading off the bottom of the ninth. On the mound was Cardinal bullpen ace Bruce Sutter, who had previously held Sandberg to one big league hit in ten at bats. A couple of swings later, a split-fingered fastball sailed into the bleachers in left-center field. Sandberg had tied up the game. Cub fans yelled themselves hoarse.

When the game went into overtime, the cheers turned to groans as St. Louis rallied twice in the top of the tenth to make it 11-9. Two were out in the Cub half when Sutter walked Bobby Dernier in what appeared to be a case of prolonging the agony.

Suddenly, Sandberg was at the plate once again. Surely lightning could not strike twice at the same spot—but it did. Ryne homered again to knot up the game at 11-11, sending the crowd into a frenzy. One inning later, Dave Owen's single knocked in Bull Durham to give the Cubs a 12-11 victory in their most exciting comeback in many a year.

Although Owen had driven in the winning run, Ryne was the real hero with his five-for-six outing and seven RBI. "I'm in a state of shock," said Sandberg, who had gathered 24 hits in his last 48 at bats and 12 in his last 16. "I don't even know what day it is. I was going up there thinking about pulling the ball against Sutter. I wasn't even thinking about hitting one out."

Prior to the game, Cardinal manager Whitey Herzog said that

Sandberg "may be the best player in the National League." After the contest, his words were, "Sandberg is the best player I have ever seen." It was the highlight of highlights in a dream season.

The Sandberg story began in Spokane's North Central High School, where Ryne excelled as a quarterback on the football team. He also played Little League and American Legion baseball.

Drafted by the Phillies in June 1978, Sandberg gained four years of minor league training at Helena, Spartanburg, Reading, and Oklahoma City. He was brought up to Philadelphia late in 1981 for his first major league trial, seeing action mainly as a late inning defensive replacement. Although he got into 13 games, he came to bat only six times, collecting one hit. On Jan. 27, 1982, Ryne and veteran shortstop Larry Bowa were traded to the Cubs for shortstop Ivan DeJesus.

Previously a shortstop, Sandberg was assigned the starting position at third base. He adjusted with grace and ease, making his defensive skills apparent from day one with his wide range and accurate throws.

With his bat, however, he stumbled off to one of the worst starts in recent memory, collecting only one hit in his first 32 trips to the plate. But manager Lee Elia refused to give up on him and more importantly, Sandberg believed in himself. Said Larry Bowa, "Ryne Sandberg never came close to panicking."

By the end of the season, Sandberg had jacked his batting average up to .271, collected 172 hits, and scored 103 times to lead the club. His 32 stolen bases set a high for a Cub third baseman, while he legged out 30 infield hits with his speed. In addition, he socked 30 doubles, five triples, and seven homers, driving home 54 runs.

Defensively, Ryne's .970 fielding average was exceeded only by the Cardinals' Ken Oberkfell with .972. In the National League Rookie of the Year balloting he finished sixth, but was given Chicago Rookie of the Year honors by the local writers.

Switched to second base in 1983, Sandberg made the transition with no difficulty, committing only 13 errors in 158 games to earn the Gold Glove Award. It was the first time in National League history that a player had won the Gold Glove his first year after being switched there from another position. His batting average slipped to .261, but he still led the club with 37 stolen bases and 94 runs scored.

The Cubs soon had a new manager, Jim Frey, who convinced Sandberg that he could improve his hitting by pulling the ball. As a result, the 1984 season became a time never to be forgotten, either for the Cubs or Sandberg.

Although Ryne started off slowly in the cold of early April, his bat soon turned into a red-hot iron. From April 24 through May 16 he hit safely in 18 consecutive games, batting .421 during the streak. He had 10 multi-hit games, including six straight three-hit contests. Sandberg ended up batting .373 for the merry month, gathering 41 hits. Since he generally batted second in the lineup behind former minor league teammate Bobby Dernier, the two became known as "the Daily Double."

Ryne began June in fine fashion, smacking two homers in a 12-3 racking of the Phillies that put the Cubs back in first place on the first of the month. In the weeks that followed his bat continued to blaze, reaching its zenith in the historic June 23 game.

By now Cub fans were calling Sandberg "the Natural" in reference to a hit movie starring Robert Redford as an amazing athlete who almost single-handedly led his team out of the briny deep into pennant contention—just as Sandberg was doing with the Cubs.

He had also become the heartthrob of screaming, teenage girls, who swooned over him the way the bobby soxers of the early 1950s did over another Cub infield gladiator, Handsome Ransom Jackson. Ryne batted .373 for June, with 47 hits, 27 runs, eight homers, and 21 RBI, earning him the National League Player of the Month honors.

Meanwhile, "Ryno" had been running a distant third in the All-Star balloting for second baseman. Dodger Steve Sax, the front-runner, stated flatly that Sandberg deserved the honors, not he.

However, when the late returns came in, Sandberg was the people's choice, passing both Sax and Alan Wiggins of the Padres. At Candlestick Park on July 10 he played the entire game, collecting a single in four trips and stealing a base as the National League emerged victorious 2-1. It was the first Cub hit in an All-Star Game since Bill Madlock singled home two runs in the 1975 classic.

At the All-Star break Ryne was batting .335 with 118 hits, 11 homers and 52 RBI. Although his second half was less productive, Sandberg continued to deliver key hits and perform miracles at second base. When the Cubs clinched the National League East title at Pittsburgh on September 24, Ryne contributed a pair of doubles and scored the winning run on a single by Gary Matthews.

Finishing the season with a club-high .314 average, Ryno led the league with runs scored (114) and tied for the lead in triples (19), the most by a Cub player since Vic Saier had a club record 21 in 1913 (tied with Frank Schulte, 1911). He was second in the National League in hits with 200 and second in total bases with 331. His 36 doubles were good for a third place tie, while his .520 slugging average gave him sole possession of third.

Sandberg's 19 home runs were the most by a Cub second baseman since Rogers Hornsby's 39 in 1929, and his 84 RBI were the best at second since Billy Herman knocked home 93 in 1936. He came within one double and one home run of becoming the first player in major league history with 200 hits *and* 20 or more doubles, triples, homers, and stolen bases (he had 32 for the year) in the same season.

Defensively, Sandberg was better than ever. He made but six errors the entire season, best in the league, and played 61 consecutive games (June 29 through September 6) without a fumble, earning another Gold Glove.

In the pennant playoffs, Ryne missed a couple of tricky bouncers that went over his shoulder, but was otherwise a hero in a losing cause, batting .368 with seven hits, two RBI, and three stolen bases. Yet all the statistics combined cannot do justice to Ryne's contributions to the Cubs in their dynamic 1984 season.

It surprised no one when Sandberg coasted to the Most Valuable Player Award on November 13, the first Cub so heralded since Ernie Banks a quarter century earlier. "I was in my room taking a shower when the call came that I had won the award," he said. "I didn't even bother to dry off. I'm a little bit amazed. It's a great feeling, no question about it."

Entering 1985, Ryne is a .282 hitter with 538 hits, 34 homers, 186 RBI, and 101 stolen bases. It is the hope of every Cub fan that his best years are both ahead of him *and* in a Cub jersey.

JAY JOHNSTONE

JOHNSTONE, JOHN WILLIAM, JR.
B. Nov. 20, 1945, Manchester, Conn.
BL TR 6′1″
190 lb.

Veteran outfielder Jay Johnstone was born shortly after the Cubs won their last pennant. Although with the team most of 1984, he was gone by the time the Cubs clinched the NL East title.

The well-traveled Johnstone entered the majors with the Angels in 1966. As an Angel, his only season as an everyday player was 1969, when he batted .270 in 148 games. In the ensuing years he played for the White Sox, A's, Phillies, Yankees, Padres, and Dodgers. He enjoyed his best seasons at Philadelphia, where he hit .329 in 1975, .318 in '76, and .284 in '77.

Signed by the Cubs as a free agent on June 1, 1982, he appeared on a semiregular basis that year, batting .249 with 10 homers and 43 RBI. The following season he was used less but batted .257 and was effective as a pinch hitter. In 1984 Johnstone came to the plate only 72 times but garnished 21 hits for a .292 average. However, he was dropped from the roster on Aug. 31 to make room for Davey Lopes. Jay is a lifetime .267 batter with 1,252 hits and 102 homers.

RON CEY

CEY, RONALD CHARLES
B. Feb. 16, 1948, Tacoma, Wash.
BR TR 5′9″
185 lb.

It took "the Penguin" to help the Cubs out of the deep freeze. Ronald Charles Cey didn't exactly swing the hottest bat, but 187 RBI in two Cub seasons proved he was no cold stiff.

As a member of the Los Angeles Dodgers, Cey would waddle into Wrigley Field and rattle the fences. For instance, on June 6, 1974, the young third baseman drove in seven runs with two homers and a single to lead LA to a 10-0 romp over the hapless Cubbies.

Whenever the Dodgers visited Chicago, the sun was always shining and the wind was blowing out.

Cey, a Dodger mainstay for 11 solid seasons, was obtained from LA on Jan. 20, 1983, for Cub farmhands Dan Cataline, an outfielder, and Vance Lovelace, a pitcher.

A native of Tacoma, Wash., Ron was originally selected by the New York Mets in the 24th round of the draft on June 6, 1966. He preferred an education and attended Washington State and Western Washington before signing with the Dodgers' organization in 1968.

Physically, Cey is a powerful 5′9″ and 185 pounds. His short arms and stocky legs, combined with his pronounced waddle earned him the nickname "Penguin."

Third base had been an enigma for 16 seasons since the Dodgers deserted Brooklyn for the West Coast. Cey was the 43rd candidate in 1972 after destroying Pacific Coast pitching, batting .328 at Spokane and .329 at Albuquerque with two year totals of 55 homers and 226 RBI.

His offensive production and defensive work ended the long search. For the next decade Cey was a big gun in the middle of the Dodger lineup. His 228 homers is a Dodger record, LA variety.

Undoubtedly, Cey's biggest and most horrifying moment came in the 1981 World Series against the New York Yankees. In the fifth game, a Goose Gossage fastball, timed at 94 mph sailed high and tight. It struck Ron on the helmet, just above the temple.

Cey crumbled in a heap. The blow rendered him unconscious and gave him a concussion. "Another inch lower and it would have been all over," recalled Cey. "I remember falling in slow motion. There was a complete explosion in my head. When the trainer came out, I asked him if any bones were protruding."

A day of travel and a rainout gave Cey ample rest. He returned for game six, wearing a protective ear flap. Cey proved he wasn't plate-shy by singling in the first inning. Afield, he made a back-handed stab of a Bob Watson liner in the second inning.

Ron then singled home the go-ahead run in the fifth inning before dizziness forced him to retire in the sixth inning. The Dodgers went on to win 9-2 and take the series.

Cey hit .350 with one homer and drove in six runs to share MVP honors with Pedro Guerrero and Steve Yeager. But Dodger management thought the team was getting too long in the tooth.

Steve Garvey at first, Davey Lopes at second, Bill Russell at short, and Cey at third, had remained intact for 10 seasons, setting an all-time record for an infield quartet.

Lopes was dispatched to Oakland and then wound up with the Cubs. Garvey, demanding a zillion, was the big cheese in the 1982 re-entry draft of free agents. The Cubs engaged in an all-out bidding war and lost to the Padres. They then set their sights on Cey.

Ron looked forward to playing at Wrigley. His wife, Fran, is a native Chicagoan, and the park seemed ideal for his hitting talent. Little did he realize he was no longer facing Cub pitching.

At the outset of the 1983 season everything went wrong. The first six weeks were the most brutal of his career. The weather was horrible, he hurt his shoulder, and the team was losing, losing, losing. Cey was an easy target for the boobirds. "Booing is something with which you try not to concern yourself," sighed Cey. "If you're booed on the road, it means the other team's fans respect you. But if you're booed at home, it's hard to feel good about it."

Eventually Cey shook his slump and emerged as the Cub clean-up hitter. He led the team in RBI with 90 and shared homer leadership with Jody Davis at 24, while batting .275. At third base, Cey displayed good instincts and a strong arm, but lacked mobility.

Cey's second Chicago season was eventful and painful. He was charged with an error in the opener against the Giants at Candlestick Park and then played the next 60 games before committing another one.

The Penguin had his customary power at the plate, but his average remained frozen—.200 and below. After hitting his sixth career grand slam against the Giants at Wrigley Field on May 8, Ron started thumping out of his slump.

Then he injured his right wrist when he was hit by the Cardinals' Ralph Citarella on June 23. X-rays showed nothing wrong, but he was bothered by pain throughout the rest of the season.

Sore wrist and all Cey led the 1984 Cubs in homers (25) and RBI (97) and even got his average up to .240. Ron had a lot to say with the Cubs making the playoffs.

STEVE TROUT

TROUT, STEVEN RUSSELL
B. July 30, 1957, Detroit, Mich.
BL TL 6'4" 195 lb.

After swimming against the tide for six sinking seasons, Steven Russell Trout finally found the pot of gold at the end of the rainbow. Trout went fishing in free agent waters before the Cubs landed him for five years at $4.5 million.

The 1984 season was a lucky season for "Rainbow" Trout, who showed his true colors with a brilliant 13-7 record and a 3.41 ERA. Prior to 1984 the enigmatic left-hander floundered with murky marks.

It wasn't until he hooked up with Cub pitching coach Billy Connors that Trout scaled the mound heights. Connors baited Trout. He worked on his mechanics, his work habits, his attitude, his confidence, and gave him a sense of pride and purpose.

Trout, 27, is the son of former Detroit Tigers' pitching great Paul "Dizzy" Trout, a right-hander, who won 170 and lost 161 games during 15 fun-filled seasons.

Combined with Steve's 60-61 record. The Trouts rank as the all-time winning father-son pitching duo in baseball history with a 230-222 record. The two Trouts top the Cleveland Indians' combo of Jim Bagby, Sr., (127-89) and Jim Bagby, Jr., (97-96) and a 224-185 mark.

The elder Trout died in 1972 when Steve was 14. "My dad told me when I was a kid, 'Whatever you do, have fun.' So I try to have fun," said Steve, who grew up in South Holland, a Chicago suburb. "People are going to cheer you or boo you. All you can do is the best you can."

Despite a brilliant sinkerball, Trout's best wasn't good enough. Signed out of high school by the crosstown White Sox in the first round of the free agent draft on June 8, 1976, (the eighth player selected overall), Trout posted a 1-3 record with the Sarasota Sox.

After whistle stops at Appleton, Knoxville, and Des Moines, the lanky, shaggy-haired blond reported to the White Sox late in 1978 and was unbeatable with a 3-0 record.

The following season Trout was 11-8, joining a left-handed quartet of Tex Wortham (14-14), Ken Kravec (15-13), and Ross Baumgarten (13-8). The four were hailed as the pitching wave of the future. Today, only Trout survives.

But he barely survived. As a power pitcher, Rainbow had neither willpower nor staying power. The next three years Trout and his sinkerball sunk to 9-16, 8-7, and 6-9 seasons.

The Sox wrapped Trout and sore-armed reliever Warren Brusstar to the Cubs for pitchers Randy Martz and Dick Tidrow, plus infielders Scott Fletcher and Pat Tabler on Jan. 26, 1983. The deal looked like a steal for the Sox.

Connors received a call the following day from General Manager Dallas Green. "I just traded for Steve Trout," said Dallas. "He's your pet project. You've got to get through to him."

The pudgy pitching coach was handed quite a project. He patted him on the back. He kicked his butt. He induced Trout to go back to his basic pitches. But the Cubs were losers and Rainbow went to post.

His 10-14 record was deserving. Trout completed only one of 32 starts, rarely got to the seventh inning, and allowed 217 hits in 180 innings. He wound up in the bullpen and was forgotten and abandoned by managers Lee Elia and Charlie Fox.

Jim Frey, the Cubs' fresh new manager for 1984, remembered Trout only vaguely from his American League days. "Good fastball and wild . . . or something like that," said Frey.

For a fellow whose promise always outweighed his production, it appeared to be Trout's final chance to stick with a big league club. Steve visited Connors in Florida prior to spring training and was warned by him.

"If you came down here to screw around, get on a plane and go home," said Connors. "I'm tired of your BS. You have a wife and baby to work for." Trout worked on Nautilus and started to eat better than in his vegetarian days. He got up to 205 pounds.

His big day came on April 13. It was the Cubs' home opener against the New York Mets and their highly touted rookie, 19-year-old Dwight Gooden. A crowd of 33,436 assembled at frigid Wrigley Field.

At the conclusion, it was a complete success for Trout, who went the route in an 11-2 Cub rout. The lefty was in command of his sinker and had the Mets beating the ball into the ground. "It was just a thing of being patient with him," said Connors. "We all go through a war. Some guy's turn comes, some don't."

Trout's best pitching performance was a 3-0 triumph over the Mets in the first game of a doubleheader at Shea Stadium on July 29. Trout recorded 16 ground outs as the Cubs took a double bite out of the Big Apple. It was Steve's first shutout since 1980, raising his record to 10-5.

Down the stretch, the Cubs hit a snag—a five-game losing streak. It was up to Trout to bail them out.

Steve came through with a seven-hit 8-1 complete game victory over the Cardinals in the opener of a doubleheader on Sept. 23 at Busch Stadium. Dennis Eckersley completed the sweep with a 4-2 triumph and the Cubs reduced their magic number to one. The next day Rick Sutcliffe provided the clincher.

Manager Frey nominated Trout to pitch the second game of the National League championship playoffs against the Padres on Oct. 2 at Wrigley Field. Trout proved a whale of a choice, going eight and one-third innings in a 4-2 victory. After walking Kevin McReynolds with one out in the ninth, Frey relieved Trout and Lee Smith got the final two outs.

That brought a smile to Connors. "He made me really proud. It's all a part of growing up. People mature at different ages," said Billy.

WARREN BRUSSTAR

BRUSSTAR, WARREN SCOTT
B. Feb. 2, 1952, Oakland, Calif.
BR TR 6'3" 200 lb.

Although Lee Smith is obviously the ace of the Cub bullpen, Warren Brusstar deserves his share of the credit. He has been effective in mid-inning and mop-up roles.

Warren began his career with Spartanburg in 1974, then moved up the ladder to Rocky Mount, Reading, and Oklahoma City before being called up to the Phillies in May 1977. During his first two seasons in Philadelphia, he was 7-1 and 6-3 with ERAs of 2.66 and 2.33.

In 1979 and '80 Brusstar spent much of the time on the disabled list and was shuffled to and from the minors. Upon returning to the Phillies for keeps, he was somewhat disappointing. Optioned to Oklahoma City in mid-1982, Warren finished the season with the White Sox.

Brusstar became a Cub on Jan. 25, 1983, when he and Steve Trout were traded for pitchers Dick Tidrow and Randy Martz, and infielders Scott Fletcher and Pat Tabler. His first year as a Cub was a comeback, as he finished with a 3-1 record and a 2.35 ERA.

Warren saw less action in 1984, finishing at 1-1 with a 3.11 ERA and three saves. Entering 1985, he is 24-13 lifetime.

CHUCK RAINEY

RAINEY, CHARLES DAVID
B. July 14, 1954, San Diego, Calif.
BR TR 5'11"
195 lb.

It was Aug. 24, 1983, as the Wrigley Field crowd held its breath. There were two gone in the ninth inning. One more out and Cub hurler Chuck Rainey would have a no-hit game over the Reds. Eddie Milner then lined Chuck's first offering into center field for a single to end the no-hitter. Rainey retired the next batter to preserve a 3-0 shutout.

Sadly, it was Chuck's only real day in the sun. Although he led the Cubs in victories in 1983 with a 14-13 mark, his ERA was a hefty 4.48. In 1984 he dropped to 5-7 before the Cubs dispatched him to Oakland on July 2 for Davey Lopes. Thus he spent only a year and a half in Cub pinstripes.

Prior to coming to the Cubs, Rainey pitched for the Red Sox from 1979 through '82, winning 23 and losing 14. In his minor league days, he made stops at Elmira, Winston-Salem, Bristol, and Pawtucket before being called up to Boston.

TOM VERYZER

VERYZER, THOMAS MARTIN
B. Feb. 11, 1953, Port Jefferson, N.Y.
BR TR 6'1"
180 lb.

Veteran infielder Tom Veryzer played second base, shortstop, and third base as a back-up man for the 1984 Cubs. However, his contributions were limited as he was on the disabled list with a broken thumb from May 18 until Aug. 7.

Veryzer entered professional ball with Bristol of the Appalachian League in 1971 and made his major league debut with Detroit late in 1973. He was the Tigers' shortstop on a more or less regular basis until 1978, when he was swapped to the Indians. Tom's first year at Cleveland was his best in the majors, as he batted .271 in 130 games.

In 1982 the Tribe traded the frequently injured Veryzer to the Mets, where he lasted one season. Coming to the Cubs in April 1983 for pitchers Bob Schilling and Craig Weissman, Tom batted .205 in '83 and .189 last year, seeing little action either season. He was hitless in his lone appearance in the playoffs. Veryzer was released from the club during spring training in 1985. He is a .243 lifetime batter with 691 hits.

STEVE LAKE

LAKE, STEVEN MICHAEL
B. March 14, 1957, Inglewood, Calif.
BR TR 6'1"
190 lb.

One of the fallacies of last year's pennant drive was the Cubs' absence of injuries. What about catcher Steve Lake? Had he been healthy all season the rifle-armed receiver could've taken some of the burden off the overworked Jody Davis.

Lake, a peppy, peppery sort, spent eight long seasons in the minor leagues before being rescued by the Cubs in 1983. After purchasing his contract from the Brewers, the Cubs thought they had the ideal backup for Davis.

Lake got off to a rousing start with seven hits in his first 10 trips. He was hitting as high as .410 before being sidelined with bone chips in his left ankle. Steve eventually wound up hitting .259 and faced ankle surgery in September.

Lake encountered worse luck in 1984. He contracted hepatitis from tainted seafood on the Cubs' first road trip of the season and was hospitalized.

His weight was down and his strength was sapped when he returned in August. Although Steve displayed his usually strong throwing arm, he dragged a weak bat to the plate, winding up with a .222 average.

"It sounded like I was using a rolled-up *Sporting News* at bat," joked the catcher in the wry. Lake hopes to limit Davis to about 130 games in 1985.

JIM FREY

FREY, JAMES GOTTFRIED
B. May 26, 1931, Cleveland, Ohio
BL TL 5'9" 170 lb.

Great Gottfried. This small-Frey resembles Harry Truman. And like Harry, he really raised some hell. The bespectacled, balding, banty battler helped turn the bumbling, loveable Cubbies into a winner in one season.

James Gottfried Frey is undoubtedly the best Cubs' manager since the reign of Leo Durocher. And Frey took the Cubs further than the Lip did in six stormy seasons.

The Ohio-born Frey is a tried and true Buckeye, born in Cleveland, reared in Cincinnati, and educated in Columbus (at Ohio State). A graduate of Cincy's Western Hills High, Frey spent 14 seasons in the bush leagues, never sipping a drop of big league coffee.

His record reads like a railroad timetable with whistle stops in Evansville, Paducah, Hartford, Jacksonville, Toledo, Atlanta, Austin, Fort Worth, Tulsa, Omaha, Rochester, Buffalo, and Columbus from 1950 through '63.

Although the left-handed hitting outfielder boasted a .302 batting average, he bounced from one big league organization to another. At times he was the property of the Braves, Dodgers, Cardinals, and Pirates.

Frey enjoyed perhaps his finest season in 1957 with Tulsa, topping the Texas League with a .336 average and winning the Most Valuable Player Award. In addition, he led with 102 runs scored, 198 hits, 294 total bases, 50 doubles, 11 triples, and tied for the lead in stolen bases with 21.

As a result he was invited to the Cardinals' spring training camp in St. Petersburg, Fla., in 1958. Frey was told by manager Fred Hutchinson that he beat out the promising Curt Flood for the center field job, but he hurt his arm and his chance was gone forever.

"I was a singles hitter," revealed Frey. "Big, fat guys used to beat me out all the time because they hit home runs. I would never say I would have been a good major leaguer. I would have been one of those guys on the fringe."

Frey started his managerial career at the bottom, spending two uneventful years at Bluefield of the Appalachian League. His teams finished fourth and fifth in 1963 and '64. He then joined the Baltimore organization as a scout, before serving a decade under Earl Weaver as a coach.

"I never thought about managing," said the soft-spoken Frey. "I was proud to be a major league coach."

Meanwhile, Kansas City dumped popular manager Whitey Herzog because the Royals failed three times to beat out the New York Yankees in the American League playoffs. Frey answered the call to manage the Royals in 1980.

Kansas City won 97 and lost 65, winning the AL West by 14 games and then swept the hated Yankees in three games, highlighted by George Brett's towering three-run homer off Goose Gossage, turning a 2-1 deficit to a 4-2 pennant clincher.

Frey clashed head-on with the Phillies, managed by Dallas Green, in the World Series and lost in six games. Then Frey faced further problems. He set up a stringent dress code and incurred the wrath of a few casually clothed players, who didn't meet his penchant for sartorial splendor.

He gave outfielder Willie Wilson a dressing down for not wearing a sport jacket as the Royals prepared for a road trip. Wilson left in a huff. In addition, the Royals' record turned ragged during the strike-shortened 1981 season.

The team record was 30-41 when Frey was replaced by Dick Howser on Aug. 31. Jim then joined the New York Mets in 1982 as coach and batting instructor. His prize pupil was Darryl Strawberry, the peaches and cream of the rookie crop of 1983.

Frey was next summoned to Chicago by Dallas Green for his second shot as a big league pilot. He became the Cubs' 41st manager with the announcement on Oct. 6, 1983. "I like the way he looks you square in the eye," said Green. Dallas must've been seated at the time because he stands 6′6″ to Frey's 5′9″.

Jimmy inherited a mediocre ballclub. The pitching staff was loaded with leftovers. The outfield defense was downright offensive. Indeed, it was an embarrassment. The left side of the infield, with shortstop Larry Bowa and third baseman Ron Cey, lacked mobility.

The Cubs compiled a 7-20 spring training record on merit. It was then that Frey began molding his winning team.

1. Outfielder Leon Durham was switched to his normal position (first base) for his own protection against errant fly balls and painful hamstring pulls.

2. Frey advised second baseman Ryne Sandberg to use his strength in driving the ball, rather than just meeting it. Jimmy, however, was well satisfied with Sandberg's glove.

3. In the outfield, he decided Mel Hall was not the answer in center field. Green answered the distress signals by trading for outfielders Bob Dernier and Gary Matthews. In Dernier, Frey got his genuine, gifted center fielder and fleet leadoff hitter. In

Matthews, Frey got his holler guy and spark plug for left field.

That created a traffic jam for the final outfield position. He decided to platoon Hall and Moreland in right and faced the consequences of placing the popular Bill Buckner on the bench.

4. The pitching. Frey turned left-hander Steve Trout over to pitching coach Billy Connors, and worked sore-armed Dick Ruthven and sore-backed Scott Sanderson into the rotation.

The rest was up to Green. Dallas rolled up his sleeves and acquired Tim Stoddard to help Lee Smith in the bullpen and then swung trades for Dennis Eckersley, Rick Sutcliffe, and George Frazier, with Buckner and Hall moving on to the American League.

It was now up to Frey. He developed a closer relationship with his players—on and off the field. He got the most out of his 25-man roster. Unlike Durocher's 1969 Cubs, the 1984 team had depth.

The National League East race was wide open and the Cubs were ready. Sutcliffe proved the team stopper with a 16-1 record, and he was ably supported by Trout, Eckersley, and Sanderson. Sandberg looked and played like Superberg. Dernier stole bases and took away hits. Matthews, Moreland, Cey, and Davis provided the punch.

But it was Frey, sitting in the shadow of the dugout, nervously chewing gum, and resting his right arm on his chin, who made most of the right maneuvers. Finally, after 39 years of frustration, the Cubs clinched the National League East title. Frey thus became the first manager in major league history to guide teams in both leagues to divisional championships his first season at the helm.

On the final day of the regular season, after the Cubs rallied for two runs in the ninth inning to edge the Cardinals 2-1, Frey marched his entire ballclub onto the field and doffed his cap to the Chicago fans. Despite their failure to punish the Padres in the playoffs, Frey was the popular choice as National League Manager of the Year.

DICK RUTHVEN

RUTHVEN, RICHARD DAVIS
B. March 27, 1951, Sacramento, Calif.
BR TR 6'3" 190 lb.

While most of the Cubs were enjoying their finest seasons in 1984, Dick Ruthven was busy overcoming obstacles. Rufus, as he is fondly called by teammates, underwent surgery on May 23 to ease a blockage of the main artery and was sidelined until July.

At 34, Ruthven is the senior member of the Cubs pitching staff. His 6-10 won-lost record last season was hardly an indication of his ability. The rangy right-hander always seemed to be drawing the likes of Dwight Gooden, Steve Carlton, Nolan Ryan, or Fernando Valenzuela as his mound opponent.

On the plus side, Ruthven was the hero of the Cubs opening-day victory over the San Francisco Giants at Candlestick Park, going seven strong innings in a 5-3 win. He was in the groove, striking out the side in the fifth to help raise his career record to 17-7 over the Giants.

Also, Ruthven is one of two Cub pitchers with more than 100 victories, compiling a 119-120 record. His top season was a 17-10 mark when the Phillies won it all in 1980.

Ruthven came to the Cubs on May 23, 1983, for left-handed pitcher Willie Hernandez. At that time the deal was a plus for the Cubs as Ruthven became their most dependable starter with a 12-9 record, winning eight of his final 13 and leading in complete games with five.

But Hernandez soon took his screwball pitch to Detroit and became a real Tiger on the mound, sweeping the AL Cy Young Award and AL Most Valuable Player honors. Ruthven, meanwhile, dropped out of the Cubs' crowded rotation and became a spot starter.

THAD BOSLEY

BOSLEY, THADDIS JR.
B. Sept. 17, 1956, Oceanside, Calif.
BL TL 6'3" 175 lb.

The Cubs are more than Thaddis-fied with Bosley's contributions in the field, on the basepaths, and at bat the past two seasons. After bouncing around the American League for almost a decade, Bosley has found a home in the ivy-covered confines.

The lanky outfielder saw duty with the Angels, White Sox, Brewers, and Mariners before the Cubs purchased his contract from the A's in 1983.

For awhile it seemed Bosley was too injury-prone for the big leagues. Seven times he was relegated to the disabled list for various ailments. As a White Sox performer Thad spent parts of three seasons batting .264, .312, and .224.

Bosley showed promise as a Cub in 1983, hitting .292 with 2 homers and a dozen RBI after being recalled from Iowa in midseason. An error in judgment dropped him from the winter roster. He was shipped back to Des Moines.

Thad was thumping .358 with 6 homers and 43 RBI at Iowa before being summoned as a replacement for the injured Richie Hebner. Bosley caught the eye of new Cub manager Jim Frey, who began using him in clutch situations.

Bosley contributed two game-winning hits in a pinch role. The first came on July 21 against the Giants when he singled home Larry Bowa with the winning run in the 11th inning at Wrigley Field.

On Aug. 19 he came off the bench in the sixth inning at Cincy and stroked a three-run homer to break a 6-6 tie. Another dramatic blow was his ninth-inning homer to tie a game 3-3 at Atlanta. The Cubs went on to win 9-3. Bosley finished his productive year with 2 homers, 14 RBI, and a .296 average.

THE 1984-1985 CUB COACHES

A ball team's coaches are the unsung heroes of the club. Although the Cub players received most of the accolades—and deservedly so—Don Zimmer, Billy Connors, Ruben Amaro, John Vukovich, and Johnny Oates played important roles in helping the Cubs win the NL East title in 1984.

In 1985 **Ruben Amaro** will begin his third year as a Cub coach. Born in Monterrey, Nuevo Leon, Mexico on Jan. 7, 1936, he is the first Cub coach from south of the border. He was a jack-of-all-trades during his professional career, but is primarily remembered as shortstop for the ill-fated 1964 Phillies, who lost a 6½-game lead with 10 games remaining in the season.

Ruben began his career with Mexicali of the Mexican League in 1954 and made his major league debut with the Cardinals in 1958. During his tenure in the majors, he also played with the Phillies (1960-65), Yankees (1966-68), and Angels (1969), finishing a .234 hitter with 505 hits. He coached for the Phillies under manager Dallas Green in 1980 and '81, and he was in charge of easing the transition of Latin American players for the Phillies in 1982 before coming to Chicago.

Cub pitching coach **William Joseph (Billy) Connors III** was born in Schenectady, N.Y., on Nov. 2, 1941. His brief major league career consisted of an 0-2 ledger with the Cubs and the Mets between 1966 and '68. No one can doubt his considerable accomplishments as a coach, however.

Prior to coming to the Cubs, Billy had coaching experience with the Mets' organization, the Phillies, and the Royals. Working with Royal manager Jim Frey in 1980, he assembled a pitching staff that carried Kansas City into the World Series. Two years later he signed as the Cubs' pitching coach.

One of Billy's foremost achievements as a Cub has been the development of Lee Smith into an ace fireman. In 1984 Billy whittled the Cub team ERA down to 3.75, the lowest by a Cub staff since 1973.

1931

Former major league catcher **Johnny Oates** was hired by Jim Frey in 1984 to take care of the bullpen duties. A .250 lifetime hitter with 410 hits in his major league days, Oates was born on Jan. 21, 1946, in Sylva, N.C. He made his major league debut with the Orioles late in 1970, and later caught for the Braves, Phillies, Dodgers, and Yankees, hanging up his spikes in 1981.

Before coming to the Cubs, Oates was a successful manager in the minors, making it to the playoffs with Nashville in 1982 (77-67) and Columbus in 1983 (83-57).

John Christopher Vukovich is the youngest Cub coach, having been born in July 31, 1947, at Sacramento, Calif. An infielder during his playing days, John signed with the Phillies in 1966 and served with them, the Braves, and the Reds as a utility man between 1970 and 1981, batting .161 with 90 hits in 227 games.

Joining the Cubs in 1982, Vukovich served as first base coach his maiden year but has been assisting in the dugout the past two seasons.

Third base coach **Donald William Zimmer** is currently on his second tour of duty with the Cubs—he was their regular second baseman in 1960 and '61. Born in Cincinnati, Ohio, on Jan. 17, 1931, he is the elder statesman among Cub coaches.

Growing up in Cincinnati during the 1940s, Don played amateur and high school ball with Jim Frey. Signed by the Dodger organization in 1949, Zimmer spent more than five years in the farm chain before making it to the parent club late in 1954. For the next several years he was their number one utility infielder, including appearances in the 1955 and '59 World Series.

Don came to the Cubs via a trade on April 8, 1960. During his two seasons in Chicago, he batted .258 and .252, including 13 homers and an All-Star selection in 1961. Zimmer later played for the Mets, Reds, Dodgers again, and finally the Senators, finishing in 1965 with a .235 average, 773 hits, and 91 homers.

Before rejoining the Cubs in 1984, Don was manager of the Padres (1972-73), Red Sox (1976-80), Rangers (1981-82) and served as a Yankee coach in 1983. His record as a manager is a strong 620-600 with two second-place and two third-place finishes.

RICHIE HEBNER

HEBNER, RICHARD JOSEPH
B. Nov. 26, 1947, Brighton, Mass.
BL TR 6'1" 195 lb.

No matter which uniform the well-traveled Richie Hebner wore, he always dug Cub pitching. Among his many slugging feats, Hebner has hit four grand-slam homers off the Cubs.

And Dallas Green has a long memory. He recalled the 1983 season. The Cubs were on a roll in mid-July, wining 13 of 17 games, until Hebner slammed a 10th-inning pinch homer off Bill Campbell for a 5-4 Pirates victory. That put the Cubs in a tailspin.

On Sept. 15, Richie added to the Cub woe by connecting for a pinch grand slam off Lee Smith. When Hebner was available, Green grabbed the off-season grave-digger as a free agent.

Hebner paid immediate dividends by sparking the Cubs in the early weeks of the season. His ninth-inning homer off Bruce Sutter broke a 2-2 deadlock with the Cardinals and then he notched his 200th homer off Greg Minton of the Giants.

He was almost a one-man bench, playing first base, third base, and the outfield until he went on the disabled list on July 13 with a shoulder injury. It was diagnosed as bicipetal tendonitis and kept him sidelined until Sept. 1.

In limited play Hebner batted .333, but could have contributed more during the dog days of summer.

The left-handed swinger began his big league career in 1968 as a third baseman with the Pirates. He left Pittsburgh after the 1976 season, serving time with the Phillies, Mets, and Tigers before rejoining the Pirates.

SCOTT SANDERSON

SANDERSON, SCOTT
B. July 22, 1956, Dearborn, Mich.
BR TR 6'5" 200 lb.

Scott Sanderson is presently the number one question mark on the Cub pitching staff. An effective pitcher when he is well, Scott could make himself worth the trade price the Cubs paid for him if only his back problems would cease.

Although born in the Detroit area, Scott spent his formative years in Northbrook, Ill. He graduated from Glenbrook North High School. Drafted by the Royals in 1974, he opted for Vanderbilt University instead, majoring in business finance and history.

Upon entering professional ball in 1977, Sanderson moved up the ladder in little time. Debuting with West Palm Beach of the Florida State League, he went to Memphis of the Southern League the following year, then on to Denver of the American Association in midseason. By the end of 1978, Scott was with the Montreal Expos. As a rookie he was 4-2 with a 2.51 ERA in 61 innings.

During his first five years with the Expos, Scott's ERAs were always respectable, but he never fully lived up to the high hopes Montreal had for him. His victory column saw double figures only twice, with a 16-11 mark in 1980—his best to date—and a 12-12 log in 1982, when he finished strong to win six of his last seven decisions. He posted a career high 158 strikeouts that season.

Then came the disastrous 1983 season. Tearing ligaments in his right thumb in a baserunning mishap at Wrigley Field on July 4, Sanderson remained on the disabled list until September 1. He finished the year with a 6-7 record and a 4.62 ERA.

The pitching-dry, fifth-place Cubs were anxious to improve their pitching staff and willing to give Scott another chance, even if he appeared to be damaged goods. Scott, then, became a Cub on December 7, 1983, in a three-team deal. The Expos acquired pitcher Gary Lucas from San Diego while the Padres soaked the Cubs for infielders Carmelo Martinez and Fritz Connally and pitcher Craig Lefferts.

In the early stages of 1984, Scott looked like he was headed for an outstanding year, winning four of his first five decisions and ranking among the league leaders in ERA. On April 28 he allowed just two hits in leading the Cubs to a 7-1 romp at Pittsburgh, facing only 28 batters.

On May 9 Scott was breezing toward a 5-0 win over the Dodgers when back spasms forced him out of the game after five innings. Although he received credit for the victory, Sanderson did not appear again until May 15. He lasted for only two batters before the spasms flared up again.

Scott rested for two weeks before pitching again on May 29 at Atlanta. He lasted just three innings before the spasms reoccurred. This time he was placed on the disabled list, spending a week in a Chicago hospital.

Reactivated on July 5, Sanderson went five and a third innings to beat the Giants 9-3, but saw little action thereafter, finishing with an 8-5 record and a 3.14 ERA In his one appearance in the playoffs, he was ineffective but decisionless. Entering 1985, Scott is a 64-52 lifetime pitcher with a 3.31 ERA.

HENRY COTTO

COTTO, HENRY SUAREZ
B. Jan. 5, 1961, Bronx, N.Y.
BR TR 6'2" 180 lb.

Henry Cotto served as a late-inning caddy for Cub left fielder Gary Matthews and was on par with Bob Dernier when the speedy center fielder was sidelined.

As a holdover from the Wrigley regime, the peppy Puerto Rican was a longshot to make the Cubs at the outset of the 1984 season. But his steady bat, defensive agility, and speed impressed incoming manager Jim Frey.

The Cubs didn't miss a step when Dernier was injured. Cotto batted safely in 17 straight games, hitting a robust .361 on 22-for-62 as an off-and-on fill-in from July 28 through Sept. 3.

The Bronx-born speedster opened some eyes last April at Dodger Stadium when he robbed Mike Marshall with a running catch at the warning track in right-center.

He was in midseason form when he plucked a Mike Schmidt drive high off the left field vines and threw out the Phillies' slugger at second base.

And who could forget his game-saving catch with his back scraping the ivy vines for the final out in the Cubs 6-3 victory over the San Diego Padres in the second playoff game at Wrigley Field.

Cotto will surely be missed. He was dispatched to the New York Yankees in late 1984 in the deal that sent left-handed pitcher Ray Fontenot to the Cubs. In his short span with the Cubs, Cotto batted .274.

GARY MATTHEWS

MATTHEWS, GARY NATHANIEL
B. July 5, 1950, San Fernando, Calif.
BR TR 6′2″ 205 lb.

It took only one season for "Sarge" to earn his stripes. Gary Nathaniel Matthews led the Cubs' charge to the top with his leadership and bubbly effervescence.

In addition, he uncorked 19 game-winning hits, scored 101 runs, coaxed a league-leading 103 walks, and seemed to be in the middle of every crucial Cub rally.

His presence in Wrigley Field's left field is an intriguing tie to the past. That's where "Old Hoss" Riggs Stephenson patrolled for a decade and sprayed enough hits for a .336 average, highest in Cub history.

It's also the same acreage where Hank Sauer was the hammering homer hero, spraying his tobacco juice as the mayor of Wrigley Field. Then there was sweet swingin' Billy Williams, flashing his V-for-Victory sign to adoring bleacher fans.

Now the Sarge is in command as he ambles out to "his territory." Bleacherites roar and rate him salutes. In return Matthews distributed "Sarge" hats in appreciation of their support.

As a youngster, growing up in the San Fernando Valley near Los Angeles, Matthews used to sneak into Dodger Stadium. "I used to change the ticket stubs, slip in behind somebody, do whatever I had to do," said Matthews. "Now, I get to play left field when I get to Dodger Stadium. It really cracks me up."

Matthews was selected by the San Francisco Giants, the 17th player grabbed in the free agent draft on June 7, 1968. But he didn't rate highly with Giant officials because of his trouble with breaking pitches.

Only Gary and batting instructor Hank Sauer kept the faith. "I can see us now," recalled Matthews, "Garry Maddox and I, swinging at slider after slider thrown by Don McMahon."

Sauer patiently stood at the batting cage, gazing at Gary in the winter mornings in the Arizona Instructional League. "I had so many blisters from hitting sliders, I thought it was the easiest pitch to hit."

Sauer's patience paid off as his pupil powdered the pill at Phoenix in 1972, batting .313 with 21 homers and 108 RBI. That earned him a promotion to the Giants, where he batted .300 and was named National League Rookie of the Year in 1973.

After five solid seasons as a Giant, Matthews declared himself a free agent and signed a fat contract with Ted Turner's Atlanta Braves on Nov. 17, 1976. "I didn't get along with Turner," confessed Matthews.

"I spoke out on things that were happening around me. When the Braves sent Bob Horner to the minors, I said 'How in the world can you send him down after he hit 30 homers last year?' "

As a reward the Braves replied, "OK, we'll just sit your butt down on the bench and watch you sulk." "That gave me a bad reputation. I learned a lesson. If somebody isn't playing, I'll just keep quiet."

At about that time Matthews taught the Cubs a lesson in hustle. There was a game in Atlanta in 1979. The Cubs had two on base with Dave Kingman up. Kong slammed a high drive to right that was labeled a homer.

Matthews raced to the chicken wire fence, leaped a la Michael Jordan, and snared the ball at the tip of his glove. The force of the drive almost knocked Gary over the fence.

Even though Matthews had a no-trade clause in his contract, he welcomed the deal that sent him to the Philadelphia Phillies for pitcher Bob Walk on March 25, 1981. He enjoyed a .301 season under manager Dallas Green and a .289 year under manager Pat Corrales.

But 1983 was an off season for Gary. His average plummeted to .258 and he was platooned. He finally responded in October, hitting .429 with 3 homers and 8 RBI to wreck the Dodgers in the National League playoffs and get the Phillies into the World Series.

Meanwhile, the downtrodden Cubbies were having their problems in spring training of 1984. Errors were turning the games into a boot camp. Fly balls resembled Frisbees or unidentified flying objects.

After watching the Cubs lose 11 in a row, with fly balls dropping everywhere in left, center, and right, new manager Jim Frey called the Cubs' outfield play "stinko."

Finally, on March 27 General Manager Green sent reliever Bill Campbell and minor leaguer Mike Diaz to the Phillies for Matthews, center fielder Bob Dernier, and someone named Porfi Altamirano.

Dernier proved to be the Cubs' first bona fide center fielder in eons. And Matthews? "We needed a screamer, a holler guy, a leader," said Green. "When I realized I could get him from the Phillies, I couldn't say yes fast enough. He talks when it's time to talk, and he produces when it's time to produce."

Matthews was off to a great start with the Cubs, hitting safely in 13 of the first 15 games, batting .360 on 18 hits in 50 trips with 16 walks. He had a four-for-five effort against the Reds on May 15, and was four-for-four against the Astros on Aug. 14.

But Matthews reached his zenith on Sept. 23 when the Cubs needed him the most. They were mired in a five-game losing streak when they took on the Cardinals in a doubleheader before 46,083 fans at Busch Memorial Stadium.

The Cubs swept the Cards 8-1 and 4-2 and reduced their magic number to one. Sarge drove in the winning runs in both games. He socked a three-run double in the first game and walloped a two-run homer in the second.

The following night the Cubs clinched the National League East Division title, beating the Pirates 4-1 behind Rick Sutcliffe, who reeled off his 14th victory in a row.

Again, it was the effervescent Matthews who was sipping and spraying champagne after picking up his 19th game-winning RBI of the season. Entering 1985, he is a lifetime .286 hitter with 1,806 hits and 197 homers.

RICH BORDI

BORDI, RICHARD ALBERT
B. April 18, 1959, San Francisco, Calif.
BR TR 6'7"
220 lb.

Rich Bordi was used as both a fireman and spot starter for the 1984 Cubs. He was effective in both roles, coming through with a 5-2 ledger.

Bordi became a Cub on Dec. 9, 1982, when he was acquired from Seattle in exchange for outfielder Steve Henderson. He began his professional career in 1980, receiving his minor league training at West Haven, Tacoma, and Salt Lake City. In between, there were decisionless, token appearances at Oakland before Seattle purchased his contract. As a Mariner, he was 0-2.

Upon coming to the Cubs, Rich was optioned to Iowa, where he spent most of the 1983 season. Brought up to Chicago late in the year, he lost his only two decisions.

Bordi was scratched from the 1984 playoff roster and made no bones about being miffed. Over the winter he was traded to the Yankees in the deal that brought lefty Ray Fontenot to the Cubs.

BOBBY DERNIER

DERNIER, ROBERT EUGENE
B. Jan. 5, 1957, Kansas City, Mo.
BR TR 6'0"
160 lb.

The best way to describe the Cubs' acquisition of Bobby Dernier is a case of highway robbery. Although only a "throw-in" as part of a trade, Bobby's brand of center field in 1984 was something Cub fans had not witnessed in a generation.

Prior to donning Cub pinstripes, Dernier was essentially a baseball nobody. Making his professional debut with Spartanburg of the West Carolina League in 1978, he moved to Helena of the Pioneer League and finished the season there. His combined batting average for 75 games was .263.

With Peninsula of the Carolina League the following year, he batted .291 and led the league in stolen bases with 77. Moving up to Reading of the Eastern League in 1980, Dernier hit .299 with a league-leading 71 steals. Late in the season the Phillies gave him a cup of coffee in the big time.

Then it was out to Oklahoma City for the final grooming at the Triple A level in the American Association. There it was much of the same for Bobby—a .302 average and 72 stolen bases to lead the league. At the end of the year, he made another cameo appearance at Philadelphia.

It now looked as if Bobby was ready for the majors, but in 1982 he was somewhat disappointing in his first full season with the Phillies. Although his 42 stolen bases made a good impression, Bobby's .249 average and 21 RBI did not. The next season, with far fewer at bats, he dropped to .231. He appeared in one game as an outfield defensive replacement during the pennant playoffs and once as a pinch runner in the World Series, scoring one run.

Dernier was still an unknown quantity on March 27, 1984, when he, outfielder Gary Matthews, and pitcher Porfi Altimarino were swapped to the Cubs for catcher Mike Diaz and pitcher Bill Campbell. It was Matthews the Cubs were after; the other two appeared to be just excess baggage the Phillies wanted to unload. When it was announced that Dernier would be starting in center field, the talented but moody Cub outfielder Mel Hall remarked, "I can't see Bob Dernier taking my job. I don't think he's qualified and I don't mind telling anyone that." But by the arrival of opening day, Dernier was in center field while Hall was moved to right en route to being exiled to Cleveland.

Bobby quickly proved himself the Cubs' best center fielder since the days of Andy Pafko, if not beyond. He covered all of his turf and then some, made breathtaking running catches, and displayed a strong, accurate throwing arm. When Keith Moreland returned to right field on a full-time basis after Hall was traded, the Cub outfield was solidified.

The best surprise, however, was that Dernier began hitting with authority, proving himself an ideal leadoff man for the big guns to blast across the plate. On May 24, 1984, he went five-for-five and stole two bases in a 10-7 victory over the Braves at Wrigley Field. He legged out two infield hits and had a bloop single to left. It was the first five-hit game by a Cub since Ivan DeJesus turned the trick against the Cardinals on April 22, 1980.

Interviewed after the game, Bobby commented nonchalantly, "It was a lucky day. It was the kind of day you sleep well after." Possibly it was not all luck, either, for on May 30 he had a repeat five-for-five outing in a 6-2 triumph over the Braves at Atlanta, stealing two bases and scoring three runs.

At the halfway point of the season, Dernier was batting a cool .316. Although his hitting tailed off thereafter, he still finished with a respectable .278 average, 149 hits, and 94 runs scored, seventh highest in the league. When he stole his 33rd base on July 21, sportswriters who had obviously not read their history books asserted that he "broke the Cubs record for stolen bases by a center fielder, surpassing Adolfo Phillips's 32 in 1966." Forgotten were Bill Lange's 41 in 1899 and Jimmy Slagle's 40 in 1902, but Bobby soon had the club position record all to himself. When he finished the year with 45 thefts—eighth highest in the league—it was the most by a Cub player since Johnny Evers swiped 46 back in 1907. Moreover, it was the general consensus that Dernier was worth having in the lineup solely for his defensive ability, even if he had batted only .200 and not stolen a base.

During the postseason pennant playoffs Bobby surprised everyone—including himself—by belting a first inning homer (he had only three during the regular season) in the series opener Oct. 2. In the Wrigley Field boxes his radiant wife beamed on national TV. Dernier had become only the second player in National League playoff history to homer in his first at bat, the other being Joe Morgan of the Reds in 1972. For the rest of the day he had a walk and a run scored in the third, and a double, a walk, and another run in a six-run fifth. The Cubs went on to trounce the Padres, 13-0, to set a record for most runs scored in a playoff game.

More heroics followed in game two, Oct. 3. Leading off the first inning with a single, he made a daring dash from first to third on Ryne Sandberg's grounder, then scored on a grounder by Gary Matthews. In the fourth inning, after forcing Steve Trout, he stole second and scored on Ryne Sandberg's double as the Cubs went on to win 4-2.

Sadly, it was to be the last hurrah that season for both Dernier and the Cubs. For the final three games at San Diego, Bobby collected only one more hit, a single, and stole no more bases as the Padres swept at home to win the pennant. Nevertheless, no one can deny that he gave Cub fans plenty to cheer about in 1984. Entering 1985, he is a .263 hitter with 299 hits and 112 stolen bases. On Nov. 27, 1984, he was given *The Sporting News* Gold Glove Award for his outstanding defense.

TIM STODDARD

STODDARD
TIMOTHY PAUL
B. Jan. 24, 1953,
East Chicago, Ind.
BR TR 6′7″
230 lb.

Tall Timothy is the lone Cub that got away. If he couldn't beat the Padres—he joined 'em. But the hefty hurler had a hearty season with the Cubs in 1984, posting a 10-6 record.

At one point Stoddard set the standard with an 8-1 mark in relief and teamed with Lee Smith as a tremendous tandem in the bullpen. Then he encountered control problems and wasn't as effective in the stretch drive.

An imposing figure at 6′7″ and 230 pounds, Stoddard was a teammate of All-American David Thompson at North Carolina State. The Wolfpack compiled a 57-1 record and downed UCLA and Bill Walton for the 1974 NCAA basketball title.

A native of East Chicago, Ind., Stoddard was originally property of the White Sox, but only pitched one inning for a 9.00 ERA. He next surfaced in the Orioles' bullpen, where he had a winning record, including a victory over the Pirates in the 1979 World Series, but spent much time on the disabled list.

He was traded to the A's for third baseman Wayne Gross on Dec. 9, 1983, and then was obtained during the spring training for two Cub minor leaguers. With his beard and bulk Stoddard was a menacing figure on the mound.

During one stretch in late June, Stoddard went on a strikeout binge, fanning 12 batters in 9.2 innings and picking up three straight saves.

As a free agent, Stoddard signed with San Diego in the winter of 1984.

DAVE OWEN

OWEN, DAVE
B. April 25, 1958, Cleburne, Tex.
BB TR 6'1" 175 lb.

Dave Owen had a hand and a bat in two of the thrillers of 1984.

The first occurred on June 23, 1984. That's the game in which Ryne Sandberg thumped two of Cardinal reliever Bruce Sutter's offerings for late-inning homers.

Lost amid all the hoopla was a bases-loaded, game-breaking single to right by Owen that beat St. Louis 12-11 in 11 innings.

And on Aug. 2, 1984, the Cubs edged the Montreal Expos 3-2 on a game-ending double play by Owen. It was no ordinary double play.

Pete Rose, still an Expo at this juncture, was at bat with the bases loaded and one out in the top of the ninth. Pete then peppered a Lee Smith pitch. The ball struck the big Cub reliever on the back and fluttered into Owen's eager arms. Dave then fired to first and, gulp, another Cub victory.

Besides those heroics, Owen batted .194 as a switch-hitting spare infielder, who filled in sparingly. Dave, a rare product of the farm system, has a brother Spike, who also fills in occasionally at shortstop for the Seattle Mariners.

Owen was optioned to Des Moines in March 1985.

DENNIS ECKERSLEY

ECKERSLEY, DENNIS LEE
B. Aug. 3, 1954, Oakland, Calif.
BR TR 6'2" 195 lb.

If anyone qualified as the hard luck man on the 1984 Cub pitching staff it was Dennis Eckersley. With just a few breaks, his 10-8 record could easily have been in the vicinity of 15-3.

It was a long trail of professional experience that eventually led Eckersley to the Friendly Confines. He began his career upon graduating from high school, signing with the Indian organization in the third round of the free agent draft on June 6, 1972.

Sent to the Tribe's farm team in Reno of the California League, Dennis did not show unusual promise his first season, but improved his record to 12-8 in 1973. Upon advancing to San Antonio of the Texas League the following year, he responded with a 14-3 mark and a league-leading 163 strikeouts.

By now Eckersley looked ready for the majors and he was.

Spending all of 1975 with Cleveland, he came through with a 13-7 record and a sparkling 2.60 ERA. The next two seasons he posted 13 and 14 wins, and in 1976 he averaged nine strikeouts per game, fanning 200 in 199 innings.

The greatest outing of Eckersley's career so far came on May 30, 1977, when he no-hit the Angels 1-0. Yet 10 months later—on March 30, 1978—he was swapped to the Red Sox with catcher Fred Kendall for pitchers Rick Wise and Mike Paxton, third baseman Ted Cox, and catcher Bo Diaz.

Eckersley's first two years with Boston were his best to date. He was 20-8 in 1978 and 17-10 the next year, posting a 2.99 ERA both seasons. Thereafter, however, his performance at the Hub was largely disappointing. His earned-run average expanded as it became a constant struggle to attain the .500 mark. In his last year and a half with the Red Sox, he began having shoulder problems as well.

Meanwhile, by early 1984 veteran Cub first baseman Bill Buckner had been supplanted by Leon Durham and desired to move on to greener pastures. On May 25 he was traded to the Red Sox for Eckersley and minor league infielder Mike Brumley. At the time, the new Cub pitcher was 4-4 with a 5.01 ERA.

Although Dennis said, "I want to go in there and show I can pitch," his start in Chicago was hardly an auspicious one. He lost five of his first six decisions as a Cub. He allowed only seven earned runs in his first three appearances over 22 innings but came away with an 0-2 ledger. It seemed that Cub power was conspicuous by its absence whenever he took to the hill. Eckersley then started getting bombed himself. By All-Star time, he was 2-5 with a 4.88 ERA.

Then came the turnaround. From the All-Star break to the end of the regular season, Dennis made 15 starts and was 8-3 with a 2.06 ERA. He lasted at least into the seventh inning in 13 of the 15 starts, while allowing two earned runs or less in 12 of his last 13 outings. On Sept. 23 his 4-2 victory over the Cardinals in St. Louis clinched a tie for the division championship.

Eckersley won one more after that to finish 10-8 as a Cub, while his overall mark of 14-12 was his best since 1979. His 3.03 ERA was second only to Rick Sutcliffe among Cub starters. He suffered five losses by one run and another two by two runs. On Aug. 9 he shut out the Expos on four hits through nine innings, only to go decisionless as the Cubs lost 1-0 in the 10th.

Sadly, in his lone appearance in the playoffs, Eckersley was ineffective. Having never faced the Padres before, he was slugged for nine hits and five earned runs in five and one third innings, getting tagged with the loss as San Diego beat the Cubs 7-1.

Entering 1985, Dennis has a 134-110 career record, the winningest total on the present Cub staff. On Nov. 28, 1984, he signed a three-year contract with the Cubs, saying, "It's a great organization and a great city to play in."

RICK SUTCLIFFE

SUTCLIFFE, RICHARD LEE
B. June 21, 1956, Independence, Mo.
BL TR 6'7" 220 lb.

Color the beard red. Paint his currency green. And pencil him in Cubbie blue for the next five years.

Never in the 109-year history of the Cubs has a player made such an impact in such a short span as Rick Sutcliffe, a gentle giant of a pitcher. At $9.5 million he is the highest-paid player in team history—more than Tinker-to-Evers-to-Chance, Hack Wilson, Gabby Hartnett, Ernie Banks, and Moe Thacker earned in their collective careers.

The Sutcliffe saga began on June 13, 1984. The Cubs gambled away their future by shipping outfielders Mel Hall and Joe Carter, plus pitchers Don Schulze and Darryl Banks to the Cleveland Indians for catcher Ron Hassey, pitcher George Frazier, and the Big Guy.

As soon as the deal was consummated, Cub third baseman Ron Cey, a Sutcliffe teammate from their Dodger days, turned to General Manager Dallas Green and said, "You're going for it, aren't you? We're ready."

"Sutcliffe is a big-game pitcher with great success," said Green. That was an understatement. In Cub livery Sutcliffe compiled a 16-1 record, including 14 wins in a row, in drum-beating the team to the National League East title.

A stopper? Seven of his victories followed Cub defeats and a pair ended four-game losing streaks. It is difficult to pinpoint his best Cub effort.

Wrigley Field patrons went into orbit when Sutcliffe showed the right stuff by fanning 14 in a five-hit 5-0 victory over the St. Louis Cardinals on June 24. Rick later set his career high in strikeouts with 15 versus the Philadelphia Phillies on Sept. 3. The Cubs won 4-3.

He saved his best in the clutch against the upstart New York Mets, the Cubs' closest pursuers. After Met rookie sensation Dwight Gooden moved down the Cubs 10-0 on a one-hitter to trim the lead to six games, Sutcliffe set the clock back to seven by ticking off a 6-0 triumph on Sept. 9 before 42,810 fans at Shea Stadium. The Red Baron was awesome, allowing only four hits and fanning a dozen.

Sutcliffe again crushed the Mets' hopes a week later on an eight-hitter with the Cubs romping 7-1. Jody Davis hit a grand slam that sent the Wrigley Field crowd home in a flag festive mood.

"Winning is the best part," said Sutcliffe, "but the fans have turned Wrigley Field into a circus. It's just fun being in the park. These Chicago fans are amazing."

The climax came on the evening of Sept. 24 at Pittsburgh's Three Rivers Stadium. The Cubs clinched the National League East as Sutcliffe allowed the Pirates two hits in a 4-1 triumph. Sutcliffe fanned nine, including the legendary Joe Orsulak with two out in the bottom of the ninth.

The victory was Sutcliffe's 14th in a row for the best Cub streak since Ed Reulbach also clicked off 14 in 1909. The all-time Cub mark is 17, set by the little-known John Luby in 1890.

Rick thus became the first pitcher since Hank Borowy to reach 20 victories in a season in both leagues. Borowy was 10-5 with the New York Yankees before being sold to the Cubs for $97,000 in midseason. Borowy led the Cubs to the 1945 National League pennant with an 11-2 record down the stretch.

Sutcliffe even topped Borowy. After getting off to a 3-1 start with the Indians, victories became harder than pulling teeth. Rick had an infected tooth, lost 20 pounds, underwent root canal surgery, and was 4-5 when he was unloaded on the Cubs.

His 20-6 combined record convinced the skeptical scribes, who voted him the NL Cy Young Award, joining Fergie Jenkins (1971) and reliever Bruce Sutter (1979) among the Cubs' previous winners.

The Cubs clinched a pennant in 1945 and a division title in 1984. On both occasions the site was Pittsburgh.

Rick was manager Jim Frey's obvious choice for the opener of the National League championship playoffs against the San Diego Padres. That October afternoon was bright and sunny as the Cubs went balmy, registering a 13-0 victory. Sutcliffe pitched seven innings and added to the festivities with a tremendous homer that cleared the right field wall onto Sheffield Avenue.

The teams were tied 2-2 as Frey led with his ace to clinch the pennant in the finale at San Diego. Rick and the Cubs led 3-0 after five innings. Then Super Sutcliffe proved he was only human. The Padres whittled the lead to 3-2 after six.

The Cubs turned to fielding flubs in the unlucky seventh, and when the dust settled, the Padres prevailed 6-3. Perhaps Frey went with Sutcliffe too long. Anyway, the Cubs wouldn't have gotten to the playoffs without the red-headed guy.

Richard Lee Sutcliffe was born in Independence, Mo., the son of sprint-car driver Dick Sutcliffe, who was known on the circuit as "Mr. Excitement." His parents were divorced when Rick was 10. He and his brother and sister were raised by their maternal grandparents, Bill and Alice Yearout.

Sutcliffe was rated All-State in baseball, football, and track when he was selected by the Los Angeles Dodgers in the first round (21st player) draft of free agents on June 5, 1974. It was reported he signed for an $80,000 bonus.

Former Cub shortstop Lennie Merullo, now a big league scout, recalls seeing Sutcliffe perform with Waterbury of the Eastern League in 1976. "Sutcliffe was more of a sidearmer then, like Ewell Blackwell, observed Merullo. "He always seemed to have a smile on his face. Now, he has that red beard and appears meaner. He really stares them down. That sinker and slider were tough to hit, even then."

Sutcliffe came up to the Dodgers to stick in 1979 and was named National League Rookie of the Year with a 17-10 record. In addition, he proved handy with the bat, driving in 17 runs and averaging .247. Ironically, Sutcliffe encountered the most trouble with the lowly Cubs, losing three-of-four contests. He also fell victim to the sophomore jinx in 1980 as his record plummeted to 3-9.

Generally affable, cheerful, and talkative, Sutcliffe became an ogre during the strike-shortened 1981 season. He spent much of the time on the disabled list, had pitched only 47 innings and was 2-2 when he was scratched from the 25-player roster for the playoffs and World Series.

That set off his fuse and the fireworks began. Rick stormed into Dodger manager Tom Lasorda's office, knocked everything off his desk, then overturned the desk. With Lasorda, that performance meant Rick wouldn't last very long with the Dodgers.

He was exiled to the Indians on Dec. 9, 1981, going with second baseman Jack Perconte for pitcher Larry White, outfielder Jorge Orta, and catcher Jack Fimple.

At Cleveland Sutcliffe pitched even better than his record indicated. Although he was 14-8, Rick was the league's earned-run average leader at 2.96. Sutcliffe should have been a 20-game winner in 1983, but had to settle for 17-11. On five occasions that Sutcliffe pitched, the Indians were shut out.

Sutcliffe was on the final year of his $900,000 per season contract, so it was a known fact that the Indians were ready to peddle him. Dallas Green took that chance, knowing Rick would be a megabucks free agent at the conclusion of the 1984 season. Sutcliffe with his agent, Barry Axelrod, filed for free agency on Oct. 19, 1984.

Then the bidding wars began. Salvos were fired from across the nation, from Atlanta, to Kansas City, to San Diego, and back to Chicago. It was down to the Braves, Royals, Padres, and Cubs for Sutcliffe's services.

Ted Turner of the Braves was a charmer. He had just lured relief ace Bruce Sutter from the St. Louis Cardinals for a contract that reportedly extended to the 21st century when Buck Rogers would likely be spritzing ray guns from the mound.

Turner, with an unlimited cable-TV bankroll, wanted Rick to join Sutter, plus sluggers Dale Murphy and Bob Horner in his gala galaxy. The Royals were relying on the hometown aspect, while the Padres were offering the sun, sea, surf of San Diego, plus the friendship of teammates Steve Garvey and Goose Gossage.

The weeks rolled by. Finally, on Friday, Dec. 14, a decision was reached. Sutcliffe would remain in Chicago. Rick met the media at Wrigley Field and expressed his loyalty to the Cubs. Green raised his right arm in triumph. And the Tribune Company shelled over $9.5 million for five years.

As the most wanted man since Dillinger, Rick stepped to the podium and smiled. Then he declared, "I owe it to Chicago. Call it a sense of loyalty or whatever you want to call it, but something happened the three and a half months I was here. It was the fans, the players, the city. We got farther than any Cub team in years, . . . but we didn't get far enough."

Although the Dodgers won the World Series in 1981 and Sutcliffe earned a series ring, it has a hollow ring. Rick doesn't wear it. He wants to be fitted with a Chicago Cubs ring.

After decades of decadence with such duds as Dobernic, Bubield, Distaso, and Dettore, the Cubs have a dandy on the mound in Rick Sutcliffe. And if things go wrong, ... he could always buy the team.

GEORGE FRAZIER

FRAZIER, GEORGE ALLEN
B. Oct. 13, 1954, Oklahoma City, Okla.
BR TR 6'5"
205 lb.

Although George Allen Frazier was born in October, he could hardly be confused with Mr. October. The World Series isn't one of his classic moments.

The righty reliever played a mop-up role for the Yankees in the 1981 edition. The Dodgers mopped him up three times. Frazier thus entered the record books alongside lefty Claude Williams as the only 0-3 series pitchers. And Williams was part of the Black Sox scheme to dump the 1919 World Series.

Frazier only pitched three and a third innings. But in that span he allowed 9 hits and 7 runs for a gaudy 17.18 earned-run average. In addition, Frazier boasted a 14-22 record with the Cardinals, Yankees, and Indians before coming to the Cubs.

George was part of the midseason, six-player swap with the Indians in 1984. He accompanied pitcher Rick Sutcliffe and catcher Ron Hassey to the Cubs and brought his strikeout pitch with him.

In Cubbie blue, Frazier fanned 58 batters in 63.2 innings. He even had a winning record, 6-3. Cub manager Jim Frey used Frazier in vital moments and, by George, he wasn't disappointed.

Perhaps his most outstanding performance occurred on Aug. 19 in near 100 degrees heat at Cincinnati's Riverfront Stadium. On that humid afternoon the fatigued Frazier sweated through five shutout innings. He gained the 9-6 victory and dropped a dozen pounds.

DAVEY LOPES

LOPES, DAVID EARL
B. May 3, 1946, Providence, R.I.
BR TR 5'9"
170 lb.

At the start of the 1985 season Davey Lopes was one homer away from his 100th in the National League. It's ironic that Lopes' milestone will be in a Chicago uniform because he was always a millstone to the Cubs.

Lopes usually had the Cubs on the ropes during his long career. He enjoyed his best day at the Cubs' expense at Wrigley Field one August day in 1974 when he had five hits, including three homers.

And who could forget his ninth inning grand-slam homer at Dodger Stadium off Cub relief ace Bruce Sutter. Now, after a dozen seasons as a tormentor, the former Dodger captain is a Cub.

Lopes was acquired from the Oakland A's on Aug. 31, 1984, and in his first at bat he doubled off the Phillies' Steve Carlton. Lopes batted .235 (4-for-17) during his September stint.

Davey figures to see a lot of action in 1985. He will play the infield and outfield and come off the bench to pinch hit or pinch run. Lopes is recognized as one of the game's leading base bandits. He reached the coveted mark of 500 stolen bases on June 5, 1985.

After joining the Dodgers for good in 1973, the chunky second baseman formed with Ron Cey, Bill Russell, and Steve Garvey an infield combo that would play together a record nine seasons. But Lopes probably won't see much action at second base. That's Ryne Sandberg territory.

BRIAN DAYETT

DAYETT, KELLY BRIAN
B. Jan. 22, 1957, New London, Conn.
BR TR 5'10"
180 lb.

A 1985 addition to the Cub roster is Brian Dayett, a utility outfielder. A relative newcomer to the majors, Brian became a Cub on Dec. 4, 1984, when the Cubs traded Rich Bordi, Porfi Altimarino, Ron Hassey, and Henry Cotto to the Yankees for him and pitcher Ray Fontenot.

Dayett began his pro career with Oneota in 1978, batting .309 in 68 games. Over the next five years his minor league hitches included West Haven, Nashville (twice), Alexandria, Fort Lauderdale, and finally Columbus.

At Columbus in 1983 Brian batted .288 with a league-leading 35 homers and 108 RBI to earn him the International League Star of Stars Award. That earned him a berth with the Yankees. He made his major league debut on Sept. 10, 1983; the following day he collected a pinch single in his first at bat. That season he hit .207 in 11 games.

In 1984, Brian was hitting .301 at Columbus when the Yankees recalled him on June 17. Appearing in 64 games, mostly as a late inning outfield defensive replacement, he batted .244 with 23 RBI.

On April 26, 1985, after going one-for-five as a replacement for Gary Woods, Dayett was optioned to the club's Triple A affiliate in Iowa. He returned with a bang, hitting a pinch grand slam on May 22 to help defeat the Reds 7-4.

RAY FONTENOT

FONTENOT, SILTON RAY
B. Aug. 8, 1957, Lake Charles, La.
BL TL 6'0"
175 lb.

Ray Fontenot is filling the Cubs' pressing need for a second left-handed starter. A former Yankee, he was traded to the Cubs in November 1984.

The Cajun lefty originally signed with the Texas Rangers' organization, making his professional debut with Sarasota of the Gulf Coast League in 1979. Dealt to the Yankee organization that winter, he spent the next three and a half seasons in such places as Greensboro, Fort Lauderdale, Nashville, and Columbus.

By mid-1983 Fontenot was wearing the familiar pinstripes of the Bronx bombers. Although his minor league statistics had not been overly impressive, he came through with an 8-2 mark and a 3.33

ERA for the Yankees in his rookie season.

Pitching 161 innings in 1984 as both a starter and reliever, Ray was 8-9 with a 3.61 ERA and 85 strikeouts. He did, however, enjoy a strong second half, winning six of his ten decisions with a 2.58 ERA through 94 innings. On Aug. 5 he combined with Mike Armstrong and Phil Niekro to one-hit the Indians. Fontenot worked the first five and two-thirds innings to notch the victory.

Entering 1985, Ray's record is 16-11 with a 3.51 ERA. His only major league shutout was over the Rangers on July 26, 1983.

LARY SORENSEN

SORENSEN, LARY ALAN
B. Oct. 4, 1955, Detroit, Mich.
BR TR 6'2" 200 lb.

Lary Alan Sorensen has perhaps the most misspelled name in the major leagues. Whoever heard of Larry with one R? Then he's caught in the middle with only one L in Alan. And, finally, most people are turned ON at the end of Sorensen.

So much for names. What about his pitching record? The University of Michigan product started out like the ace of the Milwaukee Brewers staff, winning 52 games in four seasons. Included was an 18-12 record in 1978.

He was dealt to the Cards in a big eight-player transaction on Dec. 12, 1980. The trade was popular in Milwaukee, with the Brewers receiving such names as Rollie Fingers, Pete Vuckovich, and Ted Simmons.

After a 7-7 season in St. Louis, Sorensen was sent to Cleveland. There he won 22 games in two years with a second division ballclub. Lary opted for free agency and was signed by the Oakland A's. His record sunk to 6-13. He was dropped at the conclusion of the season.

Cubs' general manager Dallas Green took a chance in early 1985 by grabbing the sinkerballer. He brings an 87-92 record to a team that will spell the oft-misspelled righty as a spot starter or middle-inning reliever.

CHRIS SPEIER

SPEIER, CHRIS EDWARD
B. June 28, 1950, Alameda, Calif.
BR TR 6'1" 175 lb.

Chris Speier signed with the Cubs during the 1985 spring training. The veteran infielder will likely be used as a back-up shortstop to Shawon Dunston.

Chris had only one year of minor league training—with Amarillo of the Texas League in 1970—before joining the Giants the following spring. Not spectacular but dependable, he was the Giants' regular shortstop for the next six years. His highest batting average was .271 in 1975, and his best overall season was 1972, when he hit .269 with 15 homers and 71 RBI.

Traded to the Expos for Tim Foli in April 1977, Chris spent seven seasons in Montreal. Over the years he slowed down considerably, due in part to two periods on the disabled list.

After going to the Cardinals in mid-1984, Speier drew his release at the end of the season. Entering 1985, he is a .246 lifetime hitter with 1,530 hits, 88 homers, and 613 RBI.

SHAWON DUNSTON

DUNSTON, SHAWON DONNELL
B. March 21, 1963, Brooklyn, N.Y.
BR TR 6'1" 175 lb.

Shawon Dunston represents the Cubs' future. The kid from Brooklyn was the top draft pick in the nation in June 1982 after batting .790 with 37 steals in 37 attempts at Thomas Jefferson High School.

Possibly the most heralded Cub rookie since Lou Novikoff, Dunston was the man in the middle of a heated exchange between Cub management and shortstop Larry Bowa, who reluctantly yielded his shortstop position to the young phenom early in 1985. Dunston hopes to fill the vital shortstop spot previously patrolled by such favorites as Joe Tinker, Charlie Hollocher, Woody English, Billy Jurges, Ernie Banks, and Don Kessinger.

The three-time All-Star and two-time MVP was the highest draft pick in New York City history. Known as "Thunder Pop," Dunston batted .380 as a freshman, .420 as a sophomore, and .450 as a junior. He was clocked at 3.7 seconds to first base.

After signing with the Cubs, Dunston was dispatched to the Sarasota Cubs and tied for the lead in stolen bases with 32 while batting .321. He was promoted to Quad Cities in 1983. There he upped his steals to 58 and batted .310.

Last season Dunston advanced to Midland and was hitting .329 when he was promoted to Iowa. Shawon found Triple A pitching more formidable, swatting only .233.

Most scouts applied the "can't miss" tag on Dunston despite his tendency to be erratic afield. But the 22-year-old youngster could be the final piece of the puzzle in making the Cubs a World Series winner. On May 15 he was sent for more seasoning to the Cub affiliate in Iowa.

As we go to press, late in June:

- Rick Sutcliffe returned in spectacular fashion on June 7 by pitching a nine inning shut out (1-0) over Pittsburgh. He had been sidelined for 19 days with a pulled hamstring.
- The next day Steve Trout returned from a bout with a sore elbow to toss seven scoreless innings in a 7-3 Cub win over Pittsburgh. He had not pitched since May 17.
- Outfielder Chico Walker is helping to fill the roster gap left by Gary Matthews, who is recovering from arthroscopic knee surgery on May 29.
- After two ho-hum starts in May, veteran lefty Larry Gura was dropped from the roster.
- Shawon Dunston was hitting close to .280 for the Iowa Cubs and fielding creditably.

Photo by Kesh Sorensen ©

CUBS WIN! CUBS WIN! Victory scene outside Wrigley Field on Sept. 24, 1984

CHICAGO CUBS 1985 ROSTER

Pitchers

No.	B	T	Ht	Wt	Birth	'84	IP	W-L	ERA
41 Brusstar, Warren	R	R	6-3	200	2/2/52	Iowa	26.2	1-1	5.06
						Cubs	63.2	1-1	3.11
43 Eckersley, Dennis	R	R	6-2	195	10/3/54	Boston	64.2	4-4	5.01
						Cubs	160.1	10-8	3.03
31 Fontenot, Ray	L	L	6-0	175	8/8/57	Yankees	169.1	8-9	3.61
39 Frazier, George	R	R	6-5	200	10/13/54	Cleve.	44.1	3-2	3.65
						Cubs	63.2	6-3	4.10
44 Ruthven, Dick	R	R	6-3	190	3/27/51	Lodi	9.0	1-0	4.00
						Cubs	126.2	6-10	5.04
21 Sanderson, Scott	R	R	6-5	200	7/22/56	Lodi	5.0	0-1	3.60
						Cubs	140.2	8-5	3.14
46 Smith, Lee	R	R	6-6	235	12/4/57	Cubs	101.0	9-7	3.65
42 Sorensen, Lary	R	R	6-2	200	10/4/55	Oakland	183.1	6-13	4.91
40 Sutcliffe, Rick	L	R	6-7	215	6/21/56	Cleve.	94.1	4-5	5.15
						Cubs	150.1	16-1	2.69
34 Trout, Steve	L	L	6-4	189	7/30/57	Cubs	190.0	13-7	3.41

Catchers

No.	B	T	Ht	Wt	Birth	'84	G	HR	RBI	Avg.
7 Davis, Jody	R	R	6-3	210	11/12/56	Cubs	150	19	94	256
16 Lake, Steve	R	R	6-1	190	3/14/57	Midland	9	0	1	.160
						Cubs	25	2	7	.222

Infielders

No.	B	T	Ht	Wt	Birth	'84	G	HR	RBI	Avg.
1 Bowa, Larry	B	R	5-10	155	12/6/45	Cubs	133	0	17	.223
11 Cey, Ron	R	R	5-9	185	2/15/48	Cubs	146	25	97	.240
12 Dunston, Shawon	R	R	6-1	175	3/21/63	Iowa	61	7	27	.240
						Midland	73	3	34	.329
10 Durham, Leon	L	L	6-2	210	7/31/57	Cubs	137	23	96	.279
18 Hebner, Richie	L	R	6-1	200	11/26/47	Cubs	44	2	8	.333
15 Lopes, Davey	R	R	5-9	170	5/3/46	Oakland	72	9	36	.257
						Cubs	16	0	0	.235
23 Sandberg, Ryne	R	R	6-2	180	9/18/59	Cubs	156	19	84	.314
28 Speier, Chris	R	R	6-1	180	6/28/50	Mont.	25	0	1	.150
						St. Louis	38	3	8	.178
						Minn.	12	0	1	.212

Outfielders

No.	B	T	Ht	Wt	Birth	'84	G	HR	RBI	Avg.
27 Bosley, Thad	L	L	6-3	175	9/17/56	Iowa	51	6	43	.358
						Cubs	55	2	14	.296
24 Dayett, Brian	R	R	5-10	185	1/22/57	Columbus	45	5	24	.301
						Yankees	64	4	23	.244
20 Dernier, Bob	R	R	6-0	165	1/5/57	Cubs	143	3	32	.278
36 Matthews, Gary	R	R	6-3	205	7/5/50	Cubs	147	14	82	.291
6 Moreland, Keith	R	R	6-0	200	5/2/54	Cubs	140	16	80	.279
25 Woods, Gary	R	R	6-2	190	7/20/53	Cubs	87	3	10	.235

A SALUTE TO THE CUBS' RADIO AND TV SPORTSCASTERS

Clark and Addison was a corner brimming with streetcars and Model T Fords on Oct. 1, 1924, when Chicago baseball made its radio debut for the first game of the Cubs-Sox City Series. Doing the play-by-play for WGN radio was the long-forgotten Sen Kaney.

The first regular season Cub game heard over the airwaves came on April 14, 1925, when Quin Ryan and WGN broadcast the season opener with the Pirates from the Wrigley Field grandstand roof. Daily radio coverage followed in 1926. At one time, five stations broadcast the games concurrently.

The Cubs have had many radio cheerleaders over the decades, including Ronald "Dutch" Reagan, who did ticker-tape recreations for station WHO in Des Moines, Iowa, before going to Hollywood in 1937. Perhaps the best remembered voice of the Cubs is the late Bert Wilson (WIND, 1943-1955), whose famous war cry was, "We don't care who wins, as long as it's the Cubs!"

In the late 1940s radio was joined by television. The first telecast of a Cub game was on April 20, 1946, with Whispering Joe Wilson calling the shots at Wrigley Field for WBKB-TV. WGN-TV, with Jack Brickhouse at the helm, did its first Cub video presentation on April 5, 1948. The Cubs, incidentally, were the first team to have all their home games televised (1946).

Today's Cub radio-television lineup includes Harry Caray, Vince Lloyd, Lou Boudreau, former Cub pitcher Steve Stone, and newcomer DeWayne Staats.

Here is the complete roster of Cubs' sportscasters from 1926-1985.

Lou Boudreau
Truman Bradley
Jack Brickhouse
Harry Caray
Harry Creighton
Jimmy Dudley
Bob Elson
Gene Elston
Bob Finnegan
Jack Fitzpatrick
Pat Flanagan
Lew Fonseca
Vince Garrity
Charlie Grimm
Alan Hale
Milo Hamilton
John Harrington
Russ Hodges
Marty Hogan
Rogers Hornsby
Len Johnson
Vince Lloyd
Johnny O'Hara
Wayne Osborne
Lloyd Pettit
Jack Quinlan
Quin Ryan
Guy Savage
Val Sherman
DeWayne Staats
Steve Stone
Hal Totten
Jim West
Bert Wilson
Joe Wilson

Index